BLACK FIRE

an anthology of Afro-American writing

edited by
Amiri Baraka
and Larry Neal

BLACK CLASSIC PRESS
Baltimore, MD

BLACK FIRE: An Anthology of Afro-American Writing

Library of Congress Card Catalog Number: 2006926897
ISBN 13: 9781574780390
ISBN 10: 1574780395

Cover design: Carles Juzang

Printed by BCP Digital Printing, Inc.,
an affiliate company of Black Classic Press

Founded in 1978, Black Classic Press specializes in bringing to light obscure and significant works by and about people of African descent. If our books are not available in your area, ask your local bookseller to order them.

Visit blackclassicbooks.com for a full list of our titles, or obtain a list by writing to:

Black Classic Press
c/o List
P.O. Box 13414
Baltimore, MD 21203

Grateful acknowledgment is made to:

Negro Digest for permission to reprint "Life With Red Top" by Ronald L. Fair, copyright © 1965 by Negro Digest; "The Fellah, The Chosen Ones, The Guardian" by David Llorens, copyright © 1966 by Negro Digest; "The Baroness and the Black Musician" by Larry Neal, copyright © 1966 by Negro Digest; "The New Breed" by Peter Labrie, copyright © 1966 by Negro Digest; "Not Your Singing, Dancing Spade" by Julia Fields, copyright © 1967 by Negro Digest; "That She Would Dance No More" by Jean Wheeler Smith, copyright © 1967 by Negro Digest.

Boss for permission to reprint "A Black Stick with a Ball of Cotton for a Head and a Running Machine for a Mouth" by Calvin C. Hernton, copyright 1967 by Reginald Gay.

Transatlantic Review for permission to reprint "Summary" by Sonia Sanchez, copyright 1966 by Joseph McCrindle.

Kulchur Press, Inc. for permission to reprint "tomorrow the heroes" by A. B. Spellman, copyright 1966 by Kulchur Press, Inc.

Dasein-Jupiter Hammon, Publishers, for permission to reprint "To the 'JFK' Quintet" by Al Fraser, which appeared originally in Dasein, copyright 1963 by Dasein Literary Society; "Man With a Furnace in His Hand" by Lance Jeffers, which appeared originally in Burning Spear, copyright 1963 by Dasein Literary Society; "Elegy for a Lady" by Walt Delegall, which appeared originally in Dasein, copyright 1962 by Dasein Literary Society.

Burning Spear for permission to reprint "Psalm for Sonny Rollins" by Walt Delegall.

American Society of African Culture for permission to reprint "Reclaiming the Lost African Heritage" by John Henrik Clarke, which appeared originally in The American Negro Writer and his Roots, copyright by the American Society of African Culture.

Student Nonviolent Coordinating Committee for permission to reprint "Toward Black Liberation" by Stokely Carmichael, reprinted from The Massachusetts Review, Autumn, 1966, and "Ain't That a Groove" by Charlie Cobb, which first appeared in Student Voice.

CONTENTS

POETRY

Contents

Contents

FICTION

DRAMA

Contents

AN AFTERWORD

Amiri Baraka

BLACK FIRE: A New Introduction

BLACK FIRE was intended as a statement, a declaration and a "roster" to inspire "recruitment". A statement, in so far as the book itself, verified that such a body of work existed. It also demonstrated as Mao sd that we could be politically revolutionary and artistically powerful.

Likewise, it was a declaration, that the assembled were artists and militants, directly involved with the struggle to liberate the Afro- American people. It was meant also as a kind of "list" of the troops, a role call of the willing!

Remember, Malcolm X had been murdered & most of us in the book were Malcolm's sons and daughters. And this was a period when "Revolution is The Main Trend In The World Today!" In fact, it was Malcolm's murder that sent many of these artists out of the Greenwich Village & other similar integrated liberal arty "cool-out" zones up to Harlem & other black communities to take up what we felt now were our "responsibility" in the Black Liberation Movement. In New York that was the setting up of the Black Arts Repertory Theater School on W 130th St and Lenox Ave in Harlem.

Most of the writers are young. This was the generation that came up after Jimmy Baldwin. Some of us were accused of actually hectoring Jimmy to return from Europe & join the struggle, which he did in a gallant way. (See "No Name In The Street").

The BARTS had fallen apart after a year of fierce & finally even gun-violent internal struggle. But as far as some of the work we pledged to do, it was an auspicious start. Six days a week we sent five trucks out across Harlem. One with Poets, one with a graphic arts exhibit. Another with actors to do some of the plays featured in this collection and others. A number of the writers in *Black Fire* rode those trucks and mounted the homemade stages painter, Joe Overstreet conceived from banquet tables, riding under The Black Arts flag designed by painter William White.

Another truck carried musicians like Sun Ra (whose poetry is in the anthology as well), Pharoah Sanders, Don Pullen, Milford Graves, Albert Ayler, Grachan Moncur, organized by Andrew Hill to vacant lots, playgrounds, parks, to bring the most advanced Black Arts to the people of Harlem. It was a wonderful summer's work.

The Black Arts Repertory Theater School self- (and FBI) destructed because "Black" is not an ideology and so the unity gained under that finally nationalist but reductionist label, though it was an attempt to locate & raise the National Consciousness, could not hold. In that emotional spontaneity there was not an advanced enough unity to maintain the eclectic entity that "Black" had brought together, Nationalists, Muslims, Yoruba devotees, Marxists, under the cover integrationists, Christians, all the above-ists. And I repeat the FBI was hard at work, Harold Cruse had two agents (we took photographs) in his political science class at the Arts.

But though that institution failed, on the immediate practical side, it was the flare sent up that marked the explosion of Black Arts institutions across the country. And this book was but one fragment of that burgeoning movement.

What we said we wanted to do at BARTS was create an art that was 1) Black by form & content, as Black as Billie Holiday or Duke Ellington. 2) An art that was Mass oriented, that could move easily in and be claimed by the Black Community as part of a Cultural Revolution. 3) We wanted an art that was Revolutionary. As revolutionary as Malcolm X or the new African revolutionaries.

From the anthology itself, it is possible to see our intentions & our contradictions and eclecticism. Still, it is a powerful document of that time & of the BLM in overview historically and yet it focuses on aspects of the struggle still very much in evidence today.

Larry Neal and I were, indeed, Comrades in struggle, although ultimately our paths diverged somewhat. Still, he was to me, a kindred spirit. He was one of the most influential publicists of the Black Arts Movement, and one of its most powerful artists, as his poems here attest.

By the time the book was put together, I had returned to Newark as BARTS imploded. The original book jacket photo of Larry & I sitting on the steps of the Spirit House, in Newark, which my wife, Amina & I had organized to continue the cultural revolution of the BARTS always has a special significance. Razor sharp, Larry Neal & the recently Dashiki wearing "Roi" Jones. It is an image, in some ways, of the united front inside the book against white supremacy & submissive "integration into a burning building" (as Malcolm and Dr. King both told us).

A Real Note: What is so frustrating, though scientifically understandable, is the muting of the most militant of these voices as well as any similarly "Black Militant" or revolutionary voices by the accumulated "covers" (record industry word), co-optations & betrayals attributable to what DuBois called "The Sisyphus Syndrome", where each time we roll the huge boulder of soi disant US democracy up the towering mountain of US hypocrisy & resistance, the "Gods" roll it back down on our heads.

The present incredibly tepid face of American (including the most media touted Afro-American) literature confirms DIS! *Black Fire* was meant to dismiss such passionless employment applications (in the racist bourgeois establishment) passing as Poetry, drama, &c But the present state of US literary affairs, which of course, mirrors the present state of US social- political affairs confirms that fact of how much another Cultural Revolution is needed here in the US & all over the world

Amiri Baraka
Newark, NJ
The Last Poet Laureate of New Jersey

Note to the first paperback edition of *Black Fire*

It is obvious that work by: Don Lee
                          Ron Milner
                          Alicia Johnson
                          Carl Boissiere
                          Katibu (Larry Miller)
                          Halisi
                          Quincy Troupe
                          Carolyn Rodgers
                          Jayne Cortez
                          Jewel Latimore
Shd be in this collection. Various accidents kept this
work from appearing in 1st edition.

We hoped it wd be in the paperback, but these devils claim
it costs too much to reprint. Hopefully, the 2nd edition of
the paperback will have all the people we cd think of. The
frustration of working thru these bullshit white people shd
be obvious.

Editors,
Black Fire
March 1969

Ameer Baraka

FOREWORD

THESE ARE the founding Fathers and Mothers, of our nation. We rise, as we rise (agin). By the power of our beliefs, by the purity and strength of our actions.

These are the wizards, the bards, the *babalawo*, the *shaikhs*, of Weusi Mchoro. These descriptions will be carried for the next thousand years, of good, and of evil. These will be the standards black men make reference to for the next thousand years. These the sources, and the constant conscious striving (*jihad*) of a nation coming back into focus.

> Throw off the blinds from your eyes
> the metal pillars of Shaitan from your minds
> Find the will of the creator yourself where it was
> Sun being eating of the good things

We are being good. We are the beings of goodness, again. We will be righteous and our creations good and strong and righteous, and teaching. The teaching and the descriptions. The will and the strength. Songs, chants, "bad shit goin down," rendered as the light beam of God warms your hearts forever. Forget, and reget. Reget and forget. Where it was. This is the source. Kitab Sudan. The black man's comfort and guide. Where we was we will be agin. Tho the map be broke and thorny tho the wimmens sell they men, then cry up hell to get them back out here agin. In the middle of my life. In the middle of our dreams. The black artist. The black man. The holy holy black man. The man you seek. The climber the striver. The maker of peace. The

lover. The warrior. We are they whom you seek. Look in.
Find yr self. Find the being, the speaker. The voice, the
back dust hover in your soft eyeclosings. Is you. Is the
creator. Is nothing. Plus or minus, you vehicle! We are presenting. Your various selves. We are presenting, from God,
a tone, your own. Go on. Now.

Essays

James T. Stewart

THE DEVELOPMENT OF THE
BLACK REVOLUTIONARY ARTIST

COSMOLOGY is that branch of physics that studies the universe. It then proceeds to make certain assumptions, and from these, construct "models." If the model corresponds to reality, and certain factors are predictable, then it can be presumed to substantiate the observable phenomena in the universe. This essay is an attempt to construct a model; a particular way of looking at the world. This is necessary because existing white paradigms or models do not correspond to the realities of black existence. It is imperative that we construct models with different basic assumptions.

The dilemma of the "negro" artist is that he makes assumptions based on the wrong models. He makes assumptions based on white models. These assumptions are not only wrong, they are even antithetical to his existence. The black artist must construct models which correspond to his own reality. The models must be non-white. Our models must be consistent with a black style, our natural aesthetic styles, and our moral and spiritual styles. In doing so, we will be merely following the natural demands of our culture. These demands are suppressed in the larger (white) culture, but, nonetheless, are found in our music and in our spiritual and moral philosophy. Particularly in music, which happens to be the purest expression of the black man in America.

In Jahn Janheinz's *Muntu*, he tells us about temples made of mud that vanish in the rainy seasons and are erected

elsewhere. They are never made of much sturdier material.
The buildings and the statues in them are always made of
mud. And when the rains come the buildings and the
statues are washed away. Likewise, most of the great Japanese
artists of the eighteenth and nineteenth centuries did their
exquisite drawings on rice paper with black ink and spit.
These were then reproduced by master engravers on fragile
newssheets that were distributed to the people for next to
nothing. These sheets were often used for wrapping fish.
They were a people's newssheet. Very much like the sheets
circulated in our bars today.

My point is this: that in both of the examples just given,
there is little concept of fixity. The work is fragile, destruc-
tible; in other words, there is a total disregard for the perpetuation of the product, the picture, the statue, and the
temple. Is this ignorance? According to Western culture
evaluations, we are led to believe so. The white researcher,
the white scholar, would have us believe that he "rescues"
these "valuable" pieces. He "saves" them from their creators,
those "ignorant" colored peoples who would merely destroy
them. Those people who do not know their value. What an
audacious presumption!

The fact is that *these* people did know their value. But the
premises and values of their creation are of another order,
of another cosmology, constructed in terms agreeing with
their own particular models of existence. Perpetuation, as
the white culture understands it, simply does not exist in
the black culture. We know, all non-whites know, that man
can not create *a* forever; but he can create forever. But he
can only create if he creates as change. Creation is itself
perpetuation and change is being.

In this dialectical apprehension of reality it is the act of
creation of a work as it comes into existence that is its only
being. The operation of art is dialectical. Art goes. Art is not
fixed. Art can not be fixed. Art is change, like music, poetry

and writing are, when conceived. They must move (swing). Not necessarily as physical properties, as music and poetry do; but intrinsically, by their very nature. But they must go spiritually, noumenally. This is what makes those mud temples in Nigeria go. Those prints in Japan. This is what makes black culture go.

All white Western art forms, up to and including those of this century, were matrixed. They all had a womb, the germinative idea out of which the work evolved, or as in the tactile forms (sculpture and painting, for instance), unifying factors that welded the work together, e.g. the plot of a play, the theme of a musical composition, and the figure. The trend in contemporary white forms is toward the elimination of the matrix, in the play "happenings," and in music, aleatory or random techniques. All of these are influenced by Eastern traditions. It is curious and sometimes amusing to see the directions that these forms take.

The music that black people in this country created was matrixed to some degree; but it was largely improvisational also, and that aspect of it was non-matrixed. And the most meaningful music being created today is non-matrixed. The music of Ornette Coleman.

The sense in which "revolutionary" is understood is that a revolutionary is against the established order, regime, or culture. The bourgeoisie calls him a revolutionary because he threatens the established way of life—things as they are. They can not accept change, though change is inevitable. The revolutionary understands change. Change is what it is all about. He is not a revolutionary to his people, to his compatriots, to his comrades. He is, instead, a brother. He is a son. She is a sister, a daughter.

The dialectical method is the best instrument we have for comprehending physical and spiritual phenomena. It is the essential nature of being, existence; it is the property of being and the "feel" of being; it is the implicit *sense* of it.

This sense, black people have. And the revolutionary artist must understand this sense of reality, this philosophy of reality which exists in all non-white cultures. We need our own conventions, a convention of procedural elements, a kind of stylization, a sort of insistency which leads inevitably to a certain kind of methodology—a methodology affirmed by the spirit.

That spirit is black.

That spirit is non-white.

That spirit is patois.

That spirit is Samba.

Voodoo.

The black Baptist church in the South.

We are, in essence, the ingredients that will create the future. For this reason, we are misfits, estranged from the white cultural present. This is our position as black artists in these times. Historically and sociologically we are the rejected. Therefore, we must know that we are the building stones for the New Era. In our movement toward the future, "ineptitude" and "unfitness" will be an aspect of what we do. These are the words of the established order—the middle-class value judgments. We must turn these values in on themselves. Turn them inside out and make ineptitude and unfitness desirable, even mandatory. We must even, ultimately, be estranged from the dominant culture. This estrangement must be nurtured in order to generate and energize our black artists. This means that he can not be "successful" in any sense that has meaning in white critical evaluations. Nor can his work ever be called "good" in any context or meaning that could make sense to that traditional critique.

Revolution is fluidity. What are the criteria in times of social change? Whose criteria are they, in the first place? Are they ours or the oppressors'? If being is change, and the sense of change is the time of change—and what is, is about to end, or is over—where are the criteria?

History qualifies us to have this view. Not as some philosophical concept acting out of matter and movement—but as being. So, though the word "dialectic" is used, the meaning and sense of it more than the word, or what the word means, stand as postulated experience. Nothing can be postulated without fixing it in time—standing it still, so to speak. It can not be done. The white Westerner was on his way toward understanding this when he rejected the postulated systems of his philosophies; when he discarded methodology in favor of what has come to be called existentialism. But inevitably, he postulated existence; or at least, it was attempted. Therefore, existentialism got hung up in just the same way as the philosophical systems from which it has extricated itself.

But we need not be bothered with that. We need merely to see how it fits; how the word dialectic fits; what change means; and what fluidity, movement and revolution mean. The purpose of writing is to enforce the sense we have of the future. The purpose of writing is to enforce the sense we have of responsibility—the responsibility of understanding our roles in the shaping of a new world. After all, experience is development; and development is destruction. The great Indian thinkers had this figured out centuries ago. That is why, in the Hindu religion, the god Siva appears—Siva, the god of destruction.

All history is "tailored" to fit the needs of the particular people who write it. Thus, one of our "negro" writers failed to understand the historicity of the Nation of Islam. He failed to understand. This was because his assumptions were based on white models and on a self-conscious "objectivity." This is the plight of the "negro" man of letters, the negro intellectual who needs to demonstrate a so-called academic impartiality to the white establishment.

Now, on the other hand, a dialectical interpretation of revolutionary black development rooted in the *Western* dialectic also will not do. However, inherent in the Western dialectical approach is the idea of imperceptible and gradual quantitative change; changes which give rise to a new state. This approach has also illustrated that there are no immutable social systems or eternal principles; and that there is only the inherency in things of contradictions—of opposing tendencies. It has also illustrated that the role of the "science of history" is to help bring about a fruition of new aggregates. These were all good and canonical to the kind of dialectics that came out of Europe in the nineteenth century.

But contemporary art is rooted in a European convention. The standards whereby its products are judged are European. However, this is merely *one* convention. Black culture implies, indeed engenders, for the black artist another order, another way of looking at things. It is apparent in the music of Giuseppe Logan, for example, that the references are not white or European. But it is jazz and it is firmly rooted in the experiences of black individuals in this country. These references are found also in the work of John Coltrane, Ornette Coleman, Grachan Moncur and Milford Graves.

A revolutionary art is being expressed today. The anguish and aimlessness that attended our great artists of the 'forties and 'fifties and which drove most of them to early graves, to dissipation and dissolution, is over. Misguided by white cultural references (the models the culture set for its individuals), and the incongruity of these models with black reality, men like Bird were driven to willful self-destruction. There was no program. And the reality-model was incongruous. It was a white reality-model. If Bird had had a black reality-model, it might have been different. But though Parker knew of the new development in the black culture, even helped to ferment it, he was hung up in an incompatible situation. They were contradictions both monstrous and unbelievable. They were contradictions about the nature of black and white culture, and what that had to mean to the black individual in this society. In Bird's case, there was a dichotomy between his genius and the society. But, that he couldn't find the adequate model of being was the tragic part of the whole thing. Otherwise, things could have been more meaningful and worthwhile.

The most persistent feature of all existence is change. In other words, it is this property which is a part of everything which exists in the world. As being, the world is change. And it is this very property that the white West denies. The West denies change, defies change . . . resists change. But change is the basic nature of everything that is. Society is. Culture is. Everything that is—in society—its people and their manner of being, and the way in which they make a living. But mainly the modes of what is material, and how the material is produced. What it looks like and what it means to those who produce it and those who accept it. And this is how philosophy, art, morality and certain other things are established. But all established things are temporary, and the nature of being is, like music, changing.

Art can not apologize out of existence the philosophical ethical position of the artist. After all, the artist is a man in society, and his social attitudes are just as relevant to his art as his aesthetic position. However, the white Western aesthetics is predicated on the idea of separating one from the other—a man's art from his actions. It is this duality that is the most distinguishable feature of Western values.

Music is a social activity. Jazz music, in particular, is a social activity, participated in by artists collectively. Within a formal context or procedure, jazz affords the participants a collective form for individual group development in a way white musical forms never did. The symphony, for instance, is a dictatorship. There is a rigidity of form and craft-practice —a virtual enslavement of the individual to the autocratic conductor. Music is a social activity in a sense that writing, painting and other arts can never be. Music is made with

another. It is indulged in with others. It is the most social
of the art forms except, say, architecture. But music possesses,
in its essence, a property none of the other forms possesses.
This property of music is its ontological procedures—the
nature of which is dialectical. In other words, music possesses
properties of being that come closest to the condition of
life, of existence. And, in that sense, I say its procedures are
ontological—which doesn't mean a thing, but that music
comes closest to being. This is why music teaches. This is
what music teaches.

The point of the whole thing is that we must emancipate
our minds from Western values and standards. We must rid
our minds of these values. Saying so will not be enough. We
must try to shape the thinking of our people. We must
goad our people by every means, remembering as Ossie Davis
stated: that the task of the Negro (sic, black) writer is
revolutionary by definition. He must view his role vis-à-vis
white Western civilization, and from this starting point in
his estrangement begin to make new definitions founded on
his own culture—on definite black values.

John Henrik Clarke

RECLAIMING THE
LOST AFRICAN HERITAGE

THERE IS a school of thought supporting the thesis
that the people of African descent in the Western World
have no African heritage to reclaim. I am not of that school.
The image of Africa was deliberately distorted by imperialists
who needed moral justification for their rape, pillage and
destruction of African cultural patterns and ways of life. It
was they who said, in spite of voluminous documents in
the libraries of Europe proving the contrary, that Africa was
a savage and backward land with little history and no golden
age.

However, many writers and scholars, both black and white,
have pointed to a rich and ancient African heritage, which,
in my opinion, must be reclaimed if American Negroes in
general and Negro writers in particular are ever to be rec-
onciled with their roots. Let us first note some of those
people who have called attention to this inheritance, then
consider a few of the more salient facts of African history
and civilization, and finally ask how Negro writers can use
this material in their historical and creative writing.

A number of white writers, keenly aware of the distorted
image of Africa, have expressed amazement at what seems
to be the indifference of the black man in the Western
World to the glory of his ancient heritage. In the following
excerpt from his book *Tom-Tom*, 1926, John W. Vandercook
speaks unsparingly:

"The civilized Negro must lose his contempt for his 'heathen' brethren in Africa and in the jungles of Melanesia and Surinam. He must learn that the fathers of the race had and still possess blessed secrets, wonderful lores, and great philosophies that rank the jungle Negro's civilization as the equal, and in many respects, the superior of any way of life that is to be found anywhere in the world."

In his column of August 8, 1933, Arthur Brisbane, then editor of the *New York American*, had these reproving words to say about "Negro Day" at the Century of Progress Exposition in Chicago:

"Next Saturday is set apart as 'Negro Day' at the Century of Progress Exposition in Chicago, with athletic sports including colored Olympic champions, a pageant at Soldier's Field called 'The Epic of a Race', and 3,000 Negro voices singing spirituals.

"The committee in charge might have reproduced on Soldier's Field the great Sphinx that stands on the Egyptian desert. That Sphinx has an Ethiopian face, proving that the Negro race was important far back in the night of time. Many colored men and women would be more proud of the fact that one of their race once ruled over Egypt than of any modern 'spirituals,' 'Green Pastures,' or athletic records."

In both the statements of John W. Vandercook and Arthur Brisbane, I detect the note of the condescending teacher. They infer that they are revealing something of which we are totally unaware. Of course this is not true. There is a tendency among the recent discoverers of African history to think that they were the first explorers on the scene.

As far back as 1881, the renowned scholar and benefactor of West Africa, Dr. Edward Wilmot Blyden, speaking on the occasion of his inauguration as President of Liberia College, sounded the note for the organized teaching of the culture and civilization of Africa and decried the fact that the world's image of Africa was not in keeping with Africa's true status in world history. I quote from his address on this occasion: "The people generally are not yet prepared to understand their own interests in the great work to be done for themselves and their children. We shall be obliged to work for some time to come not only without the popular sympathy we ought to have but with utterly inadequate resources.

"In all English-speaking countries the mind of the intelligent Negro child revolts against the descriptions of the Negro given in elementary books, geographies, travels, histories. . . .

"Having embraced or at least assented to these falsehoods about himself, he concludes that his only hope of rising in the scale of respectable manhood is to strive for what is most unlike himself and most alien to his peculiar tastes. And whatever his literary attainments or acquired ability, he fancies that he must grind at the mill which is provided for him, putting in material furnished to his hands, bringing no contribution from his own field; and of course nothing comes out but what is put in."

A year after this pronouncement by Dr. Blyden, George W. Williams, first Negro member of the Ohio legislature and founder of African Studies in the United States, wrote in two volumes his *History of The Negro Race in America*. The first volume contained 464 pages of text, of which 125 pages were devoted to the African background. The field of research in African history was later widened under the leadership of three men: Dr. W. E. B. Du Bois, beginning with his Atlanta studies; Dr. Moorland in Washington, D.C.; and Dr. Carter G. Woodson, founder of the Association for the Study of Negro Life and History. The American Negro writer's mission to reclaim his lost African heritage had begun.

What is this heritage? In the first place, the rich and

colorful history, art, and folklore of West Africa, the ancestral home of most American Negroes, presents evidence to prove that Negroes built great nations and cultures long before their first appearance in Jamestown, Virginia, in 1619. Contrary to a misconception, which still prevails, the African was familiar with literature and art for hundreds of years before his contact with the Western World. Before the breaking up of the social and political structure of the West African states of Ghana, Melle, Songhay, Kanen-Bornu, and the Mossi States and before the internal strife within these nations that made the slave trade possible, the forefathers of the Negroes who eventually became slaves in the Western World, lived in a society where university life was highly regarded and scholars were beheld with reverence.

In the years when Timbuctoo was the great intellectual nucleus of the Songhay Empire, African scholars were enjoying a renaissance that was known and respected throughout most of Africa and in parts of Europe. At this period in African history, the University of Sankore was the educational capital of the Western Sudan. In his book, *Timbuctoo the Mysterious*, Felix Du Bois gives us the following picture:

"The scholars of Timbuctoo yielded in nothing to the saints and their sojourns in the foreign universities of Fez, Tunis and Cairo. They astounded the most learned men of Islam by their erudition. That these Negroes were on a level with the Arabian savants is proved by the fact that they were installed as professors in Morocco and Egypt. In contrast to this, we find that the Arabs were not always equal to the requirements of Sankore."

Ahmed Baba, one of the greatest scholars of this period, stands out as a brilliant example of the sweep of Sudanese erudition. An author of more than forty books on such diverse themes as theology, astronomy, ethnography and biography, Baba was a scholar of great depth and inspiration. He was in Timbuctoo when it was invaded by the Moroccans in 1592 and protested against their occupation. His collection of 1,600 books, one of the richest libraries of his day, was lost during his expatriation from Timbuctoo. Ahmed Baba, although the most conspicuous, was only one of the great scholars of the Western Sudan. This is part of the African heritage that must be understood and reclaimed.

In the second place, before the European colonial period, there were already established in Africa independent nations with a long and glorious history. In the fifteenth century, when the Portuguese established trading posts along the coast of West Africa, Soni Ali—one of the greatest of Africa's empire builders—was ruling Songhay. Soni Ali was followed to the throne by Mohammed Abubaker El-Toure, founder of the Askia Dynasty of kings and later called Askia the Great. He came to power in 1493, one year after Columbus discovered America. During the reign of Askia the Great, the nations of West Africa enjoyed a standard of life which was equal to, and often higher than, that of other nations of the world.

By 1884, when the European powers with colonial aspirations in Africa sat down and agreed on a plan to divide and exploit the entire continent of Africa, the colonial period was well under way—and so was Africa's resistance to it.

The British met with continued resistance in many quarters. In West Africa, the Ashanti and other tribal wars against British rule lasted from 1821 until the eve of the First World War. In the Sudan, the Mahdi movement, founded and led by Mohammed Ahmed, cost the British some of their best officers and soldiers, the most famous being General Gordon. When the Mahdi died in 1885, the movement continued under the leadership of Abdullah Khalifa and Osman Digna, commander of the colorful Fuzzy Wuzzy warriors. Osman Digna was not captured and killed until 1928. In Somaliland, a Mohammedan religious re-

former, Mohammed Ben Abdullah—later called the Mad
Mullah of Somaliland—rose up against British rule in 1899
and was not defeated until 1920. In South Africa, the Zulu
wars of resistance lasted from the rise of Chaka in 1800 to
the last Zulu rebellion in Natal in 1906.

Nor did the French find the Africans more submissive.
Somory Toure, last of the great Mendingo warriors, fought
the French in West Africa for seventeen years. He stood
astride their path from Senegal to the Niger when the
French were trying to extend their control to the source of
this great river, then to Timbuctoo. He was captured on
September 29, 1898, by an African scout in the French
army, while he was in the midst of his morning prayers. He
died in exile two years later. The King of Dahomey, Gle-
Gle, and his son and successor, Behanzin Hassu Bowelle,
called "The King Shark," opposed French rule in their
country for over fifty years. Behanzin was defeated by the
French mulatto general, Alfred A. Dodds, and died in exile
in 1906.

Thus Africa came bleeding and fighting into the twentieth
century.

Then a new type of leader emerged. A well-known
Egyptian nationalist of Sudanese descent, Duse Mohammed
Ali, editor of the anti-imperialist magazine *African Times
and Orient Review*, extended the support of North African
nationalism to the rest of the continent. From Morocco, the
voices of El Hadj Thami El-Glaoui, the famous Pasha of
Marrakech, was heard. In West Africa men like Casely-
Hayford, John Sarbah and Dr. J. E. K. Aggrey were preparing
that area of Africa for eventual independence. From the
French-dominated territories, Blaise Diagne, Rene Maran
and Gratien Candace were heard. In East Africa and the
Congo, Paul Banda, Daudi Chwa, King of Buganda and
Apolo Kagwa lifted their voices.

In South Africa a missionary-educated native of Nyasaland

founded the Industrial and Commercial Union. A few years after its formation, this Union had a membership of nearly three hundred thousand. Two able Bantu editors, John Tengo Jabavu and Sol Plaatje, gave the founder of this Union, Clements Kadalie, the support he needed to make the I.C.U. the most powerful African trade union on the continent.

The lives of these men, and many others, went into making the emergent Africa we know today. This, too, is part of our African heritage. It is both the responsibility and good fortune of Negro writers to learn that in this heritage there is material for more books than they can write in ten lifetimes. The African story is still untold.

For the last three hundred years Africa and its people have been viewed mainly through European eyes and for European reasons. The entire history of Africa will have to be literally rewritten, challenging and reversing the European concept. It is singularly the responsibility of the Negro writer to proclaim and celebrate the fact that his people have in their ancestry rulers who expanded kingdoms into empires and built great and magnificent armies, scholars whose vision of life showed foresight and wisdom, and priests who told of gods that were strong and kind. The American Negro writer should pay particular attention to the Western Sudan (West Africa), his ancestral home.

The personalities who influenced the rich and colorful history of Africa have been natural attractions for many writers. Material on the rise and fall of the magnificent Ashanti people and their inland kingdom that cast its warlike shadow over the Gold Coast (now Ghana) for over two hundred years is staggering; yet no Negro writer in the Western World has seen fit to write a complete book on the Ashanti people. The life of the first great Ashanti king, Osei Tutu, can be retold by our writers in the form of biography, a historical novel, a grand opera, or an epic poem.

This is a scant sampling of the rich material on African life still waiting for our attention.

Countee Cullen's poem "Heritage" begins with the challenging question: "What is Africa to Me?" Our writers must expand this question in order to give a more pertinent answer. To the question, "What is Africa to Me?" we must add, "What is Africa to the Africans?" and "What is Africa to the World?" In answering these questions let us consider using as a guide the following lines from John W. Vandercook's book *Tom-Tom*. "A race is like a man. Until it uses its own talents, takes pride in its own history, and loves its own memories, it can never fulfill itself completely."

Leslie Alexander Lacy

AFRICAN RESPONSES
TO MALCOLM X

> Brother, you think your life is so
> sweet that you would live at any price?
> Does mere existence balance with the
> weight of your great sacrifice?
> Or can it be you fear the grave enough
> to live and die a slave?
> Oh brother! let it be said that when
> you're dead
> And tears are shed that your life was
> a stepping stone, which your children
> crossed upon;
> Look each foeman in the eye—
> Lest you die in vain

THUS SPOKE Malcolm X in the Great Hall at the University of Ghana-Legon, Tuesday, May 12, 1964. These were his final words. They were addressed to a hostile and young American-trained Ghanaian geologist who had accused Malcolm X, at the end of an emotional and lively question period, of bringing to Africa "the gospel of racial violence."

Suddenly, there were more words. A student who sat near the podium from which Malcolm spoke stood and pointed his finger into the area where the geologist sat and shouted passionately, *"Throw—that—useless—man—out!"*

The crowd supported the student's demand with cries and shouts of approval. Then the geologist became the victim of a special kind of violence: Three students (some said his own students) unceremoniously threw him out of the hall.

19

Before Malcolm X could take his seat and be properly thanked by the unpopular *Marxist Forum* which had presented him, the spirit of criticism which the young intellectual tried to introduce gave way to what can be called the spirit of approval. And what a spirit: It could tolerate nothing short of complete acceptance of Malcolm X. The cheers of approval came first. The students stood and shouted at the top of their voices praises in different Ghanaian languages, which produced a monotonous, steady, balanced and comforting refrain—*Brother Malcolm! Brother Malcolm! Oh! Brother Malcolm!* The cheers gave way to chants of approval and the shedding—and in some cases the destruction—of English-made wool academic gowns, which the students happily wore to such occasions; this practice the ruling Convention People's Party (CPP) had long and adamantly criticized but, due to the propaganda methods which it had employed, had been unable to change.

The cheers and chants of approval were so tremendous that it produced what Lebrette Hesse (Chairman of the *Marxist Forum* and a third-year law student) called the "Ghanaian violent elation." And it was as violent as a tropical storm—sudden, complete, collective—shaking every nail in a Great Hall which had not stood as a symbol of Ghanaian freedom and independence, but rather as a tribute and a reminder of the tradition borrowed from British intellectual history.

I watched Malcolm's face as he stood, again and again trying in his humble and somewhat awkward way to acknowledge his thanks to those who had approved of his message. The heat which the Great Hall generated had already begun to take effect on all of us. Malcolm's face was covered with perspiration, but it mixed well with the tears in his eyes and the smile on his face. I had seen Brother Malcolm's face before in America, many times and in many audiences. I had seen crowds cheer him, extol him and shout to him as their deliverer. I had seen his faces and many moods; his happy moments in Harlem and Chicago; and I had seen his face filled with depression and outrage because another black brother had sold out or, worse yet, refused to "fight" because he believed that could appeal to the conscience of white America and overcome its racism.

But there was something in his face that evening which I had never seen before. At first glance I thought it was his small beard that made the difference, for I had never seen him with one before. He had always had that clean-cut Muslim look, and somehow the beard didn't fit that image. But the second glance—a deeper look—was more revealing. Malcolm's face was new because it was filled with the youth and excitement of those black students who identified with him. And he was awkward too, like a young father who loves his newly-born son but hasn't quite discovered the correct way to pick up and hold the child; the result is that he becomes debilitated by his own happiness and forgets about his own ineptitude. And what a proud father he could be! Unlike his children of African descent in America, these children would grow up, nay, develop, in a free society. They would be black and beautiful; most would be brave and all would be free. They would create their own standard of beauty and excellence; create their own history and worship their own memories. And one day they would be men and women; have power and greatness, which, as Nkrumah said, "is indestructible because it is built not on fear, envy and suspicion; nor won at the expense of others but founded on hope, trust, friendship and directed to the good of all mankind."

These things Malcolm felt in his heart and the portrait was produced in his face. Indeed, he was a picture of self-containment and, as Julian Mayfield said later, "the white man was off his back."

But the change in Malcolm's face, though important and

heartwarming, was less politically relevant than what appeared to be a radical change in the students' behavior. Indeed, the way in which they had responded to Malcolm and all that he represented was unbelievable.

Why was their behavior unbelievable? The Legonites, as the students at the university were called, were considered by the CPP to be more conservative than the *Conservatives* and more English than the English. In fact, party newspapers and government propaganda had for years used a wide range of epithets to describe them, but the most common were: "Reactionaries," "Ivory Towerists," "Stupid Conservatives," and "Possessors of Neo-Colonialist Mentalities." The following account, taken from the major CPP news organ, the *Evening News*, was a typical editorial:

The reactionary students at the University of Ghana have failed to comprehend in clear focus the true significance and meaning of political independence and the terminology of the new imperialism. Due to this failure there has not been produced a frame of reference which is able to embrace and understand the objective conditions of Ghana and of Africa. . . . Lacking a political consciousness the Legonite is not willing and able to sacrifice himself for something larger and nobler than his own personal and private interests. . . .

The students, on their part, rejected these types of criticism as unsound and unacceptable. They felt that the CPP practiced little of what it preached; that Nkrumah's politics of the one-party state—because of its limited dimensions and political cultism—was not structurally nor ideologically flexible enough to utilize correctly the constructive and creative skills that Legon was designed to produce. The students felt that the CPP really wanted to control the university as it controlled other social institutions, using revolutionary language to create guilt feelings among the student body, while it perpetuated its true non-revolutionary character—at the expense of the Ghanaian people. Moreover, since the students were unable and afraid to register their political grievances openly, they showed their contempt for CPP rule by using party newspapers as supplementary toilet tissues, and also by intellectually harassing party or government officials who visited and spoke at the university.

Given, therefore, this political polarization and Malcolm's identification with Nkrumah, most people assumed that Malcolm's words would fall upon closed ears. However, they felt that he would probably be able to deal with the harassment, although most of the students would not understand the complexities of Malcolm's racial experience and those who did would treat them as the "irrational and bitter outburst of a frustrated Afro-American." Hence, when the students did not respond as predicted, shock and disbelief were the only clutches available for those who did not understand the inner dynamics of Party-University dispute.

Suddenly, the political polarization assumed much wider proportions. Were these the same students who had defied Osagyefo Dr. Kwame Nkrumah and cheered a total stranger? Didn't Malcolm X and their own President believe in roughly the same kind of world, extol the same political virtues and share the same spirit of exploration? I don't believe that anyone there that night wanted these questions answered . . . or perhaps no one had any answers . . . or those who did venture to answer were probably confused by their own findings . . . or, at the very least, afraid of what their answers might imply.

Only the students acted quickly and clearly. They liked Malcolm and they were showing it. And believe me, no one could have assassinated him that evening. Not only did they verbally shower him with affection, they also encircled him— to hold his hand, to touch his clothes. One young lady wiped Malcolm's face free of sweat and said to him, "Go, Brother Malcolm and rest, you are safe—you are home."

Aside from the students, another interesting group which

came out to hear Malcolm was the Afro-American community. As I watched their faces and listened to their comments, it was quite obvious that most did not *see* or *care*
about the students' reactions. Malcolm had cast a spell over
them which expressed itself in the usual non-political idiom:
"Malcolm blew!" "He sure was boss!" "He cooked," and so
on. Not that there was anything wrong with these expressions. In fact, their very use implies a certain kind of understanding and a certain level of commitment and identification. But Malcolm's words had delivered and *saved* them—
because he "told it like it was." Malcolm had not made
them *think*, but rather, had mesmerized their world of
confusion and put them in a state of tranquility. And this
was unfortunate, because they considered themselves revolutionaries.

They were indeed a strange breed of political expatriates.
Unable or unwilling to deal with racist and imperialist America from within, these black Americans had come to Ghana
to help other black people achieve their revolution. After discovering that they could not lead the revolution and becoming critical of those Ghanaians and leftwing Europeans who
did lead, they settled down into a state of psychic self-
righteousness and became either overly solicitous or hopelessly mystified.

When they reached that point, the rest was easy, for now
they could walk and talk in the corridors of black power.
From there, it meant that each Afro-American coming to
Ghana had to prove under their inspection and by the
rules of their refugee mentalities, that he was not a CIA
agent. Further, it meant that they would believe as dogma
every executive decree President Nkrumah issued even though
they held in contempt the corrupt administrators who
carried them out. In short, their personality—that tool for
social adjustment—was not well integrated to function
smoothly, and the unnecessary emotional friction generated

resulted in unhappiness, unpopularity and spiritual emptiness.

Their response to Malcolm, therefore, was natural enough. They were not really interested in the details of his speech or its ultimate effects. They had probably heard a version of it before—or thought they had—and besides, they believed in it already. What they needed from Malcolm's speech was something no revolutionary should need or want. They wanted and needed a kind of psychological underpinning to support the understandable inadequacies in their own lives and, at the same time, provide them with a new sense of cultural euphoria which would make life with malaria, inefficiency and corruption that much more bearable.

So given these political eyes, the students were still "reactionaries," in spite of the way in which they had responded to Malcolm. Their reasoning went something like this: *All black people will respond favorably to Malcolm regardless of what they believe.*

Beyond this, they were not overly concerned with student-government disputes. Malcolm X was their real political leader and they had come to Ghana not because they loved Mother Africa, but rather, because they hated Father America. And when Malcolm X and others had achieved the "revolution," they would quickly return to claim their position of leadership in the new black society.

Perhaps Malcolm X understood the socio-psychic needs of the black Americans and what his presence symbolized to them. He especially understood the needs of the women in the Afro-American community. They literally "took" Malcolm away from the students. They wanted their *man* all to themselves. It seemed as though they even resented these "reactionary" students talking to him. Malcolm, with his tremendous compassion and understanding, tried to create a climate in which both sides could express grievances and share feelings, but before long, his American sisters had led him off the podium, out of the Great Hall and into the garden, down the steps and into the car.

When we finally arrived in Accra we drove directly to the Ghanaian Press Club. Malcolm was to be the guest of honor at a press soirée that had been organized by the Association of Ghanaian Journalists and Writers. We parked our car and then proceeded to squeeze through a long line of chauffeur-driven Mercedes-Benzs and other expensive European automobiles, which were owned by party and government officials. We were greeted by Mr. Kofi Batsa, Secretary General of the Pan-African Union of Journalists and a director of the Ghana Graphic Company, Limited.

"How did you like our reactionary university?" said Kofi Batsa to Malcolm.

Malcolm smiled sympathetically and replied, "I always enjoy talking to my brothers and sisters."

As we moved to the beautifully decorated terrace, Malcolm turned suddenly and remarked, "Was Mr. Batsa serious?"

No one replied.

Malcolm's new bodyguards were very protective. Not many people could get near him, and the few who did were those very important people whom they thought he should meet. But Malcolm wanted to meet everyone, and from time to time he broke through the invisible black wall that surrounded him.

The journalists had been very nice to Malcolm since his arrival. He had been given a press conference the day before and had received excellent coverage in all of the local papers, including the *Daily Graphic*, a somewhat less radical news medium. The press soirée was fabulous. There were excellent Ghanaian dishes supported by excellent imported drinks, and the very excellent domestic palm wine. And since Malcolm never drank, he, unlike the rest of us, had more room for the delicious fried fish and fried plantains.

After a long and pleasant evening, the Malcolm X Committee, which had formed to organize Malcolm's visit, drove him back to the hotel. Our long days of preparation and planning for the arrival of Malcolm X had paid off. The Ghanaians seemed pleased and excited about him and he was pleased and excited about them.

The drive back to the hotel was a quiet one. No one spoke a word. We were all exhausted, elated, and I believe that a few of us were thinking about the students at the university. Malcolm sat in the front seat and looked straight ahead. Once or twice he turned his head to speak, but it seemed as though he could not bring himself to shatter the strange and pleasant quietness which filled our car.

The only sounds came from the roadside. Most of the Ghanaians were asleep, for morning comes very quickly in the tropics and there is always a frantic hurry to beat the noonday heat. But the night people were always there: cooking by the side of the road, bringing their goods to the public market, or praying while watching their black masters' —and sometimes white masters'—houses.

When we finally arrived at the beautiful Ambassador Hotel, a tall and proud Hausa doorman opened the car door on Malcolm's side, stood back, and Malcolm stepped down. Malcolm stretched his long arms and quietly said good night.

By the next morning, the cry of "Malcolm X!" had swept the university. Mensah Sarbah Hall seemed to be the center of excitement. This was no doubt due to the fact that the *Marxist Forum* had its headquarters there; the Chinese-style architecture which formed the three buildings into a kind of medieval courtyard made the excitement that much more real.

Since I was a member of the Malcolm X Committee, I wanted to have an early breakfast in order to take the eight A.M. bus to Accra. But I had come to breakfast early for another important reason. I wanted to hear what the students would say about Malcolm X the morning afterward. I didn't have to wait long. Students filed in by the dozens—pushing and excited as usual—shouting the slogan which they had chanted the night before: "Malcolm X! Malcolm X! Malcolm X!"

You could have been on 125th Street and Seventh Avenue. The excitement and spirit of the people were the same. And it seemed so strange. The people in Harlem cheered Malcolm because they lived and knew they would die in the world in which they all hate. These students who cheered Malcolm the night before and who kept his name on their beautiful lips the morning after came from villages and towns which Malcolm would never see; where some of their kin had died of malaria; where there was no running water and no electricity. These were children of the Second World War whose mothers and fathers had told them about the first cries of independence. These students had experienced neither the brutal world of British colonialism nor the world of quiet hell which Malcolm X had brought to them. Yet they sounded like the youth in Harlem, Watts, Rochester and Bedford-Stuyvesant; exploding with joy and giving themselves up to the "essence of thing."

Students who had publicly criticized me and debated my political views came over, shook my hands, congratulated me on the success of the *Forum* and told me how much they enjoyed Mr. X. Some said that Mr. X was dynamic; others said he was militant; but they all said, "He is so honest."

I felt very good. It was difficult not to cry. I wanted to hold each one of them because I loved them all. And Malcolm had made it all possible and none of us would ever forget that.

As I got up to leave for the bus, Harold Duggan, the first West Indian student to study at the university and the vice-chairman of the *Forum*, came into the dining hall and stood on the top of one of the center tables. He shouted,

"When a brother is beaten up in the West by a white gang . . ."

"Or East," one student interrupted.

"Or East," Duggan continued, "we shall beat one of their white brothers here. And not in gang style but man to man."

As I left the dining hall, Duggan was being carried shoulder-high. For Duggan had spoken and Duggan had been heard.

Later that day, Malcolm X spoke at the Parliament Building to members of the Ghanaian Legislature. This pleased Malcolm very much because he had never before had the opportunity to address black men who made laws for black people. I remember Malcolm standing on the steps of the Parliament Building just before his scheduled appearance, saying, "If I had grown up in a country where black men made the justice, who knows what my life would have been like."

After Malcolm spoke these words, we were carried into the main legislative chambers. The Ministers of Parliament clapped politely as Malcolm was introduced. Malcolm spoke on the degrading status of the Afro-American in the United States; repeating and reemphasizing some of the issues he had raised at the university. He described the United States as the "master of imperialism without whose support France, South Africa, Britain and Portugal could not exist." Malcolm appealed for support from all Africans for their brothers and sisters in the United States. He said, "The struggle for civil rights in the United States should be switched to a struggle for human rights to enable Africans to raise the matter at the United Nations."

He praised their President Osagyefo and said that as a result of his able, sincere and dedicated leadership, America feared Ghana.

Malcolm attacked the American press and explained how it was used to divide "people who should be united for a common cause." He further warned the Ministers of Parliament that they should be suspicious of "every American tour in Ghana."

Brother Malcolm ended his talk by saying that for the first time he felt at home; that any "Afro-American who said that he was at home in America was out of his mind." Explaining his name "X," Malcolm said that Afro-Americans bear white names—the names of their slave master—and as such had "lost their language, cultural and social backgrounds."

Although he was not cheered and applauded as enthusiastically as he had been at Legon, his very moving address was followed by a lively discussion, during which the Ministers of Parliament asked questions of topical interest.

That evening, Malcolm met many other important personalities, including Mr. Huang Ha, the Chinese Ambassador, the Nigerian Ambassador, Dr. Makonnen of Guiana, the Algerian Ambassador and Nana Nketsia, the Ghanaian Minister of Culture.

The following morning, an account of Malcolm's speech at Legon appeared in *The Ghanaian Times*. It was entitled, *Negroes Need Your Help—Says Mr. X*. The article was very favorable and stressed most of the main points in Malcolm's talk. A few individuals, however, criticized the reporting, pointing out that it stressed only those points which restated Nkrumah's overall political objectives, and neutralized many of Malcolm's arguments by quoting high American officials who had raised the same argument. There was no mention of the students' reaction to Malcolm nor the subsequent parties to celebrate Malcolm's appearance.

The last day of Malcolm's four-day visit was quite eventful: In the morning, he spoke to the students and staff of the Kwame Nkrumah Ideological Institute, at Winneba; and that afternoon, he met its founder, the ex-President of Ghana, Dr. Kwame Nkrumah.

The Ideological Institute had been established because Kwame Nkrumah felt that Africans had to create their own theories of change and their own concepts about human society. Students would be required to read and debate all existing "progressive and socialist philosophies with the intent of creating something which was *African in content, humanitarian in scope and black in spirit.*" To this end, the Winneba experiment was designed to create a new African, both intellectually and spiritually. Staffed primarily with leftwing Eastern Europeans, students took subjects ranging from Platonic metaphysics to oceanography. And after a two-year exposure, some would go on to advanced studies, while those remaining would be placed into the nation's strategic organizations and institutions.

Malcolm's message was received warmly and the students were alert, intelligent and incisive. During the question period, a young Afro-American teacher disagreed with a part of Malcolm's speech and was almost ejected from the hall. In fact, he was saved by Malcolm, who urged the students to be tolerant with those brothers and sisters who were still seeking the right path to freedom.

On the way back to Accra, someone in the car asked Malcolm, "What do you think about socialism?"

"Is it good for black people?" replied Malcolm.

"It seems to be."

"Then, I'm for it."

When we arrived in Accra, we drove directly to Christainborg Castle, the office of President Nkrumah. Malcolm went in alone, and in no time at all, he returned. Malcolm was very elated. His visit was complete, for he had seen one of the most progressive black men on the planet. And his face had changed again—he was so happy.

Malcolm then said: "Nkrumah, that man understands. He is a real believer in change. I was so impressed."

"What did he say?" Julian Mayfield asked.

Malcolm answered slowly, "He said a lot, but one thing he said which I will never forget, he said, 'Brother, it is now or never the hour of the knife, the break with the past, the major operation.' "

Malcolm left for Monrovia, Liberia, the next day.

THE AFTERMATH

Three days after Malcolm's departure, he came under serious attack in the leading government-controlled newspaper, *The Ghanaian Times*. The attack was led by H. M. Basner, a white South African professional Marxist and high-ranking political advisor to President Nkrumah. The article, *Malcolm X and the Martyrdom of Rev. Clayton Hewett*, appeared in Basner's daily column, *Watching the World from Accra*.

Using the Legon speech as the focus for criticism, Basner accused Malcolm X of "ignoring economic motivations and the class function of all racial oppression." Basner further stated:

Malcolm X discussed the Afro-American position as if he hadn't a clue how American society evolved or how it can be changed in the foreseeable future. . . . His blind racialism has made him a political cripple. . . . And if Malcolm X believes what he says, then both Karl Marx and John Brown are excluded because of their racial origins from being regarded as human liberators and must be regarded as white liberators only. . . .

Expanding on this point, Basner said that the Communist Manifesto and the Battle of Harpers Ferry have no significance for the "Colored races except to confuse and deceive them; and makes W. E. B. DuBois—greatly influenced by both—just as big a sucker as Martin Luther King, who is influenced by completely different manifestations of human solidarity."

In classic Marxist style and polemic, Basner went to the heart of Malcolm's speech:

Both human solidarity and class struggle seem to be debarred from Malcolm X's politics and until he admits these, his politics can only be of service to the American imperialists. . . . Racial conflicts are their meat and drink, and if they are extended on a global scale . . . the imperialists will have achieved all they are hoping and planning for to save their system from extinction. . . . In the United States itself, as well as in the world at large, nothing suits the capitalists more than that Governor Wallace and Malcolm X should be at each other's throats because one is white and the other black. . . .

Suppressing somewhat his Marxist objectivity, Basner brought himself to admit that Malcolm did have passion and *"it is passion which is now missing and making sterile the Negro leadership in the Civil Rights struggle."* Agreeing with Malcolm, Basner condemned the Civil Rights Bill as a betrayal and a denial of social equality for twenty-two million Afro-Americans and suggested that Rev. Clayton Hewett— the Episcopalian clergyman who went on a hunger strike with a diet of water, vitamin pills and fruit juices—had no place in the Civil Rights movement because he was not prepared to die. What Rev. Hewett was doing, continued Basner, was "reassuring the lords of racialism in the United States that the situation was well under control; that they needn't call on Senator Russell and Governor Wallace or the uniformed thugs or the police dogs because anti-racists were preparing to lie down on the road, to face prison, fire hoses and even savage dogs, but that nobody was preparing to die." And finally, H. M. Basner concluded:

As long as the Revs. Clayton Hewett and Martin Luther King remain brothers in sacrifice, there is nothing for Congress to really worry about, except that the current filibuster may inconvenience electioneering . . . . The Civil Rights Bill can be emasculated at leisure and its passage will leave things exactly as they were. . . . *All this is undeniable and Malcolm X says so with passion and with truth.* But his truth is still only a half truth, even though it is the most important half. A willingness to die for freedom is the primary necessity, but even that is useless without an understanding that freedom is indivisible—for all individuals or for none; for all races or for none.

The appearance of Basner's article stirred up a lot of controversy and caught the Afro-American community by surprise. Although they knew how Basner felt privately about Malcolm's views, Basner's views had appeared in a black, revolutionary, government-controlled newspaper. And they didn't like it. No criticism, however objective, could have ever appeared attacking Nkrumah—so why should one appear attacking their political leader? Equally outraged about the appearance of the article were the university students, who already hated Basner for his political orthodoxy and now had another reason to want him out of what they considered a confused political culture.

The day the article appeared, I was having lunch with a friend of mine in Accra. Another Afro-American whom we both knew came over to the table where we were sitting. He acted very strangely as he sat quietly shaking his head. Finally he said, "Leslie, this political situation in this country is too much. I went to the university believing what the government said about the university, and the students acted like we act in America when we hear Malcolm. Now, dig it— when the brother leaves, *a white man is allowed to correct his position in a government newspaper.* What do you think about that?"

Before I could answer, my friend sitting next to me said, "In a developing country it's always good to give people something to think about."

We ate quietly and left.

The next day, Julian Mayfield, the unofficial leader of the Afro-American community, wrote a reply to Basner's article in the same newspaper. The editor of the paper prefaced the article with the following remarks:

Malcolm X the militant Afro-American leader has never fought shy of controversy. He believes that it is useful to engage in controversy because it enables him to put the struggle of the black man to the test of scientific analysis. Yesterday, our Columnist stirred a lot of controversy about some of the ideas of Malcolm X. Today, an Afro-American writer who shares the ideas of Malcolm X takes up the issue in a debate.

Mayfield's article—*Basner Misses Malcolm X's Point*—called Basner's article a classical Marxist interpretation of U.S. racial problems. But then, Mayfield said that he agreed with this interpretation in principle, and proceeded to show from Malcolm's speech that he himself also accepted this interpretation. Mayfield stated:

I sat several rows behind Mr. Basner and I heard nothing Mr. X said to contradict this. Mr. Basner's audio reception is as good as mine and he must have heard *Malcolm say that he did not believe that the black man would ever experience full freedom under the American system . . . Is not socialism the only alternative to the system? And did not Malcolm go on to outline a campaign by which the black man in the U.S. would do all he could to destroy the present system . . . ?*

Mayfield then argued that Basner was disturbed because Malcolm's approach left little room for white workers or white progressives. Defending Malcolm's position on this point, Mayfield developed a brief history of the various alliances between blacks and progressive white groups, and showed that the white practitioners of these progressive ideologies were always incapable of throwing off the virus of white supremacy: "They, the whites had to be the leaders. They always knew what was best for the black man. To them five black comrades meeting alone represented a threat to the unity of black and white workers . . ."

To strengthen his point, Julian Mayfield cited the experiences of Cuban and Algerian revolutions, neither of which, he argued, could depend upon their respective Communist parties until the initial moves had been made by the native revolutionaries:

What we who support Malcolm X have recognized is that there can be no black-white unity until the black man himself is so organized that he cannot become the victim either of his enemies or of those whites who call themselves his friends. By making a passionate appeal to Afro-Americans to unite on the basis of racial self-interest and identify more closely with their African brother, Malcolm X is not being racialist, anti-Marxist nor showing disrespect to the memory of John Brown. He is merely using common sense. . . . Black fighters of America have neither the time nor the patience to go around with a magnifying glass searching for genuine white revolutionists . . . the vast majority of the oppressed people of the world are non-white and damn near all of the oppressors are white, and that if the vast majority could be properly channelled, a major and perhaps decisive blow could be struck against the bastion of world imperialism.

To support Julian Mayfield's position and to correct what she considered to be a criticism of her late husband, Shirley G. DuBois, Director of Television, added under another column (*Mr. X Was Not Wrong*) the following remarks:

I must take issue with Columnist Basner in his criticism of Malcolm X. Mr. Basner seems to ignore the fact that Malcolm X's vigorous protests and denunciations are against the White Government and the White Ruling Class of the United States. The leader of the Black Moslems was presented at Legon by the *Marxist Forum* which would indicate that he does not share the prevailing fear and aversion which dominates America for all things Marxist. I have never heard or read of Malcolm X attacking Marx, Engels, Lenin or Mao-tse-Tung. I know that he has always admired, I might even say revered, the works of W. E. B. DuBois . . . The truths which Malcolm X enunciates are bitter. Many people find them hard to swallow.

The *Marxist Forum* and many of the students at the university read with interest the Basner-Mayfield dispute. They accepted neither as an explanation of what Malcolm had said. Marxist in spirit but Fanonist in orientation and content, the *Forum* stated that neither had offered a realistic solution to the plight of black America. Moreover, since Basner had never visited America and Mayfield had been away too long, the young Turks in the *Forum* felt that neither was in a position to assess correctly what Malcolm meant by *new black nationalism.* On Wednesday, the day after Julian Mayfield replied to H. M. Basner, the *Marxist Forum* released the following bulletin:

Reflections on Brother Malcolm

We believe that very few white Americans and too few black Americans see and appreciate the basic questions raised by an individual like Malcolm X. He is quickly branded a fanatic or quickly worshipped as a God. Nevertheless Malcolm's message is of vital importance not only to our brothers in America whom we completely identify with, but even more to the progressive movements of the world. Malcolm's philosophy, we believe, reduced to its barest essential, is that Black America should reject *the Capitalist* and *the Marxist* rationalizations of race relations and construct a theory of change which is consistent with its racial experience. Terms like integration and separation have become anachronistic because they conceal the real American dilemma. Yet they must use caution because the problem of racial exploitation in America can only finally be settled as a part of the world proletarian struggle for real democracy. Every advance in this struggle will be an actual or potential advance for the Afro-American. Malcolm, we are with you.

But H. M. Basner had the last word. On Friday, May 29, 1964—ten days after his original article appeared—*The Conversion of Malcolm X* appeared. Basing the article on a speech that Malcolm had delivered in Chicago on his return from his African tour, Basner replied sharply to those who had disagreed with his original analysis. Basner stated, "The many people who thought I was wrong about Malcolm X

didn't include Malcolm himself . . . For in Chicago he told
an audience of 1,500 that he had experienced a spiritual
rebirth which had led him to change his views." Basner
quoted Malcolm as saying that he had seen in Africa a
spirit of unity and brotherhood between whites and Africans
that he had never seen before. Further, Basner said:

Although sudden conversions are seldom wholesome and often
dangerous . . . I do not believe that this sudden conversion is
revivalist hysteria or a desire to join the winning side. . . . It is
possible that after many years of brooding, Malcolm X at last
found the key—the class struggle and the struggle of human
society—without which all the doors to an understanding of political and social phenomena remain permanently shut. . . . What
Malcolm X must have seen in Africa—and this is why I believe
in his conversion—is the political leadership of men like Kwame
Nkrumah and Jomo Kenyatta; Africans who have slept in white
men's prisons, who have felt the lash of white supremacy over
their continent and over their people; and who, in those very
prisons, reached an understanding that it is the lust for profit and
not racial differences which make the white man behave in colonial Africa as he does. . . . All of them, Kwame Nkrumah, Jomo
Kenyatta and Nelson Mandela, must have made it clear in one
way or another to Malcolm X that no one is oppressed because of
his political weakness. . . . Political weakness makes an individual,
a community or a nation the prey of exploiting forces which need
ideological support for their economic motivation. . . .

And finally, concluded Basner:

In the next few years the effects of automation under capitalism
will swell the ranks of those millions already unemployed . . .
there is the natural army, with the Afro-American in the vanguard,
which can carry on the real fight for civil rights. . . . *I will be
told that this army cannot be assembled. I answer, it must be
because there is no other army.*

Thus ended the African response to Brother Malcolm on
May 28, 1964.

Harold Cruse

REVOLUTIONARY NATIONALISM
AND THE AFRO-AMERICAN*

REVOLUTIONARY NATIONALISM AND WESTERN MARXISM

Many of Western Marxism's fundamental theoretical formulations concerning revolution and nationalism are seriously challenged by the Cuban Revolution. American Marxism, which, since World War II, has undergone a progressive loss of influence and prestige, is challenged most profoundly. For, while most American Marxists assert that the Cuban Revolution substantiates their theories of nationalism, national liberation and revolution, in fact, the Cuban success is more nearly a *succes de circonstance*. Orthodox Marxists were unable to foresee it, and, indeed, they opposed Castro until the last minute. One would hope that such a development might cause American radicals to re-evaluate their habitual methods of perceiving social realities, but in the spate of written analyses of the Cuban Revolution one looks in vain for a new idea or a fleeting spark of creative theoretical inspiration apropos of the situation in the United States.

* The term "Negro" was always in disrepute among the Nationalists and only recently among certain other groups and individuals in the ranks of unaffiliated "revolutionaries." The accepted term among some is "Afro-American." The term "Negro" is used throughout this essay because it is convenient and more generally recognized. It was not many years ago that the term "Afro-American" was condemned by Negro intellectuals and derided for smacking of "black nationalism."

39

The failure of American Marxists to work out a meaningful approach to revolutionary nationalism has special significance to the American Negro. For the Negro has a relationship to the dominant culture of the United States similar to that of colonies and semi-dependents to their particular foreign overseers: the Negro is the American problem of underdevelopment. The failure of American Marxists to understand the bond between the Negro and the colonial peoples of the world has led to their failure to develop theories that would be of value to Negroes in the United States.

As far as American Marxists are concerned, it appears that thirty-odd years of failure on the North American mainland are now being offered compensatory vindication "90 miles from home." With all due respect to the Marxists, however, the hard facts remain. Revolutionary nationalism has not waited for western Marxist thought to catch up with the realities of the "underdeveloped" world. From underdevelopment itself have come the indigenous schools of theory and practice for achieving independence. The liberation of the colonies before the socialist revolution in the West is not orthodox Marxism (although it might be called Maoism or Castroism). As long as American Marxists cannot deal with the implications of revolutionary nationalism, both abroad and at home, they will continue to play the role of revolutionaries by proxy.

The revolutionary initiative has passed to the colonial world, and in the United States is passing to the Negro, while Western Marxists theorize, temporize and debate. The success of the colonial and semi-colonial revolutions is not now, if it ever was, dependent upon the prior success of the Western proletariat. Indeed, the reverse may now be true; namely, that the success of the latter is aided by the weakening of the imperial outposts of Western capitalism. What is true of the colonial world is also true of the Negro in the United States. Here, the Negro is the leading revolutionary

force, independent and ahead of the Marxists in the development of a movement towards social change.

THE AMERICAN NEGRO: A SUBJECT OF DOMESTIC COLONIALISM

The American Negro shares with colonial peoples many of
the socio-economic factors which form the material basis for
present-day revolutionary nationalism. Like the peoples of the
underdeveloped countries, the Negro suffers in varying degree from hunger, illiteracy, disease, ties to the land, urban
and semi-urban slums, cultural starvation, and the psychological reactions to being ruled over by others not of his kind.
He experiences the tyranny imposed upon the lives of those
who inhabit underdeveloped countries. In the words of a
Mexican writer, Enrique Gonzales Pedrero, underdevelopment creates a situation where that which exists "only half
exists," where "countries are almost countries, only fifty per
cent nations, and a man who inhabits these countries is a
dependent being, a sub-man." Such a man depends "not on
himself but on other men and other outside worlds that
order him around, counsel and guide him like a newly born
infant."*

From the beginning, the American Negro has existed as
a colonial being. His enslavement coincided with the colonial
expansion of European powers and was nothing more or
less than a condition of domestic colonialism. Instead of the
United States establishing a colonial empire in Africa, it
brought the colonial system home and installed it in the
Southern states. When the Civil War broke up the slave
system and the Negro was emancipated, he gained only
partial freedom. Emancipation elevated him only to the
position of a semi-dependent man, not to that of an equal
or independent being.

The immense wealth and democratic pretensions of the

* Enrique Gonzales Pedrero, "Subdesarollo y Revolucion," *Casa de las
Americas*, (August-September, 1960).

American way of life have often served to obscure the real conditions under which the eighteen to twenty million Negroes in the United States live. As a wage laborer or tenant farmer, the Negro is discriminated against and exploited. Those in the educated, professional and intellectual classes suffer a similar fate. Except for a very small percentage of the Negro intelligentsia, the Negro functions in a subcultural world made up, usually of necessity, only of his own racial kind. This is much more than a problem of racial discrimination: it is a problem of political, economic, cultural and administrative underdevelopment.

American Marxists, however, have never been able to understand the implications of the Negro's position in the social structure of the United States. They have no more been able to see the Negro as having revolutionary potentialities in his own right, than European Marxists could see the revolutionary aspirations of their colonials as being independent of, and not subordinate to, their own. If Western Marxism had no adequate revolutionary theory for the colonies, it is likewise true that American Marxists have no adequate theory for the Negro. The belief of some American Marxists in a political alliance of Negroes and whites is based on a superficial assessment of the Negro's social status: the notion that the Negro is an integral part of the American nation in the same way as is the white working class. Although this idea of Negro and white "unity" is convenient in describing the American multi-national and multi-racial makeup, it cannot withstand a deeper analysis of the components which make American society what it is.

Negroes have never been equal to whites of any class in economic, social, cultural or political status, and very few whites of any class have ever regarded them as such. The Negro is not really an integral part of the American nation beyond the convenient formal recognition that he lives within the borders of the United States. From the white's point of view, the Negro is not related to the "we," the Negro is the "they." This attitude assumes its most extreme expression in the Southern states and spreads out over the nation in varying modes of racial mores. The only factor which differentiates the Negro's status from that of a pure *colonial status* is that his position is maintained in the "home" country in close proximity to the dominant racial group.

It is not at all remarkable then, that the semi-colonial status of the Negro has given rise to nationalist movements. It would be surprising if it had not. Although Negro Nationalism today is a reflection of the revolutionary nationalism that is changing the world, the present nationalist movement stems from a tradition dating back to the period of the First World War.

Negro Nationalism came into its own at that time with the appearance of Marcus Garvey and his "Back to Africa" movement. Garvey mobilized large sections of the discontented urban petit-bourgeois and working-class elements from the West Indies and the South into the greatest mass movement yet achieved in Negro history. The Garvey movement was *revolutionary nationalism* being expressed in the very heart of Western capitalism. Despite the obvious parallels to colonial revolutions, however, Marxists of all parties not only rejected Garvey, but have traditionally ostracized Negro Nationalism.

American Marxism has neither understood the nature of Negro Nationalism, nor dealt with its roots in American society. When the Communists first promulgated the Negro question as a "national question" in 1928, they wanted a national question without nationalism. They posed the question mechanically because they did not really understand it. They relegated the "national" aspects of the Negro question to the "black belt" of the South, despite the fact that Garvey's "national movement" had been organized in 1916 in a northern urban center where the Negro was, according to the Communists, a "national minority," but not a "nation," as he was in the Southern states. Of course, the national character of the Negro has little to do with what part of the country he lives in. Wherever he lives, he is restricted. His "national boundaries" are the color of his skin, his racial characteristics and the social conditions within his sub-cultural world.

The ramifications of the national and colonial question are clear only if the initial bourgeois character of national movements is understood. However, according to American Marxism, Negro movements do not have "bourgeois nationalist" beginnings. American Marxists have fabricated the term "Negro Liberation Movement"—an "all-class" affair united around a program of civil and political equality, the beginnings of which they approximately date back to the founding of the National Association for the Advancement of Colored People in 1909. True, the NAACP, was, from its inception, and is still, a bourgeois movement. However, it is a distortion to characterize this particular organization as the sole repository of the beginnings of the Negro bourgeois movement. For, such a narrow analysis cannot explain how or why there are two divergent trends in Negro life today: pro-integration and anti-integration. That is to say, it does not explain the origins of the Nationalist wing, composed of Black Nationalists, Black Muslims, and other minor Negro Nationalist groupings, as an outgrowth of basic conflicts within the early bourgeois movements (circa 1900), from which also developed the present day NAACP–Martin Luther King–student coalition.

Furthermore, the Marxian version of the NAACP's origins does not explain why the Nationalist wing and the NAACP wing oppose each other, or why the overwhelming majority of Negroes are "uncommitted" to either one. There is widespread dissatisfaction among various classes of Negroes with the NAACP's approach to racial problems. On the other hand, in recent years, the Nationalists have been gaining support and prestige among "uncommitted" Negroes. This is especially true of the Muslims, the newest Negro Nationalist phenomenon.

The rise of free African nations and the Cuban Revolution have, without a doubt, stirred up the latent nationalism of many Negroes. The popular acclaim given Fidel Castro by the working-class Negroes of Harlem during his visit in the fall of 1960 demonstrated that the effects of the colonial revolutions are reaching the American Negro and arousing his nationalist impulses. Many Negroes, who are neither Nationalists nor supporters of the NAACP, are becoming impatient with the NAACP–Martin Luther King–student legalistic and "passive resistance" tactics. They suspect that the long, drawn-out battle of attrition with which the NAACP integration movement is faced, may very well end in no more than pyrrhic victories. They feel that racial integration, as a goal, lacks the tangible objectives needed to bring about genuine equality. After all, "social" and "racial" equality remain intangible goals unless they are related to the seizure and retention of objectives which can be used as levers to exert political, social, economic and administrative power in society. Power cannot be wielded from integrated lunch counters, waiting rooms, schools, housing, baseball teams or love affairs, even though these are social advances.

There emerges from this dilemma a recognizable third trend, personified in the case of Robert F. Williams. Williams was forced to take an anti-NAACP position, but he was not a Nationalist and was critical of the "Marxists." As a rebel, Williams' objectives were the same as those of the NAACP; he differed only in his *approach*. However, his seeming "revolutionary" stance is thwarted by the same lack of substance that makes a program of "racial integration" unsatisfactory to many Negroes. Williams resorted to arms for *defense* purposes—but arms are superfluous in terms of the objectives of racial integration. Arms symbolize a step beyond mere "racial integration," to the seizure of actual centers of social power. The adherents of this third trend—young social rebels who are followers of Williams' Monroe Movement—are faced with this predicament. They are neither avowed Nationalists nor NAACPers. They consider themselves "revolutionary," but are shy of having revolutionary objectives.

However, they are not a force as yet, and their future importance will rest, no doubt, upon how much influence the Nationalist wing will exert in the Negro community. In short, the main trends in Negro life are becoming more and more polarized around the issues of pro- and anti-integration.

INTEGRATION VS. SEPARATION: HISTORY AND INTERPRETATIONS

Negro historiography does not offer a very clear explanation of how the Negro has become what he is today. As written, Negro history appears as a parade of lesser and greater personalities against a clamor of many contending anonymous voices and a welter of spasmodic trends all negating each other. Through the pages of Negro history the Negro marches, always arriving but never getting anywhere. His "national goals" are always receding.

Integration vs. separation have become polarized around two main wings of racial ideology, with fateful implications for the Negro movement and the country at large. Yet we are faced with a problem in racial ideology without any means of properly understanding how to deal with it. The dilemma arises from a lack of comprehension of the historical origins of the conflict.

Furthermore, the problem is complicated by a lack of recognition even that it exists. The fundamental economic and cultural issues at stake in this conflict cannot be dealt with by American sociologists for the simple reason that sociologists never admit that such issues should exist at all in American society. They talk of "Americanizing" all the varied racial elements in the United States; however, when it is clear that certain racial elements are *not* being "Americanized," socially, economically or culturally; the sociologists proffer nothing but total evasion, or more studies on the "nature of prejudice." Hence, the problems remain with us in a neglected state of suspension until they break out in what are considered to be "negative," "anti-social," "anti-white," "anti-democratic" reactions.

One of the few attempts to bring a semblance of order to the dominant trends in the chaos of Negro history was made by Marxist historians in the 1930's and 1940's. However, it proved to be a one-sided analysis which failed to examine the class structure of the Negro people. Viewing Negro history as a parade from slavery to socialism, the Marxist historians favor certain Negro personalities uncritically while ignoring others who played vital roles. Major figures, such as Booker T. Washington and Marcus Garvey, who do not fit into the Communist stereotype of Negro heroes, are ignored or downgraded. In the process, Marxist historians have further obscured the roots of the current conflict in racial ideology.

Under the aegis of other slogans, issues and rivalries, the pro-integration vs. anti-integration controversy first appeared at the turn of the century in the famous Booker T. Washington-W. E. B. DuBois debate. Washington's position was that the Negro had to achieve economic self-sufficiency before demanding his political rights. This position led Washington to take a less "militant" stand on civil rights than did other Negro leaders, such as DuBois, who accused Washington of compromising with the racists on the Negro's political position in the South.

It is not sufficient, however, to judge Washington purely on the political policies he advocated for the Negro in the South. For Washington gave voice to an important trend in

Negro life, one that made him the most popular leader American Negroes have had. The Washington-DuBois controversy was not a debate between representatives of reaction and progress, as Communist historians have asserted, but over the correct tactics for the emerging Negro bourgeoisie.

From the Reconstruction era on, the would-be Negro bourgeoisie in the United States confronted unique difficulties quite unlike those experienced by the young bourgeoisie in colonial areas. As a class, the Negro bourgeoisie wanted liberty and equality, but *also* money, prestige and political power. How to achieve all this within the American framework was a difficult problem, since the whites had a monopoly on these benefits of Western civilization, and looked upon the new aspirants as interlopers and upstarts. The Negro bourgeoisie was trapped and stymied by the entrenched and expanding power of American capitalism. Unlike the situation in the colonial areas, the Negro could not seize the power he wanted or oust "foreigners." Hence, he turned inward toward organizations of fraternal, religious, nationalistic, educational and political natures. There was much frustrated bickering and internal conflict within this new class over strategy and tactics. Finally the issues boiled down to that of *politics vs. economics,* and emerged in the Washington-DuBois controversy.

In this context, it is clear that Washington's program for a "separate" Negro economy was not compatible with the idea of integration into the dominant white economy. In 1907, DuBois complained of Washington that:

He is striving nobly to make Negro artisans business men and property owners; but it is impossible, under modern competitive methods, for workingmen and property-owners to defend their rights and exist without the right of suffrage.

Yet, Washington could not logically seek participation in "white" politics in so far as such politics were a reflection of the mastery of whites in the surrounding economy. He reasoned that since Negroes had no chance to take part in the white world as producers and proprietors, what value was there in seeking political rights *immediately*? Herbert Aptheker, the leading Marxist authority on Negro history, quotes Washington as saying:

> Brains, property, and character for the Negro will settle the question of civil rights. The best course to pursue in regard to a civil rights bill in the South is to let it alone; let it alone and it will settle itself. Good school teachers and plenty of money to pay them will be more potent in settling the race question than many civil rights bills and investigation committees.

This was the typical Washington attitude—a bourgeois attitude, practical and pragmatic, based on the expediencies of the situation. Washington sought to train and develop a new class. He had a longer-range view than most of his contemporaries, and for his plans he wanted racial peace at any cost.

Few of the implications of this can be found in Marxist interpretations of Negro history. By taking a partisan position in favor of DuBois, Marxists dismiss the economic aspects of the question in favor of the purely political. However, this is the same as saying that the Negro bourgeoisie had no right to try to become capitalists—an idea that makes no historical sense whatsoever. If a small proprietor, native to an underdeveloped country, should want to oust foreign capitalists and take over his internal markets, why should not the Negro proprietor have the same desire? Of course, a substantial Negro bourgeoisie never developed in the United States. Although this fact obscured and complicated the problems of Negro Nationalism, it does not change the principles involved. Washington sought to develop a Negro bourgeoisie. He failed. But his failure was no greater than that of those who sought equality through politics.

Washington's role in developing an economic program to

counteract the Negro's position is central to the emergence
of Negro Nationalism, and accounts for much of his popu-
larity among Negroes. Yet Aptheker makes the error of assessing Washington purely on political grounds. On this
basis, of course, Aptheker finds him not "revolutionary" or
"militant" in the fashion that befits a Negro leader, past or
present. He rejects the historico-economic-class basis of
Washington's philosophy, although these are essential in
analyzing social movements, personalities, or historical situations. Aptheker has not seen Washington in the light of what
he was: the leading spokesman and theoretician of the new
Negro capitalists, whom he was trying to mold into existence.
All that Aptheker has to say about Washington is summed
up by him as follows:

Mr. Washington's policy amounted objectively to an acceptance
by the Negro of second-class citizenship. His appearance on the
historical stage and the growth of his influence coincided with and
reflected the propertied interests' resistance to the farmers and
workers' great protest movements in the generations spanning
the close of the nineteenth and the opening of the twentieth
centuries. American imperialism conquers the South during these
years and Mr. Washington's program of industrial education,
ultra-gradualism and opposition to independent political activity
and trade unionism assisted in this conquest.

Thus is the Marxian schema about the "Negro people"
projected back into history—a people without classes or dif-
fering class interests. It is naive to believe that any aspiring
member of the bourgeoisie would have been interested in
trade-unionism and the political action of farmers. But
American Marxists cannot "see" the Negro at all unless he
is storming the barricades, either in the present or in history.
Does it make any sense to look back into history and expect
to find Negroes involved in trade unionism and political
action in the most lynch-ridden decade the South has ever
known? Anyone reading about the South at the turn of the

century must wonder how Negroes managed to survive at all, let alone become involved in political activity when such politics was dominated by the Ku Klux Klan. According to Aptheker, however, the Negroes who supported Washington were wrong. It was the handful of Negro militants from above the Mason-Dixon line who had never known slavery, who had never known Southern poverty and illiteracy, the whip of the lynch-mad KKK, or the peasant's agony of landlessness, who were correct in their high-sounding idealistic criticism of Washington. These were, Aptheker tells us, within a politically revolutionary tradition—a tradition which had not even emerged when Washington died!

After the Washington-DuBois debate, DuBois went on to help form the NAACP in 1909. Washington died in 1915. The controversy continued, however, in the conflict between the NAACP and the Garvey movement.

In 1916, Marcus Garvey, the West Indian-born Nationalist, organized his "Back to Africa" movement in the United States. Garvey had, from his earliest years, been deeply influenced by the racial and economic philosophies of Booker T. Washington. Adopting what he wanted from Washington's ideas, Garvey carried them further—advocating Negro self-sufficiency in the United States linked, this time, with the idea of regaining access to the African homeland, as a basis for constructing a viable black economy. Whereas Washington had earlier chosen an accommodationist position in the South to achieve his objectives, Garvey added the racial ingredient of Black Nationalism to Washington's ideas, with potent effect. This development paralleled the bourgeois origins of the colonial revolutions then in their initial stages in Africa and Asia. Coming from a British colony, Garvey had the psychology of a colonial revolutionary and acted as such.

With the rise of Nationalism, DuBois and the NAACP took a strong stand against the Garvey Movement and against revolutionary nationalism. The issues were much deeper than mere rivalry between different factions for the leadership of Negro politics. The rise of Garvey Nationalism meant that the NAACP became the accommodationists and the Nationalists became the militants. From its very inception, the Negro bourgeois movement found itself deeply split over aims, ideology and tactics, growing out of its unique position of contending for its aims in the very heart of Western capitalism.

Neither the nationalist side of the bourgeois movement nor the reformist NAACP wing, however, were able to vanquish the social barriers facing Negroes in the United States. The Garvey Movement found its answer in seeking a way out—"Back to Africa!" where the nationalist revolution had elbow room, where there was land, resources, sovereignty—all that the black man had been denied in the United States.

The Garvey era manifested the most self-conscious expression of nationality in the entire history of the Negro in the United States. To refrain from pointing this out, as Aptheker does in his essays on Negro history, is inexcusable. In his essay, "The Negro in World War I," Aptheker says: "What was the position of the Negro People during the years of Wilson's 'New Freedom'?" He then mentions the activities of the NAACP, the National Race Congress of 1915, and the formation in 1915 of the Association for the Study of Negro Life and History. But in discussing the racial unrest of the time, Aptheker fails to mention the Garvey movement, despite the fact that it had organized more Negroes than any other organization in the three years following its establishment in 1916. The causes for these omissions are, of course, apparent: orthodox Western Marxism cannot incorporate nationalism into its schema.

With the NAACP and the Garvey movement growing apace, the "Negro People" had two "Negro Liberation Movements" to contend with. Never was an oppressed people so richly endowed with leadership; the only difficulty was that these two movements were at bitter odds with one another. Furthermore, within the Negro community, prejudice about lighter and darker skin coloring also served as a basis for class stratification. Thus, when retaliating against DuBois' criticisms of his movement, Garvey attacked him on the basis of his skin color, and assailed the assimilationist values of the upper-class Negro leadership. In addition, the Garvey "blacks" and the NAACP "coloreds" disagreed as to which was the true "motherland"—black Africa or white America.

During the period when the Communists looked upon the Negro question as a national question, some Communist writers perceived the positive, as well as the negative, aspects of Garvey's appeal. Harry Haywood, for example, wrote that the Garvey movement "reflected the widening rift between the policies of the Negro bourgeois reformism and the life needs of the sorely pressed people." He sees in Garvey's "renunciation of the whole program of interracialism" a belief that the upper-class Negro leadership was "motivated solely by their desire for cultural assimilation," and that they "banked their hopes for Negro equality on support from the white enemy." Haywood sympathized with this position, seeing in the "huge movement led by Garvey" a "deep feeling for the intrinsic national character of the Negro problem."

In 1959, the Communists withdrew the concept of "self-determination" in the black belt, and sidestepped the question of the Negro's "national character." Instead, they adopted a position essentially the same as the NAACP. Their present goal is to secure "with all speed" the "fullest realization of genuinely equal economic, political and social status with all other nationalities and individual citizens of the United States"—this is to be accompanied by "genuinely representative government, with proportionate representation

in the areas of Negro majority population in the South."
This position is essentially no different from that supported
by the NAACP.

Thus, it is not surprising that it is difficult to understand
the present conflict within the Negro movement; the roots
of the conflict have been obliterated. While most historians
do not attempt at all to bring order to the chaos of Negro
history, those that have—the Marxists—find it convenient
from a theoretical standpoint to see Negroes in history as
black proletarian "prototypes" and forerunners of the "black
workers" who will participate in the proletarian revolution.
This Aptheker-Communist Party mythology, created around
a patronizing deification of Negro slave heroes (Denmark
Vesey, Nat Turner, Sojourner Truth, Frederick Douglass,
etc.), results in abstracting them from their proper historical
context and making it appear that they are relevant to
modern reality. Of course, there will be those Marxists who
will argue that their inability to come to terms in theory
with Negro Nationalism does not arise from an error in their
interpretations of the role of the Negro bourgeoisie, of
Washington, or of DuBois. They will defend all the historical romanticism and the sentimental slave hero worship
of the Aptheker Cult. They will say that all this is "past
history" and has no bearing on the "new situation." But
if one takes this position, then of what value is history of any
kind, and particularly, of what value is the Marxist historical
method? The inability to view Negro history in a theoretical
perspective leads to the inability to cope with the implications of Negro Nationalism.

NEGRO NATIONALISM AND THE LEFT

To the extent that the myth of a uniform "Negro People"
has endured, a clear understanding of the causes of Negro
Nationalism has been prevented. In reality, no such uni-
formity exists. There *are* class divisions among Negroes, and

it is misleading to maintain that the interests of the Negro working and middle classes are identical. To be sure, a middle-class NAACP leader and an illiterate farmhand in Mississippi or a porter who lives in Harlem, all want civil rights. However, it would be far more enlightening to examine why the NAACP is not composed of Negro porters and farmhands, but only of Negroes of a certain "type."

What we must ask is why these classes are not all striving in the same directions and to the same degree of intensity. Why are some lagging behind the integration movement, and still others in conflict with it? Where is the integration movement going? Into what is the integration movement integrating? Is the Negro middle class integrating into the white middle class? Are integrated lunch counters and waiting stations commensurate with integration into the "mainstream of American life"? And what exactly *is* the "mainstream of American life"? Will the Negro ten per cent of the population get ten per cent representation in the local, state and national legislatures?—or ten per cent representation in the exclusive club of the "Power Elite"?

Why are some Negroes anti-integration, others pro-integration, and still others "uncommitted"? Why is there such a lack of real unity among different Negro classes towards one objective? Why are there only some four hundred thousand members in the NAACP out of a total Negro population of some eighteen to twenty million? Why does this membership constantly fluctuate? Why is the NAACP called a "Negro" organization when it is an *interracial* organization? Why are the Negro Nationalist organizations "all Negro"? Why do Nationalist organizations have a far greater proportion of working-class Negro membership than the NAACP? Finally, why is it that the Marxists, of all groups, are at this late date tail-ending organizations such as the NAACP (King, CORE, etc.), which do not have the broad support of Negro workers and farmers? We must consider why the interests of the

Negro bourgeoisie have become separated from those of the Negro working classes.

Tracing the origins of the Negro bourgeoisie back to the Booker T. Washington period (circa 1900), E. Franklin Frazier, a Negro sociologist and non-Marxist scholar, came to the enlightening conclusion that "the black bourgeois lacks the economic basis that would give it roots in the world of reality." Frazier shows that *the failure of the Negro to establish an economic base in American society served to sever the Negro bourgeoisie, in its "slow and difficult occupational differentiation," from any economic, and therefore cultural and organizational ties with the Negro working class.* Since the Negro bourgeoisie does not, in the main, control the Negro "market" in the United States economy, and since it derives its income from whatever "integrated" occupational advantages it has achieved, it has neither developed a sense of association of its status with that of the Negro working class, nor a "community" of economic, political, or cultural interests conducive for cultivating "nationalistic sentiments." Today, except for the issue of "civil rights," no unity of interests exists between the Negro middle class and the Negro working class.

Furthermore, large segments of the modern Negro bourgeoisie have played a continually regressive "non-national" role in Negro affairs. Thriving off the crumbs of integration, these bourgeois elements have become de-racialized and de-cultured, leaving the Negro working class without voice or leadership, while serving the negative role of class buffer between the deprived working class and the white ruling elites. In this respect, such groups have become a social millstone around the necks of the Negro working class—a point which none of the militant phrases that accompany the racial integration movement down the road to "racial attrition" should be allowed to obscure.

The dilemma of the Negro intellectual in the United

States results from the duality of his position. Detached from the Negro working class, he tries to "integrate" and to gain full membership in a stagnating and declining Western society. At the same time, failing to gain entry to the status quo, he resorts to talking like a "revolutionary," championing revolutionary nationalism and its social dynamism in the underdeveloped world. But this gesture of flirting with the revolutionary nationalism of the non-West does not mask the fact that the American Negro intellectual is floating in ideological space. He is caught up in the world contradiction. Forced to face up to the colonial revolution and to make shallow propaganda out of it for himself, the American Negro intellectual is unable to cement his ties with the more racial-minded sections of the Negro working class. For, this would require him to take a nationalistic stand in American politics—which he is loath to do. Nevertheless, the impact of revolutionary nationalism in the non-Western world is forcing certain Negro intellectuals to take a "nationalist" position in regard to their American situation.

Although Frazier does not delve into the nature of Nationalism or connect the rise of Nationalism with the failure of the Negro bourgeoisie to establish the "economic basis" of which he writes, it can be seen that the sense of a need for "economic self-sufficiency" is one of the causes for the persistence of nationalist groupings in Negro life. The attempt to organize and agitate for Negro ascendency in, and control of, the Negro market is expressed in such racial slogans as "Buy Black." The Negro Nationalist ideology regards all the social ills from which Negroes suffer as being caused by the lack of economic control over the segregated Negro community. Since the Nationalists do not envision a time when whites will voluntarily end segregation, they feel that it is necessary to gain control of the economic welfare of the segregated Negro community. Moreover, many Negro Nationalists, such as the Black Muslims, actually believe that "racial separation" is in the best interests of both races. Others maintain this separatist position because of the fact of the persistence of segregation.

Thus, when Communists and other Marxists imply that "racial integration" represents an all-class movement for liberation, it indicates that they have lost touch with the realities of Negro life. They fail to concern themselves with the mind of the working-class Negro in the depths of the ghetto, or the nationalistic yearnings of those hundreds of thousands of ghetto Negroes whose every aspiration has been negated by white society. Instead, the Marxists gear their position to Negro middle-class aspirations and ideology. Such Marxists support the position of the Negro bourgeoisie in denying, condemning or ignoring the existence of Negro Nationalism in the United States—while regarding the reality of Nationalism in the colonial world as something peculiar to "exotic" peoples. The measure of the lack of appeal to the working classes of the Marxist movement is indicated by the fact that Negro Nationalist movements are basically working class in character while the new Negroes attracted to the Marxist movement are of bourgeois outlook and sympathies.

Ironically, even within Marxist organizations Negroes have had to function as a numerical minority, and were subordinated to the will of a white majority on all crucial matters of racial policy. What the Marxists called "Negro-white unity" within their organizations was, in reality, white domination. Thus, the Marxist movement took a position of favoring a "racial equality" that did not even exist within the organization of the movement itself.

Today, the Marxist organizations which advocate "racial integration" do not have a single objective for the Negro that is not advocated by the NAACP or some other reform organization. It is only by virtue of asserting the "necessity of socialism" that the Marxist movement is not altogether superfluous. It could not be otherwise. For Marxism has stripped the Negro question of every theoretical concern for the class, color, ethnic, economic, cultural, psychological and "national" complexities. They have no program apart from uttering the visionary call for "integration plus socialism" or "socialism plus integration."

However, when Marxists speak of socialism to the Negro, they leave many young Negro social rebels unimpressed. Many concrete questions remain unanswered. What guarantee do Negroes have that socialism means racial equality any more than does "capitalist democracy"? Would socialism mean the assimilation of the Negro into the dominant racial group? Although this would be "racial democracy" of a kind, the Negro would wield no political power as a minority. If he desired to exert political power as a racial minority, he might, even under socialism, be accused of being "nationalistic." In other words, the failure of American capitalist abundance to help solve the crying problems of the Negro's existence cannot be fobbed off on some future socialist heaven.

We have learned that the *means* to the *end* are just as important as the end itself. In this regard, Marxists have always been very naive about the psychology of the Negro. It was always an easy matter for Marxists to find Negro careerists, social climbers and parlor radicals to agree with the Marxist position on the Negro masses. However, it rarely occurred to Marxists that, to the average Negro, the *means* used by Marxists were as significant as the ends. Thus, except in times of national catastrophe (such as in the depression of the Thirties), Marxist means, suitable only for bourgeois reform, seldom approximated the aspirations of the majority of Negroes. Lacking a working-class character, Marxism in the United States cannot objectively analyze the role of the bourgeoisie or take a political position in Negro affairs that would be more in keeping with the aspirations of the masses.

The failure to deal adequately with the Negro question is

the chief cause of American Marxism's ultimate alienation from the vital stream of American life. This political and theoretical deficiency poses a serious and vexing problem for the younger generation who today have become involved in political activity centered around the defense of Cuba. Some accept Marxism; others voice criticisms of Marxist parties as being "conservative," or otherwise limited in their grasp of present realities. All of these young people are more or less part of what is loosely called the "New Left" (a trend not limited to the United States).

It is now the responsibility of these new forces to find the new thinking and new approaches needed to cope with the old problems. Open-minded whites of the "New Left" must understand that Negro consciousness in the United States will be plagued with the conflict between the compulsions toward "integration" and the compulsions toward "separation." It is the inescapable result of semi-dependence.

The Negro in the United States can no more look to American Marxist schema than the colonials and semi-dependents could conform to the Western Marxist time-table for revolutionary advances. Those on the American Left who support revolutionary nationalism in Asia, Africa and Latin America, must also accept the validity of Negro Nationalism in the United States. Is it not just as valid for Negro Nationalists to want to separate from American whites as it is for Cuban Nationalists to want to separate economically and politically from the United States? The answer cannot hinge merely on pragmatic practicalities. *It is a political question which involves the inherent right accruing to individuals, groups, nations and national minorities, i.e, the right of political separation from another political entity when joint existence is incompatible, coercive, unequal or otherwise injurious to the rights of one or both.* This is a principle that must be upheld, all expedient prejudices to the contrary.

It is up to the Negro to take the organizational, political and economic steps necessary to raise and defend his status. The present situation in racial affairs will inevitably force nationalist movements to make demands which should be supported by people who are not Negro Nationalists. The Nationalists may be forced to demand the right of political separation. This too must be upheld because it is the surest means of achieving Federal action on all Negro demands of an economic or political nature. It will be the most direct means of publicizing the fact that the American government's policy on "underdeveloped" areas must be complemented by the same approach to Negro underdevelopment in the United States.

It is pointless to argue, as many do, that Negro Nationalism is an invalid ideology for Negroes to have in American life, or that the Nationalist ideas of "economic self-sufficiency" or the "separate Negro economy" are unrealistic or utopian. Perhaps they are, but it must be clearly understood that as long as racial segregation remains a built-in characteristic of American society, Nationalist ideology will continue to grow and spread. If allowed to spread unchecked and unameliorated, the end result can only be racial wars in the United States. This is no idle prophecy, for there are many convinced Negro Nationalists who maintain that the idea of the eventual acceptance of the Negro as a full-fledged American without regard to race, creed or color, is also utopian and will never be realized. These Nationalists are acting on their assumptions.

Can it be said, in all truth, that Nationalist groups such as the Black Muslims are being unrealistic when they reject white society as a lost cause in terms of fulfilling any humanistic promises for the Negro? For whites to react subjectively to this attitude solves nothing. It must be understood. It must be seen that this rejection of white society has valid reasons. White society, the Muslims feel, is sick, immoral,

dishonest and filled with hate for non-whites. Their rejection
of white society is analogous to the colonial people's rejection of imperialist rule. The difference is only that people in
colonies can succeed and Negro Nationalists cannot. The
peculiar position of Negro Nationalists in the United States
requires them to set themselves against the dominance of
whites and still manage to live in the same country.

It has to be admitted that it is impossible for American
society as it is now constituted to integrate or assimilate the
Negro. Jim Crow is a built-in component of the American
social structure. There is no getting around it. Moreover,
there is no organized force in the United States at present,
capable of altering the structural form of American society.

Due to his semi-dependent status in society, the American
Negro is the only potentially revolutionary force in the
United States today. From the Negro, himself, must come
the revolutionary social theories of an economic, cultural and
political nature that will be his guides for social action—the
new philosophies of social change. If the white working class
is ever to move in the direction of demanding structural
changes in society, it will be the Negro who will furnish the
initial force.

The more the system frustrates the integration efforts of
the Negro, the more he will be forced to resolve in his own
consciousness the contradiction and conflict inherent in the
pro- and anti-integration trends in his racial and historical
background. Out of this process, new organizational forms
will emerge in Negro life to cope with new demands and
new situations. To be sure, much of this will be empirical,
out of necessity, and no one can say how much time this
process will take to work itself towards its own logical ends.
But it will be revolutionary pioneering by that segment of
our society most suitable to and most amenable to pioneering
—the have-nots, the victims of the American brand of social
underdevelopment.

The coming coalition of Negro organizations will contain Nationalist elements in roles of conspicuous leadership. It cannot and will not be subordinate to any white groups with which it is "allied." There is no longer room for the "revolutionary paternalism" that has been the hallmark of organizations such as the Communist Party. This is what the "New Left" must clearly understand in its future relations with Negro movements that are indigenous to the Negro community.

AUTHOR'S NOTE
This essay was the first theoretical attempt to deal with the reality of Afro-American nationalism after World War II. It was written primarily to open up the question for further exploration and development. It was not intended to be definitive; neither does the author agree with all of its conclusions today. Some of its historical analyses are not wholly consistent with fact.

—H.C.

Peter Labrie

THE NEW BREED

TODAY, within the black ghettoes of America, a new generation is making its presence felt. Its presence has far-reaching implications for the survival of the society at large, yet has not been sufficiently described and explained by the many observers and writers of the black communities. But perhaps the best way to understand it is not through the works of writers and scholars, but through certain changes occurring within the fertile music of the black communities.

Rhythm and blues, gospels and spirituals, and to a lesser extent, jazz, comprise some of the most significant components of black culture in America. Within their sounds and lyrics, are contained all the hurt, pain, and good times which black people share through their daily experiences. There is hardly an area of community life which escapes the contact of this music, and the musicians and vocalists, through their sounds, have come to function as powerful agents of moral and cultural influence on black behavior. Black music, then, is an integral thread which knits together, invigorates, and gives substance to the personal and collective experiences of the black masses.

However, since World War II, and particularly since the mid-fifties, important changes have begun to take place within black music. The rhythms have become more varied and complex. Black artists are getting more and more 'way out' with their sounds. The form and expression of black music is taking off in all kinds of directions.

These changes can be readily seen in jazz with the emergence of such artists as Ornette Coleman, Albert Ayler, Archie Shepp, and Sun Ra. LeRoi Jones writes how one of these artists "wants to play past note, and get them purely into sound . . . into the basic element, the clear emotional thing, freed absolutely from anti-emotional concept."

Another more important change has been in the direction of a fusion between the blues and the spirituals. It is now practically impossible to distinguish between the two. The spirituals now contain the 'big beat' and the blues the cries and humming of the spirituals. The whole career of the late Sam Cooke, in fact, exemplifies this blend. Starting out with a gospel group, the Soul Stirrers, he later branched into rhythm and blues and continued to record and influence music in both areas until his death. However, the big hit, "The Night Time is the Right Time," by Ray Charles and the Raylettes, is probably the prime single example of the blend between gospels and the blues. Produced in 1957, it marked the complete popularization of the gospel-blues sound in the black community.

That sound, so prevalent today, is clearly distinct from the blues of earlier years. The Clovers, the Orioles, Charles Brown, and particularly the older country blues singers, were producing a more secular song. Some of the older country blues singers, in fact, have reacted strongly against the more spiritual-oriented blues singers of today. It is well known how upset Big Bill Broonzy was over Ray Charles. As he said of Ray, "He's got the blues. He's crying sanctified. He's mixed the blues with the spirituals. I know that's wrong."

The mixture of the spirituals and blues, the new expressions in jazz, all are indications of deeply rooted ferment within black culture. Old forms are being discarded or improvised upon. New, different, and freer forms are being created. Recently there was a side out called "The New Breed." James Brown, in his hit recording "Papa's Got a Brand New Bag," refers to a 'new breed.' Beneath the pulsating changes in black music one can feel the absorption of new ingredients into black life, one can discern the emergence of a new breed of black man making his influence felt over the black ghetto.

It behooves us then to ask: Who is this new breed? What conditions have gone into his formation? What kind of consequences does his presence have for the society at large? What, in effect, is the new breed saying?

One way to begin to identify the emerging generation is through statistics. Reliable statistics tell us that one of the fastest growing population components in the United States today is the Negro now living in cities who was also born in cities. Before World War II, most blacks lived in the rural South, and most of those who did live in the North had been born in the South. They all had direct contact with the South. But today we find a completely new phenomenon: large, rapidly growing black populations who are indigenous to city life. These home-grown urban populations, while rural and Southern in the culture transmitted by parents, relatives and friends, have had no direct contact with the rural South. They are subjected to the rigorous ordeal of the urban way of life from birth and in that sense truly represent the 'new Negro.'

Yet, the statistics cannot give a complete picture, for they omit the cultural, social, and human experiences which surround the emergence of urban blacks. To get into a broader and deeper area of facts one must inquire into the black world itself, into the belief and authority structures that have held together the black community in America.

Every nation, tribe or natural community is ruled less by external forces from without than by internal forces from within. Compulsive internal images in the form of beliefs and moralities deeply embedded in the collective experiences which a natural group has shared in common regulate behavior among the members of the group and achieve thereby a necessary amount of cohesion and cooperation without which the group could not survive. It is these internal laws, generally called customs, folkways and mores, which make a person feel most comfortable among his own kind and less so among outsiders. The security and reliability which they furnish to one's environment enables the development of his personality. Every man owes his life, his moral and material condition, to his family and nation, for it is through these groups that he becomes human. Born helpless and dependent, he wins control over himself only through the education and sustenance given him by his people.

Our purpose here is to inquire into some of the vital internal forces that have traditionally structured the black community in America. Outside of a few exceptional cases, it is widely acknowledged that black people, from slavery to at least World War II, lived in a severely limited, isolated, and relatively static world. The status of the black man at the bottom of white society was well defined and strongly entrenched. The general orientation of his life and of his subjective mind was that which had been shaped by the slave-like conditions of the Southern plantation system. Although after World War I many black people migrated to cities, even those in the cities remained, by and large, a Southern people. The moral habits and cultural norms internalized in their consciences were essentially the same as those shared by their relatives and friends left behind in the South.

The particular belief structures that we want to bring out are those buttressed by two prevailing authorities: that of the church and that of the white ruling powers. Christianity, as taught and administered by the folk and storefront preachers, has always provided the dominant religious nourishment for the spiritualistic black masses. The church, its teachings and its activities have been not only the main religious institution, but also one of the major social institutions of the black community. Now, this is not to say that all black people went to church and lived by the Bible. For there has always been a large element of black 'sinners' who have lied, stolen, and done wrong. But the point is that even they did not really escape the church influence under which most of them came up. In fact, in most cases they probably looked upon themselves as 'sinners' and almost certainly would never have challenged the divine authority of Jesus or the Bible. Life had just become too cruel and hard for them to remain in the church or to live according to its teachings. They were 'wrong' and knew it. But if they ever decided to live 'right,' or if there ever was a 'right' way to live, it would be by the teachings of the church.

Just as the divine authority of Jesus was rarely questioned, so was the authority of the white people to rule black people rarely questioned. The black masses were so downtrodden, so poor, illiterate, and ignorant, and the white man's power over them so omniscient, that any thought of their rising to an equal status with the white man could not possibly have been taken serious for long. Whether it was at home, at church, at work, in the schools, in government, or in business, the authority of the white man hovered over their lives. It was always he who held the main strings to their well-being. In such a situation there was little alternative left for the black man except to acquire a slave mentality, to look upon himself as inferior and upon the white man as superior, and to accept the white way of doing things as the right way. After all, such an outlook corresponded to almost everything which he observed and experienced in real life. True, there were sporadic black rebellions, but none of these seriously threatened the dominant position of the white powers. In the end they probably only confirmed to most blacks that it would be impossible to break down the white man's domination over them.

The prevailing authorities of the church and the white man, then, were two dominant pillars of the traditional black world. The beliefs and moralities which they imprinted upon black behavior severely constricted and stunted the mental and moral development of the black population.

However, between the pre-World War II period and now, many things have come to pass: the Depression, two major wars, erratic but large-scale occurrences of industrialization and urbanization, economic and employment stagnation, etc. It would be impossible to measure the influence which all these complex societal forces had upon the black community, but one result is obvious; namely, that most black people have acquired a different basis for the existence of their community life. This basis, the slums of large American cities, was to prove quite different from the type of life which black people knew previously in the agricultural South. In the industrial cities the black people would have to adjust to more complex, but still oppressive, conditions of life.

The most far-reaching consequence of this adjustment has been the breakdown in the traditional authority and belief structures of the black ghetto. Today the church and ruling white authorities no longer hold the grip they once held on the minds of the black population. The Christianity preached under the slave conditions of the South simply cannot have any relevance or real meaning to the black youth coming up under the complex industrial systems of the cities. Young people today often know more about the world around them than do the preachers. The religious teachings of the black preachers have now become no more than a means of deluding the ignorant black masses so that the preachers themselves can become rich. New, college-trained 'sociologist' preachers are attempting to fill the vacuum left by the increasingly outcast uneducated preachers, but their formal style and presentation has no real attraction to black tastes. Thus, the influence of the black church has steadily decreased as black preachers have failed to keep up with the time and demands of the younger generation.

Another development of equal, if not more, significance is the rise to prominence of other religious groups, particularly the Nation of Islam. Although these groups may not have been very successful in recruiting great numbers of Negroes into their fold, they have been very effective in disseminating their special ideas. This means that they have questioned and repudiated some of the basic tenets of black Christianity. Arguments against the divinity of Jesus and the Bible and the justice of the Christian god, which previously would have been taboo, are now circulating freely within the black community. And the result is easy to see. A typical black youth today does not believe that he was born into a world of sin, that Jesus died 2000 years ago for his salvation, and that if he lives right now he will go to heaven when he dies. If anything, instead of believing that he owes God something, he believes that God owes him something. Young people want to enjoy life now and are not prepared to suffer and endure as their parents did. Unaccustomed and unable to meet these requirements of the young generation, the spiritual authority of the black church, like the influence of its preachers, has diminished.

The other belief structure to fall has been that of the authority of white domination; as James Baldwin has put it, "the American Negro can no longer, nor will he ever be controlled by White America's image of him." The mental subjection, the 'nigger' stigma, which the white power structure had imposed upon the black man, is now a thing of the past. A new pride in being black is growing. Light-skinned Negroes who might formerly have tried to pass for white are now glad to be *black*. Negroes no longer conceive of the world as one in which the white man has to be on the top and the black man on the bottom. For today there are black nations in Africa and a powerful yellow nation in Asia. Moreover, militantly charismatic and popular leaders, such as Malcolm X, have revealed to the masses the responsibility of the white power structure for their downtrodden condition. The white man's treachery, hypocrisy, and deceit in his exploitation of the black man has been brought into the open and his significance in a world populated by the darker races has been belittled. Thus, the determination of the U.S. government and military to win the war against the yellow people in Vietnam tends to confirm the now prevalent opinion in the black community that the white man will do almost anything to maintain his domination over the darker races.

The black world has changed so dramatically since before World War II that it would be impossible for a youth coming up today to have the same view of the world and himself which his father had. In the turbulent, lawless cities of America, the rhythm of life is quicker and more varied and complex for the masses. Life becomes a game in which one has to learn at an early age to be flexible, to scheme and hustle if he is to survive. 'Use or be used.' 'Stay one up on people or they'll take advantage of you.' Besides this necessity of scheming in order to make it, one also becomes exposed and attracted to a wide variety of social sets: storefront churches, hustling on the streets with pimps and prostitutes, black college crowds, integrated civil-righters and beatniks, the 'fingerpopping' and 'good times' groups, black nationalists.

When one moves between any of these sets he has to 'go through changes.' He has to change roles, to change his game so that he can get 'in' on a particular set. From hustle to hustle, from set to set—such is the pace of black life in the cities. The chaos and disorder which is a part of it makes it easy to understand why some of the new jazz sounds are becoming 'chaotic.' For, after all, in these sounds the musicians are often expressing no more than the various personal experiences which they have known in the disorder of American living conditions. It is also easy to understand how the spirituals become mixed up with the blues. The black singers coming up through the church take their singing, but not the religion, seriously. Eventually the forces of black life on the streets pull them into the world of secular music, and they carry their church sound and feeling, and sometimes even the church moralities, into the blues.

The tense, fast-driving demands of the rat race in modern America is pushing Negroes to do things which their fathers never would have thought of doing, and this is changing their music and their whole way of life. On the streets the young 'headshakers' used to just talk aloud, drink wine, and steal from and fight among each other. Today, besides drinking wine they are getting loaded on weed and other things. Instead of fighting among one another they are stabbing white people on the subways.

It is clear that the black nation today is in a state of profound flux. The collective conscience of the people is being shaken to the very core of its being, thereby causing black music and black culture to take off into so many different directions. The pathos, violence, and disorder involved in this period of severe cultural and social disruption are often shocking to older-generation Negroes.

One old-timer, Arna Bontemps, who had pleasant and memorable experiences in Harlem during the Negro Renaissance of the Twenties, was shocked and frightened by the conditions he found on Harlem streets in 1942. As he puts it, "At least one reason for avoiding Harlem night streets in 1942 would have been the fear of muggers. Where poets went about singing in the days of the new awakening, angry, frustrated boys now prowled. Where 'primitive' children had danced on the sidewalks, hungry, evil-eyed little criminals lurked in doorways. . . . Outlandish cults were meeting in some of the housefront churches where the moaning and shouting had formerly been spontaneous and filled with joy. What, in God's name, had happened?"

Actually, those conditions Bontemps was observing in 1942 were only the emerging conditions which produced the young generation of today. The fright and shock is largely in his own mind because he is looking at a younger generation through the lens of the older generation. The lawlessness which he observes is, by and large, no more than the breakdown of the cultural folkways and norms which he had known during his time. Although those norms may have provided some emotional and psychological security to his generation, they cannot do so for the present generation because they do not apply to the social realities of today.

New folkways, new mores are being developed. But before they become structured the old ones must be vomited up. This means a process of shock, disruption, and transformation. It can be a violent and frightening process. But it is not as destructive as Bontemps puts it, for there is a deeper, more creative and constructive aspect to it. For example, one can note that with the destruction and breakdown of law that have occurred during the riots in black communities, a deep sense of unity and brotherhood always asserts itself afterwards. People who have been in a black community in the aftermath of rioting have witnessed how the residents become more polite to each other on the streets, how they are not so quick to lose their temper with one another. There is a steady growth in their sense of community and a profound realization that they are sharing a common cause and a common destiny. The era of the new breed, then, is one of order in disorder, clarity in confusion, unity in disunity. The forces of violence and destruction become superceded by those of liberation and brotherhood.

Some have pointed out how Negroes, in throwing off the shackles of their 'slave mentality,' are responding to deep psychological needs for human dignity and self-respect. There is undoubtedly some truth to this, but more should be

added. The changing attitudes among the younger generation are more than a psychological quest for human dignity;
they express also a greater will to power.

Although many young blacks have come up in some of
the worst kind of squalor and poverty in the country, most
of them still have not had to work as hard as their parents
to make a living. The young people today not only do not
know what it is to labor all day in the fields under the hot
sun, they have no intention of doing so. They are not willing
to slave all day like their parents for only a few coins, when
they see white people all around them with easy jobs and
a lot of money. For these young people know how wealth,
success, and prestige are really earned in white society. The
white man with whom they have had experiences is not the
one who is openly evil, but the one who is double-faced, who
will smile in your face while he sticks a knife in your back.

In moving among the many social sets of the cities, these
ghetto blacks have come to find out that behind the rigid,
staid smile of the white woman is often no more than an
insecure, aggressive, and sexually deprived girl; that behind
the overfriendly air of the white man is frequently a neurotic,
power-driven adult with a childlike mentality. Negroes today
know well the type of lives which white people really live and
what they do behind the doors. That is why, unlike their
parents, they are not impressed by the examples set by white
people. Their actual experiences have taught them that
there is nothing genuine behind the examples and ideals of
white society. When a person had been 'turned out,' when
he has experienced life as it really exists, he just cannot
appreciate the artificial copy. He reacts against phony sets
and phony people. This is the environmental situation of the
new breed.

With his experiences under oppression and into the
deeper and more subjective realms of life, with his knowledge of the white world around him, it becomes almost im-

possible for him to be moral in any conventional sense. To have someone tell him to go to college so that he can get a good job, to be patient and grateful until some 'charity' organization gives him something, is an insult. If he wants something, he will take it in whatever way he can and by any means necessary. This is his will to power which goes beyond conventional morality.

The 'power' attitude among the young breed is what makes them so violence-prone. When the sun is hot, when there is no place to go and nothing to do because you don't have the means, it only takes a small incident of police brutality to set things off. Mass rioting and looting becomes an easy way to give vent to your pent-up anger and frustrations and to get the things you want and need.

It is this threat of violence among the young breed which makes them a highly political group. They are political not because they may like to go on demonstrations or engage in organized political activities, but because certain of their actions have far-reaching political consequences. Their willingness to use force and violence to get what they want upsets the traditional socio-economic organization of American cities. The white business and political leaders of the cities cannot stand for widespread looting and rioting because it means destruction of their properties and disturbing their political and social positions. This they fear much more than they do peaceful demonstrations and thus become willing to make token concessions to the black community.

Since the white power structure, through its black spokesmen, has lost its ability to control the black masses and keep them peaceful, it has now recognized a necessity to do something, quick. 'Good housing, schools, and jobs—these are the concrete essentials which the Negro needs.' Hence a host of shotgun crash programs: the War on Poverty, Neighborhood Youth Corps, apprenticeship training programs, neighborhood improvement centers, etc.

Yet it is becoming apparent that even these programs

can not cope with the situation at hand. One basic reason
is that the private economy can't create enough jobs and
decent houses for everyone. But another, more subtle, reason
has to do with the utilitarian nature of the solutions. It is
typical of white Americans to reduce everything to matters of
economic needs and basic commodities and to neglect
thereby the related human factors. After all, when one deals
with houses and jobs, one inevitably must confront the people
who are going to live in the houses and occupy the jobs.
So today, when one talks about housing and jobs for Negroes
he sooner or later will have to face up to black people themselves, which means facing up to attitudes of the younger
generation. And it is here, at the attitudes and emotions of
young blacks, that the shotgun poverty programs are likely
to fail. For their wants are not easily satisfied. If you offer a
young black a job, he might take it; then again, he might
not. He might not feel like working at the time. He is too
cool, too resentful, and too reckless to be easily satisfied.
He takes things in his own stride and is not prepared to
shape up to the hasty and ill-prepared demands of the white
man.

The attitudes, dispositions, and sounds of the new breed
are with us. No one can escape their influence. The penetrat-
ing glares, the pulsating rhythms, the down-to-earth beat—
those elements which have always been a part of music and
culture—have been reinvigorated and given a new distinct
overall quality. It is a quality which cannot be sufficiently
described in words, but whose end effect is unmistakably
clear. The end effect is one of completely unmasking the
listener, of piercing beneath artificial forms to the raw emotions and bare essentials.

The effect of new-breed music is part and parcel of the
total social situation created by the new breeder's influence.
With the development of his style of life, his actions and
will to power, everybody's front is broken and there is no-

where to hide. The white ruling interest can no longer hide behind their promises and declarations of freedom, democracy, and racial equality. No one believes their declarations any more. Now they stand fully exposed, resting on nothing but naked power, that power which was experienced so brutally by the black residents of Watts and which operates so blatantly in Vietnam and Santo Domingo. The black so-called leaders—the preachers, lawyers, and entertainers—no longer impress people with statements of what they can do and will do because everybody knows they can't back up what they say. Amid the masses of black people, the 'field Negroes,' stirred up by the younger generation, have shed their slave mentality and stand face to face with their real plight in the country. In the background one can hear the voices, the shouts and cries of the new breed.

What is the new breed saying? They are saying what the Bible prophesied long ago. 'We shall reap what our fathers have sown.' 'We are the last who shall be first.' The new breed has expressed a willingness to act. They are hostile and restless, ripe for militant black leadership. Can such leadership emerge? This is the central question which the new breed poses to the black ghetto in America today.

Calvin C. Hernton

DYNAMITE GROWING
OUT OF THEIR SKULLS

THE CEASELESS and unmitigated bigotry, torture, lawlessness and killing that American white men and women have historically inflicted upon black people in this country is now producing a species of black men, women and teenagers who are possessed with the psychology of the damned. Their view of America is the view of those who have been made into monsters. For it is now obvious that they have been designed as permanent victims for America's madness. They are beginning to feel that they are the *anointed* ones. Within the next few years, the nightmare that America has visited upon the lives of these people shall boomerang, and they will be more inhuman, more insane, than all the years of terror and violence that will have produced them.

When this happens America will be struck dumb, outraged. Local, state and national militia will be dispatched to the scene. But the scene will be everywhere. White men will be at a complete loss to understand why so many black people have gone mad. Because the white man looks at the world through the eyes of the white man, he understands, sees and feels only what his skin allows him to understand, see and feel, and according to whatever perversities with which he is afflicted.

Standing on top of the rest of humanity, from his upside-down position, the white man sees (W-W) the Wonders of the World. From the bottom of the heap, looking at things

WHITE AMERICA

NEGRO MASSES

right side up, the downtrodden Negro in the street sees
(M-M) the Madness of Mister Charlie. When the Negro
says that he wants to be a member of mankind, the upside-
down white man takes it to mean that the Negro wants to
sleep with white women. Up and down the line there is a
feedback on the M-W equation that causes static in communication, which functions to maintain the status quo,
which deludes white people into thinking that everything is
all right, which enrages the Negro.

When I say the record of the white's relations with the
Negro in America is a record of ceaseless slaughter, I mean
what the ordinary black folks in the South and in the
Northern ghettos mean. I am looking at the world through
their eyes, their lives; I feel what they feel, I am one of
them, and I mean what, for instance, my grandmother
means who is almost a hundred years old, and she ought to
know. I also mean what the contemporary millions of black
men, women and children mean, who view America through
an avalanche of mud being kicked into their faces. Two
hundred and fifty years of slavery . . . another hundred
years of lynching, flogging, intimidation, threats, murder,
humiliation . . . freelance acts of cruelty committed by individual white men as well as institutionalized crimes committed by groups of white men . . . and the wholesale viola-
tion of black women. Make no mistake—every time you see
a lower-class Negro, that Negro is thinking in the underground of his mind about *all* of these things; his everyday life,
so to speak, his sleep, is never as carefree as you force him
to pretend. But this is not all. The horror of horrors is the

fact that the American culture itself, when it comes to the average black man, is a civilization of violence. How else has it been possible to hold a group of people in the slime of oppression for the greater part of four centuries!

Slavery was established and enforced by violence and threats of violence. So too, segregation, discrimination, denial of fair employment and equality of opportunity, and the exclusion of Negroes from the processes of government, are obtained and perpetuated by methods of terror and lawlessness. The laws themselves—predominantly those in the South—which sanction and give moral fibre to practices of inhumanity against the Negro, along with the local courts which decide on the legality of the black man's humanity and citizenship, are criminal and immoral. The bulwark of persecution and tyranny against black people in America is the police force. With machine guns, rifles, shotguns, tear gas, armed trucks, helicopters, waterhoses and Nazi dogs, the police is maintained and cultivated for the suppression of the millions of dark people, most of whose lives are gestapoed and terrorized by the police every day and every night within the smoldering confines of the black ghettoes throughout America.

What is so uncanny, so terrifying, about all of this is that white people are doing these things, yet they claim ignorance of them; most of them deny outright that such despicable deeds are going on even as they watch them over television or, better yet, even while they are doing them. This denial of reality goes beyond the M-W equation. It strikes deep into the very psyche of American culture, which is a thing that intends to vilify and maim the *ethos* of downtrodden Negroes. The gut-bucket music of lower-class black people, their dance, their art, their divergent patterns of speech, their sexual spontaneity, their capacity for enjoyment in life even while suffering, their particular style of living—all have been the objects of scorn, ridicule, caricature, and devaluation by the folkways, myths, values and ideologies of the white world. When some aspect of the ethos of Black People (middle-class Negroes do not have an ethos) is accepted—their dance or music, for instance—it is accepted with pseudo appreciation, and embezzled from them for the exploitative purposes of making money for white people. Or it is accepted as being "exotic." Ray Charles, Mahalia Jackson, Lightning Hopkins, Little Richard—sex, soul, honkytonk!—it all represents something that will turn white folks on, something that will gratify their perversities.

The culture of the white world constitutes a violence against the mass of black people which is, in many ways, far more vulgar than outright acts of physical brutality. Everybody who is black is ugly. Beauty and femininity have been denied to Negroes on the basis that their hair, for instance, is not like the hair of white people, or their lips are not thin, or the color of their eyes is not blue. Because the Negroes who do the most frowned-upon type of work in America, which is the most valuable work and the least rewarded, along with those who are deprived of any work whatever; because these people cannot afford chic, effeminate, Ivy League clothes and expensive suburban boxes that might be free of rats and roaches, and must live four and five to a room; and because they exemplify a lust for life, including a less pathological attitude about reproducing themselves than white folks and middle-class Negroes—because of these things, white America conceives of these people as being uncivilized apes. In the area of the popular media—from reading the newspapers, for example—one would have to conclude that, until recently, the vast majority of black people in America were rapists and criminals. In that case, if such things were true, they would be highly commendable; even now one gets the impression that it is the black people who are causing all of the trouble, rather than the universal system of American violence against black people.

In the movies and works of fiction, both light and serious,

the rule has been to portray the black man of the masses as an inmate in prison, a laughing monkey or an obsequious servant. Of late, the rule is to picture him as a "problem," causing trouble for white folks.

In the social sciences, particularly in what passes for history, the black man is either excluded altogether or he is portrayed as an ignoramus incapable of executing social, political and moral responsibility. Richard Wright and Chester Himes are among the ten greatest writers that America has produced, and rank with the great writers of the world. Like the works of Dostoevski and Joyce, those of Wright and Himes are classics in the ethos and turbulent lives of common people. Yet it is rare indeed that you find their names, let alone their works, in the standard literature courses of American high schools and colleges.

W. J. Cash, a Southerner, wrote a very impressive book entitled *The Mind of the South*, in which he painstakingly dissected the economic, religious, political, moral, and all other sectors of thought in the South. At the time Cash wrote that book—slightly more than two decades ago—there were at least eight million black people in the South. Nowhere in Cash's huge book did he see fit to mention, let alone to incorporate, anything regarding the thoughts of the Negro. Ergo, the purpose of the book was to deny systematically not only the thought of, but the existence of, eight million people without whose presence, ironically, there would have been no "mind" of the South, certainly not the mind that Cash wrote about. This propagandizing in the social sciences and the literature constituted a significant portion of the education of every white child in America, and it has been employed in the Negro schools to teach black children to hate and degrade and feel ashamed of their own humanity.

The violence in the culture of America against black people forces the Negro into what psychiatrists Gregory Bateson and

R. D. Laing call the "double bind." The culture seeks to do harm to the Negro—if the Negro refuses to submit he is cast into the role of the criminal. The black man is expected to pledge allegiance to a civilization which openly destroys him every day. The black man is conscripted into the Army and ordered to kill people who, it would seem, are far less harmful to him than those in his own country. Black men are expected to do violence to other men—the majority of whom are colored—in the service and promotion of a system whose very purpose and function are to do violence to black men.

The alienation of a man in this manner succeeds not only in alienating him from the culture in which he has his birth-right, but expels him from the integrity of his death. To demand that a man accept your views of his experiences under your oppression is to deny that man the validity of his own feelings, along with the meaning of his suffering. Such a man, whether he is downtrodden or rich, walks around haunted by the forbidden knowledge that he is living in a republic of terror and violence every second of his life. If that man lives for a hundred years and manages to acquire a million dollars, he never really experiences within himself what we call a sense of inner security. Not once.

But, what happens to the biography of a single black man who might survive in America for a hundred years is nothing, compared with what happens to the humanity of millions of people who live under a system of universal terror and violence for almost four centuries! The junctures at which biography and society encounter each other determine the psychological nature, as well as the human nature, of the homo sapiens. This is what C. Wright Mills was trying to demonstrate all of his life. Assuming that black people are homo sapiens—i.e., rational, biological entities malleable to environmental circumstances—three hundred and fifty years of hatred and mayhem have wrought within the Negro *three distinguishable species of contemporary black men and women.*

The definitions and roles of the Negro that are propagated and expected by American society and culture are as follows.

1. Black people are violent by nature . . . BUT, in their attitudes and behavior towards white people, these same black people are by nature childlike, docile, and affable.

2. Black people are possessed with unlimited potency and primitive sexual energy . . . BUT, these same black people are impotent and sexless when it comes to white women.

3. Black people live under conditions of extreme and prolonged oppression . . . BUT, these same black people are happy this way, and actually appreciate and love their oppressors.

4. More than ninety-nine per cent of the light-skinned black people in America, who now constitute at least seventy-five per cent of all black people, are the result of white men mating with black women . . . BUT, it is the black man who is the cause of mongrelization of the races.

These and other contradicting definitions of the black man and his situation, plus the violence employed to enforce these paradoxes upon and within the Negro, have produced a kind of black man who is nothing more than the function of the white man's insane definition of what is going on. Consequently, we hear many Negroes saying they are invisible, or that they do not know who they are. They do not know what their names are, what color they are, or what sex they are. They experience, and consider, themselves as a conundrum, a puzzle whose pieces are blowing in the wind, which in the final analysis is true, and pitiful. I call these Negroes the Species of the Self-Riddled Negro.

More puzzling, however, is the emergence of an unprecedented phalanx of Negroes who advocate measures and policies for doing away with oppression that would have caused Spartacus to vomit. Hate yourselves—love your oppressors. Let your blood flow—not the blood of your enemies. Though they maim and murder you, even as you lie prostrate beneath the hard heels of their boots, you must not raise a finger to defend yourselves, for you would be worse than your enemies are. I call these Negroes the Species of the Non-Violent Negro.

The self-riddled Negro requires no discussion. He is transparent to everybody; his problem is metaphysical, or metasexual, which is the same thing. As long as he remains self-riddled he is dangerous to no one, he is merely a riddle to himself. But the non-violent Negro is out here in the middle of things trying to grapple with the real world. He is not only weird, but controversial as well.

Non-violence, as an instrument of protest, has never been spared of underground criticism; recently, however, the philosophy and tactics of non-violence have become game for open controversy. Since the disillusioning aftermath of the March on Washington, outright dissension and denunciation have mounted, especially among the ranks of younger Negroes who are rapidly developing into, or casting their lot with, the Third Species of contemporary black people—the Existential Negroes—to whom I will come when I finish with the species of non-violent Negroes.

Negro oppression is part and parcel of the history of the growth and development of American civilization; similarly, the species of the non-violent Negro, and the movement itself, must be dissected and evaluated as a product of historical oppression and violence against black people in America. But first, it is necessary to shed some light on the biography and the milieu of the Negro who is the fountainhead of the movement, and the archetype of the species.

Dr. Martin Luther King, Jr., was born in Atlanta, Georgia in a twelve-room house situated in the heart of downtown Atlanta on Auburn Avenue, a street which, according to

King's biographer Lerone Bennett, occupied then and now
a position in the Negro community similar to the Wall
Street of the white community. After completing his early
education in the Atlanta public school system, King enrolled
in Morehouse College, an all-boys school famous for its
emphasis on Negro adaptation of white, Protestant middle-
class success. King graduated from Morehouse with honors
and matriculated with equal success in two high-ranking
Northern universities, Crozer Theological Seminary and
Boston University, where, at the latter, he received his
Doctorate degree in Divinity before he was thirty years old.
The father-in-law of King's father was pastor of the famed
Ebenezer Baptist Church in Atlanta. King's father inherited
this church, and later King himself served as assistant pastor
under his father. The Ebenezer Baptist Church is an institution attended mainly by well-off, highbrow Negroes. The
Dexter Street Baptist Church in Montgomery, Alabama, for
which King himself served as pastor, is, according to King's
biographer and friend, "an upper income congregation composed largely of professionals and teachers." Lerone Bennett,
in *What Manner of Man*, states: "Martin Luther King, Jr.,
belongs to the Negro leadership class . . . true to his Black
Puritan heritage of *noblesse oblige*, he argued passionately
for the hard and narrow path of duty, a straight and narrow
path that led to the high mountain of fame." Dr. King
attempted suicide twice in his youth; on one occasion, when
his grandmother died, he threw himself out of the window
from the second story of his house.

The well-off, highbrow class of Negroes constitute what
E. Franklin Frazier called the "Black Bourgeoisie." A student of Frazier, Dr. Nathan Hare, has described the middle-
class Negro as a "Black Anglo-Saxon." These Negroes represent, in every way permitted by white society, the attitudes,
values and aspirations that are associated with the white-
Protestant middle class in America. A great deal of stress is

put on success, on exemplifying good manners, keeping their hair trim, dressing presentably, refraining from loudness and over-indulgence. Indeed, they are preoccupied with trying not to appear like plain ordinary black people, to whom they often refer in private as "niggers." In many cases, they are ashamed of so-called run-of-the-mill Negroes. In all regards, both in his behavior and aspirations, the middle-class Negro practices restraint and refinement.

The universalization of violence against the Negro, which is inherent in American culture, affects the very socialization process of the Negro child, especially the child in the black bourgeois setting. As the child is being tutored in the refinements, restraints and weaknesses of the so-called better class of Negroes, he is simultaneously being trained to accept the violence of white society as a way of life. Lorenzo Patterson—West Indian scholar, lecturing before a group of London psychiatrists studying the political aspects of schizophrenia—observed this same phenomenon in the rearing of West Indian children. The West Indian mother wants her child to be good, to stay out of trouble, which means that she passes on to him—perhaps through the acceptance of her violence as discipline—the acceptance of the violence of the system. When you see the docile, laughable, folk-minded, cajoling, mother-directed Negroes from the West Indies, you are looking at the effects of the pseudo-paternalism of the violence of slavery being handed down through the mothers in a time when legal slavery has long passed. So too, the black child in America is robbed of manhood because the mother and father, especially those of the middle class, fear that if they let him keep his manhood—his instinct to assert himself—it will get him into trouble, with white men and women! The Negro child learns to annihilate himself, to grow limp, before Mister Charlie and Miss Ann. The middle-class Negro child is trained to be a sissy.

The emergence of the species of non-violent Negroes to the forefront of the freedom movement came shortly after the success of, and even during, the Montgomery bus protest movement in the mid-1950's. Dr. King was then extremely young, well-educated, and considered one of the new young "radical" Negroes. There were disputes among the older leaders about Dr. King's role as leader; but in time, the opposition was thoroughly removed, owing partly to the success of the boycott and, more significantly, to the way King had handled an explosive incident which occurred during the heyday of the boycott—the bombing of his home. On that night, a mob of young and lower-class Negroes gathered outside King's house with clubs, bottles, knives and possibly guns, too; the word echoed through the crowd: "Let's get the white man!" Tremors went over the city. The angry blacks were talking back to the police, and the police got scared, because Negroes constitute a large part of the population in Montgomery and they could have made that city look as if General Sherman had marched to the sea again. Dr. King emerged on the bombed ruins of his porch that night and told the Negroes that they must forgive and learn to love the doers of violence, such as the bomb throwers who had barely missed killing him and his family. Instantly, throughout the nation, the press acclaimed this remarkable new species of the Negro; all of the liberals, and even some Southern moderates and diehards, praised the philosophy of love and non-violence as the best brand of Negro protest. From that night on, there was no question in the minds of white people as to who was the new leader of black people in America.

After the bus movement, when things quieted down, Dr. King went on a speaking tour, lecturing on non-violence, and his name was continually in the press. A few years later the sit-ins and wade-ins and freedom rides were launched by a newer, younger and even more "radical" group of Negroes, mostly students, white and black, from South and North. Dr. King flew to the scenes, organized the Southern Christian Leadership Conference (SCLC) and assumed the leadership of the new upheaval. At this very moment, commanding a large organization of men (SCLC), many of whom are well-salaried, Martin Luther King, Jr., is not unlike the president-director of an American corporation with a network of vertical and horizontal subsidiaries, functionaries and lesser workers crosscutting on down the ranks.

In the beginning, the species of non-violent Negroes so revitalized the plight of black people in America that, while most whites were giving lip service to the non-violent brand of protest, many of them were deeply suspicious. Permeated by corruption themselves, they could not keep from wondering what those Negroes were up to now; that is, beside getting their rights, what were their "real" motives?

The phenomenal success of the Montgomery bus boycott and the equally unprecedented publicizing of the Negro's situation, are, unquestionably, achievements of the non-violent movement. Beyond these, however, the role of the non-violent Negroes has diminished with each new solemn parade or bloody bath that has occurred. Many Negroes now hold the philosophy of non-violence—not to mention its exponents—in utter contempt, accusing it of grave breaches of responsibility. To employ certain tactics in a battle of social reality, involving the immediate well-being as well as the future of millions of people, when those tactics and the philosophy underpinning them seem to work more for the protection of the haters and doers of violence than they do for those who are being hated and maimed and murdered, smacks of blindness, if not something even more tragic. The lie-down-before-your-oppressor philosophy is now a treadmill upon which the Negro is running but getting nowhere fast. Everywhere the non-violent Negroes go—Birmingham, Selma, Chicago, Washington, California, Cleveland—the downtrodden blacks parade themselves and get beaten up, but rarely is anything really achieved when the deal goes down. The obsession with love-your-enemy and do-not-fight-back makes it appear that the black man is the criminal if he so much as lifts a finger to shield himself from getting his balls kicked in.

The main function of the non-violent Negroes appears now to be that of keeping the other Negroes in their places. This is precisely what a lot of white people desire—that by being non-violent, Negroes cooperate in the very violence that is being heaped upon them. Richard Wright pointed out years ago that this is the "Ethics of Living Jimcrow." It is founded upon the dictum that a Negro must never strike a white man, no matter what the circumstances may be—the white man can insult, kick, beat, kill a black man or even rape a black man's wife or daughter, and the Negro is supposed to drop his head, tuck his tail between his legs and scurry away like a little black puppy.

Every time white men want Negroes to conform to these ethics, they call the non-violent Negroes to the scene. Check the record. When the blacks were rioting in parts of New York, for instance, Mayor Wagner, ignoring the local leaders, summoned Dr. King all the way from Georgia, when in fact, King has not spent over two weeks at a time in New York in all of his life and does not have as much influence among Negroes in that city as perhaps the Mayor himself! The non-violent Negroes are being used to deflect the Negro struggle away from the needs of the masses of black people; they are being used to direct the struggle more along the lines of the black bourgeoisie, most of whom are sitting in their mortgaged homes in Negro suburbia, watching, over their twenty-one-inch TV screens, lower-class blacks being brutalized in the debris-laden streets of the ghettos.

The style of leadership of the non-violent Negroes derives from their Black Puritanical Bourgeois milieu. The planks in the platform of their leadership aspire to what all middle classes of oppressed people aspire to—civil rights for themselves, integration with the dominant class, and equal participation with the dominant class in exploiting their own people along with the exploitation of anybody else in the world. We do not need a Karl Marx to tell us this. It is as plain as day to every black man in the streets. It is not nice or cultured for middle-class Negroes to fight, to be aggressive; they do not want to "embarrass" their oppressors, they do not want to appear "rude and uncultured" by confronting their oppressors head on. I know, I have been there. So they participate with the white man in censoring the leaders and spokesmen of the downtrodden people, such as happened to John Lewis during the great march on Washington. Typically, middle-class Negroes, as well as those who are aspiring, refer to the blacks who are starving with the rats in the dilapidated tenements of high-rent ghettos as "hoodlums." These people are preyed upon by facile forces of violence from both the white world and the petty bourgeois world of their own race.

The species of the non-violent Negro, as a progressive social force towards the liberation of black people in America, has been eclipsed by the very forces that have called the species into being and yet prevail against it—the forces of compromise, corruption, hate and violence. Then, too, the socio-economic, political and cultural organism that is America, is a powerful octopus. It has proved itself capable of absorbing crisis after crisis throughout the world; and it has literally swallowed up the non-violent movement, which now represents, at best, nothing more than obsolete idealism.

Historically, the personality of the non-violent Negro represents the social evolution of the "New Species of the House Negro." Any Negro, usually the bastard descendant of his master, who works as a servant in the Big House around the family and peers of the master, who thereby acquires the

manners and feelings and aspirations of the master class, or
who, through the liberal paternalism of the master class,
may actually receive a formal education—any Negro who does
not want those rough, uncouth blacks who slave in the
fields to endanger either the place he has been given in the
master's house or his chances of becoming even more similar
to the oppressors of his race—is a House Negro. Repeat: the
majority of middle-class Negroes are creatures of hypocritical
white Protestantism and perverted socio-moral puritanism.
The philosophy that compels any man to lie down before his
enemies when he knows they are going to tread on his flesh—
the flesh with which he makes love to his women—seems
rather queer to me. I fail to find anything creative, anything
socially or spiritually uplifting in that form of loving your
enemy. What I find in it is the repudiation of one's body,
one's manhood—precisely what the racists desire of the
Negro. I do not think it is only coincidental that it has been
almost impossible to get critical discussions published about
the non-violent Negroes in the respectable nationwide media.
If we are going to be non-violent, let us all be non-violent,
whites as well as blacks. Nobody has endeavored to set up
Mahatma Gandhi workshops among the white mobs and
murderers in the South. I do not expect the President of the
United States to do it, as everybody knows that he believes
in using bombs. But Billy Graham flies all over the world
preaching about the blessings of the Holy Father and the
milky-white way. I know because I make a point of keeping
track of influential people. Graham is influential; recently he
was in England, in Kent and Birmingham, preaching the
love of the white mushroom to British workers, frustrated
housewives and other sinners—and he brought thousands to
their knees. Yet I recognize how useless it would be to suggest
that Billy Graham use his influence, his great voice—voice of
America—on the white men, women and teenagers throughout the deep and not-so-deep South who are screaming pro-

fanities as they beat and mutilate hymn-chanting black people, throw bombs on little black girls praying in the house of God . . . young girls whose lips will never know the touch of a kiss. I know that Billy Graham knows out of whose blood and flesh his bread is transubstantiated into money and wine.

The same goes for the middle-class, non-violent, obsessed Negroes who are set up as leaders of the black people. Roy Wilkins, Leon Sullivan, Whitney Young, Absent Clayton Powell, Cecil Moore, A. Philip Randolph, James Farmer (Who ever heard of a leader retiring, with benefits!), to name a few of those operating on a wide scale.

What I cannot accept is that of all the bourgeois Negroes who so unilaterally condemn black people defending themselves against racists and murderers, not one of them has denounced with equal fervor the violence that Americans, white and black, are heaping upon huge portions of humanity outside of the United States. The Nobel Prize winner for Peace refused to make a statement on the extraterritorial wars being waged by America until he was pressured into doing so. After he conferred with several respectable, big-moneyed white people, he came out with some milk-warm, ambiguous oratory.

The underlying meaning of the continued enforcement upon black people—and it is an enforcement—of the philosophy of love and non-violence, for the white men and women who are victimizing and killing these people as well as for a government which permits all of this, is but the furthering of the alienation of black men and women from the society in which they suffer and from the very psyches and physical bodies upon which this suffering is being inflicted. But the ideology which decrees that the black man is at best his own enemy and at worst a downright criminal if he should defend himself against hate and tyranny boomerangs after awhile.

Every attempt at mystifying black people as to the cause of their oppressive circumstances, as well as how best to get rid of these circumstances, leads to clarity in the end, a bitter clarity. For the black man in the street has always known his enemy—"Ofay!" That word came from the language of the streets, a language originally unknown to whites and middle-class Negroes alike; it could not be learned at Boston University or Howard University. Pig Latin: *Ushhay puay erehay omescay aay hiteway anmay. Hiteway anmay siay hetay nemyay foay lackbay eoplepay.* Translation: "Hush up here comes a white man. White man is the enemy of black people." The old langauge has been discovered and it no longer serves the needed function. But there is a new language comprising everyday symbols which seem harmless enough to most whites but which are saturated with terrible meaning for every black man in the street. James Brown screaming: "Money Won't Change You But Time Will Take You Out." Ray Charles: "You Know The World Is In An Uproar, The Danger Zone Is Everywhere."

The instinct for self-preservation is granted to the lowest of animals. To deny or prohibit, by any means, the spontaneous reaction of a human being to protect himself is to turn that human being into an obsequious victim—but only for a little while—from the outset you run the risk of contradicting your purpose, you run the risk of producing in that man a monster, a demon, that will break loose and kill you even if it means killing himself.

From the beginning, from slavery, unlike the house Negroes, the ordinary blacks worked and lived in the fields. They were the "field Negroes." They were abject slaves. They existed for no other purposes except to be worked, beaten, raped and sold. In all other respects they were ignored. The only time they were given serious thought was when the masters learned, usually from one of the house Negroes, that a revolt—"trouble"—was stirring among them, a revolt which, if not brutally put down, was appeased through some kind of meaningless "reform," and usually through the cooperation of the house Negroes. Because it was the house Negroes who, if anybody did, benefited most from the "reform."

The same situation applies today. One can recite example after example. In fact, most of the ordinary Negroes in present-day America still live in the fields, the geographical fields as well as the social and cultural wastelands of the United States. In the South, the Negro section of town is always across the railroad tracks. In Kosciusko, Mississippi, James Meredith's hometown, the pavement disappears when you come to the part of town where Negroes live. After being away for ten years I went back to my hometown, Chattanooga, Tennessee, and found that the air in my particular neighborhood was as foul from the sewer ditch as it was when I was a boy; the boys and girls of my generation had grown up, those who had survived, to be replicas of the wretched men and women I remembered when I was a child; my stepfather had managed to put himself in debt for the rest of his life by buying a new house in a better neighborhood, and the sewer ditch there, too, vomited up stagnant water onto the lawn and under the house; the better neighborhood was mazed with its symbolic share of dirt roads and those that were paved were done so carelessly that soon they would be full of guts and ditches. Nashville, Tennessee is the same way; so is Birmingham, Jacksonville, Florida, Mobile and Savannah—the entire South is this way. Newark, New Jersey is this way; socially and culturally every ghetto in America is this way; Washington, D.C. is this way—generation after generation, the wretchedness of the average black man and woman in the street gets worse. It is uncanny.

When I worked for the New York Department of Welfare as a social investigator, my beat was Harlem. Every time an investigator left the office to visit the clients he wrote on his

time card that he was going to the "field." I walked the
streets of Harlem for over a year, in and out of every kind
of time bomb that you can imagine—that is what most of
the tenements in Harlem are, time bombs. A light-skinned
Negro woman owned a five-story dilapidated tenement; the
eight-by-ten, unfurnished, unheated, roach- and rat-infested
rooms were rented mainly to unwed mothers for as much as
twenty-two dollars a week. The woman also owned a chicken
shack around the corner from the building. One afternoon
I went in there to ask her if she knew the whereabouts of
two of my clients who lived in her building. She looked at
me boldly, saying that today was Friday, that usually the
girls went to the "field" for the weekend, and she smiled.
Another landlady of similar practicality told me point-blank
that she would give me the first two weeks' rent for every
welfare recipient I sent to her for a room, provided the
recipient was a female who had no objection to working in
the "field."

The conditions of contemporary black people, and the attitude that the rest of America has towards these people,
make them analogous to their ancestors of nearly four centuries ago—field Negroes. Now, however, the men, women
and children in the "fields" of the ghettos constitute the
embodiment of *all* of the hurt, depravity and anger stemming
from three-and-a-half centuries of ceaseless inhumanity
against black people on the part of white America. Get this
and get it straight: When you meet a black man on the
street, you are not looking at *a* Negro of *a* particular generation; no, you are looking at an accumulation, an historical
phenomenon, a dialectical synthesis of nearly four centuries
enclosed in a single black skin, and—if he is not a middle-
class, non-violent Negro, which he is likely not to be—you
are looking at dynamite. I give you the Third Species of contemporary black men, the Existential Negro.

Right now, in concert with the violence being visited

upon black people, permitted by the American government as well as by the black-man-don't-defend-yourself philosophy of Negro leaders, the ghettos of America are manufacturing men and women who are becoming more pathological, and far more capable of violence, than the system of oppression in which they are being victimized and bled of hope. I recorded a discussion with twenty Chicago Negroes, one of whom said:

The only way Negroes like me are going to get a chance to live like human beings instead of like niggers—yeah, niggers, that's what we live like—the only way is if some foreign country comes over here and put the white man in his place, put him out of business! Before we ever get our freedom Sam's got to be conquered by a foreign power. The way I see it it's got to be Africa or the Chinamen, because ain't nobody else going to do it. Not Russia, shit, Russia is white and all white people are against colored people when the shove comes to push. But Africa and China ain't strong enough to whip Sam, not yet, not for a long time, and we ain't got no time, things are getting too hot over here, things are coming to a head. The man keeps messing over us and keeps bulljiving around. All that a boot like me can do is go mad, crazy, kill until I get killed, and I won't be running and jumping and hiding when that day comes, either.

The man who made that statement has a wife and three daughters, and has worked as a department store janitor for ten years. He goes to church, he is not flat broke, he earns sixty dollars a week, and he has a hustle on the side— you know, he can get you a television or maybe a studio couch for a third of the price. The thing that keeps bugging this man, and millions like him, is that every time he encounters himself in the mirror, or in his thoughts, or in the face of someone else, or in the smile of one of his daughters, he encounters a symbolic thing which is the object of perpetual rejection, hatred and violence of white America. It is impossible to know the quantity and intensity of violence that white people have let loose against Negroes, say, since the desegregation of Central High School in Little Rock, Arkansas. If we begin with that situation, highlighting Meredith's three years at Mississippi University, then Birmingham, Selma, and the recent madness that gripped Granada, Mississippi when black children went to the wrong schoolhouse, we would have enough violence and slaughter to compare with the reign of terror during the French Revolution. Noticeable among the mobs are hordes of screaming women, but even when the mobs are predominantly all male, one still gets the impression that they are mobs of hysterical females. One wonders deeply why the government of the United States seems to be unable or unwilling to prevent or control the mobs, when some middle-class, non-violent Negroes and a few white liberals and white hipsters have been murdered, and the murderers unapprehended or set free.

But for the unwed mothers, the hustlers, the vice-preyed-upon youth, the hoodlums of the street, the unemployed and the under-employed with families, and the plain, hard-working, ordinary black folks—as far as these people are concerned, the Negro Revolution is a mockery. Desegregated schools, colleges, lunch counters, HARYOU, ACT, the Civil Rights Bill, the War on Poverty, and the rest—these are the fruits from the marching and singing and getting beaten and murdered; and all these things mean is that a few Negroes have been granted the opportunity of associating with whites (integration!), that several more of the middle-class ones have gotten jobs (graft!), that some militant ones have been bought off (bribed!), and that a lot of liberals and bigot perverts wearing familiar disguises are working-socially among the heathen blacks. A young black poet, well known in New York, who is working for the President's War on Poverty, wrote me a letter:

When I first came to this program straight from San Francisco and Acapulco, my head was blowing and I was a bit enthusiastic about being able to help out in the ghetto. BUT I WAS NAIVE . . . I'm at the top of my wits to merely pass through this laugh show every week. . . . It is not a war on poverty, it is a war on the poor folks . . . militant blacks are being bought out right and left by this here war. . . . Everybody is getting bread from the war . . . the Catholics are weird, some very radical and some very conservative. They showed us all the radicals at first but then now the conservatives leak in. . . . I published a raggy raggy Harlem newsletter. Published the janitor of the school . . . he writes plays . . . met me at Baldwin's . . . so I published this here poem of his on raggy mimeo and the cat gets euphoric, starts talking about his opportunity. . . . Also I brought *Manchild In The Promised Land* in by Claude Brown for the kids to read. Claude still lives in the area (I'm on 141 between 7th and 8th). . . . The kids flipped that the book was there and they could read it, the brothers and sisters were so impressed it made me a little sad. They are ignored and impoverished . . . everyone is bullshitting, trying to get the money. . . . The people know it, everyone knows it.

The persistent corruption and bad faith that characterize America's relationship with the Negro—especially with the bottom rungs of the black people—but which have been hidden in the past, are now so blatant that little children can see what is going on. In *Three Years In Mississippi*, James Meredith, with an openness that five years ago few Negroes would dare, writes about the initial attitude of cooperation and game-playing on the part of the late President Kennedy and Governor Wallace, and even the readiness of the NAACP, in the courts, to sell Meredith short of his full rights as a citizen of Mississippi and a student of that university. The classic example of game-playing in (or *with?*) the Negro struggle was the march on Washington. It was a mammoth game. The original idea germinated among the field Negroes in the ghettos subsequent to the disillusioning bloodbath in Birmingham: Negroes got mad and started talking about storming the White House, tying up Congress and even lying down on the runways of the airports. As soon as the white folks heard about this, they called a meeting with the chiefs of staff of the non-violent Negroes in the Carlyle Hotel in Manhattan and mapped out plans for "shaping up" the march on Washington. An organization was formed, the Council for United Civil Rights Leadership (Wow!); Whitney Young was made chairman and Stephen Currier was the co-chairman. Stephen Currier, a white millionaire philanthropist, gave the Negroes eight hundred thousand dollars, made available to them the top public relations experts, opened up the news media across the nation for their disposal, and promised them seven hundred thousand dollars more, which he gladly gave after the march was over. During that time (1963), Adam Clayton Powell alluded to the affair rather bitterly in a speech he made in Cobo Hall. It seemed that he had been on one of his Puerto Rican vacations, for which he is famous, and had been excluded from the game.

The existential Negroes are being driven beyond the zone of faith, and not only in reference to Negro leaders and liberal whites: They are far on the road to losing faith in the American Dream. On the afternoon of the loss of faith comes the death of hope . . . eternal night engulfs the mood of the Negro. "My man, what drags me about the Audubon Ballroom scene," said a big, black, well-dressed man standing in front of Small's Paradise, "is that it was not Luther King instead of brother Malcolm who got washed away." Several months before the big Negro said this to me, I had been in South Carolina, in the home of people I considered to be middle-class Negroes. They have a sixteen-year-old son who had won a scholarship to Yale University. We were watching the police and the black people of Watts over television when, suddenly, without a word, the son got up and kicked in the face of the set. In my hometown of Chattanooga, I sat with a boyhood friend who had returned from Chicago to see his mother. One of his legs was missing, from the Korean war. He said that if Uncle Sam can rebuild an entire country like Germany within ten years, after two wars, there was no reason in the world for the continued existence of the ghettos in America—except one: the Germans are white, the ghettos are black.

The wretchedness of every downtrodden Negro in the United States is inextricably linked, in theory and fact, with the existence of the big-city ghetto. Everybody knows this, or ought to know it, but nobody is doing anything that will wipe the ghettos from the face of America, because, they say, they do not know what to replace the ghettos with. Therefore—contrary to what they all say, and due to the circumstances, which I know are hard—the continued existence of the ghettos is the best thing that can possibly happen to the Negroes who suffer within the ghetto confines. The big-city Negroes are existential Negroes fullblown; they are the liberating oppressed. The existence of the ghetto shall frustrate them and enrage them to the point of explosion— the point of no return. They shall rise up and, without worrying or even thinking about what to replace the ghettos with, destroy them. The ghettos in the big cities of the South and the North are the dynamos of oppression, but they are also the volcanos of liberation!

Violence, only violence, smoldering within the dark pits of the psyche, will at once be the tool of liberation as well as the experience which will recreate a sense of manhood and human worth within the souls of black folk. When I worked for the New York Department of Welfare, I discovered on the wall of the room of one of my Harlem unwed mothers, a painting by one of her bastard sons, a twelve-year-old school dropout who was then doing time for burglary. The painting was of a group of Negroes being beaten with sticks and clubs and guns by a gang of respectable-looking whites (their faces were smiling almost ecstatically), including what I took to be a few policemen in blue uniforms with huge distorted silver badges. The Negroes were bleeding and some were sprawled on the pavement; there was a lot of green paper flying around—money I supposed—and hanging out of the pockets of the white men who, incidentally, had big pot-bellies. The painting was done in oil color, heavy reds and greens and blues with thick splotches of black. In a circle, with an arrow pointing to the mouths of the white men, were scribbled some words: "You niggers love us, don' you." The mother told me it was her son's painting. I noticed something about the Negroes—that their hair stood up on their heads in rod-like plaits with blood on the tip ends. I remarked about this, and the mother corrected me. "That's not hair with blood on it," she said, "that's dynamite growing out of their skulls."

The spark that will set off the dynamite which is being cultivated within the Negro may well be the slightest incident, some little mishap, which, in the minds of most Americans, will have no connection with the explosion that shall ensue. But it will have a connection; it will be the boomerang, having gained momentum, returning to the source of its origin—the prodigal violence. Unlike most Americans, the existential Negroes are not blind to, or blinded by, reality; they have been grappling with the most horrible realities all of their lives. They know America from both inside and out, they are Americans and they are not Americans, they are possessors of double vision, double lies, double truths; they are not alienated from America, they are alienated within America; they are aware, more aware, of the presence of the Bomb than most white people are, and sense that annihilation haunts the entire human race; they discern the presence of violence in a society which has lost its community, its humanity—as when thirty human beings stand by as a woman is repeatedly attacked and finally murdered, or the assassination of the President, the murder of Medgar Evers, the maiming of those three young civil rights workers, and the killing of people in foreign lands (sometimes by accident and sometimes as if for sport). The existential Negroes know the meaning of these things, for they *are* the meaning of these things; their violence will not be their violence alone, their violence will be America's violence.

There will be no plot, no organized gangs or secret societies for violence or sabotage, except for perhaps a few misled individuals who will be quickly disposed of by the FBI and other agencies. The violence will be spontaneous, without leadership, without control; the fuse will be the chains of depravity running from heart to heart, connecting the subconscious labyrinths of hurt, anger and rage festering in the psyches of these people for centuries, and setting them off like a million live wires unleashed at last from all stations of censorship and better judgment. Everybody will be a guerrilla—men, women, teenagers and some children—individual guerrillas urged on by social contagion and the relentless wellsprings of utter insanity. As the collective mind, supraorganic, pitting itself against the mythologized odds of an unsurmountable monster, this demon will rise, for only demons can destroy demons and thereby become human again. The sense of fear will be wiped from their consciousness, reason will disappear, emotions will evaporate, fear of death will be meaningless, for they have been dead all of their lives. Nor will they care about winning, not in any understandable sense of the word, for in and through the act of destroying and killing and dying they shall be winning, a sense of life will be born anew within them. There may be some looting at first, some rapes, and other immoral deeds, but after the first few days their madness shall reach beyond good and evil, deep into the mysteries of Being.

Their madness will no longer be attached to any identifiable norm, value or nonvalue—neither money, hate, freedom or revenge. For, having been purged of faith in all human values, in all normal behavior, their madness will be the only god in whom they can put their fidelity without being deceived and betrayed. No doubt, according to the way America will look at them, they will appear as raving blacks on a rampage of ruin and riot . . . nothing new, for America has always looked at them this way. But from their side of the M-W equation, phenomenologically, they shall be gods, answerable to no one.

Then nobody will be able to make them turn in their knives and guns and bottles and Molotov cocktails and—most of all—their bodies. The respectable, middle-class Negroes will be helpless to quell the furies of the blacks. The white mobs will be ignited. Chaos will sweep the nation. Flame, blood, destruction—Chicago, Birmingham, Harlem, Brooklyn, Atlanta, San Francisco, Philadelphia, Newark, Miami, Washington, D.C.—the great powder keg will erupt. Nothing will stop the blacks, except to kill them. Freedom will not appeal to them, for it will be an irrelevant thing—everything you might offer them will be irrelevant, for how do you give a people back their manhood, their souls? These things must be gotten back in the same way that they were lost—they have to be *taken* back! Soon, all of the youths, from high-brow, middle-class, 'goodnigger' families will revolt, violently, and join the ranks of, or will actually become, existential Negroes—it is already happening! Why? Because America would rather lose the world than treat black people like human beings . . . then thousands of whites will be killed, thousands will be wounded, the Army will step in, the world will be charged . . . and then we'll see.

James Boggs

BLACK POWER—
A SCIENTIFIC CONCEPT
WHOSE TIME HAS COME

BLACK POWER. Black Power. This is what is being written about and talked about in all strata of the population of the United States of America. Not since the spectre of Communism first began to haunt Europe, over one hundred years ago, has an idea put forward by so few people frightened so many in so short a time. Liberals and radicals, Negro civil rights leaders and politicians, reporters and editorial writers— it is amazing to what degree all are fascinated and appalled by "Black Power."

The fact that these words were first shouted out by the little-known Willie Ricks and the now world-famous Stokely Carmichael to a crowd of black marchers during a march to Jackson, Mississippi, last spring [1965], has heightened the tension surrounding the phrase. For, earlier in the year, the Student Non-Violent Coordinating Committee (SNCC), which Carmichael heads and of which Ricks is an organizer, had issued a public statement on American foreign policy, condemning the war in Vietnam as a racist war and solidarizing the black movement in this country with the anti-imperialist movement in Asia. In that same period SNCC had begun to analyze the role that white liberals and radicals could play in the ongoing movement, aptly characterizing their role as that of supporters rather than decision-makers.

Coming after these statements, the cry of "Black Power" was seen by most people as deepening the gulf between the pro-integrationists and the nationalists. Whether or not Carmichael had intended this cannot really be determined, since the phrase had scarcely left his lips before the press and every so-called spokesman for the movement were making their own interpretation to fit their own prejudices or program.

When Malcolm X was assassinated in February of 1965, every radical in the country and every group in the movement began to seize upon some slogan Malcolm had raised or some speech he had made or some facet of his personality to identify themselves with, or to establish support for some plank in their own program. The same process of attempted identification is now taking place with Black Power. The difference, however, is that Black Power is not just a personality or a speech or a slogan, as most radicals, liberals and Negro leaders would like to regard it. In this connection, the immediate and instinctive reaction of the average white American and the white extremists or Fascists is far sounder than that of the liberals, radicals and civil rights leaders. For these average whites reacted to the call for Black Power simply and honestly by reaffirming White Power. Their concern is not civil rights, which are, after all, only the common rights that should be guaranteed to everyone by the state and its laws. They are concerned with power, and they recognize instinctively that once the issue of power is raised it means one set of people who are powerless replacing another set of people who have the power. Just as Marx's concept of workers' power did not mean workers becoming a part of, or integrating themselves into, capitalist power, so Black Power does not mean black people becoming a part of, or integrating themselves into, white power. Power is not something that a state, or those in power, bestow upon or guarantee those who have been without power, because of morality or a change of heart. It is something that you must make or take from those in power.

It is significant that practically nobody in the U.S.A. has tried to seek out the extensive theoretical work that has been done on the concept of Black Power. Actually, most of those writing for and against Black Power do not want to investigate farther. They would rather keep the concept vague, than grapple with the systematic analysis of American capitalism out of which the concept of Black Power has developed. In my book, *The American Revolution: Pages from a Negro Worker's Notebook,* I stated my belief that if Marx were living today he would have no problem facing the contradictions which have developed since his original analysis, because Marx's method of analysis was itself historical. I said, further, that I considered it the responsibility of any serious Marxist to advance Marx's theory to meet today's historical situation in which the underdeveloped (i.e., super-exploited) nations of the world who are in fact a world underclass, confront the highly-developed capitalist countries in which the working classes for the most part have been incorporated or integrated into pillars of support for the capitalist system. Yet such an analysis has not been seriously attempted either by European or by American Marxists. European Marxists have not seriously grappled with 1) the fact that Marx specifically chose England, at that time, industrially, the most advanced country of the world, as the basis of his analysis of the class struggle in terms of the process of production; and 2) the fact that at the same time that the European workers were beginning to struggle as a class against the capitalist enemy at home, this same class enemy was expanding its colonial exploitation of Africa, Asia and Latin America, thereby acquiring the means with which to make concessions to, and integrate the working class into, the system at home. Therefore, the working classes in the advanced countries were to a significant degree achieving their class progress at home at the expense of the under-class of the world. It was Lenin who dealt with this question most seriously when the European workers supported their capitalist governments in the first imperialist world war and it was Lenin also who, finding it necessary to deal seriously with the anti-colonialist revolutionary struggle after the Russian Revolution, recognized the nationalist and anti-colonialist character of the Negro struggle in the United States. Yet, today, nearly a half-century after the Russian Revolution and after two generations of European workers have shown themselves as opposed to independence for the peoples of Africa and Asia as their capitalist oppressors, European Marxists are still using the slogan "Workers of the World, Unite"—and evading the scientific question of which workers they are calling upon.

Who is to unite? With whom? The underclass of Africa, Asia and Latin America who make up the colonized, ex-colonized, semi-colonized nations? Or the workers of highly-developed Europe and America whose improved conditions and higher standard of living have been made possible by colonial exploitation of the world underclass? Is it not obvious that the working classes of Europe and America are like the petty-bourgeoisie of Marx's time who collaborate with the power structure and support the system because their high standard of living depends upon the continuation of this power structure and this system?

The United States has been no exception to this process of the developed nations advancing through exploitation of an underclass excluded from the nation. The only difference has been that its underclass was inside the country, not outside. In the United States, black men were brought into the country by a people dedicated to the concept that all blacks were inferior, subhuman savages and natives to be used as tools in the same way that machines are used today. The "all men" defined in the Constitution as "created equal" did not include black men. By definition, blacks were not men but some kind of colored beings. It took 335 years, from 1619 to 1954, before an effort was made to extend the definition of manhood to blacks. Yet American radicals have sought to propagate the concept of "Black and white, unite and fight" as if black and white had common issues and grievances, systematically evading the fact that every immigrant who walked off the gangplank into this country, did so on the backs of the indigenous blacks, and had the opportunity to advance precisely because the indigenous blacks were being systematically deprived of the opportunity to advance by both capitalists and workers.

The United States has a history of racism longer than that of any other nation on earth. Fascism, or the naked oppression of a minority race not only by the state but by the ordinary citizens of the master majority race, is the normal, natural way of life in this country. The confusion and bewilderment of old radicals in the face of the Black Power concept is therefore quite natural. United States and European radicals accept white power as so natural that they do not even see its color. They find it perfectly natural to exhort blacks to integrate into white society and the white structure but, as I pointed out in my article on "Black Political Power" in the March, 1963 issue of *Monthly Review*, they cannot conceive of its being the other way. Integration has been an umbrella under which American radicals have been able to preach class collaboration without appearing to do so. Under the guise of combating the racism of whites, they have actually been trying to bring about collaboration between the oppressed race and the oppressing race, thus sabotaging the revolutionary struggle against oppression, which by virtue of the historical development of the United States, requires a mobilization of the oppressed blacks for struggle against the oppressing whites.

There is no historical basis for the promise, constantly

made by American radicals to blacks, that the white workers will join with them against the capitalist enemy. After the Civil War, the white workers went their merry way homesteading the West while the Southern planters were being given a free hand by Northern capitalists to re-enslave the blacks systematically. White workers supported this re-enslavement just as the German working class supported Hitler in his systematic slaughter of the Jews. The gulf between blacks and white workers in the United States is just as great as that between the Jews and the German workers under Hitler. The difference is that Hitler lasted only a few years while the systematic oppression and unceasing threat of death at the hands of ordinary whites has been the lot of blacks in the United States for nearly four hundred years. The present so-called "white backlash" is just white people acting like white people, and just as naturally blaming their white hate and white anger not on themselves but on the blacks wanting too much, too soon.

Despite their slavish allegiance to the concept of "Black and white, unite and fight," most United States radicals and liberals are well aware that they do not constitute a serious social force in the United States. Few, if any, of them would dare go into a white working-class neighborhood and advocate the slogan. They would be about as safe doing this in South Africa. It is just another example of how naturally they think white, that they go so naturally into the black community with the slogan but steer clear of white communities with it. For whether they admit it to themselves or not, if anyone wanted to build a quick mass organization in a white working-class neighborhood today, his best bet would be to go in as a Ku Klux Klansman or White Citizens' Council organizer to mobilize white workers to unite and fight against blacks. Out of this self-mobilization, white workers have already come up with the slogan "Fight for what is white and right!"

Revolutionaries must face the fact that the black revolt is now underway, that it is not waiting for that "some day" when the white workers will have changed their minds about blacks. Like it or not, they must face the fact that the historical and dialectical development of the United States, in particular, has made the blacks the chief social force for the revolt against American capitalism and that the course of this black revolt itself will decide on which side the white workers will be. The more powerful the black revolt, the more blacks move towards Black Power, the greater the chances of the white workers accepting revolutionary change. On the other hand, the more the black revolt is weakened, diluted and deluded by class collaboration (e.g., "Black and White, unite and fight" and "Integration"), the more chance there is of the white workers remaining counterrevolutionary.

Black Power in the United States raises the same question that Stalin could not tolerate from Mao. Would the revolution in China come from the urban workers or from this peasantry? Mao pursued his theory, based upon the specific conditions in China, and was proved right by the revolution itself. In the United States today, the question is whether the blacks, over seventy-five per cent of whom are now concentrated at the heart of the nation's largest cities, will lead the revolution or whether they must wait on the white workers. In the twentieth century, the United States has advanced rapidly from semi-urban, semi-rural society into an overwhelmingly urban society. The farms, which at the beginning of the century still employed nearly half the working population, have now become so mechanized that the great majority of those who formerly worked on the land have moved into the cities. Their land is now the city streets. Meanwhile, industry itself has been automated so that black labor, which over the centuries has been systematically deprived of the opportunity to become skilled, has become socially unnecessary. Unemployed or underemployed, the now-expendable blacks are a constant threat to the system. Not only must they be fed in order to cool off the chances of their rebelling, but they occupy the choicest and most socially critical land at the heart of the nation's cities from which the racist white population has fled in order to remain lily-white. Moreover, since they have become a majority of the inner-city population, they are now in line to assume the political leadership of the cities in accordance with the historical tradition whereby the largest ethnic minorities have successively run the cities. As we explained in the April issue of *Monthly Review*, the city is now the black man's land and the city is also the place where the nation's most critical problems are concentrated.

Confronted with this dilemma, the power structure, all the way down from its highest echelons to the middle classes, is seeking to incorporate or integrate a few elite Negroes into the system and thereby behead the black movement of leadership. At the same time it has devised ingenious methods for mass "Negro removal." Under the pretext of "Urban Renewal," it condemns and breaks up entire black communities, bulldozes homes and scatters the black residents to other black communities which in turn are judged to require "Urban Renewal." Meanwhile, under the auspices of white draft boards, black youths are sent as cannon fodder to die in the counterrevolutionary wars which the United States is carrying on all over the world as it replaces the old European colonial powers. Today, the sun never sets on the American Empire, which maintains its bases in at least fifty-five different worldwide locations. The war in Vietnam today is a war of sections of the world underclass fighting one another; for it is the poor, uneducated, unemployed who are drafted and the privileged—mainly white—who are deferred. This United States counterrevolution all over the world has the support not only of the general United States population but of organized labor. A peace demonstration in any white working-class or middle-class neighborhood brings out the mob, which is sure to come, even when the peace demonstrators are allegedly guarded by police.

Those progressives who are honestly confused by the concept of Black Power are in this state of confusion because they have not scientifically evaluated the present stage of historical development in relation to the stage of historical development when Marx projected the concept of workers' power vs. capitalist power. Yesterday, the concept of workers' power expressed the revolutionary social force of the working class organized inside the process of capitalist production. Today, the concept of Black Power expresses the new revolutionary social force of the black population, concentrated in the Black Belt of the South and in the urban ghettos of the North, a revolutionary social force which must struggle not only against the capitalists but against the workers and middle classes who benefit by, and support, the system which has oppressed and exploited blacks. To expect the Black Power struggle to embrace white workers inside the black struggle is in fact to expect the revolution to welcome the enemy into its camp. To speak of the common responsibility of all Americans, white and black, to fight for black liberation is to sponsor class collaboration.

The uniqueness of Black Power stems from the specific historical development of the United States. It has nothing to do with any special moral virtue in being black, as some black nationalists seem to think. Nor does it have to do with the special cultural virtues of the African heritage. Identification with the African past is useful insofar as it enables black Americans to develop a sense of identity independent of the Western civilization which has robbed them of their humanity by robbing them of any history. But no past culture ever created a revolution. Every revolution creates a new culture out of the process of revolutionary struggle against old values and culture which an oppressing society has sought to impose upon the oppressed.

The chief virtue in being black at this juncture in history

stems from the fact that the vast majority of the people in the world who have been deprived of the right of self-government and self-determination are people of color. Today, these people of color are not only the wretched of the earth but people in revolutionary ferment, having arrived at the decisive recognition that their underdevelopment is not the result of ethnic backwardness but of their systematic confine ment to backwardness by the colonial powers. The struggle against this systematic deprivation is what has transformed them into a social force or an underclass.

The clarion call, "Black people of the world, unite and fight" is only serious if it is also a call to black people to organize. The call for Black Power in the United States at this juncture in the development of the movement has gone beyond the struggle for civil or equal rights, to a call for black people to replace white people in power. Black people must organize the fight for power. They have nothing to lose but their condition as the wretched of the earth.

The call for Black Power is creating, had to create, splits within the movement. These splits are of two main kinds. The first split is between the Black Power advocates and the civil rights advocates. The civil rights advocates, sponsored, supported and dependent upon the white power structure, are committed to integrating blacks into the white structure intact without any serious changes in that structure. In essence, they are simply asking to be given the same rights which whites have had and blacks have been denied. By equality, they mean just that and no more—being equal to white Americans. This is based on the assumption that the American way of life and American democracy is itself a human way of life, an ideal worth striving for. Specifically and concretely and to a large extent consciously, the civil rights advocates evade the fact that the American way of life is itself a way of life that has been achieved through systematic exploitation of others—chiefly the black people inside this country and the Latin Americans—and is now being maintained and defended by counterrevolutionary force against blacks everywhere, and particularly in Asia and Africa.

Inside the Black Power movement there is another growing split between the idealists or romanticists, and the realists. The romanticists continue to talk and hope to arouse the black masses through self-agitation, deluding themselves and creating the illusion that one set of people can replace another in power without building an organization to take the active steps towards power, while at the same time agitating and mobilizing the masses. Mass support comes only when masses of people not only glimpse the desirability and possibility of serious improvement in their condition, but recognize force and power able to bring this about.

The realists in the movement for Black Power base themselves first and foremost on a scientific evaluation of the system and of revolution, knowing that Black Power cannot come just from the masses reacting when they feel like it, but only from the painstaking, systematic building of an organization to lead the masses to power. The differentiation now taking place inside the Black Power movement between idealists and realists is comparable to the classic differentiation which took place inside the movement towards the Russian Revolution, between the Mensheviks who were opposed to building a disciplined organization, and the Bolsheviks who insisted upon discipline inside the organization.

The organization for Black Power must concentrate on the issue of political power, refusing to redefine and explain away Black Power as *Black Everything except black political power.* The development of technology in the United States has made it impossible for blacks to achieve economic power in the United States of America by the old means of capitalist development, accumulating capital through private enterprises that exploit the masses. The ability of United

States capitalists today to produce in abundance not only makes competition with them on an economic capitalist basis absurd, but has already brought the United States of America technologically to the threshold of a society where each can have, according to his needs. Thus, Black Political Power, coming at this juncture in an economically-advanced United States of America, is the key not only to black liberation but to the introduction of a new society to emancipate economically the masses of the people in general. For Black Political Power will have to decide the kind of economy and the aims and direction of that economy for the people.

"The City is a Black Man's Land" (*Monthly Review*, April, 1966) laid the basis for the development of the type of organization which would be in tune with the struggle for Black Power. Such an organization must be distinguished clearly, and not only from the traditional civil rights organizations which have been organized and financed by whites to integrate blacks into, and thereby save, the system. It must also be distinguished from the *ad hoc* organizations which have sprung up in the course of the struggle, arousing the masses emotionally around a particular issue and relying primarily on the enthusiasm and good will of their members and supporters for their continuing activity. By contrast, an organization for Black Power must be a cadre-type organization whose members have a clear understanding, allegiance and dedication to the organization's perspectives and objectives, and who have no illusions about the necessities of a struggle for power.

In every revolutionary period it has been possible to achieve *some* social, political and economic reforms without resorting to the methods by means of which every ruling group has achieved power and by which, in the last analysis—or when it is really threatened—it maintains its power But no revolutionary struggle for power (i.e., to replace one group in

power by another) has ever been successful without resorting to these means. Violence, persuasion of the masses and
by the masses, protest, demonstrations, negotiations, are all
means to an end—when the end is the power to rule.

A cadre organization cannot be made up of just enthusiastic and aroused people. Its essential core must be cold,
sober individuals who are ready to accept discipline and
who recognize the absolute necessity of a strong leadership
which can organize and project a strategy of action to
mobilize the conscious and not-so-conscious masses around
their issues and grievances for a life-and-death struggle
against those in power. Such a cadre must be able to continue the revolutionary struggle despite the setbacks that are
inevitable in every serious struggle, because the members of
the cadres feel that it is only through the revolution that
their own future is assured.

At the same time that it recognizes the inevitability of
setbacks, such an organization must build itself consciously
upon a perspective of victory. This is particularly necessary
in the United States, where the idea of defeat of the black
man has been so systematically instilled into the black
people themselves that a tendency to self-destruction or
martyrdom lurks unconsciously within the organization unless it is systematically rooted out of every member, leader
and supporter. The movement for Black Power cannot afford
another Malcolm, another Emmett Tills, another Medgar
Evers, but must build, first and foremost, the kind of organization which has the strength and discipline to assure
that there will be no more of these.

Nor can such an organization build itself on the counterrevolution's mistakes or abuses of the masses as the civil
rights movement has done. Rather it must seriously plot every
step of its course, when to act, when to retreat, when to seize
upon an issue or a mistake by the ruling power, and when
not to.

Within such a cadre there must be units able to match every type of unit that the counterrevolution has at its disposal, able not only to pit themselves against these but to defeat them. Colonialism, whether in Asia, Africa, Latin America or inside the United States of America, was established by the gun and is maintained by the gun. But it has also been able to hold itself together because it had skilled, disciplined colonizers and administrators, well-versed in the art of ruling and able to make the decisions inseparable from rule.

There will be many fundamental questions and problems to face such an organization as it moves toward power. How will it create new national and international ties with other people within the country and without? What will it do about the armed forces and how will it win them over? In what cities or localities should a base first be built? What shall it do when confronted by those in power as they respond to the threat of replacement? What segments of the old apparatus can be useful and which should be destroyed? And most important, how can it expose its alleged friends as the real enemies that they are? These are all questions of strategy and tactics which every serious organization for power has to work out, but which no serious organization for power would write too much about.

As I said in *The American Revolution: Pages from a Negro Worker's Notebook*, the tragedy is that so few see the urgency of facing up to this reality. But, as I also said, that is what makes a revolution: two sides, the revolution and the counterrevolution, and people on both sides.

Stokely Carmichael

TOWARD BLACK LIBERATION

One of the most pointed illustrations of the need for Black Power, as a positive and redemptive force in a society degenerating into a form of totalitarianism, is to be made by examining the history of distortion that the concept has received in national media of publicity. In this "debate," as in everything else that affects our lives, Negroes are dependent on, and at the discretion of, forces and institutions within the white society which have little interest in representing us honestly. Our experience with the national press has been that where they have managed to escape a meretricious special interest in "Git Whitey" sensationalism and race-war-mongering, individual reporters and commentators have been conditioned by the enveloping racism of the society to the point where they are incapable even of objective observation and reporting of racial *incidents*, much less the analysis of *ideas*. But this limitation of vision and perceptions is an inevitable consequence of the dictatorship of definition, interpretation and consciousness, along with the censorship of history that the society has inflicted upon the Negro—and itself.

Our concern for black power addresses itself directly to this problem, the necessity to reclaim our history and our identity from the cultural terrorism and depredation of self-justifying white guilt.

To do this we shall have to struggle for the right to create our own terms through which to define ourselves and our relationship to the society, and to have these terms rec-

ognized. This is the first necessity of a free people, and the
first right that any oppressor must suspend. The white fathers
of American racism knew this—instinctively it seems—as is
indicated by the continuous record of the distortion and
omission in their dealings with the red and black men. In
the same way that southern apologists for the "Jim Crow"
society have so obscured, muddied and misrepresented the
record of the Reconstruction period, until it is almost impossible to tell what really happened, their contemporary
counterparts are busy doing the same thing with the recent
history of the civil rights movement.

In 1964, for example, the National Democratic Party, led
by L. B. Johnson and Hubert H. Humphrey, cynically un-
dermined the efforts of Mississippi's black population to
achieve some degree of political representation. Yet, whenever the events of that convention are recalled by the press,
one sees only that version fabricated by the press agents of
the Democratic Party. A year later, the House of Representatives, in an even more vulgar display of political racism,
made a mockery of the political rights of Mississippi's Negroes when it failed to unseat the Mississippi Delegation to
the House which had been elected through a process which
methodically and systematically excluded over 450,000 voting-
age Negroes, almost one-half of the total electorate of the
state. Whenever this event is mentioned in print it is in
terms that leave one with the rather curious impression that
somehow the oppressed Negro people of Mississippi are at
fault for confronting the Congress with a situation in which
they had no alternative but to endorse Mississippi's racist
political practices.

I mention these two examples because, having been directly
involved in them, I can see very clearly the discrepancies
between what happened, and the versions that are finding
their way into general acceptance as a kind of popular mythology. Thus the victimization of the Negro takes place in

two phases: first it occurs in fact and deed, then—and this is equally sinister—in the official recording of those facts.

The "Black Power" program and concept that is being articulated by SNCC, CORE, and a host of community organizations in the ghettoes of the North and South has not escaped that process. The white press has been busy articulating their own analyses, their own interpretations, and criticisms of their own creations. For example, while the press had given wide and sensational dissemination to attacks made by figures in the civil rights movement—foremost among which are Roy Wilkins of the NAACP and Whitney Young of the Urban League—and to the hysterical ranting about black racism made by the political chameleon that now serves as Vice-President, it has generally failed to give accounts of the reasonable and productive dialogue which is taking place in the Negro community, and in certain important areas in the white religious and intellectual community. A national committee of influential Negro churchmen affiliated with the National Council of Churches, despite their obvious respectability and responsibility, had to resort to a paid advertisement to articulate their position, while anyone shouting the hysterical yappings of "Black Racism" got ample space. Thus the American people have gotten at best a superficial and misleading account of the very terms and tenor of this debate. I wish to quote briefly from the statement by the national committee of churchmen which I suspect that the majority of Americans will not have seen. This statement appeared in *The New York Times* of July 31, 1966.

We an informal group of Negro Churchmen in America are deeply disturbed about the crisis brought upon our country by historic distortions of important human realities in the controversy about "black power." What we see shining through the variety of rhetoric is not anything new but the same old problem of power and race which has faced our beloved country since 1619.

. . . The conscience of black men is corrupted because, having no power to implement the demands of conscience, the concern for justice in the absence of justice becomes a chaotic self-surrender. Powerlessness breeds a race of beggars. We are faced now with a situation where powerless conscience meets conscience-less power, threatening the very foundations of our Nation.

. . . We deplore the overt violence of riots, but we feel it is more important to focus on the real sources of these eruptions. These sources may be abetted inside the Ghetto, but their basic cause lies in the silent and covert violence which white middleclass America inflicts upon the victims of the inner city.

. . . In short; the failure of American leaders to use American power to create equal opportunity *in life* as well as *law*, this is the real problem and not the anguished cry for black power.

. . . Without the capacity to *participate with power*, *i.e.*, to have some organized political and economic strength to really influence people with whom one interacts—integration is not meaningful.

. . . America has asked its Negro citizens to fight for opportunity as *individuals*, whereas at certain points in our history what we have needed most has been opportunity for the *whole group*, not just for selected and approved Negroes.

. . . We must not apologize for the existence of this form of group power, for we have been oppressed as a group and not as individuals. We will not find our way out of that oppression until both we and America accept the need for Negro Americans, as well as for Jews, Italians, Poles, and white Anglosaxon Protestants, among others to have and to wield group power.

Traditionally, for each new ethnic group, the route to social and political integration into America's pluralistic society, has been through the organization of their own institutions with which to represent their communal needs within the larger society. This is simply stating what the advocates of Black Power are saying. The strident outcry, *particularly* from the liberal community, that has been evoked by this proposal can only be understood by examining the historic relationship between Negro and white power in this country. Negroes are defined by two forces, their blackness and their powerlessness. There have been traditionally two communities in America: the white community, which controlled and defined the forms that all institutions within the society would take; and the Negro community, which has been excluded from participation in the power decisions that shaped the society, and has traditionally been dependent upon, and subservient to, the white community.

This has not been accidental. The history of every institution of this society indicates that a major concern in the ordering and structuring of the society has been the maintaining of the Negro community in its condition of dependence and oppression. This has not been on the level of individual acts of discrimination between individual whites against individual Negroes, but as total acts by the white community against the Negro community. This fact cannot be too strongly emphasized—that racist assumptions of white superiority have been so deeply ingrained in the structure of the society that it infuses its entire functioning, and is so much a part of the national subconscious that it is taken for granted and is frequently not even recognized.

Let me give an example of the difference between individual racism and institutionalized racism, and the society's response to both. When unidentified white terrorists bomb a Negro church and kill five children, that is an act of individual racism, widely deplored by most segments of the society. But when in that same city, Birmingham, Alabama, not five but five hundred Negro babies die each year because of a lack of proper food, shelter and medical facilities, and thousands more are destroyed and maimed physically, emotionally and intellectually because of conditions of poverty and deprivation in the ghetto, that is a function of institutionalized racism. But the society either pretends it doesn't know of this situation, or is incapable of doing anything meaningful about it. And this resistance to doing anything meaningful about conditions in that ghetto comes from the fact that the ghetto is itself a product of a combination of forces and special interests in the white community, and the groups that have access to the resources and power to change that situation benefit, politically and economically, from the existence of that ghetto.

It is more than a figure of speech to say that the Negro community in America is the victim of white imperialism and colonial exploitation. This is, in practical economic and political terms, true. There are over twenty million black people comprising ten per cent of this nation. They, for the most part, live in well-defined areas of the country—in the shantytowns and rural black-belt areas of the South, and increasingly in the slums of Northern and Western industrial cities. If one goes into any Negro community, whether it be in Jackson, Mississippi, Cambridge, Maryland or Harlem, New York, one will find that the same combination of political, economic and social forces is at work. The people in the Negro community do not control the resources of that community, its political decisions, its law enforcement, its housing standards; and even the physical ownership of the land, houses and stores *lie outside that community*.

It is white power that makes the laws, and it is violent white power in the form of armed white cops that enforces those laws with guns and nightsticks. The vast majority of Negroes in this country live in these captive communities and must endure these conditions of oppression because, and only because, *they are black and powerless*. I do not suppose that at any point the men who control the power and resources of this country ever sat down and designed these black enclaves, and formally articulated the terms of their colonial and dependent status, as was done, for example, by the apartheid government of South Africa. Yet, one cannot distinguish between one ghetto and another. As one moves from city to city, it is as though some malignant racist planning-unit had done precisely this—designed each one from the same master blueprint. And indeed, if the ghetto had been formally and deliberately planned, instead of growing spontaneously and inevitably from the racist functioning of the various institutions that combine to make the society, it would be somehow less frightening. The situation would be less frightening because, if these ghettoes were the result of design and conspiracy, one could understand their similarity as being artificial and consciously imposed, rather than the result of identical patterns of white racism which repeat themselves in cities as far apart as Boston and Birmingham. Without bothering to list the historic factors which contribute to this pattern—economic exploitation, political impotence, discrimination in employment and education—one can see that to correct this pattern will require far-reaching changes in the basic power-relationships and the ingrained social patterns within the society. The question is, of course, what kinds of changes are necessary, and how is it possible to bring them about?

In recent years, the answer to these questions which has been given by most articulate groups of Negroes and their white allies—the "liberals" of all stripes—has been in terms of something called "integration." According to the advocates of integration, social justice will be accomplished by "integrating the Negro into the mainstream institutions of the society from which he has been traditionally excluded." It is very significant that each time I have heard this formulation it has been in terms of "the Negro," the individual Negro, rather than in terms of the community.

This concept of integration had to be based on the assumption that there was nothing of value in the Negro community and that little of value could be created among Negroes, so the thing to do was to siphon off the "acceptable" Negroes into the surrounding middle-class white community. Thus the goal of the movement for integration was simply to loosen up the restrictions barring the entry of Negroes into the white community. Goals around which the struggle took place, such as public accommodation, open housing, job opportunity on the executive level (which is easier to deal with than the problem of semi-skilled and blue-collar jobs which involve more far-reaching economic adjustments), are quite simply middle-class goals, articulated by a tiny group of Negroes who had middle-class aspirations. It is true that the student demonstrations in the South during the early Sixties, out of which SNCC came, had a similar orientation. But while it is hardly a concern of a black sharecropper, dishwasher, or welfare recipient whether a certain fifteen-dollar-a-day motel offers accommodations to Negroes, the overt symbols of white superiority and the imposed limitations on the Negro community had to be destroyed. Now, black people must look beyond these goals, to the issue of collective power.

Such a limited class orientation was reflected not only in the program and goals of the civil rights movement, but in its tactics and organization. It is very significant that the two oldest and most "respectable" civil rights organizations have constitutions which *specifically* prohibit partisan political activity. CORE once did, but changed that clause when it changed its orientation toward Black Power. But this is perfectly understandable in terms of the strategy and goals of the older organizations. The civil rights movement saw its role as a kind of liaison between the powerful white community and the dependent Negro one. The dependent status of the black community apparently was unimportant since— if the movement were successful—it was going to blend into the white community anyway. We made no pretense of organizing and developing institutions of community power in the Negro community, but appealed to the conscience of white institutions of power. The posture of the civil rights movement was that of the dependent, the suppliant. The theory was that, without attempting to create any organized base of political strength itself, the civil rights movement could, by forming coalitions with various "liberal" pressure organizations in the white community—liberal reform clubs, labor unions, church groups, progressive civic groups, and at times one or other of the major political parties—influence national legislation and national social patterns.

I think we all have seen the limitations of this approach. We have repeatedly seen that political alliances based on appeals to conscience and decency are chancy things, simply because institutions and political organizations have no consciences outside their own special interests. The political and social rights of Negroes have been and always will be negotiable and expendable the moment they conflict with the interests of our "allies." If we do not learn from history, we are doomed to repeat it, and that is precisely the lesson of the Reconstruction. Black people were allowed to register, vote and participate in politics because it was to the advantage of powerful white allies to promote this. But this was the result of white decision, and it was ended by other white men's decision before any political base powerful enough to challenge that decision could be established in the southern Negro community. (Thus at this point in the struggle Negroes have no assurance—save a kind of idiot optimism and faith in a society whose history is one of racism—that if it were to become necessary, even the painfully limited gains thrown to the civil rights movement by the Congress will not be revoked as soon as a shift in political sentiments should occur.)

The major limitation of this approach was that it tended to maintain the traditional dependence of Negroes, and of the movement. We depended upon the goodwill and support of various groups within the white community whose interests were not always compatible with ours. To the extent that we depended on the financial support of other groups, we were vulnerable to their influence and domination.

Also, the program that evolved out of this coalition was really limited and inadequate in the long term, and one that affected only a small select group of Negroes. Its goal was to make the white community accessible to "qualified" Negroes and presumably each year a few more Negroes armed with their passport—a couple of university degrees—would escape into middle-class America and adopt the attitudes and life styles of that group; and one day the Harlems and the Wattses would stand empty, a tribute to the success of integration. This is simply neither realistic nor particularly desirable. You can integrate communities, but you assimilate individuals. Even if such a program were possible, its result would be not to develop the black community as a functional and honorable segment of the total society, with its own cultural identity, life patterns and institutions, but to abolish it—the final solution to the Negro problem. Marx said that "the working class is the first class in history that ever wanted to abolish itself." If one listens to some of our "moderate" Negro leaders, it appears that the American Negro is the first race that ever wished to abolish itself. The fact is that what must be abolished is not the black community, but the dependent colonial status that has been inflicted upon it. The racial and cultural personality of the black community must be preserved and the community must win its freedom while preserving its cultural integrity. This is the essential difference between integration as it is currently practised and the concept of Black Power.

What has the movement for integration accomplished to date? The Negro graduating from M.I.T. with a doctorate will have better job opportunities available to him than to Lynda Bird Johnson. But the rate of unemployment in the Negro community is steadily increasing, while that in the white community decreases. More educated Negroes hold executive jobs in major corporations and federal agencies than ever before, but the gap between white income and Negro income has almost doubled in the last twenty years. More suburban housing is available to Negroes, but housing conditions in the ghetto are steadily declining. While the infant mortality rate of New York City is at its lowest rate ever in the city's history, the infant mortality rate of Harlem is steadily climbing. There has been an organized national resistance to the Supreme Court's order to integrate the schools, and the federal goverment has not acted to enforce that order. Less than fifteen per cent of black children in the South attend integrated schools; and Negro schools, which the vast majority of black children still attend, are increasingly decrepit, overcrowded, understaffed, inadequately equipped and funded.

This explains why the rate of school dropouts is increasing among Negro teenagers, who then express their bitterness, hopelessness and alienation by the only means they have—rebellion. As long as people in the ghettoes of our large cities feel that they are victims of the misuse of white power without any way to have their needs represented—and these are frequently simple needs: to get the welfare inspectors to stop kicking down your doors in the middle of the night, the cops from beating your children, the landlord to exterminate the vermin in your home, the city to collect your garbage—we will continue to have riots. These are not the products of Black Power, but the absence of any organization capable of giving the community the power, the black power, to deal with its problems.

SNCC proposes that it is now time for the black freedom movement to stop pandering to the fears and anxieties of the white middle class in the attempt to earn its "goodwill," and to return to the ghetto to organize these communities to control themselves. This organization must be attempted in Northern and Southern urban areas as well as in the rural black-belt counties of the South. The chief antagonist to this organization is, in the South, the overtly racist Democratic

Party, and in the North, the equally corrupt big-city machines.

The standard argument presented against independent political organization is, "But you are only ten per cent." I cannot see the relevance of this observation, since no one is talking about taking over the country, but taking control over our own communities.

The fact is that the Negro population, ten per cent or not, is very strategically placed because—ironically—of segregation. What is also true is that Negroes have never been able to utilize the full voting potential of our numbers. Where we could vote, the case has always been that the white political machine stacks and gerrymanders the political subdivisions in Negro neighborhoods so the true voting strength is never reflected in political strength. Would anyone looking at the distribution of political power in Manhattan, ever think that Negroes represented sixty per cent of the population there?

Just as often, the effective political organization in Negro communities is absorbed by tokenism and patronage—the time-honored practice of "giving" certain offices to selected Negroes. The machine thus creates a "little machine," which is subordinate and responsive to it, in the Negro community. These Negro political "leaders" are really vote-deliverers, more responsible to the white machine and the white power structure than to the community they allegedly represent. Thus the white community is able to substitute patronage-control for audacious Black Power in the Negro community. This is precisely what Johnson tried to do even before the Votings Rights Act of 1966 was passed. The National Democrats made it very clear that the measure was intended to register Democrats, not Negroes. The President and top officials of the Democratic Party called in almost one hundred selected Negro "leaders" from the Deep South. Nothing was said about changing the policies of the racist state parties, nothing was said about repudiating such leadership figures as

Eastland and Ross Barnett in Mississippi or George Wallace in Alabama. What was said was simply, "Go home and organize your people into the local Democratic Party—*then* we'll see about poverty money and appointments." (Incidentally, for the most part, the War on Poverty in the South is controlled by local Democratic ward heelers—and outspoken racists who have used the program to change the form of the Negroes' dependence. People who were afraid to register for fear of being thrown off the farm are now afraid to register for fear of losing their Head Start jobs.)

We must organize black community power to end these abuses, and to give the Negro community a chance to have its needs expressed. A leadership which is truly "responsible" —not to the white press and power structure, but to the community—must be developed. Such leadership will recognize that its power lies in the unified and collective strength of that community. This will make it difficult for the white leadership group to conduct its dialogue with individuals in terms of patronage and prestige, and will force them to talk to the community's representatives in terms of real power.

The single aspect of the Black Power program that has encountered most criticism is this concept of independent organization. This is presented as third-partyism, which has never worked, or a withdrawal into black nationalism and isolationism. If such a program is developed, it will not have the effect of isolating the Negro community, but the reverse. When the Negro community is able to control its local office, and negotiate with other groups from a position of organized strength, the possibility of meaningful political alliances on specific issues will be increased. That is a rule of politics and there is no reason why it should not operate here. The only difference is that we will have the power to define the terms of these alliances.

The next question usually is, "So—can it work, can the

ghettoes in fact be organized?" The answer is that this organization must be successful, because there are no viable alternatives—not the War on Poverty, which was at its inception limited to dealing with effects rather than causes, and has become simply another source of machine patronage. And "Integration" is meaningful only to a small chosen class within the community.

The revolution in agricultural technology in the South is displacing the rural Negro community into Northern urban areas. Both Washington, D.C. and Newark, New Jersey have Negro majorities. One-third of Philadelphia's population of two million people is black. "Inner city," in most major urban areas, is already predominantly Negro, and with the white rush to suburbia, Negroes will, in the next three decades, control the heart of our great cities. These areas can become either concentration camps with a bitter and volatile population whose only power is the power to destroy, or organized and powerful communities able to make constructive contributions to the total society. Without the power to control their lives and their communities, without effective political institutions through which to relate to the total society, these communities will exist in a constant state of insurrection. This is a choice that the country will have to make.

C. E. Wilson

THE SCREENS

THE CHANGING world often makes some terms obsolete and requires new names and concepts in order that men can communicate with one another. The growth of a new Negro group who help enforce the present racial order of things (status quo) demands a new name to describe that group. The term "Uncle Tom" is no longer apt, and its use only adds more heat than light to arguments within the Negro community. A more suitable term for this new group might be *Screens*.

There is nothing unique about the employment of such people by the ruling majority. Conquering and ruling peoples have always found it advantageous, even necessary, to employ individual members of the conquered group to do their bidding and assure their continued rule. The ruling clique of the United States uses this technique on all its national groups with a skill and finesse that the ancients might well envy. In dealing with its non-white population, white America utilizes many different cadres to enforce and maintain the established socio-economic system in the least brutal, most refined and most profitable ways possible. The Ku Kluxers and the rightwing groups, the rural sheriffs and the metropolitan police, the professional and business groups specializing in Negro clienteles, private and public welfare boards, and boards of education are all examples of these cadres. Increasingly, however, whites have had to recruit willing, middle-class Negroes to do their dirty work for them, i.e., to keep social unrest under control. These recruited Negroes disarm the victims, blunting their awareness by their similarity of coloration. The enforcement of the standards of the majority, however, proceeds by all necessary means. The recruits function as perfect Screens, camouflaging racism's unpleasant reality from the victims and from the unfeeling section of the general public as well as from the deeply prejudiced, who would prefer to ignore the facts anyway.

WHO ARE THE RACIAL SCREENS?

Screens, regardless of color—and whites serve just as faithfully as blacks—are often personally attractive, beautifully turned out, with credentials that would assure their success in any other system. The black Screens, however, face definite limits in job and status within America's system, which Charles Silberman for one, author of *Crisis In Black and White*, has called "deeply racist." Their favorite values are patience and long-suffering hard work, super-patriotism, naive opportunism, eloquence without relevance—all deeply imbedded within a penny-in-the-pocket mentality. They share one outstanding conviction, a basic assumption that this current national, economic and social order has only one slight flaw—the so-called race problem.

Screens, then, are not "Uncle Toms," "Handkerchief Heads," or "Aunt Jemimas." Consciously, they loudly deny their loyalty to the white Boss Man, affirming for all who would hear—"We Shall Overcome." Screens are rarely conscious spies or race traitors. If they do let the group down it is because they are betrayed by their own personal weaknesses, single-minded bourgeois ambitions, yearning for recognition, and desire for the good things of life. As able, solid citizens with academic and business credentials comparable to levels of leadership within the white community, Screens simply try to realize their potential through the only available avenues. In a word, they are "taking advantage of the disadvantages."

RECRUITMENT AND PROCUREMENT OF SCREENS

However chosen, by election or appointment, Screens generally perceive their personal success as a great victory for America and their race. They see themselves as models for black youth. (Now the kids can look up to someone and be just like them.) They see their appointment as a liberalization of the system. White liberal elements glory in the Screens' triumph; government agencies, private and goodwill uplift groups take deep bows; even conservatives nod their approval. Each group has individual reasons for their postures of joy and congratulations. Liberals are happy because the Screens' success maintains the game of tokenism. The government and goodwill groups are overjoyed because the Screens' advance positively demonstrates white good faith. Uplift groups, Negro as well as white, are gleeful because the Screens' success promises rewards, if blacks will only work harder than everybody else. Conservatives are relieved for they recognize that Screens are safe, useful and racially naive, however brilliant and able.

Screens are recruited from every stratum and sector of the minority community—social work, welfare, technical fields, business, labor, education, politics, community affairs, lay religious work, clergy, housewives, the unemployed, even the racial militants. Certain professional occupational categories, however, seem prime training grounds for Screens. Educators, and others with backgrounds in education, are especially welcome Screens because Americans have always looked to their educators to provide the panacea for all her social system's inequities. The educators conveniently see change in long, long-range terms—meaning current postponement. Social workers, too, make ideal Screens. The orientation of the social work profession—to help the individual adjust to the society—leads logically to tokenism and welfare colonialism on a large scale, and does not seek disturbing adjustments *by* society. Negro ministers may be ideal Screens because the Negro minister's orientation encourages him to believe that he, as a leader, can really do something meaningful. In reality, the Negro minister's presence and involvement provide a moral cover to the society's basic immorality.

Into these traditional standbys, a new group of have-resumé-will-travel professionals—the poverticians—have shouldered their way. As Janes and Johnnys-come-lately on the colonial-control gravy train, the poverty people will try any tactic to keep their particular projects going. This struggle to maintain their status and projects makes the poverty-boys and -girls endlessly useful to the current ruling circles.

The recruitment of Screens whose roots lie outside the particular geographic area or political jurisdiction in question is the best guarantee of the continuance of the racial status quo. A local candidate can be chosen only if the power circles are certain, as a result of exhaustive investigation, that the individual is safe, conservative, and untainted by the idea that he should represent the Negro group and be responsive to its demands. Age is an important qualification for the role of a Screen—the older, the safer. However, since conservatism in the black bourgeois is not a respecter of chronology and because there are definite publicity advantages attached to the appointment of a "bright, young, level-headed Negro," the white power structure sometimes takes this calculated risk.

Sometimes, Screens receive jobs for which they have been trained; and other times they are offered jobs for which they are overtrained, sometimes even jobs about which they know little. Key to the appointment is exposure (let everybody see who he is). Screens are ideally suited for symbolic number-two jobs on impossible tasks, for projects with little hope of success, for tentative tasks, for hot spots, and for cold dead ends. Screens are convinced, first, that their single *individual* efforts are going to make a difference, and second, that they can outfox their employers; and in a corner of their minds, they realize quite well that if they don't take the job, someone else will. Therefore, they prove extremely useful and generally compliant to the wishes of their masters. The more effective Screens, as far as the power order is concerned, are generally those unconscious of, or pretending to be unconscious of, the true motivation behind their appointment, a form of convenient ignorance. Only the truly crass or extremely sharp ones will admit that they are there for the money alone. Even when they acknowledge the hopelessness of their position, very few have the courage to talk about resigning, and even fewer, if any, ever actually do resign.

RECOGNIZING A SCREEN

The words and the style of action and thought reveal the various kinds of Screens for what they are. The language of the Screen is particularly distinctive—their watchword is "individuality"—Screens labor at the thankless task of showing whites that blacks are not all alike. Then there is *optimism* (things are going to improve), *caution* (do nothing to make the majority angry), *control* (leave no stone unturned, so that the minority people will not have a say), *propriety* (everything must be extra-special and proper), *What can I do?* (whispered admission of powerlessness), *I can't jeopardize my position* (confession of personal ambition), and, finally, *professionalism* or *professional status* (a frank admission of naiveté and confusion). Regardless of their attainments, Screens are still members of the minority as far as the white majority is concerned.

The styles of Screens may be accommodationist, or moderate, or the classic style of the Negro Establishment—militant-conservative—or on rare occasions, even militant. Each different style can be useful to the power order, depending on the particular situation. In some vulnerable areas, one style is preferred to another. Since the goal is always one which has been established for him by other persons or groups, the Screen is the easy victim of exploitation, an exploitation of which the Screen is not always aware and which he is seldom able to counteract.

The accommodationist, as a Screen, merely says "yes" to the demands of the power structure, or pretends not to know the racial consequences implicit in his functioning. The accommodationist often prefers to be above the race issue, which means parenthetically that he is floating in far outer space. As a type of accommodationist, Screens are prestige and token leaders who have the best and most extensive contacts with influential white leaders and whose presence in particular offices represent the power order's passing acknowledgement of the unwelcome presence of Negroes in their midst. Seldom are they involved in any aspect of the race problem at the time of their appointment and many of them have functioned as white-collar errand boys—some prominent person's liaison man with colored people—prior to their appointments. The time spent in public office or in the limelight, by accommodationist Screens, merely continues their original pattern of behavior. The style of the racial moderate who acts as a Screen is that of a highly skilled professional bargainer whose manner is cautious and proper and whose outlook is pessimistic about the employment of compulsory or radical means to solve a radical problem like the race problem. His words are a hymn of hope, of friendly persuasion. The moderate Screen is a quiet gradualist who prefers to keep race issues in the background and deal with individual points of conflict in, as he terms it, "a wider context." Preferred by the white conservative because he shares the same point of view ("Let's not spoil a good thing.") as well as the same style (conservative about everything but the race problem), the moderate Screen sees the world as it is and tries not to rock the boat or disturb the relationships of the status quo. Hence the moderate Screen is an ardent champion of status quo—afraid of Communist or radical agitators, even afraid of change itself, for change would threaten his own functioning.

The Negro Establishment's classic militant-conservative style is an ideal cover for Screens. Since only the words are militant while the actions are conservative, cautious and conciliatory, the power structure may even prefer Screens drawn from this arena. Here, but for the accident of skin color, would be a highly prized *Liberal*. These Screens are actually liberal in outlook, moderate in performance, and cautious without daring or imagination. On most issues, they have both feet planted on the liberal side while their heads float in the clouds. Their militant protests mask their inaction and their own true fears, even from themselves. Jim Crow is attacked with a sheaf of telegrams, exploitation routed savagely by petitions, racial murder punished by letters to Congressmen, discrimination flogged by eloquent phrases, lynching avenged by mass meetings. The militant-conservatives prefer to pretend that they possess the support of the masses rather than bothering to organize them (those people). In office, militant-conservatives substitute motion for thought, and these Screens frequently go from pillar to post and back again, flying thither and yon in the pursuit of racial harmony.

Even the loud-talking racial militants can make excellent Screens in certain proscribed situations . . . provided, of course, that they promise not to go too far either in dramatizing, organizing, debating or educating. Within limits, militant Screens are excellent safety valves. If gifted, militant Screens are truly magnificent. If, as is so often the case, the militant perceives racial issues in simplistic form, hinges his whole attack on the moral issue, dismisses ideological questions as "not relevant," speaks boldly and belligerently without investing energy in non-spectacular organizational work, after a long frustrating period of seasoning the militant is stamped as potentially useful to the white power structure. Of all the various types of Screens, the militant most effectively blurs the distinction between opposing ideas, groups and individuals. All opposing whites are prejudiced, all co-operating whites are white liberals and all Negroes are saints and victims. The steady stream of accusations, plus his very posture, keep reality safely hidden from the militant and from those around him.

This militant group produces, also, its share of racial devils, persons whom everyone uses to scare fainthearted individuals in the power structure into some minor concession or talk of concession. The posture or façade of militancy is *the* thing to the militant and may cause him to be considered unreliable by the power order. For the militant to hurdle this image barrier, whites must be convinced that he is really only an actor, really tame and easily pleased, with no world point of view, save on the "race issue."

Office-holders are the most conspicuous Screens for the cultural system, but Screens are found on every level. The Negro policeman who, because of his guilt and anger about the high levels of Negro crime, is rougher on Negro prisoners, may be a Screen. The Negro teacher who sets higher standards for Negroes than for whites may function as a Screen, regardless of how ingeniously he (or she) rationalizes this behavior. Those who flock to join the countless boards and committees of the ghettoes may be Screens. Their participation, no matter how impeccable their behavior, may serve to obscure the fact that society's attempts at social remediation are usually too little, much too late.

Screens may be found among the countless black Anglo-Saxons who have introjected the values of the white society, including acceptance of their own debasement, to the point that they dream of assimilation on the terms of that society and work feverishly to that end. These persons are ideal Screens. In reality, they are little more than prized Judas goats. In this retreat from reality, the black social-set Screens huddle together for mutual support and succor. In the designation as the only Negro of a professional society or in an important Negro "first," these Screens hide most successfully.

SCREENS—THE SYSTEM'S DEPENDABLES

The individual issue, whether national or local, isn't important to the behavior of the Screens—Vietnam, Black Power, self-defense—the entire gambit. Each issue is resolved for the Screens in terms of the values, needs, goals and aspirations of the dominant white society. Screens can be counted on by their exploiters to be as highly dependable as the postman, whom neither rain nor snow, nor dark of night can stay from his appointed rounds.

In the Vietnam debate, Negro Screens chose not to come out against an obviously immoral war. By this act of loyalty to their psychological as well as physical white masters, they condemned sixty thousand or more Negro troops to fight against an anti-colonialist struggle for the rights and liberties of the Vietnamese, when these very Negroes cannot enjoy the same rights and privileges in America. After years of picturing their own struggle for equality in America as a "moral issue," on the issue of Vietnam these Screens reveal a "moral bankruptcy." But the Screens have rationalized their behavior as the only practical one, since the Negro had been struggling for decades before the Vietnamese began their struggle.

On the issue of Black Power, Screens have adopted a similar, predictable position. As if on cue, each of the old-line leaders (Paramount Screen par excellence) described the new cries for Black Power, Negro control of Negro organizations, as something un-American, unthinkable. NAACP Executive Director Roy Wilkins suggested that the new focus was similar to South African apartheid policy, only topsy-turvy. Whitney Young, Jr., Urban League's Executive Director, intimated that Black Power is indistinguishable from the bigotry of Bilbo, Talmadge and Eastland. James Nabritt, Jr., Howard University President, on leave, and now United States Permanent Deputy Representative to the United Nations, went so far as to equate the demands for Black Power with a declaration that the Negro minority doesn't need the help of the white majority.

These are just a few conspicuous examples of the behavior of Screens. To hide their moral bankruptcy, Screens conform to the very standards that debase them. To hide their lack of a sound political and cultural theory, Screens adopt a single-issue orientation. Actually, Screens disdain theory and praise the practical. They want a program without valid assumptions. Screens choose to be without a theory or point of view because they are intellectually lazy. Yet nothing is so practical as a sound theory.

So while the dominant white society pictures Screens of whatever level as Negroes who can be counted on—black society must see Screens, Negro or white, as individuals who must be counted out.

Screens spare the establishment the tedium of having to explain inequality as an integral part of the system. More important, they blunt the protest of the victims, keep their fingers on the public pulse for their employers or patrons, divert the hopeless with false hope, and present a mirage to those who so desperately wish to believe that racial progress is finally here. Screens are in effect modern Gunga Dins—forever carrying the water, guns or whatever needs to be carried, for *their masters.*

Black Screens then, are by no means the first of their species and, as history indicates, will not be the last. As long as status, prestige, money and a little authority can be dangled in front of a few to keep the many in line, the practice will continue. For the Screens in any system protect that system from its own contradictions and save it from having to bother much with those groups it exploits.

William Mahoney

TRAVELS IN THE SOUTH:
A COLD NIGHT IN ALABAMA

W E RACED from Phoenix City, the old Mafia town, through Tuskegee and on to Selma to be off the highway before the sun went down. In the evening the road was dangerous.

Alabama life is regimented. It is regulated precisely by the rising and setting of the Southern sun that tells farmers when to plant and hoe. It is regulated by a gang of owners who tell people what to plant.

There were no white-haired gentlemen on the porticoed porches of the mansions drinking mint julep. In a real sense there never were. The Faulknerian South is actually a façade which hides a sinister intelligence.

The average Alabaman has an eighth-grade education. The one thing they do know very well is a perverted morality. They follow rules of social conduct as carefully as a spider web.

Travel in the tightly controlled state is made tortuous by the complicated local customs. One must move within one of two communities—either the white community or the black community. The traveler's view of the state is, necessarily, colored by the people surrounding him.

If you travel with either blacks or whites, you can find those who've succumbed to the dulling facts of Alabama life. The whites who work at their farm labors for an average of $2516 a year, boots sunk into the mud, know they will be allowed to live only if they kill all hope for themselves and for Negroes.

The various dreary systems of life are a manner of intelligence. More than intelligence, there is an emotional set one must fit if he is to live in the South. One must not only think and act according to prescription, one needs have correct feelings. Misfits such as myself live in constant danger of being discovered.

In the gray steel cities of Bessemer and Birmingham, whites prostitute themselves to earn $5779 a year. It is significant that children of Alabama whites forget how to smile and by the time they reach their teens, their thin mouths are drawn into permanent tight sneers. By the time they are fifteen they have developed all the cunning needed to live in a jungle.

Only the black community can still revel in life. The sheer honesty of the impoverished who say "no" to the cruelty of sharecropping and ghetto life is beautiful. There is hope in the black community for it is the only community that is willing to struggle. In that struggle alone is found bravery and genius.

There is a sweetness about Alabama. It is the sweetness of rotten grapes. Revived ante-bellum mansions scattered throughout the state give no hint of roots in the past. But they rather seem to be a part of modern Alabama. They suggest a strong upper class is thriving in that fearful state.

Integrated among large mansions along the highways sit hosts of eight- to ten-room houses of early 1900 vintage and modified gothic style. In little pockets throughout the town and on the outskirts of town are the shot-gun houses of the poor working class. And in the rural areas of the country are the shacks of sharecroppers; bare boarded structures raised on blocks to keep the water out.

It was in one of those shacks on the edge of the Selma community that we spent the night. We stood around the fire talking, afraid to get into bed and face the cold and long night. All there would be to do would be to think— and it would be too cold to sleep or think.

We started singing, "Will the circle be unbroken? By and by Lord, by and by?/I was standing by my window on a moonlit summer night/When I saw a torch a-flaming and a mob all dressed in white./ As they started toward my window . . ."

Erich stood warming himself by the fire, staring quietly at us from behind the dark glasses he was forced to wear because of eye trouble. Erich was an organizer in Wilcox County. Some time ago it had been hard in Wilcox.

When a group of Negroes appeared at the courthouse and asked the registrar if they might register to vote, he ran from the office. Once out in the street he leaned against a lamppost and gasped incoherencies at passersby.

The registrar was hysterical. The Negroes within the court-house might just as well have announced they were intending to fly, for the difference it made to him. The rigid intelligence of the registrar is what many times is mistaken for stupidity.

Erich had stopped in Selma on his way to Wilcox to investigate the murder of Daniel Colson; Colson had been killed January 31, in front of Antioch Church, a half-hour before a meeting on the poll tax was to start.

Stokely Carmichael warmed his hands in the red glow of the gas heater. Stokely is a leader. He was born in the slums of Trinidad, fought his way through adolescence in a Bronx Italian neighborhood, and led students in revolt at Howard University in Washington, D.C. Through his struggle Stokely has come personally to embody the movement.

The fire reminded me of a hot, late summer day in that small river town. It was years past. Lines of people waiting to vote at the courthouse were surrounded by deputies. A white man leaped from the rank of deputies into the midst of the students. Fists clenched in the air, he shook a writhing, green snake. Like a shadow from a troubled, mythical past, he thrust the reptile into the faces around him and retrieved it, waved and whirled and retrieved the tongue-flicking snake.

A girl cried out and fainted. The man tried to force the snake into a boy's mouth. When the youngster gritted his teeth and pursed his lips, the man laughed and tried to stuff his sickness down other throats.

Some of the posse laughed too; others hid their delight behind stolid, policeman stares. When, desperately, a victim threw out an arm to protect himself, knocking the snake to the street, the man grew wide-eyed with shock and indignation. Two of the deputies came dashing forward. They led the Negro to a squad car. At the stationhouse, Sheriff Jim Clark's deputies charged him with assault and jailed him.

The drama of the Negro as a victim was thus, once again, publicly acted out. Losing, but fighting back. The important thing is that these stories of the movement are low tragedy. A people's character is laid bare by the stories they tell.

Gloria stood solemnly by the fire, her hands folded near her lap. Her mind was far away. A question was posed on her thin, delicately etched black face.

At times, during the most absurd encounters—commonplace in the movement—she smiled. Her habitual ironic smile was a womanly defense against all the world's men who would use her.

"They took his death well," she said. She had just been with the family of an organizer who was killed in Tuskegee.

Erich left the room. For some of us, talk of those who were dead was sacrilegious. Will, the youngest, strutted around the room picking up his clothes. The light glistened upon his green earring. He acted as though he hadn't heard. A couple of fellows couldn't hide their fright and laughed stupidly.

Most of us refused to confront the reality of death. When the subject came up once at a meeting one fellow was publicly criticized for being frightened. He refused to work in Mississippi. The project director then drew a ring around death and examined it. Everyone in the meeting had a different level of understanding of death. When they were all brought to the same level of understanding, they no longer criticized their frightened co-worker.

"Those who understand life can better understand death," someone in the circle of light said.

"No one wants to die for anything," another said. "But we must demand to live in freedom."

The fire-talk tired us. The women were given the room. They accepted complacently. Neither of them asked to be treated with deference, but when treated as women, they acquiesced.

The rest of us slept in double-decker beds in the large cluttered hallway of the shack. There was another room, but it had no fire.

An agitation somewhere between my throat and chest made me cough, waking me. When my nose started running, I felt much better.

I went in morning light into the bathroom and found the tap frozen. Ice hung from the faucets. One of the bathtub taps worked. I washed with numbing cold water and my fingers turned blue.

The bathroom had a coal stove and if there had been coal it could have heated the room. I rinsed the soapy ice water from my body and briskly dried with a rough towel and washed out some underwear. After I hung up the clothes, I went back to the blue flame flickering in the gas stove in the hall.

Soon we'd be heading on to the tents to work with evicted sharecroppers camping just down the road.

Lindsay Barrett

THE TIDE INSIDE, IT RAGES!

THE MEMORIAL POSITION

The situation of the black man in the western world today, is that of a man in the midst of an open war without the benefit of a complete knowledge of the weapons he holds. And an added difficulty in combat is the fact that his memorial history, although it might refute and repel the advances of a white sensibility whose historic justification can record in relation to him only a knowledge of unjustified slavery, is by nature elusive, since its natural state of being involves the Negro who seeks the root of it in a kind of dance-game with motion and solid shape. In other words, the memory of sensuality that one black man might detect in a solo in jazz as played by another black man whose experience is at the basic point similar to his, could elude him completely when his environmental history, clouded by white Western thoughts and analyses, forces him to attempt a technical breakdown of the pure sound on musical terms. Musical terms, in this sense, allude to the Western tonic chordal systems in which, following on his pure and unbridled expression of a feeling, the musician, through social, ideational, and other conformities, is expected to explain the form of his desire. And since the desire of the musician, who is basically a brother-in-combat to the listener, runs parallel to that of the listener, a metamorphosis along similar lines is forced on the ear as well as on the feeling for the sound that moves the listener to specific, although un-planned, points of admiration and appreciation.

If a black man could grasp a Coltrane solo in its entirety
as a club, and wield it with the force that first created it
centuries before the white man moved Coltrane's and his
ancestors from the cave of history out into the bright flats of
their enslavement, the battle would be near ending and in
his favour.

WHITE ON WHITE BREAKS THE BACK

Our life, governed by black, has been so far a chronicle
of understressed violence, since the outer government of our
actions has been dictated by something explainably white and
yet irrationally selfish in its hold on our existence and pos-
session of the commodities that are essential to the simple
and necessary business of survivial. The white man, whether
friend or enemy, has denied the Negro any recognition of the
simple separation and difference between the business of
survival on the one hand, and the far more private and
personal business of existence, on the other. Today, what the
artistic sensibility of the black man spreads before the world
as evidence of his social and historic dilemma, is really the
articulation of a protest against the white denial of the
possibility or existence of black light, and the superimposi-
tion, on his knowledge of this black light, of the hostile
white light of Western history. The screams that a jazzman
sends out into the world through his horn are not merely
juxtapositions of notes, but the screams of a thousand lost
and living voices whose existence has begun to demand the
release of the soul's existence from the demands of the
body's survival. The necessity that drives the black artistic
personality towards the specific goal is viable. It is capable
of maintaining a life of its own quite apart from, and outside
of, the petty desires that attack and tempt it. Thus, the
technical problems of playing a horn does not prevent black
power from loosening itself but sets up a challenge that,
when overcome, becomes the force that solidifies the motion
and makes the unreal dream the valid reality. Coltrane's

long screams or Rollins' spot shots are built unconsciously along this course. But today's demands, as the white man refuses to see it, and cannot imagine it, are demands that suggest a need in the black man for not just the full recognition of the black light that illuminates the shapes contained in a Rollins or a Coltrane—or for that matter a solo by the old master Coleman Hawkins—but also a need for the elimination of the whiteness of the social normalities that surround him. It is no longer feasible that the black man may break the chains that bind him by accepting the white light and then searching for his own light. Instead, it seems inevitable that all white confrontations must be reddened in order to be lived with and yet overlooked, and that this reddening must arrive on all levels now. The historic reality of the black man's presence in the white world has armed him with a certain knowledge of the white man that is undoubtedly an asset in his reaction against, and forced destruction of, this avaricious white presence. And yet, his strongest weapon in the actual destructive process is not this knowledge but that elusive and yet inherent knowledge of himself. Where the white man has tried to dominate, for example, our reaction to an appreciation of African sculpture and music and jazz, we are now definitely obligated to assert our own personal symbolism, and memorial feeling, in any new and honest evaluation of it. It is only the white man's fault, and certainly his guilt that has made any such assertion of honest black knowledge within the white community, of necessity an assertion of violence, for he has forged such a prison of symbols, terms and educational values around us without regard for our personal desire, that we must first destroy this prison of pure survival form in order to face, with any directness, the reality of our deeper sense of existence. It is here that even in the matter of thought, the blood must flow, and the reddening of white take place. Thus, this process, as demonstrated in the development of jazz in America, is a prophesy of the final physical reality as it has to be; and in its urgency, in fact, is a frantic finger showing the black man that the time which has always been here is still here. Hawk and Pres and Bird, on these terms, are no different from Ornette, or Trane, or Rollins, or Cecil Taylor: thus the long line and the call for imperative action that is represented in that central unchanging shape that any sensitive black man will hear always, in jazz of any period, but which any hip-minded ofay will deny. Duke Ellington and Coleman Hawkins have held that line a long time, and their contribution to the historic drama of our urgent reality and desire to be free of the white sensibility that ropes its way about the alleys of our brain is even today indispensable to our need for a battle cry (even though there always is a cry). We overhear our dreams spilling from his white-made horn. And to hear this is to believe in the reality of the overturning world. And the overturning world, when it overturns, brings the superficial bottom, strangely enough, to the real and valid upper level of the broad-based existence.

WADE IN THE WATER

Like wielding a Coltrane solo as a club. Like seeing all white as red. Like breaking heads with words. Like this language wasn't mine and is mine now. The river runs in the head. All the years a sound of floods. Roars and the blind edge of water breaking on shifting sand. And sand bursting white and suddenly sinking subsiding. All these years. And the sight in the head. All these years. The water. And as the flood rages on, a vile tide, a lone and young black son, wading in the water. Up river. Wading. And the course of the stream uphill against the slope and the sound all these years and the child alone wading in the water of the tide. A decisive dream.

THE COURSE OF FRIENDSHIP

Why do we understand our losses to be primarily thefts? As far as our inner knowledge of the Western white society that houses us can see, the historic stance of the white man towards the feeling of black is one of awe and irrational fear hidden by an equally irrational denial of any positively virtuous values in the overall nature of the black thing. Thus, while the presence of black within the white community has been its source of mysterious exotica for some time, the demands of unreal politesse and assumed morality declare the essence of blackness to be the color of evil. In spite of the reality with which black faces him each day as a standard form (black lines abound in nature . . . the edge of a green leaf or the shape of a shadow) the white man who first endowed the elusive quality in natural black with the mythical fantasies that his ignorance of it creates in his mind, then scares himself into denying its validity within any area of existence but that of myth, which is, in this case, the fanciful area of mind and manner that houses such vague values as sin and propriety and politesse. The white eye refuses to see any good but that which is white, and then scares itself into complete blindness in the area of black since the preoccupation of white sensibility, down through the ages, with the matter of form and survival over and above the matter of desire and existence, has developed a society that cannot admit its hypocrisies without undermining its realities and necessities. The natural white mind leans closer to the idea of planned search in its conception of progress. But the black mind, left with a memorial history rather than a formal chronicle of guilt to work with, leans much closer to the area of broad and undirected search. Thus, where the white man sees progress primarily as up from down, the black man (in relation to how much of the white man's moral camouflage he has shed), sees progress as a course that runs in all directions, up from down, then down, and then around . . . and destination for the black man is a belief rather than an inflexible form. The white man who first titillated his sensual hunger with the myth that all Negroes have rhythm, is too scared and blind in his efforts to prove that he has progressed beyond this fallacy to a point of tolerance. So, in his so-called liberal manner, he denies the existence of the black thing, denies the existence of the general black rhythmic sensibility as separate from the less elemental white sensibility of cautious reaction, and announces that the black man is worthy to be the white man's friend—not because he is a dissimilar though equal man, but because according to the irrational white blindness he is a similar man. But black is black, and white no longer quite white!

The tide inside the black soul may flood whiteness to drowning point and yet never overwhelm it unless that final gate is broken. If the shape of the sound of jazz is governed by a spread of force rather than by the preconceived vertical stretch of form, the message and vision within any essential solo is extended way beyond the borders and boundaries that the white standard's values and systems would impose on it and judge it by. But Western musical taste has been nourished on such an inverted (and, in fact, perverse, because of its elemental narrowness) scale of values, that to accept or acknowledge the musical excursions of the most adventurous of those explorers who have entered the cave of the black self and memory, would be to underscore the impotency of those studiously narrowed symphonic excursions of Western atonal greats—and so point out in actual black and white the basic separation of personalities that exists within what has been portrayed always as a world directed by a singular, white, *right* personality. The rightness of whiteness, if even slightly challenged on the unimportant grounds of it being really white, must crumble, since its main reinforcement and body of defense has always been its ability to seem unapproachable. Our music, when seen as a solid black shape that has challenged this unapproachability on one level and successfully overwhelmed it there, is in actuality the clearest directive we hold today in the matter of how to conduct the actual necessities of inner combat!

THE PRICE OF FACES

Sweat, pain and kindness are universal values. Faces are personal and by reason of identity mirrors of the wave. The tide is not just a wash of blood and water. A flood of tempered flesh and faces flushed to laughter with the happiness of young knowledge is roaring in the course of this wild and wary river.

And the manner of our black existence has made the faces of our young much more than the faces of our old. The press is on the young wave's terror and the tidal wash of laughter that sees more laughter in a far place and will rip laughingly through fallow walls of white to gain the black pain. The black child is the era's black face. And because the memory that our immediate history offers the child is a memory of less than laughter, even this memory of ours will bleed at the hands of our children. The black child can no longer believe the white game is all there is to play. In fact, the black child will now reject the white playground and cavort about the less fashionable but more familiar black slum yard, because the essence and fulfilment of the pleasure that he seeks lies with familiar faces burnt by familiar laughter in familiar places . . . and a unity of joy. The awareness of generations grows closer to the heart always in relation to the face that the era presents to its generation. And children are always being born. A black son of the era that produced Charlie ("Bird") Parker is nourished in growing by the same set of rhythms and broken melodies that the black experience meant to Parker. But whereas this basic essential experience is the guide that controls or suggests the essence of the sensibility of experience, the young black one is encouraged by the white world to push it to the far reaches of the rear of the country of knowledge in order to cram the forefront of the head with white values, moral stances and ideas which are sold under the cloak of necessary education. But today, as can be heard in the music of the latest and most original forces in jazz, the increased pressure that the white man has brought to bear on the black life within his community, in an effort to have this life de-blackened, leaves the black sensibility, true to form, engaged in a process of reinforcement and constructive destruction. In other words, by involving more of the singular personality in the business of collective improvisation, the communal existence, as vitality, depends less upon common and standard terms and forms for the successful impressions of the soul, and so by constructing new paths without overwhelming amounts of common reference, which by right of situation would automatically fall from white heights, the black musical leaders are naturally destroying more and more of the white influence in the communal native experience of the beleaguered Negro. And so, the child whose native experience is less reality than dream and less presence than memory, picks up on such elemental forces as that described above, and grows with it. And, as he grows, he sheds or retains as much or as little of this force as he can in relation to the nature of his actual experiences against his natural memorial force. The pleasure of black children in games lies never with the plan and always with the sound. This is a general observation. We used to love to play moonlight games with no planned rules—only rhythmic songs to keep them burning in the black night gone blue with a flood of moonlight and grave great images reeling in the memorial mind.

THE DAUGHTER OF A DARK WIND

Born black to a slap and crying. Growing black. No more weeping. Growing to be a mother . . . black . . . but loving childhood. Her eyes have them. Tears are no longer flowers of the faith. No weepers wade this floor of fire. And then growing to be another mother. Mother black and beautiful. Black. Daughters. And to wish for a doll. This pretense is the gate to parenthood. Oh, for a doll to be a child's first child. But why are they white? Black dolls are clowns or golliwogs. Why? All children aren't white, so why are all child dolls white? Tell me, Mummy. Because the great lie and because. The death of reason is the life of love! I love my memory. Is that really your baby?

THE COLOR OF DESPERATION

A green light blazes in the head. And the leaves of our historic trees flame yellow, blue, red and then black and covers us with the enormous sound of our blues. Desperation is a vile and welcome weapon here. The force of blackness has been driven to a point at which desperation is more than just necessary, is, in fact, compulsory. The white world, dominated by a survival urge and therefore, in the capitalist society, a money urge rather than a moral one, encloses the Negro in an automatically vicious cocoon, in which existence on almost any level is spelt W-E-A-L-T-H and wealth is spelt M-O-N-E-Y. And with the black force being augmented by a new desperation of the soul, in which existence demands that it be spelt F-R-E-E-D-O-M and freedom that it be spelt M-O-V-E-M-E-N-T, the black line is a straight line only in the sense that it leads straight ahead to given points of future memory and existence. And because of the inherent confusion of our actual situation, our straight line must wind about various curves. Obstacles confront us. We no longer choose to break the force of our energy by attempting to break through them. Instead, we curl around them and continue straight ahead. Abbey Lincoln has expressed this in a song in which she sings the line, « Straight ahead the road is winding/Stony hard and dimly lit ». In other words, movement, that movement that we consider and accept as personal freedom, is the multi-directional movement that in heading straight branches out into all possible areas of space. To understand this, think of each black personality as the separate branch, as beginning where it ends and winding and twisting in space until it arrives with eventual direction at the crook of the trunk and merges into the huge unit trunk. Now, think only of the branches in space without the trunk, as seen by a bird in flight. By the similarity of existence, material and force, the trunk is a presence, a reality. So each branch is nourished by a quality of desperation. And so the trunk is a conglomerate force of collective desperation directed by the valid though hidden presence of the roots. And the trunk is black as the branches are black, and the roots are eternally hidden though real, and therefore eternally memorial; and as the memorial presence is itself black, it is not hard to know what color is the color of black desperation.

IN FINALITY WHERE TO GO IS WHAT TO DO

And we know now how our direction is: not back to beginning but on to constant commencement. And, if desperation and movement together give birth to desperate movement, and construction is of necessity destruction, our violent need must give birth to violence and destructive moods in which blood must glow and then flow and our children must inherit by their own will the further presence of our loving laughter without tears and exist within spots of black light burning. And, if we have lived and loved ourselves through fire, it is time now to extinguish this fire and continue to burn on our own into vast eras unknown and yet felt, and let the black mother laugh the way we love to laugh. . . . The sons who die must live, too, and the daughters be mothers and in eventuality we must arrive at that place where construction is construction and with the white wall removed there can be no need for destruction. I love your laughter and mine, black mother. If the tide rages . . . I rage and laugh . . . so if we must break the demon's back, we must break it with laughter and live.

A. B. Spellman

NOT JUST WHISTLING DIXIE

Marion Brown, an alto saxophonist who is as articulate with words as he is with his horn, made an incisive observation when he remarked, "One of the main reasons that white intellectuals are attracted to this music is that they can't believe a black man's mind can work so abstractly." True; and taken one step further, it is the desire to penetrate and comprehend that abstraction that attracts anyone to this music.

Certainly, the New Music is an abstract extension of the historical forms of jazz. A cursory comparison of the New Music with its most immediate antecedent, bebop, reveals a general disregard on the part of the New Musicians for the rules of improvisation that were established in the bebop era, though this was indeed a period of great musical liberation. Charlie Parker, who was twenty years ahead of his time, remains the father of modern saxophone playing, though few of the new reed men play Bird licks, as the cool and hard boppers always did. In fact, the New Musicians often refer to Bird as much as a teacher of life, as of music. It was Parker's revolutionary approach to self, society and existence that illuminates those brilliant arpeggios and lays the basis of his genius. Thus, it was considered hip and honorable to "live like Bird," even if this allowed for a certain self-indulgence and self-destructiveness, since, as we shall later see, this hipster life style one-upped those elements of society that thought they were on top.

It is a similarly revolutionary impulse, though different

in style and identity, which colors the highly emotive sound and techniques of the New Music. As a movement, it can be seen as the latest in a fifty-year series of all-pervading shake-ups of the jazz esthetic. Some critics, anxious to tie jazz to European music, have divided jazz into primitive, baroque, rococo, classical, romantic and atonal periods. The approach that this writer will take is that the New Music is the artistic signal of the imminent maturation and self-assertion of the black man in an oppressive American society.

To begin at the beginning, the frenetic religiosity of Afro-American slave music was clearly an attempt at establishing a vocabulary of release by a people whose languages were conscientiously taken from them by slave owners, who even went so far as to destroy their drums, a major means of communication. It is from this perspective that the development of Afro-American music must be viewed: as the progressive refinement of a sublimated vocabulary, wherein that which is most heartfelt is stated loudly and clearly but never directly, never in so many dangerous words. If the New Jazz is abstract, if it defies notative analysis, the same could be said of slave music. Take, for example, the words of Abolitionist Lucy McKim Garrison, who in 1862 wrote one of the first musicological essays on slave music. Miss McKim admittedly could not pinpoint that abstract quintessence that made black music, even then, the most interesting in America:

. . . I despair of conveying any notion of the effect of a number singing together, especially in a complicated shout, like I Can't Stay Behind My Lord. . . . There is no singing in *parts*, as we understand it, and yet no two appear to be singing the same thing—the leading singer starts the words of each verse, often improvising, and the others, who "base" him, as it is called, strike in with the refrain, or even join in the solo. . . . When the "base" begins, the leader often stops, leaving the rest of his words to be guessed at, or it may be taken up by one of the other singers. And the "basers" themselves seem to follow their own whims, beginning when they please and leaving off when they please, striking an octave above or below . . . or hitting some other note that chords, so as to produce the effect of a marvellous complication and variety, and rarely with any discord. And what makes it all the harder to unravel a thread of melody out of this strange network is that, like birds, they seem not infrequently to strike sounds that cannot be precisely represented by the gamut, and abound in slides from one note to another, and turns and cadences not in articulated notes. It is difficult to express the entire character of these negro ballads by mere musical notes and signs. The odd turns made in the throat, and the curious rhythmic effect produced by single voices chiming in at different irregular intervals are as impossible to place on the score as the singing of birds or the tones of the Aeolian harp.

If such perplexity sounds familiar to the reader who is familiar with modern jazz criticism, it is because Miss McKim was in precisely the same position as her twentieth-century counterpart. White, she could acknowledge vaguely, but not explicate, the background of emotive manners of African musicians; liberal, but patronizing despite her good intentions, she attached no social relevance to the music other than the discomforts of gigging in the rice fields and the desire to escape to heaven; ignorant of African traditions, she could not uncover the cultural sources of those "odd turns made in the throat" which were so "impossible to place on the score"; equipped with irrelevant disciplines, she was thrown by techniques developed with little reference to Europe; ready to appropriate as well as to preserve, she appended a footnote from the Georgia lady who wished "that some great musical composer could hear these semi-savage performances . . . one or two barbaric chants might be evoked from them that would alter the fortune of an opera." She was, in short, confronted with a music that would, in another context, be said to be too avant garde for her. Certainly she merits applause for transcribing the music for us in her book of slave songs, but it fairly can be said that she was just too far from the musicians to get the real point of the music, which is, "I am oppressed beyond description in a barbarous world that is far from my home. I will sing with my brothers because song is the only language left to us."

This is the most important and most negative aspect of black folk music up until the jazz musician achieved the role of vanguard artist in the 1940's: that only exceptional Negroes ever felt free to describe the oppression that was foremost on their minds. Many of our parents, particularly in the South, could not conceive of political action, but those who were musicians could channel all those energies into song.

Apart from the total irrelevancy of most criticism as exemplified by the ongoing search for white hopes who will "prove that jazz is everyone's music," this has been the fatal flaw in white appreciation of black art. The music has been seen too much as art for art's sake and devoid of anything other than mildly liberal social significance. Samuel Charters puzzled over the question of why racial subjugation had not been the subject of more blues, when Bessie Smith was able to sing a song as socialistic as:

Mr. Rich Man, Mr. Rich Man, open up your heart and mind.
Mr. Rich Man, Mr. Rich Man, open up your heart and mind.
Give the poor man a chance, help stop these hard, hard times.
While you living in your mansion, you don't know what hard
    times mean.
While you living in your mansion, you don't know what hard
    times mean.
Poor working man's wife is starving, while your wife is living like a
    queen.

The obvious answer to Mr. Charters' question is that you could get damned shot up for attacking the south's racial institutions, while Bessie, by restricting her subjects, could at least be assured of dying a natural nigger's death. This is why LeRoi Jones' hero in Dutchman tells his white lady antagonist, "If Bessie Smith had killed a few white people she wouldn't have had to sing the blues." He was talking about the sublimation of the true meaning of Afro-American, about the attempt to accomplish through music what only action can accomplish.

But there *are* specific references to white racism in the black music in pieces such as Lightnin' Sam Hopkins' *The Black Man Told The Devil*, in which a black man being chased by a devil (obviously not another black man) looks back over his shoulder facetiously and tells the devil "You can't run, we sho having a lot of fun." Billie Holiday's description of a lynch scene in the song, *Strange Fruit*, is another example.

Contemporary musicians, given the contest of a large mass political movement, have been excellent on such artistically dangerous projects as Max Roach's ballet, *We Insist On Freedom Now* and Archie Shepp's *Malcolm, Malcolm Semper Malcolm*, in which jazz word and jazz sound deliver a clear political message. The New Musicians also use their titles in wordless works to carry the listener's ear in a given social direction, as in Roach's *Garvey's Ghost*, Coltrane's *Alabama* and *Africa*, Ornette Coleman's *Old Black Joe* (which turns that image completely around), and many others; trumpeter-composer Bill Dixon even named a series of concerts that he produced, *The October Revolution in Jazz*.

The true value of the New Music is in the expression of the whole man, the whole black man, in a society that affords him no comparable release. Roberto Matta, the Chilean Surrealist painter who has spent most of his life working toward an art that would facilitate the total liberation of the human potential, heard tenor Pharaoh Saunders at a SNCC benefit, and described him as "an incredibly generous man, exactly what an artist should be!", meaning that Pharaoh was giving a lot of himself in performance and that there is no other artistic gift possible. That self becomes, in performance, a less private sector of the artist's being.

We live in a time of massive social breakdown, and this breakdown is related in the breakdown of the forms of art. European art forms have afforded the black artist useful media of expression, and all European forms, creative and performing, have been mastered to the point of excellence by at least a few black artists. However, all of the writings of Ellison, Jones, Baldwin, et al., all of the paintings of Lawrence, do not weigh as much as one John Coltrane solo in terms of the force of its thrust, the honesty of its statement, and in the originality of its form.

The reason is that poem, play, novel and canvas are, for us, learned forms. We may find useful parallels in our culture which may add a certain amount of originality to our use of those forms, but they remain, after all, the forms of European culture, meaningful to Europeans and to non-Europeans with European values. This is not the exclusive predicament of the Afro-American artist—the exponents of negritude in Africa and the Indies have spent years dealing with it. Novelist Eduard Glissant of Martinique had an extremely difficult time reorienting his style to develop a fictional form that conformed more to the oral folk tale than to the French novel. Glissant's compatriot, poet Aimé Cesaire, feeling trapped in a European language, went back into Surrealism to find an anti-French French, which would, in a sense, punish the colonialists for forcing him to write in a European language. There is a school of young African painters who have never seen a European painting and who refuse to be shown one.

The problems of Afro-American painters and poets is that they are hunting for a form which relates to their traditions in a useful way. Poets have blues, true, but the difference between the concept of poetry and the concept of blues is that poetry is conceived as a permanent record, etched in stone, while the blues is the literature of performance, the great body of it sung to the breeze, and then gone. Lightnin' Hopkins claims that he never remembers his words from one performance to the next, and that he always makes up new ones. The African tradition of sculpture might perhaps have been transmuted into some Afro-American form as original as jazz had not the artisans of New Orleans, Charleston and other Southern cities been replaced by whites and then by immigrants after Reconstruction. This is conjecture, of course, but it must be remembered that jazz developed as a form of work, as a job. I imagine the painters of the Italian Renaissance must have regarded their commissions in much the same way.

For the Afro-American, however, music was a weapon of survival ever since that unnamed Dutch frigate landed (the year before the *Mayflower*, for what that's worth) at Jamestown, Virginia, with a cargo of African slaves. We are too poor a people to have a culture of literacy, but music is rescue and release, and the slaves proved it was possible to dance in chains.

So, when America takes credit for jazz as its only indigenous art form, it is only flattering itself for its ongoing slaveholder tradition. The work song was as functional for the master as for the slave, as it improved the quality and quantity of the work. The same is true of blues and religious music—if you deprive a man of *both* testicles, he can no longer procreate, and you will have no more baby slaves.

The context in which jazz had to survive is germane, here. If it were not for the unbelievable sexual depravity of the white aristocracy in New Orleans, there would have been no Storeyville. Jelly Roll Morton and Louis Armstrong would never have had a gig to play and nurture their music

on. Likewise, the extreme alcoholism of the Twenties provided a modicum of security for Duke Ellington, Count
Basie, Fletcher Henderson and all of the geniuses whom
they employed. Now, these were not shallow men, and they
must have had strong feelings about their working conditions, though their biographers would have you think that
they thought that everything was just hunky-dory. Even if
this was so, there was a great deal of frustration among these
pre-bop musicians about the actual form that was forced on
their music so that it would satisfy its social function. Duke
was always writing suites, ballets and concerti of various
kinds; Fletcher Henderson adapted Liszt; James P. Johnson
wrote an opera, and so on. The point is that, perverse as it
may seem, frustration fructifies the music in so far as it
gives the musician something to blow about.

The bebop revolution saw the jazz musician adopting an
entirely different social posture. As LeRoi Jones wrote in
Blues People (unquestionably the best book on jazz yet
written), "The young Negro musician of the Forties began
to realize that merely by being a Negro in America, one
was a non-conformist." Here, for the first time, a black
artistic vanguard assumed whole styles of comportment, attire and speech which were calculated to be the indicia of a
group which felt that its own values were more sophisticated
than, if not superior to, the mores of the American society
at large. The music and the manner developed concom-
mitantly, which indicates that the musicians were aware
that each musical innovation was a new way of commenting
on the world around them. Their alienation was cultivated
to the extent that many of them, emulating Charlie Parker,
adopted a drug (heroin) which blots out all interaction of
self and outer world. When the high hipster played "Out
Of This World," he wasn't just whistling "Dixie." (whew!)

Bebop was, then, the beginning of a realization on the part
of the jazz musicians that if they wanted to be artists in

America, and not just entertainers, they would have to accept the lot of the artist in industrial society—as if they needed another handicap. This meant the sacrifice of any financial security they might have had, as the music was not the best for social dancing and would ultimately prove to be unsuitable for promoting the sale of alcohol.

All that's sufferable, but, unfortunately, alienation is a part of the artist's situation in capitalist industrial society. For the black musician, it meant alienation from his black brothers, since he was born alienated from whites. The emergence of the white hipster as an important market for the music, created, in New York, a neutral turf, first in Midtown and then in Greenwich Village. This was probably an inevitability. There simply are no institutions set up in the ghetto to facilitate the growth of black art, no matter how relevant that art is to the conditions of ghetto life, no matter how much brotherhood is felt by the musicians for the family of black men.

The twin problems of alienation and economic control of jazz by white men, are the two most distressing problems confronting the New Music. It would not be such a drag that white America has not accepted the music if black America loved it; it would not be so horrible that there's so little money to be made if the musicians themselves had control of such money as there is. The most rewarding feature of the New Music is that it has so much to say about the dignity of man, and it is the black man who most needs this message. But the reality is that it was Greenwich Village which heard the evolution of the New, not Harlem. The man standing in line for the Otis Redding show at the Apollo almost certainly never heard of tenor saxophonist Albert Ayler, and wouldn't have the fuzziest idea of what he was doing if he did hear him. Yet the roots of Ayler's music are largely the same as Otis Redding's.

This is the kind of problem which characterizes black

America at this stage of its development. Though our condition hasn't changed that much, we have come a long way as a people since Miss McKim tried to figure out just how those colored people sang that weird music. But there is still that missing chord that will tie together the various dynamic elements of our community. The man who strikes it will be a major mover.

David Llorens

THE *FELLAH*,
THE CHOSEN ONES,
THE GUARDIAN

"In the presence of the Guardian, the Chosen One is allowed to act like a fellah only if the Guardian is acting like a fellah—and exceptions to this rule are extremely rare"

I N HIS powerful work, *The Wretched Of The Earth*, which has been called a revolutionary bible, Frantz Fanon made this brilliant observation:

Now, the *fellah*, the unemployed man, the starving native do not lay a claim to the truth; they do not *say* that they are the truth, for they *are* the truth.

Fanon's words were written with direct reference to the masses of natives vis-à-vis the native intellectual or the native who had adopted the "forms of thought of the colonialist bourgeoisie." At the time of the writing, Fanon was one of the most articulate spokesman for the Algerian Revolution.

But inherent in Fanon's writings was a profound concern for oppressed blacks—the "colonized"—the world over, including this land that he described as a former European colony that "decided to catch up with Europe."

According to Fanon, "It succeeded so well that the United States of America became a monster, in which the taints, the sickness and the inhumanity of Europe have grown to appalling dimensions."

It is interesting to note that his early death by cancer, which occurred on these shores, might possibly have been avoided had he not feared coming to this country for treatment. A bit ironic, perhaps, but his fears were not so unreal, nor were they based on myth.

"For they *are* the truth"—so simple, so mighty, and so many implications! And the *fellah* Fanon spoke of very definitely inhabits this land, and he is—in this land—no less the truth than in Fanon's adopted Algeria. We have, for so many years, attempted to avoid him, to not see him, and upon seeing him we have pretended that we did not. But we know who the *fellah* is in this country!

But the *fellah*, in recent times, has forced us to look at him, to see him, and he has made it increasingly difficult for us to deny his presence and his condition. Moreover, he has forced us to listen to him, to hear him—albeit our response to him more often than not makes one wonder!

We have seen him erupt in Harlem and Watts and we heard him through the voice of Brother Malcolm—and to think that Malcolm did not speak for the *fellah*, simply because they were not card-carrying followers, is really not to think at all.

Let us, for our purposes, define the Chosen Ones: quite simply, those blacks among us who, in words, actions (inaction), and indifference—and we know who we are—lay a claim to the truth. The *fellah* also knows who we are.

After all, we are so easily identified. But the marks of identification that come to mind are not so superficial as the clothes we wear or the houses we live in. More precisely, the Chosen Ones are given to a pattern of thought and reflex that is indeed pronounced.

One of the more obvious marks of identity of the Chosen Ones is the predictable nature of their *telling* comments on the *fellah*. The Chosen Ones' comments on the *fellah*, for the most part, lack validity and are often quite unintelligent—although the Chosen Ones think themselves rather learned—however, they are indeed telling. To be sure, they are *telling* about ourselves.

Another mark of identity is the Chosen Ones' reaction(s) to the *fellah*—his words, his actions, and his very existence (the right to which is often challenged by the reactionary nature of the Chosen Ones).

But, alas, the Chosen Ones manage to sympathize with the *fellah* when he rebels. Or do they? Perhaps it is more accurate to say that the Chosen Ones experience a vicarious orgasm of the soul when the *fellah* rebels. For you see, in a very real sense, the *fellah* is rebelling for the Chosen Ones who, with such painful ramifications, have conceded the right to rebel for the right to be among the Chosen Ones— the right to serve the Guardian!

And the Guardian, of course, is the white man (and to elaborate on the exceptions is to indulge in futile exercise). Whitey is the Guardian who, not out of kindness or brotherhood or any such myth, but out of intense fear, has taken upon himself the Chosen Ones in a desperate attempt to protect himself from the *fellah*. With unequaled resolve, he has designed, in this valley of rampant timidity, a peculiar niche wherein the Chosen Ones reside in all their misery. And the suffering of the Chosen Ones is apparent for many reasons.

Paramount among the reasons for their misery is the inescapable fact that in each of the Chosen Ones there dwells some *fellah*. That same fury is cradled in his psyche, that same desperation buried in the pit of his belly, but, unlike the *fellah*, when his emotions demand that he rebel, his debt to the Guardian—those special dues of the Chosen Ones—demands that he repress.

Although the indocrination of the Chosen Ones has insured certain mechanical reactions to given situations involving the *fellah*, his emotions do not, and perhaps cannot, respond to this specific indoctrination. Emotionally, the Chosen One remains a *fellah*, hence his emotional response is in direct conflict with his physical response, resulting in a vicious paradox.

Witness the language of the Chosen Ones within the confines of safety: They will talk of things being soulful, nitty-gritty, and funky—but they will unfailingly avoid this ethnic behaviour whenever the atmosphere suggests that their "place" might be jeopardized. In the presence of the Guardian, the Chosen One is allowed to act like a *fellah* only if the Guardian is acting like a *fellah*—and exceptions to this rule are extremely rare. Let the *fellah* choose the "wrong" time and place to become emotional (or funky) and witness the Chosen Ones squirm and cringe as their roots become like terrible, scorching fires.

A young black lady, a very Chosen One who, in her words, belongs to a "very high class church," recently conveyed the following incident to me:

One Sunday morning, in the presence of a white friend, she turned on the TV, only to be confronted with the spectacle of a Negro church service where "they" (*fellahs* one guesses) were "carrying on." She confided that it made her "very ashamed." I inquired why, and asked her if there was something wrong with people praising their God in *their* way?

She allowed that there was "really nothing wrong with it," but that she just thought "we should keep such things to ourselves." It is rather interesting that she, a Chosen One, should use the pronoun "we." But, nevertheless, not at all surprising. For even the most Catholic, Episcopal, Unitarian, or what have you, among the Chosen Ones, cannot avoid identification with the Holy Rollers. Although in complete control of the physical characteristics or manifestations of the *fellah* in themselves, the Chosen Ones are unable to contain its inevitable rise, and, at its mildest, the *fellah* in them is much more Baptist than Catholic!

But, through further questioning, I discovered there was much more to her shame. It seems that her white friend's head drooped at the spectacle, alas, embarrassed. Of course, the Chosen One's obligation to protect the Guardian is, at that precise moment, primary. What follows might well be described as emotional prostitution. It is sad enough that the Chosen Ones' bag requires that they stand before the Guardian begging for that thing called freedom, but what is even more sad is that they think it their responsibility to free the Guardian from the self-inflicted psychology—the guilt—that makes a Guardian's head droop at the sight of those uninhibited Holy-Rolling *fellahs*.

And the head-droopers and their would-be saviours, in their collective misery, are seemingly incapable of reasoning that if the *fellah* did not spend all that precious time Holy Rolling, it is quite possible that he would spend it making Molotov Cocktails—(and there are those who would suggest that the production of such might produce more *real* Christians than all of the "high class churches" have managed to produce, to date, in this land).

Each of us who has, at some juncture, played the role of the Chosen One—whether by choice or circumstance—can recall at least one cringing experience.

About ten years ago, while riding a bus en route to school, a shabbily dressed black man sat next to me. He proceeded, without apparent qualm, to pull out a hamburger—and began feasting. Well, it so happened that there was a shortage of "brothers" on that bus. But there were many Guardians present! Now, let's face it, if that had been a bus full of brothers I probably would have said something like: "dig, baby, my man's goin' for himself"—which translated is like proclaiming the cat soulful or something similar—and my emotions would have been quite safe. At any rate, I *would not* have been embarrassed by such an incident on a bus full of "brothers"—and what "brother" would have been?

But *with all those Guardians present,* and my head filled
with all that phenomena that once passed as values, I did
what all good Chosen Ones would have done then—and still
do today—I squeezed against the side of the bus, face flush
against the window, and did my damnedest to pretend that
either I or my hamburger-eating "brother" (the *fellah*) did
not exist, and that the incident was not really happening.
What choice did I have? How else might I have preserved
the pride of the Chosen One? And what's a squashed nose
when so much is at stake?

But, and I find this very sad, it was perhaps four or five
years later before I was finally able to question my reaction
to the incident, before I began to understand it. On that
harsh day, it was so simple for me to condemn the *fellah*
for causing me such great pain. (He caused me pain?) Well,
blinded by the cruel plight of the Chosen Ones, I certainly
thought he did. After all, I would not have eaten a hamburger on a bus (well, perhaps on a bus full of brothers,
maybe) and therefore it was wrong—certainly not very *cultured!* Is that not the usual method employed by the Chosen
Ones to condemn the *fellah?—I would not have done it!* I
suggest that such was indeed the usual method, and it
remains so.

And the Guardians have bestowed upon the Chosen Ones
that Great Rationale for such God-playing exercises—"Values
and Culture." The Chosen Ones have accepted—for better
or for worse—the values of the Guardian. And, they have no
other choice, short of abdicating their curious status.

And the products of this tormenting marriage, both the
Chosen Ones and the Guardian, have the unadulterated
arrogance to subject the *fellah* to those values in a manner
that is perhaps without precedent as one man's brazen
declaration of superiority over another. Year after year after
year they persist, with inimitable audacity, in demanding
that the *fellah* respect, uphold and keep sacred those dubious

values which have, to this date, in this land, served the
fellah's interest not one damn bit.

The result of this vile web, the condition of American life
today—that which all the surveys are about—rather compels
one to search and search for a rationale that will deem the
Guardian and the Chosen Ones something other than the
most merciless duo to ever inhabit the earth. But the web
is so full of lies and the search, alas, is in vain.

Moreover, the accusers—those who deny the *fellah's*
humanity by condemning him for the sins they have committed against him—claim the right to their vicious under-
taking. They have manipulated the teachings of their "high
class churches" so as to defend their incredible impositions
and judgments on the grounds of a strange, barren morality.
But it is no secret that they are not half as vehement in their
efforts to make of themselves, and their values, something
worth respecting.

The distorted nature of their morality can be witnessed,
for example, in their pretentious inability—throughout America's cities—to persecute slum landlords with the same tenacious will that they have employed all these years in their
persecution of the very people whose stench, degradation,
and deaths will forever haunt the souls of those same landlords. This is but one example of the horror of the American
double standard that one might depict, *ad infinitum!* And
such is the noble status of the sons and daughters of the
Chosen Ones and the Guardian. And the *fellah* is hep to
them, and they know it.

But the Chosen Ones cloak their guilt with all the affecta-
tions of the catalogue culture, and its *peculiar* dignity. What
is more American than mail-order houses and catalogues?
You see it, you want it, you order it, it's yours, you have a
lifetime to pay for it, and in all probability it isn't worth
a damn—but everyone has one, so!

So it is with the culture that is valued by the Chosen Ones

who have received, from the Guardian with his blessings, the catalogue which carries with it the right to order those things deemed necessary by the Guardian to insure complete control of the Chosen Ones. Anyone, given the opportunity, can grasp all that jazz that is at once a claim to fame and the source most often used to deny the *fellah's* humanity. *It is just as easy as that.* It is nothing more than a catalogue culture. All one really needs is the catalogue!

But the "cultured" ones have not yet proved that they have the basic decency—in spite of Brotherhood Week—to share the catalogue with the *fellah*; a fact which implies that they are somehow terribly afraid that the *fellah* might pass the course in six easy lessons, quite like they did before him, and no longer would the Chosen Ones and the Guardian loom so mighty in their timid, make-believe minds. For, as Fanon so wisely observed, the *fellah* is the truth—*about the rest of us!*

If we are fortunate, the nature of love and hate being so entwined, perhaps the *fellah* will eventually save us from ourselves. To expect the *fellah* to join this fraternity of hypocrisy and self-deception, at this late date, is to believe in miracles. This dreary coalition has conspired to starve men, and has sealed the conspiracy with faith, hope, charity, good intentions and a yet-unfound democracy. But time has worked against us and caught us naked. For the masses of victims to join—NOW—would be to defy human nature.

Fanon suggested: "Come, then, comrades . . . we must find something different." And the *fellah* will—it is only a matter of time—but what hope is there for the Chosen Ones and the Guardian? Perhaps the starting point is to look at ourselves, finally to question our existence.

In *Another Country*, through the voice of the preacher sermonizing over the dead Rufus, a suicide victim, James Baldwin spoke profoundly:

And I tell you something else, don't none of you forget it: I know a lot of people done took their own lives and they're walking up and down the streets today and some of them is preaching the gospel and some is sitting in the seats of the mighty. Now, you remember that. If the world wasn't so full of dead folks maybe those of us that's trying to live wouldn't have to suffer so bad.

And he *was not*—when he spoke of dead folks—talking about the *fellah!*

Nathan Hare

BRAINWASHING OF
BLACK MEN'S MINDS

As a boy I used to hear old folks laughing and talking about the way white folks tricked Negroes to America as slaves with stories of a land where creeks were overflowing with molasses and flapjacks grew on trees. While hardly anybody seemed really taken in by that myth, it did have, as most jokes have of necessity, a certain tone of truth: that the Negro in America has been everlastingly misled, tricked and brainwashed by the ruling race of whites.

It seems certain, as recorded history bears out, that white conquerors supplemented more deadly weaponry by falling back on ideological warfare in confrontations with other races in the lands they "explored." Guns were used, as in Hawaii, for example, but not guns alone. Explorers, trailed by missionaries and other warriors, first sought to convert "natives" to the Christian religion. Then, failing to "save" the pagan chief, they merely proceeded to convert a "commoner" and provide him guns with which to overthrow the chief. This well-known tactic of divide-and-rule is proving just as efficient to this day. "Why" is still the question.

Africans in the know have finally come to realize that: "Once we had only the land. The white man came and brought us the Bible. Now we have the Bible, and they have the land." To accomplish this piracy—and retain the loot indefinitely—it was of course necessary to control the minds and bodies of the subjugated blacks. Indeed, control over the body is one basic means of manipulating thought. This was accomplished even more successfully in the case of American blacks, compared to Africans, because of the fact that brainwashing is best implemented by removing the subject from his normal setting, severing his social relations and identities ordinarily sustained only by regular interaction with family, friends and "significant others." Communication is then restricted—in the case of the Negro slave, it was virtually destroyed—and the "stripping process," the process of self-mortification (the destruction of identity and self-esteem) is then almost a matter of course.

Not only were slaves cut off from contacts and lifelines of old, they were restricted in their social relations with one another (sold apart as well from their families on the whims of their "masters") and forbidden to congregate without the presence of a white "overseer." Even after they were permitted to enter the confines (pun intended) of Christendom, pastors of Negro churches such as First Baptist in Petersburg, Virginia, seat of a violent slave uprising, were at first typically white. Ritualistic deference (such as keeping eyes downcast in the presence of whites, addressing them as "Mr.", "Sir" or "Suh," and other means described in Bertram Doyle's *Racial Etiquette in the South,* also aided in undermining the slave's self-respect and stimulating his glorification of the white man's world which in turn made him more inclined to bow down to the Great White Society.

A University of Chicago history professor, Stanley Elkins, in a book called *Slavery,* has likened the practices and consequences of the slave plantation to the Nazi concentration camp. This fits in with the basic principles of brainwashing in the setting of "total institutions" (prisons, asylums, concentration and POW camps) set forth by University of California sociologist Erving Goffman in the book, *Asylum.* The slave plantation was a total institution in that a large number of persons were restricted against their will to an institution which demanded total loyalty and was presided over and regimented by an "all-powerful" staff, and "master."

Even the language of white America has exhibited a built-in force destructive of the black man's self-image. Blacks were taught to worship a god who was always painted white, and then, to sing that they wanted to "be more and more like Jesus" who would be "riding six white horses when He comes." While the color white symbolized purity (Negroes may be found singing in church houses, even today, that they are going to be "washed white as snow in the blood of the lamb"), black stood—stands now—for evil and derogatory referents. You "blackball" a person from your club; an employee is "blacklisted"; phony magic is "black magic"; illegal commerce comprises a "black market"; you are in a "dark mood" or "blackhearted" on "Black Thursday"; especially if you are behind the eight-ball, which of course is painted black in pool. If a chartreuse cat or a polka-dot cat crosses your trail, it is no cause for alarm, but if a black cat crosses your trail, you are doomed to bad luck. We refer here only to the cat that purrs. Admittedly women may be in trouble when some black cats cross their trails.

It seems no accident, in any case, that a romance word for "black"—"Negro" (capitalized only in the past four decades)—was attached to a group which, owing to the white man's sexual drives and his Christian manipulation of the sexual and familial relations of his slaves, soon became a *potpourri* of colors and racial derivations. The word "black" was used by the English to describe a free man of color while a "Negro" was used to designate a black slave. Naturally, the word "Negro" eventually assumed a connotation of low esteem regardless of, but not exclusively independent of, the color or biological characteristics of the individual to whom the appellation was applied. This allowed some Negroes of "fair" features to "pass" (also a word for the act of death, just as a Negro who passed was called a "harp"—which he was going to play when he got to Heaven). Confusion arose requiring laws fixing a white person's race as Negro if it was known that he had even the remotest bit of white ancestry. Today's experts still stammer in their efforts to clarify the concept: *Webster's Collegiate Dictionary* finally winds up declaring a Negro anyone with "more or less Negro blood" and the 1960 Bureau of the Census instructions directed interviewers to classify as Negro any descendant of a black man, or a black man and any other race, *unless the Negro is regarded as an Indian in the community!* This was a concession to the white-Negro-Indians of the Carolinas and Oklahoma where I have known Negro women of the Aunt Jemima variety to wear a wig (long before it was the fashion), marry an Indian, fry their offsprings' hair, and send them to a white or/and Indian school, except when the childen were bounced back as a bit too black.

The standard of beauty, so essential to a group's self-image, also was derogatory to the Negro. Not only were mulatto descendants of white masters given special privileges and higher status among slaves, all beauty queens and men of power were visibly white. Even today, "Miss Washington, D.C.," where Negroes are in the majority, for example, is likely to live in the suburbs, in Fairfax, Virginia or Silver Spring, Maryland, and, regardless of her residence, she is certain to be white.

On top of all of the foregoing, there has been a massive effort, deliberate and persistent in speed, to keep the black man in ignorance. During the early days of slavery, it was illegal to teach, aid or abet a black slave to learn to read, for fear he might find out how he was being treated. Books, newspapers, periodicals and other media of information have consistently been published or controlled, in almost every case, by white men. The King James' version of the Bible, the only book many Negroes ever read, also plays down the black man; for example, "black but (nevertheless) comely."

Negro worshippers are exhorted to tuck in their whimpering tails and conform to white society by such tidbits as: "The meek shall inherit the earth," "Thou shalt not covet they neighbor's goods . . . ," "We'll all be one when we get over yonder" and "To him who hath shall be given, and to him who hath not, *even that which he thinks he hath*, shall be taken away."

Most other books, too, including those on the Negro— especially those promoted and accepted in the United States —are not only published but also generally written by white men. Thus the Negro is led to depend on the white man to tell him what to think even about himself! During Negro History Week last February (known as "Brotherhood Week" now that we are "integrated"), I happened to notice in the lobby of Howard University's Founder's Library a set of twelve books on display as "books about the Negro." I knew, because of my special interest in literature on the race issue, the names of eleven of the authors. All were white. I walked over to the circulation desk and asked the black gentlemen behind it: "How about a book about the Negro by a Negro?" He laughed and thought the matter one big joke.

Children (learning to read on white Dicks and Janes) internalize the hatred of black men early in life. Although some black Anglo-Saxon Negroes will claim that they never knew there was a difference made between whites and Negroes until they were going on seventeen or had "got grown." Only a moment ago, even as I was writing this article, I learned that a black schoolteacher in Washington, D.C.'s summer school program got mad at a white teacher and called her a "black Jew!" With teachers like that, our children don't have a chance.

I once sat on a churchhouse step and watched a band of boys about ten years old stand beside their bicycles on the sidewalk and swap black epithets for thirty minutes by the clock. "You black as tar; can't get to heaven on an electric wire." "You so black your mamma had to throw a sheet over your head so sleep could slip up on you." Thus they grow up to look down on their own kind and idolize, mimic and conform to white standards of behavior.

Consequently, the black man's passive approval of the control of media of communication by white men in this mass society makes it virtually impossible for a black leader to emerge except through the white press. Accordingly, aspirants as well as established "spokesmen" for the Negro must slant their strategy toward capturing the spotlight of the white press.

W. E. B. DuBois, for example, had to contend in his day with white promotion of Booker T. Washington, now widely known as an Uncle Tom. DuBois sought to persuade Negroes to do half-a-century ago—though he later realized his error—what the NAACP eventually did, but, by that time, still fifty years ahead of his time and having fallen into disrepute with the white establishment, was not even invited to the NAACP's fiftieth anniversary, according to newspaper reports. Schools fail to carry his name, in spite of his legendary attributes as a scholar, just as E. Franklin Frazier, in spite of his acceptance by the white sociological establishment, has been overlooked. Instead, acceptable Negroes such as Booker T., Ralph Bunche, George Washington Carver, Charles Johnson and Marian Anderson, along with Abraham Lincoln and Franklin D. Roosevelt, are symbols for the Nation's black schoolchildren. Although Rev. King is not a name for a school—to my knowledge yet while he lives—he eventually will join his brethren as a white-groomed Negro leader, as indicated by the plethora of prizes and honorary degrees already bestowed upon his crown.

Conversely, all the pretense of not understanding "Black Power" (a simple phrase) is merely an effort to whitewash the tardy awakening of black men in America and deter them from any attempt to acquire or utilize power to their own advantage.

White theorists have disseminated a number of false theories readily gobbled up and parroted by hoodwinked Negroes. One is that the Negro should not be bitter, whereas Anna Freud, in *Ego and the Mechanisms of Defense*, suggests that it is natural to be bitter in a bitter situation. For instance, if somebody sticks a pin in a portion of your anatomy and you do not yell out, then something is wrong with you or that portion of your anatomy. Another erroneous theory, geared to keeping Negroes conformist, is that Negroes are hopelessly outnumbered in America and must act to gain white sympathy, to "change white hearts and souls." This led to the assimilationist craze now increasingly apparent on the part of the Negro's "civil rights" movement before SNCC and CORE sought to put some sense into the movement. LBJ, in a recent effort to scare rioting Negroes, made a big ado about the Negro comprising only ten per cent of the population (actually he comprises at least eleven per cent, according to the Government's own figures) but white boys never get their facts straight about the Negro. The truth is that, regardless of their numbers, white men rule—two per cent in South Africa or Jamaica, forty per cent in Washington, D.C. or Mississippi or ninety-nine per cent in Maine or Montana. It is a mental attitude—not numbers. What excuse, then, had black men in Rhodesia (who grumbled privately when Smith took over but grinned and cowardly tucked their tails whenever a white person passed by for fear he might overhear them)? Outnumbering whites twenty-three to one, they could have taken each white man—one each grabbing a finger, ten others a toe, one the head and two whatever portion pleased them—and pulled him apart.

But, of course, black men are supposed to be non-violent in conflict with whites, while violent in his behalf and with one another. The non-violent hypocrisy has been perhaps the most ridiculous and appalling farce ever perpetrated upon and swallowed by a supposedly sane group of human beings. Only recently have black people begun showing signs of shedding this preposterous shackle.

It is amusing to watch the media's effort to commit the Afro-American to the Vietnam fiasco. While Afros virtually never make the daily press in a laudatory manner—not to mention the front page—they frequently find themselves turning up there now in uniform, holding up some wounded white "buddy," eating chicken, turkey or goose on Thanksgiving Day, or saving a Bible from perspiration and harm by wearing it under the band around their helmets. It is enough to cause a man to hang his head in shame.

Even on the home front, news about the Afro is slanted and sorted to suit the white power structure's purposes. William Worthy, for example, foreign correspondent for the *Afro-American* newspaper, was gagged by white newspapers when he ran afoul of then-Attorney-General Robert Kennedy's great white liberal graces after going to Cuba, and reporting that Castro was solving the race problem exported there by United States-dominated industry. William Worthy was believed to be the first newsman to test the right to go abroad, write home the news, and come home again—and though the white press is forever crying crocodile tears over "freedom of the press"—the press fell curiously silent in this case. So much so, that some brainwashed Negro students in a class of mine, during a discussion on mass communications, insisted that the United States has a free press. Yet, when I placed the name of William Worthy on the board—at a time when his case was current—along with five multiple-choice descriptions of his identity, only six in a class of twenty-four were able to choose the correct answer.

These students were, in the full sense of the word, pathetically "miseducated," in the manner described by Carter G.

Woodson, in his *The Miseducation of the Negro*. They, like most Negroes, are merely products of generations of the most efficient and gigantic system of brainwashing the world has ever known. Thus, while they once merely chanted desires of being "more and more like Jesus," they now typically long and struggle to be more and more like "whitey" as a group. No doubt their brains, at least, at last have been *"washed white as snow. . . ."*

Poetry

Charles Anderson

FINGER POP'IN

I was spinning with Earth and a foul wind was blowing.
    Finger pop!
I was drinking wine and the rats skipped across my floor.
    Finger pop!
Rev. King sent a lot of children to jail to make his religion
    work.
    Finger pop!
Was freedom ever found behind bars or in the philosophy
    of an Indian failure?
    Finger pop!
I was listening to the radio and Nat King Cole said,
    "Don't be a litter bug—"
    And one more finger pop!
I heard Bobby Kennedy charge, publicity is the Freedom
    Riders' cause.
    And his finger popped!
His daddy is well-known exploiter, a thief—dig?
    And their fingers popped loud!
And all around fingers were popping and gum-chewing white
    liberals were encouraging youth, white and black, to fill
    the jails while they paid off their mortgages and Hi-Fi
    payments.
    And their fingers popped, too!
I was spinning with Earth and a foul wind was blowing.
    Finger pop!
While in Monroe, a Dixie grave was being prepared for
    Robert Williams.
    And the white man's finger popped!

And all too many happy songs were being sung in a folk
disguise of the black man's burden.
And a paternalistic white liberal's fingers were popping!
And, in their plush offices, Judas black lawyers and doctors
maneuvered a wayward path.
And their fingers popped, but with green dollars!
And the Earth continued to spin into a greater frenzy as
President Kennedy plotted his atomic stockpile to replace
a fading prestige.
And the fingers of "the reformed" West Germans
popped!
And blood continued to flow in a bonded, aborted Africa,
while the ghost of Lumumba observed from a cobalt
grave,
And the long fingers of imperialism popped!
And the rats skipped across the floor!
Finger pop!
And at Playa Giron, widows and orphans were replacing new
housing projects, destroyed by Yankee bombs.
And "Tio Sam's" finger popped, somewhat—
And, in Washington, President Kennedy lumped up a billion
dollars to suppress a hundred and forty million people.
And the fingers of Latin tyrants popped!
And the rats skipped across the floor.
Finger pop!
And in Israel a monster was put on stage, in a blood cam-
paign to sell bonds in order to buy more bombs to drop
on Cairo.
And the rats skipped across the floor.
Finger pop!
And Dr. Edward Teller's new merit badges were made into
a fine circle around his old Iron Cross.
And the rats skipped across the floor.
Finger pop!

* * *

PRAYER TO THE WHITE MAN'S GOD

I've been prayin' for centuries
To some God up in the sky.
Lord, what's the delay?
Help me live today.
God said, Go 'way, boy
I don't want to hear you cry,
But I know Jesus heard me
Cause he spit right in my eye.

Richard W. Thomas

AMEN

Night has secreted us
Out of herself
Black against black
Song against song
We travel hard upon the asphalt
Towards ourselves
Humming the tunes of our fathers
Hugging the breath
Blown forth out of our mothers' brown nostrils
We birthed ourselves
We bury ourselves
We cry and curse for selves
Beyond our birthing and burial:
Those who wear the middle skin
We live
Hour upon hour
Thump upon thump
Until we drop into space
Through the funnel of graves

* * *

THE WORKER

My father lies black and hushed
Beneath white hospital sheets
He collapsed at work
His iron left him
Slow and quiet he sank
Meeting the wet concrete floor on his way
The wheels were still turning—they couldn't stop
Red and yellow lights flashing
Gloved hands twisting knobs—they couldn't stop
And as they carried him out
The whirling and buzzing and humming machines
Applauded him
Lapping up his dripping iron
   They couldn't stop

* * *

INDEX TO A BLACK CARTHARSIS

Get this now!
Listen to the stomp and thunder of the long trip home
Here we come down our own uterus
Paid for in cash.
                    No more lay-ways
Or white Christ
And we at the opposite pole
Begging tickets
To kingdoms burning on the sand and cardboard.
Get this now!
No more gray folks
Playing cool with new nickles under our crosses
Between black thieves (playing black with gray hungers)
Hollering
For the elixir
Of burning pink flesh slumming.
Get this now!
Cancel the cement. This thing coming down
Now! With or without the flashes from treetops.
This bus is full. Catch another or run by mail to uglyland
     because
The weather getting bad.
Get this now!
The machine age is over; we can pray.
Glorify the messenger; kiss the East
And hurry the hybrid of the consequences.
My sister's new baby and yours.
Willie got married on the shores
Columbus dug it and cried

Some sun sat in our West; the universe convulsed with our
    new zoo.
(I'm feeling good now) get this now! (gonna solo a taste)
    If I die before you wake
                    Love me
After the third day I woke
Banged on the rock
Got out.
Saw Mary and Mamma crying.
Took them home
Felt my freedom deep
My signature!

REVOLUTION!!

We will not die for nothing.
Not anymore.
Our deaths shall be noisy and beautiful to the last swing.
And deep
Evenly spread all over; without a wrinkle or a tear.
We shall die properly, all at once!
No more inch by inch,
Day by day,
Or by the hour. There shall be one crash and one crash only!
We shall go spirits first,
Leaving our bodies dragging in your sleep of us,
While folks cry at our funeral
For themselves in us
But, not us! Not anymore baby; no good!
We ain't radical or high;
We've thought it all over, and
Its marked on your calendar
Burning on our foreheads. . . .

* * *

JAZZY VANITY

She was really neat, man.
Great mind . . . bearing . . . purpose.
I felt something was missing,
Wasn't sure what or where in her the thing was Loose.
Ran my spirit all through her.
Couldn't find it!
Air, beauty and mind, brother, that was all. Tough!
What a shame. A mellow lady. Out of sight. Really together,
    baby.
But, had to cut her loose! Something was missing. She wasn't
    wrapped up
Tight enough.
Where was it?
I wonder could it have slipped through that crack
In my jar!

Ted Wilson

MUSIC OF THE OTHER WORLD

Soul dust with particles of
interplanetary messages
filtering down into self
Reminders of purpose
One-pointedness
Moving downward to earth's atmosphere
BLOW SUN-RA
Moon Soul dance
Blow zodiac feeling
to emotionless, contained carrots
Outside the system
Inside of self
Inside of feeling
Inside of Life
Blow sounds of yesterday
that they call tomorrow
Blow love-calls in your foreign language
which is common to all
in your sphere of life
Notes and chords of cosmic rhythm'n'blues
Gut-bucket tunes from the year ∞
360° —➤ aspiration—ultimate—all-knowing
Back into time

Moving ahead to modeerf—360°

Something that hasn't been conceived
in shape, in form, or substance
BLOW SUN-RA
Music of the other World
THE UNIVERSAL WORLD——360° —➤ aspira-
      tion

* * *

COUNT BASIE'S

Count Basie's place
90 cents beers
Bourgeois slicksters
Prostitutes with degrees
Zanzy faggots
Hip white boys shootin' on black broads
being slicked out of their beards
Hip noses and their dough
Count Basie's place
Slick music
Hip-swingin', finger-poppin'
Cool folks
Embracing
    one another
because it's what's happenin'
Count's joint
Diamonds
Decadence
    and
        Disease

* * *

S, C, M,

     Sound
Mighty Drums echoing the voices
of Spirits determining the movement
of human forms
These sounds are rhythmatic,
The rhythm of vitality,
The rhythm of exuberance
and the rhythms of Life
These are sounds of blackness
Blackness—the presence of all color
     Color
The color representative of the
sound
Hi sounds = bright colors
Low sounds = sombre colors
Rhythmatic sounds thrown together
are harmonious
Colors thrown together in prints
with scales & wheels all their own
     Movement
Sound & Color = Movement
Rhythmatic sound, print harmonious colors = Movement
indicative only to Blackness
These times of Easternness
are where we must go
for this is from whence we came

James T. Stewart

Poem: A PIECE

My mother plays an Oud
My mother plays an Oud
I threw the hitch,
the stock butts bad
Ngwenyana is my father.
. . . awaits the white eyes
and longs for 2000 atavistic cows
to give your father (dead)
back to plants
back to plants,
spells terrorist pussys
at Jung's hotel (Broad&South)
and make churches
performances toward now,
jams twenty bitches
in mohair
conch shells
for cinder eschatology
and mashed potatoes.
There is nothing keener
nothing finer
to bank bishops with
while musicians squat in cars.

* * *

ANNOUNCEMENT

I'm a hammer
you see some lame thing to do
to stuff pink cotton candy in
your child's fist,
to blackjack James Brown—
I'll sandbag all you white motherfuckers,
and then I'll pee,
I'll pee wet patterns on granite walls
drop a money-seed in a blind man's cup
and run with glee and do a buckwing
o-wee
For half a man I'd snuff twenty Armenians
and tell their Episcopalian mothers
to be on guard
and find linoleum stratagems
getting to your buns.
I saw you Benin bold on Sunday.

* * *

POEM

We drank Thunderbird all night,
and rode the subway from Snyder to Olney
and back,
and made occasional love.
We went for a whole day through the white stores: Gimbels,
    Sterns and Wanamakers,
and to Robin's bookstore on Thirteenth street;
and rubbernecked at sweazy faggots we chance to see,
and I thought while I stroked your legs
about the sweet hype,
the sweet smell of pot
    through the El window along Market around 56th
and how we sat sedately
while a toilet flushed somewhere.
Oh and the revolutionary sheets
        and your calibrated belly
            (the children came too soon
                You'll never wear a Bikini
                at Coney Island)
            where seasons of hairs make a steeple
            in your thighs—
a whole day.
A whole day to go reconnoitering
the rummage sales (you bought me a pair of pants and we
    saw a silver casserole you wanted)
down the brittled pavements,
to see our tar-baby jesus
in the Moorish Temple window,
and saw a floor where black arabesques

flowered at your feet as you stepped out of bed.
Fully I see you now,
before footlights, in a lineup,
for some greedy hustler's game
and I drink Sterno
and quietly die.

Calvin C. Hernton

JITTERBUGGING IN THE STREETS

to Ishmael Reed

There will be no Holyman crying out this year
No seer, no trumpeter, no George Fox walking barefoot
    up and down the hot land
The only Messiah we shall see this year
Staggers
To and fro
On the LowerEastSide
Being laughed at by housewives in Edsel automobiles
    who teach their daughters the fun of deriding a terror
    belched up from the scatological asphalt of America
Talking to himself

An unshaven idiot
A senile derelict
A black nigger
Laughter and scorn on the lips of Edsel automobiles
    instructing the populace to love God, be kind to puppies
    and the Chase Manhattan National Bank
Because of this there will be no Fourth of July this year
No shouting, no popping of firecrackers, no celebrating,
    no parade
But the rage of a hopeless people
Jitterbugging
    in the streets.

Jacksonville, Florida
Birmingham, Atlanta, Rochester, Bedford-Stuyvesant
Jackson, Mississippi, Harlem, New York

Jitterbugging
   in.
   the streets
To ten thousand rounds of ammunition
To waterhoses, electric prods, phallic sticks
   hound dogs, black boots stepping in soft places
   of the body—
Venom in the mouths of Christian housewives, smart young
   Italians, old Scandinavians in Yorkville, suntanned
   suburban organization men, clerks and construction
   workers, poor white trash and gunhappy cops every-
   where:
"Why don't we kill all niggers
Not one or two
But every damn black of them. Niggers will do anything.
I better never catch a nigger messing with my wife, and
most of all never with my daughter! Aughter grab 'em up
   and ship every black clean out of the country . . .
   aughter just line 'em up and mow 'em down
MachineGunFire!"
All Americans—housewives, businessmen, civil service
Employees, loving their families, going to church, regularly
   depositing money in their neighborhood bank
All Fourth of July celebrators belched up from the guilt-
   ridden, cockroach, sick-sex terror of America
Talking to themselves
In bars
On street corners
Fantasizing hatred
At bridge clubs
Lodge meeting, on park benches
In fashionable mid-town restaurants.

No Holyman shall cry out upon the black ghetto this year
No trombonist
The only Messiah we will know this year is a bullet
In the belly
   of a Harlem youth shot down by a coward crouched
   behind an outlaw's badge—

Mississippi
Georgia
Tennessee, Alabama
Your mother your father your brothers, sisters, wives
    and daughters
Up and down the hot land
There is a specter haunting America
Spitfire of clubs, pistols, shotguns, and the missing
Murdered
Mutilated
Bodies of relatives and loved ones
Be the only Santa Claus niggers will remember this year
Be the only Jesus Christ born this year
    curled out dead on the pavement, torso floating
    the bottom of a lake
Being laughed at by housewives in Edsel automobiles.

You say there are four gates to the ghetto
Make your own bed hard that is where you have got
To lay
You say there is violence in Harlem, niggers run amuck
    perpetrating crimes against property, looting stores,
    breaking windows, flinging beer bottles at officers
    of the law
You say a certain virgin gave birth to a baby
Through some mysterious process, some divine conjure,
A messenger turned his walking cane into a serpent
    and the serpent stood up and walked like a natural man
You say . . .
America, why are you afraid of the phallus!

I say there is no "violence" in Harlem.
There is TERROR in Harlem!
Terror that shakes the foundation of the very assholes
    of the people
And fear! And corruption! And murder!

Harlem is the asphalt plantation of America
Rat-infested tenements totter like shanty houses
    stacked upon one another

Circular plague of the welfare check brings vicious wine
every semi-month, wretched babies twice a year, death
and hopelessness every time the sun goes down
Big-bellied agents of downtown landlords with trousers
    that fit slack in the crotch
Forcing black girls to get down and do the dog before they
    learn to spell their names
If you make your own bed hard

He said he was fifteen years old, and he walked beside us
    there in the littered fields of the ghetto
He spoke with a dignity of the language that shocked us
    and he said he had a *theory* about what *perpetrated* the
Horror that was upon us as we walked among flying bullets,
    broken glass, curses and the inorganic phalluses of
    cops whirling about our heads
He said he was a business major at George Washington High
And he picked up a bottle and hurled it above the undulating
    crowd
Straight into the chalk face of a black helmet!

Thirty-seven properties ransacked, steel gates ripped from
    their hinges, front panes shattered; pawn shops, dry
    cleaners, liquor stores
Ripped apart and looted—

"Niggers will do anything. Aughter grab 'em up . . . If they
    ever try to eat my children I'll personally get a
    shotgun and mow down everyone I set eyes on."

And if your church don't support the present police action,
In dingy fish-n-chip and bar-b-que joints
Niggers will be doing business as usual—
From river to river,
Signboard to signboard
Scattering Schaefuer sex-packs all over the ghetto,
Like a bat out of hell,
Marques Haynes is a dribbling fool.

TERROR is in Harlem.
A Fear so constant

Black men crawl the pavement as if they were snakes,
    and snakes turn to bully sticks that beat the heads
    of those who try to stand up—
A Genocide so blatant
Every third child will do the junky-nod in the whore-scented
    night before semen leaps from his loins—
And Fourth of July comes with the blasting bullet in the belly
    of a teenager
Against which no Holyman, no Christian housewife
In Edsel automobile
Will cry out this year
Jitterbugging
    in the streets.

* * *

A BLACK STICK WITH A BALL
OF COTTON FOR A HEAD AND
A RUNNING MACHINE FOR A MOUTH

Will it be like this, Charlie
In life's other solidified enterprise?
Stiff in the strut of the dead
Bituminous shirt,
Carbonic boots and spider web,
Cling to our flesh more fierce
Than instinct.

We are a stampede of late supplicants
Who have found no love in swaddling clothes
But the mummy of a worthless radiator
In a cold tenement.

Oh, Charlie! When we have crossed under this death—
Paranoid cells explode rural areas of the psyche—
Will it be the same in life's other formaldehyde
Metropolis?

We hate crippled people, you and I, Charlie.
Deformed, in wheelchair, dragging their
Vestiges along streets, soliciting money,
Soliciting sympathy—
We hate jews and niggers and dagoes
And polaks and japs and those who humiliate
Us by affronting our guilt
With their hypochondriatic scars—
We hate them, and they hate us.

Oh, how will it be
When we have crossed under into utopia's other hate king-
 dom?
Sundown suit of sweat
Static dance, staccato pain.
Do you really love your life, Charlie,
Coming down Bleaker Street
Past monuments
To medicine riddle organisms
Singing paint-paint-paint,
Discovering paint is chiseled agony
On the triangle of your profile in the
Village East?

Hate lean epileptic,
The head gyrates like the ass of a whore;
Mouth, rehearsed medieval lips of hangman,
Rattles solicitation like a talking machine—
 The Shamrock! Come into the last angle of
 This ugly beauty, and get your
 Village entertainment.
 Genuine! Bohemian!
 Poet, folksinger, Barrelhouse Mary!
 No naked girls, no boo. no cover charge,
 no shitting around!

Poor Charlie. . . .
We are ejaculating stone,
We are here where
Bones do not connect with bones.

SAGA OF RESISTANCE

Resist me ————
Make me strong.
Resist me ————
Make me strong.
For since I cannot be what you will
I shall always be that much more so
What I will.
Resist me ————
Repulse my dreams.
Thus is a spark brought from nothing . . .
Stone rubbed against stone
Upon the thirsty grass,
Dried and baked by a burning son . . .
Then suddenly: flame.
Flame feeding flame.
. . . Now, nothing is the same:
   The stones are blackened ————
   The grass is ashes
   The burning sun is still no less itself
   But all else is changed
   Nor ever shall be as it was before.

* * *

"THE VISITATION"

In the early days of my visitation,
Black hands tended me and cared for me . . .
Black minds, hearts and souls loved me . . .
And I love them because of this.
In the early days of my visitation,
Black hands tended me and cared for me;
I can't forget these things.
For black hearts, minds and souls love me—
And even today the overtones from the fire
of that love are still burning.
In the early days of my visitation
White rules and laws segregated me . . .
They helped to make me what I am today
And what I am, I am.
Yes, what I am, I am because of this
And because of this
My image of paradise is chromatic-black.
And chromatic-black again.
Those who segregate did not segregate in vain
For I am,
And I am what I am.

* * *

OF THE COSMIC-BLUEPRINTS

If it was not slavery——
It was rather complete service to humanity,
Unstinted humble-effort
Foolishness to the world
But bolder and braver
Than any of history's warriors.
If it was not slavery—
It was the activation
Of the Cosmic-blueprints . . .
Sowing seeds of cosmos rare
Casting ever down to ever lift above.
If it was not slavery
It was freedom not to be
In order to ready for the discipline-plane
From other-greater-worlds.

* * *

WOULD I FOR ALL THAT WERE

Would I for all that were
If all that were is like a wish.
Would I for all that were
If all that were is that which never came to be;
For the image of the world that was
Is the light of the darkness today . . .
And all that were is not what I wish it were.
So would I for all that were
All that swirls anon in the world of dreams
Boundless in thought to fruitful reminisce.
Would I for all that were
All that words cannot express
All that pleasant dreams cannot remember . . .
The enchantment and warmth of rare content.
Would I for these and these alone
That I might live as Cosmic thought insists I should
As it were right to be as I wish I were.
Would I for this wondrous thing
A new decree of happiness
Better than, any liberty this world has ever known.
A Cosmic weigh
That opens the way to the worlds that are: ——
The Kosmos worlds of endless galaxies.

* * *

NOTHING IS

At first nothing is;
Then nothing transforms itself to be air
Sometimes the air transforms itself to be water;
And the water becomes rain and falls to earth;
Then again, the air through friction becomes fire.
So the nothing and the air and the water
And the fire are really the same—
Upon different degrees.

* * *

TO THE PEOPLES OF EARTH

Proper evaluation of words and letters
In their phonetic and associated sense
Can bring the peoples of earth
Into the clear light of pure Cosmic Wisdom.

* * *

THE IMAGE REACH

To
The territory of the non-memory
The realm of the moving potential
of that which is not—
To
The state beyond the image-reach
The magic life of myth
And fantasy
I speak
And say "Welcome.
I welcome thy presence
As a very Cosmic gift
of sheer happiness.
The happiness I have known
Are no longer mine.
I cast them to the world";
And say "Take These,
As you have taken all else from me,
For I have one foot upon
The threshold of other realms
And wings"

* * *

THE COSMIC AGE

This is the Space Age
The age beyond the earth age:
A new direction
Beyond the gravitation of the past.
This is the space age.
This is the disguised twin of tomorrow
Striking upon the earth
With relentless power
Like a perpetual whip.
This is the Space Age—
Prepare for the journey!
You have a rendezvous
With the living wisdom
of the unadulterated fate.
Prepare for the journey!
Like a happy child
You will step out of the pages
of the blinding-blend of the book,
And gaze astounded at
The Endless space of the Cosmic Void.
Your new course is the Cosmic Way—
Your new vehicle is the Cosmic plane;
You will learn to live the Cosmic Way,
You will learn to journey with courage—
With the fiery aim to reach
The even greater day
of the even greater tomorrow
The greater tomorrow of the Cosmic Age.

The second main is the master key
From the heaven of Outer-Space.
The second main
Is the second principal
The principle:
Cosmic-Timelessness of the Cosmic Age.

Lethonia Gee

BY GLISTENING, DANCING SEAS

By glistening, dancing seas
On ancient time-spun sands
Black woman bends her wooly head
And thinks about her man

In the ghost house of the ghetto
With folded, wrinkled hands
Black woman bends her tired head
And thinks about her man

On ugly, cement, city streets
Or quiet village-lands
Black woman has one heavy thought
And it's about her man

BLACK MUSIC MAN

As a Masai warrior
With his Burning Spear
Blessed by the Gods
The epitome of man
BLACK MUSIC MAN
In smoke-filled cafés
The sound of your golden horn calls
to me
You blow, sad, sorrowful, and blue
But cannot know
That my throat pains
As sound bursts forth

Your mournful prose you offer to me
Yet, you cannot feel
My heart as it dies

You cry
But do not see
That tears fall from my eyes

You think that all is lost
You rip away your soul
And fling it naked to the world
And I stand bleeding
But you do not look

Then you stop
(when the soul is torn away the body lives no more)
You walk the streets
Cold, quiet, alone
Never once do you turn

Never once do you know
That behind you I walk
And in my arms
I carry your soul

K. William Kgositsile

IVORY MASKS IN ORBIT

For Nina Simone

these new night
babies flying on ivory wings
dig the beginning

do you love me!

son gawdamm
i saw the sun
rise at the midnight hour

300 sounds burn
on the ivory bespeaking
a new kind of air massive
as future memory

this like a finger moves
over 300 mississippies
rock the village
gate with future memory
of this moment's riff

the sun smiles of new
dawn mating with this
burning moment for the memory
can no longer kneel-in

do you love me!

88 times over lovely
ebony lady swims in this
cloud like the crocodile

in the limpopo midnight
hour even here speaking
of love armed with future
memory: desire become memory
i know how you be tonight!

THE AWAKENING

My sleep was like a prenatal death.
After 300 years I thought something in me was awake
But then I couldn't have been awake
Because nothing sounded clear—
Nothing sounded good enough
Unless it had a white background.
I flirted with Marx
Kept my ear open to Tshaka,
Moshoeshoe, Dingane, Garvey, DuBois.
Then came Nkrumah's voice,
Heraldic of bearings flowery as spring.
Lumumba, Kenyatta, Mandela, Sobukwe,
Kaunda, Babu, Castro, Tour, Mao—
Twentieth century recipe
For a grass roots favorite dish.

Then came I to America,
Twentieth century capital of the living dead
Petulant whores fighting to make me a phallic assimilado
A sexcessful relic of the house nigger.

Amidst sit-ins, kneel-ins, sleep-ins and mass mis-education
Brother Malcolm's voice penetrated alienated bloodcells
Teaching Black manhood in Harlem USA
Endorsing "Bandung,"
Retrieving Black balls cowering in glib Uncle Tomism
Forcing me to grow up ten feet tall and Black
My crotch too high
For the pedestal of Greco-Roman Anglo-Saxon
adolescent Fascist myth.

Now I see everything against a Black background
As Black and proud as Melba
Breaking the blood-dripping icons of Western congenital
  chicanery
Enthralling me like the cataract of a cosmic orgasm.

TOWARDS A WALK IN THE SUN

THE WIND IS CARESSING
THE EVE OF A NEW DAWN
A DREAM: THE BIRTH OF
MEMORY

                                    Who are we? Who
were we? Things cannot go on much as
before. All night long we shall laugh
behind Time's new masks. When the moment
hatches in Time's womb we shall not complain.
Where, oh where are
The men to matches
The fuse to burn the
Snow that freezes some
Wouldbe skyward desire
    You who swallowed your balls for a piece
    Of gold beautiful from afar but far from
    Beautiful because it is colored with
    The pus from your brother's callouses
    You who creep lower than a snake's belly
    Because you swallowed your conscience
    And sold your sister to soulless vipers
    You who bleached the womb of your daughter's
    Mind to bear pale-brained freaks
    You who bleached your son's genitals to
    Slobber in the slime of missionary-eyed faggotry
    You who hide behind the shadow of your master's
    Institutionalized hypocrisy the knees of your
    Soul numbed by endless kneeling to catch

The crumbs from your master's table before
You run to poison your own mother. You too
Deballed grin you who forever tell your masters
I have a glorious past . . . I have rhythm
. . . I have this . . . I have that. . . .
Don't you know I know all your lies?
The only past I know is hunger unsatisfied
The only past I know is sweating in the sun
And a kick in the empty belly by your fatbellied master
    And rhythm don't fill an empty stomach
        Who are we? All night long
        I listen to the dream soaring
        Like the tide. I yearn to
        Slit throats and color the
        Wave with the blood of the villain
        To make a sacrifice to the gods. Yea,
        There is pain in the coil around things
Where are we? The memory . . .
And all these years all these lies!
You too over there misplaced nightmare
Forever foaming at the mouth forever
Proclaiming your anger . . . a mere
Formality because your sight is colored
With snow. What does my hunger
Have to do with a gawdamm poem?
THIS WIND YOU HEAR IS THE BIRTH OF MEMORY. WHEN
THE MOMENT HATCHES IN TIME'S WOMB THERE WILL BE NO
ART TALK. THE ONLY POEM YOU WILL HEAR WILL BE THE
SPEARPOINT PIVOTED IN THE PUNCTURED MARROW OF THE
VILLAIN; THE TIMELESS NATIVE SON DANCING LIKE CRAZY TO THE
    RETRIEVED RHYTHMS OF DESIRE FADING INTO MEMORY

David Henderson

NEON DIASPORA

For the famous rhythm and blues quartet, the Drifters

The Drifters are in Harlem
The Drifters are at the Theresa
Staring over the soot-stained ghetto
Just as Castro did in '60
    The Drifter's suite—just as Castro's was—is directly
Over Chock Full O' Nuts, the distinction being twelve stories
of elevation, of stained brick and crevices.
These fine slickheaded ghetto boys have wheeled
   their agony through streets of iron, beast, blood
   and fire singing *their* songs of freedom to the blackbelted
   bucks of our America.
     There Goes My Baby through Atlanta, *Let the Music*
    Play
    Through Birmingham, Jackson, *Up On the Roof* through
    Los Angeles, Jacksonville, *On Broadway, The Rat Race*
    Chicago, Illinois, Manhattan—the Theresa built upon
    base of Chock Full O' Nuts—*Let The Music Play just*
a little longer.
    The Drifters are in the foul auricle of the city
walking no freedom orgasm to wave of biblical firehose.
    The Drifters are in the Palm Café strutting for the
    aristocracy
the Post Office Employees, the Parks Department truck
    drivers, the
Transit Railroad Clerks and policemen. The nurses, the Fish
    and

230

Chips' shack owners
The fully employed, steady working hands of Harlem. The
    Drifters
are in the Palm Café to wave and shout, stomp and lead the
privileged, the responsibles
    to the Apollo
    along with the rest.

II

The Drifters are in the fetid bosom of Manhattan
Rocking the Apollo like an exploding battleship:
The bobbing black crowd reach long upwards,
The short-skirted young girls dog in the aisles . . . .
    The Drifters are in the big Apple tonight
Sing us a song . . . SANG!

I see the enigmas of our Neon Diaspora

The Drifter's lashing gleaming red and black hair elongated
    Crushed in waves like a murky manic sea. White hand-
    kerchiefs
    billowing outward draw gasp from the crowd, mop brightly
    brown faces and then are released above the orchestra to be
    ripped to pieces in terms of love.
I see the lead singer of the Drifters (his teeth too big for
    his mouth), react to his plasmic nickname. The Drifters
    are legs encased in silver, they are pop-collared shirts
    flowing
    outward at the breast, they are blazing orange jackets exact
    in tightness from shoulder to buttocks—holding all in
    along the aorta line.
These hightop demons of the Quarter strip
    do not dance
These incantators of neon disasters
    do not clown
These imbibers of barbecue and Gordon's Gin

    are not from Liverpool

    When I see them strut to the footlights, faintly
smiling amongst themselves, giving measured "cool" response

to the screaming, the dancing, the reaching, and then looking into the crowd and darkness, swagger a retreat with that Elemental sexuality (that has been our only hope for so long) I love those black bastards with all the heart I dare.

* * *

BOSTON ROAD BLUES

Boston Road is as wide as a boulevard
but lacks the classic grandeur of verdure
Tenements and bleacher-like stoops
line the cobblestone expanse through Mid-Bronx
the cars & trucks sound faster than they go
often
     cobbled stone runs up into pink brick
of the Housing Authority's stadium

ride a Bonneville speeding
along this main street
and you will see the Negroes waiting on either side
on stoops on dinette and aluminium beach chairs
like the retired
           bop-cap and sneakered Jews
of the Grand Concourse

at 149th St. Boston Road passes perpendicular
under the El
then the Shadow Box Cabaret, Freddy's, the Oasis,
Sylvia's Blue Morocco, Paradise Club, Goodson's
on to Crotona Park
where one summer of the fifth decade
the burning Enchanters bopped down
on the Crowns, the Bathgate Avenue Stompers,
and the Scorpion from PR
in rapid fury & succession
and now   where the same adolescents
play softball for the youth Board.

and the inlet to Public School 55
the swinging "Cadillacs" always took

Earl at the fishtail wheel
responding to 'hey Speedo' when in reality
his real name was Mister Earl
singing as he was
                    his teeth jumbled & contorted
the Cadillacs personnel tall and short
sundry and aloof
gleaming bemused hair
the only top to the convertible
the only road map to the sun.
parked in front of all-girl Jane Addams
their marijuana their argot their ornate auto
routed by a militant lady principal.
All the quartets sang louder
when the Cadillacs cruised Brook Avenue—
P.S. 55 is to be integrated this Autumn
the Cadillacs have passed (Earl now with the Coasters)
and the housing Authority has arrived
as influential as Jesus
as gigantic as the Tennessee Valley Authority.
1501 Boston Road is Bronx C.O.R.E.
      (stompers have risen to politics)
Herb Callender   Isaiah Brunson   knife riding
      shit talking   genius pacifist—
The road swirls until ghetto limits
where   above two hundred street
            it becomes tar smooth   single similar double
            family homes
and Boston Road becomes Boston Post Road.

                              II
When I was a singer
I stayed on Boston Road
among the cabarets & the singers: the Dells,
the Mellotones, the Cadillacs . . .
      our quartet calling ourselves Starsteppers
      (perhaps to insure a goal
                              other than a ghetto)

evinced no concept of space save
                  where the cobblestone Road
and the bleachers-on-residence tapered to a point
where the Road became post itself.
by twilight the clubs released their exotic lures
Sylvia's Blue Morocco sheds blue light both neon & real
on sidewalk and cobblestones between Shabazz Beauty Parlor
& Denzil's Fabulous candystore
Velvet Blue drapes hang ceiling to floor
and all to be seen inside is the spotlighted face
of the singer   the dim blue faces of the music
the soloist   the master of ceremonies   —heads
                          truncated in blackness
puppeted by galloping Hessians from Scarsdale

And Freddy's white enamel front white lights
all outward   upward
harlem jazz exude bandstand tall   /mixing
                  with moth & mosquito insect-serendipity
all white light reflected spill over bleacher sitters
parked car residers, vigillers, standees dispersed
                  and reassembled.
The tenements soar skyward
half white light half black dwindling to sky
stars dismissed by energy of mortals.
     & for a moment Club 845 the combo in the window
     (display)
sunday combination cocktail sips jam sessions
for bored number players 4pm to 8pm
after church and before chicken.

III

We Starsteppers
               wore the same type cord suit blue
and as a rhythm 'n blues singer my PAT BOONE endorsed
one afforded uniform discomfort as just reward
for being in a hurry in an 125th Street clothing store
(probably thinking the street was in Harlem)
and contributing to the corny man (:Patrick Alphonse Boone
               Columbia University 1959)

who stole Little Richard's tunes
& parodied them into a fortune.
Little Richard receiving lyricist royalties
but no TV show
no life insurance & old age compensation
only a backwater church Southern
the God
the Holy Ghost
The Son
                              of a pagan country.
The Starstepper organization carried four singers
three managers and a lopsided Cadillac
                  Let's take a cocktail sip
        and talk of the crippled '55 Caddy in 1960
                  — the epoch of reform —
Buddy, our main manager, wrote and recorded a song
called "SCHBOOM"
then the Crewcuts swept away the bread
the Man couldn't use a colored group on TV 1954
Buddy got the writer's royalties
                              tho
and I would suppose that Sunset Boulevard
in a brand new white caddy convertible
things travel quickly
as that colored group did in L.A.
singing the Crewcuts' song.
                  Spenser —yet another manager—
    torpedo-head lank lipped   sold "Let The Little Girl
    Dance" for one hundred
Fat Billy Bland & three young colored girls took over
and Spenser
because he had a hit record (moneywise not his)
sported his long red conk all over Tin Pan Alley
haranguing the Brill Building   and shit—
borrowing the single-axled Cadillac
by day
to return at night
hair out of gas   car out of gas
spent

IV

So
after record hops (anyone and every one)
community center and house party gigs
background harmony (of our own invention) for
BIG TIME RECORD COMPANY
ten dollars a day
steady gigging Goodson's (gay) Little Club
on Boston Road-by-Randolph
                    (The clientele loved fresh young talented
                    they said, Goodson too)
We recorded Broadway in a white Cadillac
High School boys & old hustlers
Handkerchiefs Sabu over Pozner-fresh conk
black   and   red
Then one day I told Goodson, sir
the Starsteppers have a recording out now
and we are not accepting anymore club dates
on Boston Road, our managers have instructed me
to tell you.
                    ZAP!
Outside the "Little" club on the Road that last night
I watched the tiny attracter light
swing its eerie ascorbic beam twenty times yellow
a minute
            to the street stones of steep 167th
long across Boston Road   the island in front of A&P
through the trees   catching the tenements high
then diffused and broken runs to rewing
the tiny canopy of Goodson's Little Club
                    then down 167th again
        (which in the Bronx has a common level of under-
        standing)
take Sunset Boulevard
                    to give a sense of dimension
Later
the higher forms of publicity
our managers had subsequently informed

Mr. Goodson of
consisted of giving all available copies
of our hit to friends
occasional pilgrimages downtown
for pep talks about word-of-mouth
waiting day   waiting nights
New York Radio stations   New Jersey Stations
            (WVNJ played it at six one morning)
            JOCKO   MURRAY THE K   ALLEN FREED,
            CLAY COLE DR JIVE BRUCE THE MOOSE
            announcing to their
         boys & girls the new boss hit by the starsteppers
"You're Gone"   the flip side that you'll wig over
"The First Sign Of Love"
We were told
it often takes months   up to a year
for a record to be picked up on
sometimes they start big on the Coast
we waited
six months   a year
reading CASHBOX weekly
we waited (never to Goodson again)
we waited
and after a while
started singing to ourselves once more.

KEEP ON PUSHING
(Harlem Riots/Summer/1964)

The title taken from a recent hit recording
(Summer, '64) by the famous rhythm & blues
trio, Curtis Mayfield and The Impressions.

Lenox Avenue is a big street
The sidewalks are extra wide—three and four times
    the size of a regular Fifth Avenue or East 34th
    Street sidewalk—and must be so to contain the
unemployed vigiling Negro males, the picket lines
and police barricades.
Police Commissioner Murphy can
muster five hundred cops in fifteen minutes.
He can summon extra
tear gas bombs, guns, ammunition
within a single call
to a certain general alarm.
For Harlem
reinforcements come from the Bronx
just over the three-borough Bridge.
    a shot   a cry   a rumor
can muster five hundred Negroes
from idle and strategic street corners
    bars   stoops   hallways   windows
Keep on pushing.
I walk Harlem
I see police eight per square block
crude mathematics

eight to one
eight for one
I see the store owners and keepers—all white
and I see the white police force
The white police in the white helmets
and the white proprietors in their white shirts
talk together and
look around.
 I see Negro handymen put to work because of the riots
boarding up smashed storefronts
They use sparkling new nails
The boards are mostly fresh-hewn pine
and smell rank fresh.
The pine boards are the nearest Lenox Avenue will ever have
to trees.
 Phalanxes of police
march   up   and   down
They are dispatchedandgathered   helmet heads
Bobbingwhiteblack and blue.
They walk around—squadroned & platooned.
groups of   six   eight   twelve.
Even in a group
the sparse Negro cop walks alone
or with a singular
talkative
white buddy.
                    keep on pushing
 Am I in the 1940's?
 Am I in Asia? Batista's Havana?
where is Uncle Sam's Army? The Allied Forces
when are we going to have the plebescite?

                              III
I walk and the children playing frail games seem
like no other children anywhere
they seem unpopular   foreign
as if in the midst of New York existed
a cryptic and closed society.
 Am I in Korea?

I keep expecting to see
companies of camouflage-khakied Marines
the Eighth Army
Red Crosses—a giant convoy
through the narrow peopled streets
jeeps with granite-faced generals colonels
marching grim champions of the free world
Trucks dispensing Hershey Bars and Pall Malls
Medical equipment
nurses doctors drugs serums to treat
The diseased and the maimed
and from the Harlem River
Blasting whistles horns
volleying fire bombs against the clouds
the 7th fleet
                    but the prowling Plymouths
          and helmeted outlaws from Queens
          persist
                    Keep On A' Pushing

                              IV
I see plump pale butchers pose with their signs:
          "Hog Maws 4 pounds for 1 dollar"
"Pigs ears 7 pounds for 1 dollar"
"Neck Bones Chitterlings 6 pounds for 1"
Nightclubs, liquor stores bars 3, 4 & 5 to one block
3 & 4 shots for one dollar
I see police eight to one
          in its entirety Harlem's 2nd Law of Thermodynamics
                    Helmet to barehead
                    nightsticks bullets to barehead
                    black reinforced shoes to sneaker
Am I in Korea?

                              V
At night Harlem sings and dances
and as Jimmy Breslin of the *Herald Tribune* says
they also pour their whiskey on one another's heads.
They dog and slop in the bars
The children monkey in front of Zero's Record Chamber

on 116th and Lenox
They mash potatoes and madison at the Dawn Casino,
Renaissance Ballroom, Rockland Palace, and the Fifth
  Avenue
Armory on 141st and the Harlem River
      Come out of your windows
dancehalls, bars and grills Monkey   Dog in the streets
like Martha and the Vandellas
Dog for NBC
The *Daily News* and the *Christian Science Monitor*
Dog for Adlai Stevenson
And shimmy a bit
for 'the boys upstate'
                              'cause you got soul
                              Everybody knows . . .
                              Keep on Pushin'

                              VI

This twilight
I sit in Baron's Fish & Chip Shack
Alfonso (the counterman) talks of ammunition
and violence   The *Journal American* in my lap
headlines promised 'exclusive battle photos'
by a daring photographer they call Mel Findlestein
through him they insure "The Face Of Violence—The most
    striking Close-ups"
WWRL the radio station that serves
the Negro community
tools along on its rhythm and blues vehicle
The colorful unison announcers
declare themselves "The most soulful station in the nation"
Then the lecture series on democracy comes on
The announcer Professor Robert Scalapino for this series
    doesn't sound soulful
          (eight to one he's white, representing management)
We Negroes are usually warned of the evils of Communism
and the fruits of democracy, but this evening he tells us
that in this troubled time we must keep our heads

and our law
and our order
he says violence only hurts (and he emphasizes hurts)
        the cause of freedom and dignity. He urges the troubled
restless residents of Harlem and Bedford-Stuyvesant to stay
in their homes, mark an end to the tragic and senseless
    violence
a pause
then he concludes
and a rousing mixed chorus ends with
            "And the home of the brave."
Alfonso didn't acknowledge the majestic harmony
he hears it every hour on the hour.
The rhythm and blues returns
a flaming bottle bursts on Seventh Avenue
and shimmies fire across the white divider line
helmets
and faces white as the white fluorescence of the street
bob by   BLACK
Prowl cars speeding wilding wheeling
the looney tune of the modulating de-modulating sirens
climb the tenements window by window.
Harlem moves on an automatic platform.
The red fish lights swirl the gleaming storefronts
there will be no Passover this night
and then the gunfire high
in the air   death static
        over everything
ripped glass
shards   sirens   gunfire
down towards 116th
        Then Jocko scenes radio WWRL
late at night he hustles wine: Italian Swiss Colony Port
sherry and muscatel. Gypsy Rose and Hombre "The man's
Adult western drink,"
but by day and evening
his raiment for Harlem's head is different
zealous Jocko coos forward

his tongue baroque-sinister
snakes like fire   "Headache?   —Take Aspirin"
                         "Tension?
                               . . . . take Compoz!"
Keep on a' pushin'
Someway somehow
I know we can make it
with just a little bit of soul.

A. B. Spellman

THE BEAUTIFUL DAY #9

for rob't mcnamara

the beast's backing up. his ass
is grass. have him. in hue
they say taylor can be had
with a gallon of gas. in the congo
they say tshombe leaning
on the beast is leaning on air.

stateside shades
watching the beast in his jungle
biting blackness from the sides of
ibo, shinto, navajo, say
no mo, charlie.

by biting i mean standing before
all that is human
ripping the shadow from a man's back
throwing it in his face
& calling it him.

but what if that shadow was the beast
gray as the grave, hanging on?
what if his mirror was blackness
the knife of the shadow
the thaw of the times?

sexless & fragile, frail
as machine, his energy made, whiter
than air, strength leaking from every
hole, & richer than god, what do
you do with him?

pour color in his circuits, where
love armed with nature like gas
in his veins will smoke out
his tubes. or as they say who hate the
octopi, put out the octopus' eye

* * *

tomorrow the heroes

tomorrow the heroes
will be named willie. their
hair will the bushes that grow
everywhere the beast walks. america

is white. america is not. white
is not the slow kerneling of seed
in earth like the willies, the grass
the roots that grapple the beast

in the swamps. the williecong are earth
walking. ile-ife succor the williecong.
there is no other hope.

* * *

friends i am   like you   tied

friends i am   like you   tied
to you & the delicate chain   knots
us each to all the moving points
together   apart   making "the thing"
knotted chain   links awkward in knots
knots notted   trying to move on impulse
beyond the "us" of us   fungus
of the self that eats races whole   like you
i am tied

a.b.   break something   action   i've
acted   who mans the far end of the i?
that fellow violently inert so placed
so moved   from the chair its eye
to filthy window   to filthy air to
filthy curb   redolent with skid piss
curb street curb skid piss houston st.
moving on down the line   you   now   we
us   how stay clean in this   place
do not eat soap   relevance pays   there squats
mundanity   kick it in the nuts   its crotch swallows
your foot now where are you footless
hiss of the hideous   you goofed in the tactic   a.b.
you're still too quiet   break something larger

who started this war   who said   there are folk
with culture and good looks   let's fry the niggers
in texan shit   johnson?   kennedy?   trumanhoover-
    hower?
kid you're ugly ok   i told him   but don't flatter yourself

248

you're uglier than that   there is no "this" war
there is no "all" war   either   the west turned
moribund   with marco   the east woke up
with mao   there is war   friends
with sickness and dying   with dying
and hating it   twisting the chain into knots

poem at thirty

it is midnight
no magical bewitching
hour for me
i know only that
i am here waiting
remembering that
once as a child
i walked two
miles in my sleep.
did i know
then where i
was going?
traveling. i'm
always traveling.
i want to tell
you about me
about nights on a
brown couch when
i wrapped my
bones in lint and
refused to move.
no one touches
me anymore.
father do not
send me out
among strangers.
you you black man
stretching scraping

the mold from your body
here is my hand.
i am not afraid
of the night.

summary

no sleep tonight
not even after all
the red and green pills
i have pumped into
my stuttering self or
the sweet wine
that drowns them.
                 this is
a poem for the world
for the slow suicides
in seclusion.
somewhere on 130th st.
a woman, frail as a
child's ghost, sings.   oh.
                    oh. what
can the matter be? johnny's
so long at the fair.
           / i learned how
              to masturbate
thru the new york times.
i thought
shd i have
thought anything
that cd not
be proved. i
thought and
was wrong. listen.
                    fool
    black

                    bitch
of fantasy. life
is no more than
                                                            gents
              and
                   gigolos (99% american)
      liars
      and
      killers (199% american)
                                        dreamers
                      and drunks (299% american)
(ONLY GOD IS 300% AMERICAN)
                              i say
is everybody happy?
this is a poem for me.
i am alone.
one night of words
will not change
all that.

Q. R. Hand

And I can Remember still your first lies America
When I too was at Lexington in Massachusetts and the South
  Pacific too
You Motherfuckers
When Bataan fell and then Corregidor I was on the Death
  March
The Fascist *Journal American* scooped a center piece of
  beheadings
Americans burying others alive
Realer than John Wayne and Robert Preston
Or was it the Italian Campaign Anzio Monte Casino Salerno
Blood and guts Mark Clark or was it Patton
Wasn't it in Italy they allowed Black Americans to fight,
Or was it Oran or Casablanca?

I didn't realize then when there were no "Murdering Reds"
  at Stalingrad what it might mean to be dead except
For that "Stars and Stripes Forever" valhalla where all of
  our heroes negroes too went
I didn't know the difference between the well-disciplined
  valiant Marines who waded and floated the bloody jaws of
  hell at Tarawa
Under the withering death dealing murdering cowardly
  (That's what you called it) hellfire crossfire of those yellow
  slant-eyed rats
And the . . . or is it now fools of Midway and Wake . . .

(And speaking of Wake and wakes and the like America the
  tide of your blood spilt in revenge . . .
Do you begin to see it yet . . . ? . . . a riptide . . . and the
  wake . . .
Do you really drink it America? . . . manic vampire ten red
  galloned he-men . . .)

Who would have thought who was in the third grade then
that lend-lease was life insurance for zombies,
Who would have thought who was in the third grade then
America that you were more full of shit than the Christ-
mas Turkey?
Sure BING, yeah I know, it was a good tune, made thou-
sands for DECCA AND . . . I'll be home for Christmas . . .
And they didn't make it,
I mean those Mississippi Black Boys dead of too much
freezing sea or air in the lungs in the North Atlantic, you
dirty lying motherfuckers,
Your boats U-boats but not our boats,
I wonder how many died wondering if now they belonged,
finally, at last, while their brothers drove trucks over the
Via Appia and
Did things they would have been Lynched for at home (balls
cut off and all) and were under the threat of court-martial
for at the front
ME-109's breathing down their necks with rapid-fire fixed 50
caliber bullets (which Hollywood later did in LIVID
color— you know what that is— "The Black— I mean
Red-Ball-express— before McCarthy you know!")
History is now a monument to your deceit,
At whose base sits the sack-suited button-downed ex-OSS
men (Yes . . . I saw that one too)
Who manage and direct how many of your companies who
manage and direct how many of whose countries who
manage and neglect how many of whose citizens who manage to stay alive don't ask me how all over the world,
And remember FOLKS, an empty little belly in Chile or Peru
is worth at least Two full ones at home,
Support Fascism at home and abroad it keeps your split-
level mind from owning up to its mortgage value in blood
While your soul turns cartwheels policing or is it caressing
the globe with your compulsive green leprosy
Let me tell you I had a Black ancestor at San Juan Hill
(still alive, in the NAACP, lost an eye, would you believe
it, from a bow and arrow delivering mail on an island

(Staten) where he had to fight to stay, whose grandson was
  wounded and fights for money in Vietnam
And who because I am human and black can understand cannot put down but I sure wish he'd turn his gun around at
  least once)
And I don't mean to let you get away with that one, at all.

I had a friend once who told me how his tears frooze his
  beard solid on the strategic withdrawal from the Chosen
  reservoir,
Signed up to be a frog-man at 15 a killer at 17 on land in the
  sea and I'm sure if he could have flown in the air
And yet I'll always remember his smile of glee when he told
  me how (now get this, from a decorated "gyrene")
He had blown away a top sergeant from Georgia just a few
  steps ahead of him just because he said "Niggrahs" a little
  too funny-like.
I mean that's a real Uncle Tom.

When the 17th rode the plains hard the Kiowa never took
  a CONKED scalp but no wooly-haired brothers were on
  the right side at the little big horn.
Experience teaches us that experience is at least the worst
  teacher, if not worse than that.
It's too bad that's a premise a forgetful beginning the demise
  of memory the death of the vengeful heart which can at
  times be the rebirth (if you have that kind of power, but
  who has?)
When a stimulus continually provokes or is it evokes the
  response that negates the acts (the former)
Why is it that the latter upon further appraisal means little
  or no thoughts of reprisal.
With all of the condemning evidence before us a chorus of
  supplicant no's stifle all sense
When the conversion of the convulsive into beautiful fluid
  energy of much-beloved hates begins to feed on our very
  selves,
When the gnaw of centuries of ill-drawn dreams of joy leaps
  into the hand of the impotent slaves of our civilization,

Why do we do the dance of life rather than the dance of
their death?

Why do we die for them rather than them for us when the
ineluctable talk of their hearts is the sign of their sub-
humanity to which we are so subject.

Since when did our culture mean such goodness and such
love of death?

And the bearers the true bearers of it (the word-logos-logic-
their word) benefit so little from their labors,

The collective effort in soul so seemingly rewarding in body
and spirit so enervating [in reality]

That our humanity seems less than it is even to those to
whom we should be as examples

where love flows forth like the cornucopia of a myriad dreams
of fecund beautiful great-hipthighed women

And we would rather forge music to strengthen the soul
rather than destroy the bodies of our enemies who by their
very fleshy being keep us and themselves and the world
enslaved in the roles of master and slave

While soul and body yearn for the freedom of the earth
as the flowers of the jungle warm red and orange Bougain-
villea

Flow in the ethereal and substantive cries of the saxes of the
masters of the tunes of our times while millions listen and
the few that hear don't heed the message,

Yes it is that terrible

Yes love is that hard to come by

Yes meekness inherits all of the earth but none of its life

And our creativity

that green and yellow and gold crescendo of anger and opium
under the gray skies of that old

(Yes I'm back to that again)

American dream,

Must spurt forth again like a thousand coming hardons

Amongst a thousand coming warming cunts

Destroying forever the lie of that dream

FOREVER creating the YES of that good . . .

What was that we were fighting about, anyway? [Was that
what we were fighting about?]
YOU SEE . . . ? . . .
what I'm talking about,
how easy it is to forget . . .

* * *

"I WONDER"

I wonder:
How many Little or Big Black Sambos totter-teeter-titter-
tatter at the cakewalk justice of their American dreams?

Can the rage of just one tottering Black Sambo Wino run
a North American distillery for a year or maybe in a minute
do a lifetime's worth of killing of every North-American
White?

. . . that is, of course, if it could be harnessed either way.

The burning madness of blackness in whiteness can esca-
late a race in space and more— but it is more that counts.

Ron Welburn

EULOGY FOR POPULATIONS

Any of the several names,
who sit on the hands
they use to speak with—
the fingers' many expressions,
many carved topographies
and perspectives. They walk
into the corners of themself
when we scream . . . about
anything. One (if not the only)
beauty of their souls
is the shadow, dancing.
                    And
as though this culture had
a decrement to it, if to everything
there exists an evil half, a section
wavering like a ghoul (there is
a great possibility that the dead
will be buried with secrets
This scares me.

* * *

FIRST ESSAY ON THE
ART OF THE U.S.

Andy Warhol,
  there are empty cans of Campbell soup
  lying along the roadsides; this is called
  the art of the united states.

There are faces, cans/figures
    solid geometry.
This is a dying stare from a hollow world,
an existence of decay having so little hope
  (I must be subjective about America,
    the wasteland above Mexico,
  here I am birthed
  here I am the revival, the messianic
  holy spirit to your society).

And the death of your art, the impeccable surfaces
  of duplicate faces,
    (people who are like ghosts
      or less,
            without spirit
            without a Soul)
  is the product of
a complicated theory of art.

Each day things become clearer to me,
the air becomes easier to breathe—
  it has excitement, tension, it smells
  of death and sickness;
and I call this evil 'politics'.

The politics of revolution are rooted
in the art of my people, are rooted
   as yours is even now without roots,
   such a thing as dead trees or yet
   the mind from the heart.
   as yours has the artificial eyes
   fed by a vision (that makes one dig himself
                 and see that his reality
                 is decadent, obscure,
                 that his reality is without
                 the energy or chaos we live
                 in.
Only your chaos is in the scattering of Man
in fright, in Watts/Harlem, in Africa or
Vietnam or however hip you are your art reflects
You, reflects the first thesis of what a Man is
who cannot escape the chaos he mindlessly creates.

Joe Goncalves

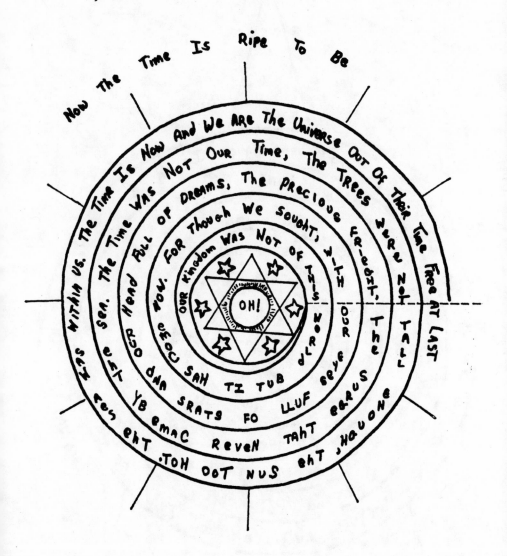

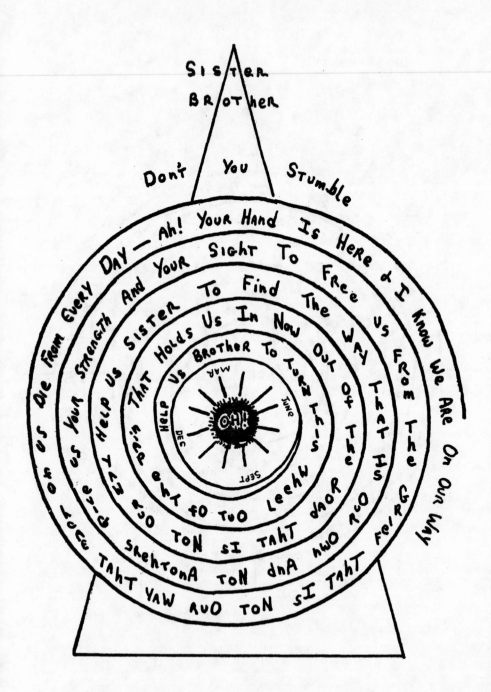

THE WAY IT IS

June or July—I'm not really sure—In
Meridian Mississippi, where you read of white girls (front
page) Raped in periwinkles and their dresses tied up over
Their heads. The detail. And a black boy
Is found by a roadside, mangled,
An "auto accident."
  But it's Boston, really, early 1940 Boston—at least
These four blocks are, where we live. Where we
Stop awhile. A café with tiny black and white squares
For floor; the stools; the footrest, the old mirror, a fan
Beating the heat. And at the hotel, an antique smell,
And photos on the wall—so faded—brown. The heat.
the movie (horror movies): 40¢; 10¢ for kids.
Like early 1940 Boston.
The three who were killed
Came out of here
And went to Philadelphia where
(a middle-aged black man tells us) they
Had set a trap to get some of them
Civil rights workers.
  And the journey here, through Louisiana. The
Stink of water and weeds, decay.
Death, I tell myself. Life, I tell myself. Meridian.
Mid-way Mississippi. Like early 1940 Boston.
Down here, now, 1965, when black people say, good luck,
  baby,
On your trip, they really mean it.

Marvin E. Jackmon

THAT OLD TIME RELIGION

Malcolm.
The Saint
   behind our skulls
in the region of fear and strength
Nothing but a man, who threw fear away
and caught something greater . . . life
And the price of life is death
protect ourselves from the beast
and he went un-protected
by the will of allah
most merciful
a lost leader
though we have found his spirit
   behind our skulls
   in the region of fear and strength
Malcolm held our manhood
   he said what we knew but feared
   we feared to name the beast
   who is a man; who has a number
   and the number is 666 spoken of
   in Revelations of the Bible.
   Ready or not . . . God is here
      LET THERE BE BLACKNESS OVER THIS LAND
      LET BLACK POWER SHINE AND SHINE.

* * *

BURN, BABY, BURN

TIRED. SICK AND TIRED.
TIRED OF BEING SICK AND TIRED.
LOST. LOST IN
THE WILDERNESS OF WHITE AMERICA.
ARE THE MASSES ASSES?
COOL. SAID THE MASTER
TO THE SLAVE, "NO PROBLEM,
DON'T ROB AND STEAL, I'LL
BE YOUR DRIVING WHEEL."
COOL.
AND HE WHEELED US INTO
350 YEARS OF BLACK
MADNESS—TO HOG GUTS,
CONKED HAIR, QUO VADIS
BLEACHING CREAM,
UNCLE THOMAS, TO WATTS
TO THE STREETS, TO THE
KILLLLLLLLLLLL . . . . . .
BOOOMMMMM . . . . . .
2 honkeys gone . .
MOTHERFUCK THE POLICE
AND PARKER'S SISTER TOO.
BURN, BABY, BURN*******
COOK OUTTA SIGHT*******
FINEBURGS, WINEBURGS,
SAFEWAY, NOWAY, BURN . . . . .
BABY, BURN

THE SINGER

I don't know how you died.
I'm not sure where you died.
Or even sang. Or what you looked like.
Young, fat, skinny, old—you
Changed.
I know you came and suffered.
I know you suffered for them
(And us), and I know you
Died for us, and I hope not for them.
Now they cream over your corpse.
They like to listen to you die,
Like they would like to listen to
All of us die.

* * *

MY BROTHER

You tell me they only do to us
What we would do to them
If we were on top. You are the
Product of their bad fantasy.
You are the nigger legislator
Who is drunk and deflowers white
Womanhood. Look at yourself,
With your little moustache and greased hair
And looking more like a Spaniard every day,
You fear the nigger
In you, and most of all
You fear we are all niggers like you
And you don't want to give a nigger
A chance. You are a nigger's nigger:
A white man in the head.

Al Fraser

TO THE "J F K" QUINTET

I dug you
off red and brown
in the light behind,
five bundles of controlled panic
short-suited, fire brained, and young.
I dug you
tear from startled notes
nascent little secrets of blue
so fast, I thought that you
might stumble.
I dug you
loud like young cats are
bitch-snatching, hip, and crazy
pimp a crooked avenue of sound,
hit a groove and cook.
I dug you
screaming bitter blue boys
deep underground;
dug you and knew that I
was like you—
short-suited, fire brained, and young.

Lance Jeffers

MY BLACKNESS IS THE BEAUTY
OF THIS LAND

My blackness is the beauty of this land,
my blackness,
tender and strong, wounded and wise,
my blackness:
I, drawling black grandmother, smile muscular and sweet,
unstraightened white hair soon to grow in earth,
work-thickened hand thoughtful and gentle on grandson's
head,
my heart is bloody-razored by a million memories' thrall;
remembering the crook-necked cracker who spat on my
naked body,
remembering the splintering of my son's spirit because
he remembered to be proud
remembering the tragic eyes in my daughter's dark face
when she learned her color's meaning,

and my own dark rage a rusty knife with teeth to gnaw my
bowels,
my agony ripped loose by anguished shouts in Sunday's
humble church,
my agony rainbowed to ecstasy when my feet oversoared
Montgomery's slime,
ah, this hurt, this hate, this ecstasy before I die,
and all my love a strong cathedral!
My blackness is the beauty of this land!

Lay this against my whiteness, this land!
Lay me, young Brutus stamping hard on the cat's tail,

gutting the Indian, gouging the nigger,
booting Little Rock's Minniejean Brown in the buttocks and
    boast,
        my sharp white teeth derision-bared as I the conqueror
        crush!
Skyscraper-I, white hands burying God's human clouds
    beneath the dust!
Skyscraper-I, slim blond young Empire
        thrusting up my loveless bayonet to rape the sky,
then shrink all my long body with filth and in the gutter lie
as lie I will to perfume this armpit garbage,
While I here standing black beside
wrench tears from which the lies would suck the salt
to make me more American than America . . .
But yet my love and yet my hate shall civilize this land,
this land's salvation.

* * *

BLACK SOUL OF THE LAND

I saw an old black man walk down the road,
a Georgia country road.
I stopped and asked where the nearest town might lie
where I could find a meal.
I might have driven on then to the town nearby
but I stayed to talk to the old black man
and read the future in his eyes.

His face was leathered, lean, and strong,
gashed with struggle scars.
His eyes were piercing, weary, red,
but in the old grief-soul that stared
through his eyes at me
and in the humble frame bent with humiliation and age,
there stood a secret manhood tough and tall
that circumstance and crackers could not kill:
a secret spine unbent within a spine,
a secret source of steel,
a secret sturdy rugged love,
a secret crouching hate,
a secret knife within his hand,
a secret bullet in his eye.

Give me your spine, old man, old man,
give me your rugged hate,
give me your sturdy oak-tree love,
give me your source of steel.
Teach me to sing so that the song may be mine
"Keep your hands on the plow: hold on!"
One day the nation's soul shall turn black like yours
and America shall cease to be its name.

* * *

MAN WITH A FURNACE
IN HIS HAND

From the ocean filled with sand inside of me,
from the mountaintop that snows my brain,
from the volcano overflowing with my viscera,
from the blood that clots my rain,
from the pleading last song of my jesus-nightingale,
    a-snare in a soul within my soul,
from the crippled hands that stretch for mercy in my heart,
from my consecrated stone of frozen tears,
from every buried vein that anguishes my blood,
from every nerve that groans my hell,
from every well sunk deep into my loins
flies the hawk that longs to tear.

Flies the hawk that emptyhearted tears at my flesh,
flies this leopard with black beating wings,
flies the enemy of all humanity,
fly famine, humiliation, fear.

Flies the hawk: his beak and scissor-eye are as cruel
    as the mother who spat upon her child's grief.
The hawk is slavery still alive in me,
    my testicles afloat in cottonfield.
The hawk is the West astride my mighty back—
    my love the beaten Comanche's bitter shame.
The hawk is the snarl of the sahib in the East—
    my love the Aztec crucified.
The hawk and my love are in the smoke of human flesh:
    SEE? Choking up from Hiroshima shore.

The hawk and my love are in the dumb and tortured maw
　　of my idiot grandchild of the Bomb.
The hawk is a future of the devil on the throne:
　　Cortez: his buttocks set in man's face.
My love is a furnace to burn him screaming alive,
　　hands tender to caress the human race.

Walt Delegall

PSALM FOR SONNY ROLLINS

This vibrant, all-embracing, all-pervading
Sound which bleeds from the vinylite veins
Of my record, steals into the conduits of my heart
Forces entrance into the sanctuary
Of my soul, trespasses into the temple
Of my gonads. In a lifespan-while, I am
Absorbed into the womb of the sound.
    I am in the sound
    The sound is in me.
    I am the sound.
I am your tears that you shed for forty days
And forty nights, Theodore. I am
Your pain who you accepted as
Your bedfellow. I am your hunger and
Your thirst, which purified your
Soul, Theodore. I am your sorrow that
You won in a raffle. Pick up your axe
And let us blow down the Chicago citadels
Of convention. "You just can't play like that in here."
Let us blow down the Caucasian battlements
Of bigotry. "But we don't hire Colored musicians."
Open your tenor mouth and let
Us blow into oblivion the insensible
Strongholds of morality.
"And I'm sure he's an addict."
Blow down thunder and lightning
And White People!! Blow down moons
And stars and Christs! Blow down

Rains and trees and Coltranes! Blow down
Shirleys and Star-eyes and West Coasts!
Walk naked into a 52nd street basement
And show Them the "Bird" in your thighs.
Open your Prestige mouth and let them see
The "Hawk" in your voice. Recite ten
Stanzas of blackeyed-pead *Bluing*. Sing
A hundred choruses of South Street
Solid. Paint a thousand canvases of *Dig*
For Joe White. Lead us you Harlem
Piper with a Selmer pipe. The black
Boned children of tomorrow follow
You through space and time
  Lead us to truth,
  To order, To Zen.
  Lead us to Poetry,
  To love, to God.

     * * * * * *

Ring hallelujahs from a sombre past.
Roll hallelujahs to a buoyant dream.
Breathe hallelujahs for a solemn few.
Hallelujah! Hallelujah! Hallelujah!!
     * * * * * *

ELEGY FOR A LADY

I

"It cost me a lot
But there's one thing I've got,
It's my man. . . ."

* * *

Bare and bow your Christian
Heads in sixteen blue bars of
Silence, a Lady's dead. A Lady's
Dead, and yet no flags fly
At half mast. No trumpets lament
Her finale with reverent taps
Her only salute is the twenty-one
Tears which shatter the still
As they fall from
My cheeks to the ground.

A lady's dead and a
Gentleman killed her. A
Gentleman named morality or
Maybe life, I'm not exactly
Sure, but he killed her. He
Killed her in South Philly back
In "47" at the Attucks Hotel. He
Killed her in Baltimore in 1928.
He snuffed out her life with
New York cabaret licenses. He
Murdered her with judges and
Federal Women's Penitentiaries. He
Battered her with Afro

Headlines in 48 point Gothic
Type. He strangled her with
Slander and pointed fingers. He
Killed her and dragged her by
Her heels from the end of his
Chariot. And her only anodyne
Was the naked blues and her
Only relief was to use and use.
Percy baby, she paid her dues!

II

A Lady gropes up the nocturnal
Stairs towards a carrion
Perched on the moon. The
Sombre sound of an old
Upright piano sighing a
Blue-black dirge in B-flat
Pervades the air. And the
Darkness digests the light.
The ubiquitous darkness
Absorbing us also, seeps
Into the conduits of our
Being and fills our mouths
And nostrils with the
Cold clay of black
Nothingness. And as we
Dissolve and become one
With the darkness, for the
First time we see. We
See with an inner eye and
Mark an end to the blind
Stumbling of paltry existence.
Yielding up our lives in order
To live; closing our eyes in
Order to see, to see
Pan, to see "Prez".

And now in the eternal indigo
Night as we mourn the passing of

Day, a deluge of blue tears
Fall from a cloudless sky.
Weep. Weep for the day,
Which in our youth gave
Wonderland reality to lollipop
Dreams. Weep for day in which
We got "high" and almost discovered
The unknowable why. Weep for
Day which, with pain and poverty,
Purged our souls of external
World squalor. Weep for
Day which will never break again,

III
Tonight, perhaps along South
Street or Lenox Ave. or
   Maybe 7th and 'T', a gaunt
   Black man, with a crepe on his
Soul and a smell of port wine
In his pores, will wake
   Up in some consecrated gutter
   And with a pig's foot
Sticky hand, pick up the
Wilted white gardenia beside
   Him, which is all that
   Remains of a Lady.

Welton Smith

malcolm

i cannot move
from your voice.
there is no peace
where i am. the wind
cannot move
hard enough to clear the trash
and far away i hear my screams.

the lean, hard-bone face
a rich copper color.
the smile. the
thin nose and broad
nostrils. Betty—in the quiet
after midnight. your hand
soft on her back. you kiss
her neck softly
below her right ear.
she would turn
to face you and arch up—
her head moving to your chest.
her arms sliding
round your neck. you breathe deeply.
it is quiet. in this moment
you knew
what it was all about.

your voice
is inside me; i loaned
my heart in exchange
for your voice.

in harlem, the long
avenue blocks. the miles
from heart to heart.
a slobbering emaciated man
once a man of god sprawled
on the sidewalk. he clutches
his bottle. pisses on himself
demands you respect him
because his great grandmother
was one-eighth cherokee.
in this moment, you knew.

in berkeley the fat
jewess moves the stringy brown
hair from her face saying
she would like to help you—
give you some of her time.
you knew.
in birmingham "get a move
on you, girl. you bet'not
be late for sunday school."
not this morning—
it is a design. you knew.

sometimes
light plays on my eyelashes
when my eyes
are almost closed—
the chrome blues and golds
the crimson and pale
ice green   the swift movements
of lights through my lashes—
fantastic—
the sound of mecca
inside you. you knew.

the man
inside you; the men

inside you fought.
fighting men inside you
made a frenzy
smelling like shit.
you reached into yourself—
deep—and scooped your frenzy
and rolled it to a slimy ball
and stretched your arm back
to throw

now you pace the regions
of my heart. you know
my blood and see
where my tears are made.
i see the beast
and hold my frenzy;
you are not lonely—
in my heart there are many
unmarked graves.

The Nigga Section

slimy obscene creatures. insane
creations of a beast. you
have murdered a man. you
have devoured me. you
have done it with precision
like the way you stand green
in the dark sucking pus
and slicing your penis

into quarters—stuffing
shit through your noses.
you rotten motherfuckin bastards
murder yourselves again and again
and call it life. you have made
your black mother to spread
her legs   wide
you have crawled in mucous
smeared snot in your hair
let machines crawl up your cock
rammed your penis into garbage disposals
spread your gigantic ass from
one end of america to the other
and peeped from under your legs
and grinned a gigantic white grin
and called all the beasts
to fuck you hard in the ass
you have fucked your fat black mothers
you have murdered malcolm
you have torn out your own tongue
you have made your women
to grow huge dicks you
have stuffed me into your mouth
and slobbered my blood
in your grinning derangement.
you are the dumbest thing
on the earth   the slimiest
most rotten thing in the universe
you motherfuckin germ
you konk-haired blood suckin punks
you serpents of pestilence you
samboes you green witches nawing the heads of infants
you rodents you whores
you sodomites you fat
slimy cockroaches crawling to your
holes with bits of malcolm's flesh
i hope you are smothered
in the fall of a huge yellow moon.

interlude

we never spent time in the mountains
planting our blood in the land planting
our blood in the dirt planting our blood
in the air   we never walked together
down Fillmore or Fifth Avenue
down Main Street together
Friend we never sat together as guests
at a friend's table   Friend
we never danced together as men
in a public park   Friend we never
spent long mornings fishing or laughed
laughed falling all down into the dirt
laughed rolling in the dirt   holding
our stomachs laughing rolling   our mouths
wide open   huge fat laughter
our black bodies shaking   Friend
we never laughed like that together

Special Section for the Niggas on the Lower Eastside or: Invert the Divisor and Multiply

you are the lice
of the lower eastside
you are deranged imitators
of white boys acting out a
fucked-up notion of the mystique

of black suffering. uptown
they believe they are niggas
here you have explanations—
psychological, cultural, sociological,
epistomological, cosmological, political,
economic, aesthetic, religious, dialectical,
existential, jive-ass bullshit explanation
for being niggas   you are
deranged slobbering punks lapping in the
ass of a beast
in the bars you recite
slave rebellions you recite egypt
you recite timbuktu you stand
on your head and whine anger
you are frauds   trying to legitimatize
what they say you are
you are jive revolutionaries
who will never tear this house down
you are too terrified of cold
too lazy to build another house

you lick every cranny in tompkins square
you slurp every gutter from river to river
you are gluttons devouring
every cunt in every garbage can on avenue b
you hope to find
an eighty ton white woman
with a cock big enough
to crawl inside
you don't just want a white woman
you want to be a white woman
you are concubines of a beast
you want to be lois lane, audrey hepburn, ma perkins, lana
    turner, jean harlow, kim stanley, may west, marilyn
    monroe, sophie tucker, betty crocker, tallulah bankhead,
    judy canova, shirley temple, and trigger
you frauds: with your wire-rim glasses and double-breasted
    pin striped coats, and ass choaker pants

you sing while your eyes are scraped from their sockets
you dance while flares are rammed into your ears
you jive mercenary frauds
selling nappy hair for a party invitation
selling black   for a part in a play
selling black   for a ride in a rolls
selling black for a quick fuck
selling black   for two lines on page 6,000 in the new york
    times
selling babies in birmingham for a smile in the den

turn white you jive motherfucker   and ram the bomb up
    your ass.

interlude

            screams
            screams
            malcolm
            does not hear my screams
            screams
            betty
            does not hear my screams
            screams scraping my eyes
            screams from the guns
            screams
            screams
            the witches ecstasy
            screams screams
            ochs sulzberger oppenheimer
            ecstasy luce ecstasy johnson
            galbraith kennedy ecstasy
            franco ecstasy bunche

ecstasy king ecstasy salazar rowan ecstasy
screams
screams
in my nights in st. louis
screams in my nights
screams
screams in the laughter of children
screams in the black faces
schlesinger lodge ecstasy conant ecstasy
stengel nimitz ecstasy screams
screams in my head screams
screams six feet deep.

The Beast Section

i don't think it important
to say you murdered malcolm
or that you didn't murder malcolm
i find you vital and powerful
i am aware that you use me
but doesn't everyone
i am comfortable in your house
i am comfortable in your language
i know your mind   i have an interest
in your security. your civilization
compares favorably with any known
your power is incomparable
i understand why you would destroy
the world rather than pass it to lesser
people. i agree completely.
aristotle tells us in the physics
that power and existence are one

all i want is to sit quietly
and read books and earn
my right to exist. come—
i've made you a fantastic dish
you must try it, if not now
very soon.

LeRoi Jones

THE WORLD IS FULL
OF REMARKABLE THINGS

for little Bumi

Quick Night
easy warmth
The girlmother lies next to me
breathing
coughing
sighing
at my absence. Bird Plane
Flying near Mecca
Sun sight warm air
through
my air foils. Womanchild
turns
lays her head
on my
stomach. Night aches
acts
Niggers rage
down the street. (Air
Pocket, sinks
us. She lady
angel brings
her self
to touch me
grains & grass & long

silences, the dark
ness my natural
element, in
warm black skin
I love &
understand
things. Sails
cries these
moans, pushed
from her by my
weight, her legs
spreading wrapping
secure the spirit
in her.
    We begin our
ritual breathing
flex the soul clean
out, her eyes slide
into   dreams

*   *   *

THREE MOVEMENTS AND A CODA

THE QUALITY OF NIGHT THAT YOU HATE MOST IS ITS BLACK
AND ITS STARTEETH EYES, AND STICKS ITS STICKY FINGERS
IN YOUR EARS. RED NIGGER EYES LOOKING UP FROM A BLACK
   HOLE.
RED NIGGER LIPS TURNING KILLER GEOMETRY, LIKE HIS EYES
   ROLL UP
LIKE HE THOUGHT RELIGION WAS BEBOP.

> LIKE HE THOUGHT
> RELIGION WAS BEBOP
> . . . SIXTEEN KILLERS
> ON A LIVE MAN'S
> CHEST . . .
> > THE LONE
> > RANGER

IS DEAD.
THE SHADOW
IS DEAD.
ALL YOUR HEROES ARE DYING. J. EDGAR HOOVER WILL
SOON BE DEAD. YOUR MOTHER WILL DIE. LYNDON JOHNSON,

> these are natural
> things. No one is
> threatening anybody,
> that's just the way life
> is,
> boss.

Red Spick talking to you from a foxhole very close to the
Vampire Nazi's lines. I can see a few Vampire Nazis moving
   very quickly

back and forth under the heavy smoke. I hear, and perhaps
you do, in
the back ground, the steady deadly cough of mortars, and
the light shatter
of machine guns.

BANZAI!! BANZAI!! BANZAI!! BANZAI!! BANZAI!!

Came running out of the drugstore window with
an electric alarm clock, and then dropped the motherfucker
and broke it. Go get something else. Take everything in there.
Look in the cash register. TAKE THE MONEY. TAKE THE MONEY.
YEH.
TAKE IT ALL. YOU DON'T HAVE TO CLOSE THE DRAWER. COME
ON MAN, I SAW
A TAPE RECORDER BACK THERE.

These are the words of lovers.
Of dancers, of dynamite singers
These are songs if you have the
music.

* * *

ELECTION DAY

(Newark, New Jersey)

The lies of young boys are to be heard about, or read about,
or perhaps
generally tolerated, but the lies of an old man. Of a man
growing bald
and fat. These are the lies of death. And the cloak of death
they spread.
We can die from them. Like choked by underbrush, heavy
weeds. We see him.
Pull the election lever, and men die in Greystone, elec-
trocuted, or are
beat to death on the corners of dirty cities. By heroes. These
are the
killers' heroes. Wd that they were our own. And not the
mad races killing
us. We have a nigger in a cape and cloak. Flying above the
shacks and whores.
He has just won an election. A wop is his godfather. Praise
Wop from whom
all blessings flow. The nigger edges sidewise in the light
breeze, his fingers
scraping nervously in his palms. He has had visions. With
commercials. Change
rattles in his pockets. He is high up. Look, he signals. Turns,
backup, for
cheers. He swoops. The Wop is waving. Wave Wop. He
swoops, he has a metal

mother-sister, loves him, made him from scrap iron. Taught
him to fly. Wave
Metal sister. Grump and waddle. Grouch at heaven, love and
God. Metal woman
wave the nigger in. He sails. Wopwaves. Crowds of neckless
italians whistle
and tell jokes. Leaving rings around the East River. They
swim with the goods.
"Hellow, this is Heroin Plant Sardinia, How many bags you
want Jefe??"
He is leading us, through the phonecalls and shootups. He
is flying ahead,
giving being losing a head. I love him. He is made of iron
and is steered
by a huge white joint. Fly councilman. (WEST). He loves
us. We are his people
Look
he waves and sails. Tho the breeze is wind is gale and stiff
and turns him
back and up against his will. Wave will. And sister ironhole.
And neckless
ton of Wop. Wave. Look. He loves and beckons to us. He
is preceded far
ahead, in purple fading rheumatic wings, by the aluminum
coon. Long dead,
but pushed in the same heavy storm. His dry fly wings batting
sideways
useless, lips eyes fingers squeezing shut and open wings flaking
loose
in the wind. He is the old leader killed from booze and electricity. He is
The Flag, and turns his votes into pizzerias. The "new man"
has a guideline
leads from alum to him, from ass to nose, and through the
spine, and tied
with chains to the white quivering dick shoved halfway up
his ass, its tip

like an enormous fishmouth is the victorious candidate's
    tongue. Talk vic
torious candidate, when you land, or while you fly. Talk,
    and wave. We moving
now. We see all of you hovering above us, gods of the un-
flushed commode.

Victorious candidate, we are your lowly slovenly ignorant
    people, and we
need no help. We are merely the scorekeepers for your hip
    enterprises. Oh,
victorious roundshouldered nigger candidate
daughter of a victorious roundshouldered nigger
mother-father. We are no
bodies. We are no merit.
We are to be used and killed
and lied to. Don't mind us, oh
victorious roundshouldered imitation
whiteman, fly on in your vacumn-packed commode, do not
    fear us, we are
garbage, we are filth, listen to our dirty mouths, look at our
    loud
clothes and bad grammar. We are indeed scum, yr honor,
    lock us up.
We aint shit, baby. We aint nothin. Don't mind us, partner,
    jus go on head
where you gon' go. All we can do is watch, that's all my man,
    just watch,
and maybe pray

* * *

Bludoo Baby, Want Money,
And Alligator Got It To Give

say day lay day may fay come some bum'll
take break jake make fake lay day some bum'll
say day came break snow mo whores red said they'd
lay day in my in fay bed to make bread for jake
limpin in the hall with quiverin stick
he's hiney raised, in a car by the curb,
licking his yellow lips, yellow snow yellow bubs
yellow eyes lookin at the dark, hears his whisper
says, "come down goily i give you a stick . . . da da da
     come down goily i give you a pinch . . . da da da
     come down goily i sit in my car . . . da da da
     come down goily to where we grey guys are . . .
                   da da da .
                   da da da .
                  da da da .
                   da da da .
she's not thinkna him, seein nim, seen people like him
dazed out there, suckin heavy vapors, her butt throw off,
like stick-it-in nitetime, for the dough, chile, for the money
baby, look at him down there, lookn up at me . . . da da da
she and jake
look

da cuppd flame
fat claws, motor batting
outside miss workamo's house.

shd she go down she's pulling the coat
gainst the wind, will she let him, ol good guy
get in.
for the dough
mr tom
for your woman
in the mirror

shakin like a storm

psst oh miss, oh miss, oh oh, yellow, vapor butt got him
hung out the window
look down
jake jr.
and mr roy
there, look kin you help . . . da da da
kin you give me
somethin
can you make me
beautiful
with your bullshit
can you
love me
nigger
she askin us, jake jr
sis betty, where we at, at the pin of the stare, curld flag of
    misery,
oh the hip walk on that chile
fat sister, swashing that heavy ass
psst psst
oh miss miss,

yellow
cloud it up
stick it in
and jab down
under the wheel . . . da da da

miss
oh miss

stumbling down the stairs
when she turns to go back
and stick her head in the car
the motor's running, she already know the money's in her
slide
we throwin rocks and garbage cans
barry draggin the motherfucker out
stomp
bompa dee dee da, and run your heaviest
game,
baby, baby, take
it take it,

run on way,

baby, baby, take it
take it, baby

run on way,

money on the ground

blood on the ground

the first step

we protects
provides

the example
plain

when the sun
come up
again

BLACK ART

Poems are bullshit unless they are
teeth or trees or lemons piled
on a step. Or black ladies dying
of men leaving nickel hearts
beating them down. Fuck poems
and they are useful, they shoot
come at you, love what you are,
breathe like wrestlers, or shudder
strangely after pissing. We want live
words of the hip world live flesh &
coursing blood. Hearts Brains
Souls splintering fire. We want poems
like fists beating niggers out of Jocks
or dagger poems in the slimy bellies
of the owner-jews. Black poems to
smear on girdlemamma mulatto bitches
whose brains are red jelly stuck
between 'lizabeth taylor's toes. Stinking
Whores! We want "poems that kill."
Assassin poems, Poems that shoot
guns. Poems that wrestle cops into alleys
and take their weapons leaving them dead
with tongues pulled out and sent to Ireland. Knockoff
poems for dope selling wops or slick halfwhite
politicians Airplane poems. rrrrrrrrrrrrrrrrrrrr
rrrrrrrrrrrrrrr. . . . tuhtuhtuhtuhtuhtuhtuhtuhtuhtuh
. . . .rrrrrrrrrrrrrrr. . . . Setting fire and death to
whities ass. Look at the Liberal
Spokesman for the jews clutch his throat

& puke himself into eternity. . . . rrrrrrrrrr
There's a negroleader pinned to
a bar stool in Sardi's eyeballs melting
in hot flame. Another negroleader
on the steps of the white house one
kneeling between the sheriff's thighs
negotiating cooly for his people.
Aggh. . .stumbles across the room. . .
Put it on him, poem. Strip him naked
to the world! Another bad poem cracking
steel knuckles in a jewlady's mouth
Poem scream poison gas on beasts in green berets
Clean out the world for virtue and love,
Let there be no love poems written
until love can exist freely and
cleanly. Let Black People understand
that they are the lovers and the sons
of lovers and warriors and sons
of warriors Are poems & poets &
all the loveliness here in the world

We want a black poem. And a
Black World.
Let the world be a Black Poem
And Let All Black People Speak This Poem
Silently

or LOUD

Barbara Simmons

SOUL

Tell me about Soul
Do you know? Have I got it?
Do you have it? Can you touch mine?
I'll touch yours.

Soul is a plastic man
who lives in an invisible shell
and drifts to heaven or to hell
when you get shot or trip or slip
on a banana peel left living in the street.
Naw man!
Soul's a trumpet playin, Baby!
Eyes closed and cryin NOTES
spottin hizself
hiz inside self
and groovin and cryin
there's gonna be/ gotta be
AN EXPLOSION

an there is:
women cryin, heels tappin,
no nappin, no foolin, no drinkin, no talkin,
or smokin

just beatin hard hearts
made softer
a moment

SOUL SOUL SOUL
YO SOUL/ MI SOUL/ HE SOUL/
FA SOUL/ LA SOUL
WHEEEE
   SOUL
is way down deep in the bucket
Soul's way up high floatin around
Soul's sittin on the subway
   you see me
   I see you
but nobody's lookin.
Soul is Screamin/ Screechin
   TINTINNABULATION! That's Soul!!

Ring bells oh
RING LAWDY LAWDY
You can't touch it or feel it
but you touch it and feel it
it moves ya when you see it,
and you feel it when it moves ya
cause you can't see it if it
moves ya

It's the holy ghost
It's the seven seas
It's chicken pie
and a bloody nose

It's the rhythmic beat
of two flat feet
thumpin and bumpin
out soul
SOUL SOUL
will beat ya
in a minute

if you're highfaluttin
round in it
Listen:
   A beautiful south sea island,
the whistle of the waves,
grass skirts, the whistle of,
a liner docks, smiling faces
You're here! Mr. & Mrs. Westerveal
Duddly Hammington, you're here

staying at the HILTON,
registered and fed, you take a "dip"
at the hotel pool
WHATA LIFE! WHATA LIVIN!
A dance? A drink from a ceramic coconut
A piece of mint thrown on the side A flower
in Miz Duddlys' hair? That's Soul?
(You're told).
But in the distance:
drums beatin, natives retreatin,
night grows darker,
fires starta glowin,
somethin magic gets ta goin
heat gettin hotta,
somethin swellin deep inside ya,
hips movin and groovin,
this ain't art
It's Real/Movin!
DO YOU HEAR ME, MR. DUDDLY?
ARE YOU SWINGIN AND SWAYIN
WITH MIZ DUDDLY IN HER CORSETED MOO MOO?

COULD YOU DIG IT IF YOU KNEW IT
YOU SPENT YOUR MONEY AND YA BLEW IT!
TAKE THE LINER WITH DINAH (SHORE) SINGIN 49ER,
NOOO SOUL.

Soul is the titular head of your emotional household
something in man believed to be the source
of his spiritual being
Yeah, man!
Soul is the holy rollers
and all the unholy rollers
groovin in their own kinda way
Soul is the swish and swash
of a fat bahind with somethin good
on her mind
Please understand it!
You can't go round spillin
out pat definitions
on Soul
Cause Soul is goin down
in the gutter down
and comin up/ STRONG
a rose with a gutter smell
and ya love that smell
wont lose that smell
cause it's where ya been
and ya might go back
Heard a man say,
"I laughed all the breath out my body."
Now that's Soul
Soul is burnin for learnin
and learnin ta burn
and singin
for singin, no more
Soul is an honest livin
legal or illegal when you're honest
with yourself about life
Soul is a heart cut out of watermelon rind
screamin, "I wanta VOTE!"
while the vein of a country
the A-okay order, chokes off it's breath

See
how deep Soul can go.
Anyhow, for those who don't understand
Soul, there is this word,
you never will.

Larry Neal

THE BARONESS AND
THE BLACK MUSICIAN

Tangled in sea weed minutes;
her eyes suck your blood.
the baroness glides into the Harlem houses,
leaves her touch on the lips
of the young blacks.
spits out your manhood with Chase
Manhattan check books—is a lover of *Negro* art.
Sea weed minutes. winter-white bleaknesses.
the icy ride of her touch up toward
the place where your penis once was.
Franks on 125th st:
      the silhouettes of our salvation
      drift rhythmically by
      as occasional strokes of laughter
      compete with the match between
      your face and her's.

FOR OUR WOMEN

Out of the Earth, this love
moved rivers
sang joy songs, these women wrapped
in the magic of birth;
deep rivers formed your innocence—
knew no evil
knew beyond what knowing
has come to mean
wordlessly knew.

Black women, timeless, are sun breaths
are crying mothers
are snatched rhythms
are blues rivers and food uncooked,
lonely villages beside quiet streams,
are exploding suns green yellow moons,
the story of the snake and the turtle.
lonely roads.
night-rider. see-see rider. easy men
who got lost returning to you,
blues in our mothers' voices
warning us.
blues people bursting out.
Like it is, I tell it,
and there are towns that
hang lonely in some man's
memory and you are there
and not there.
blackened in the soil of earth-time,

southern towns that release
their secrets to you
and then retreat, returning later
to rape.
you are there and not there.
Looming magic out of endless dreams—
our continuousness.

I see you announce their doom,
and the breath of your life
sustains us
sustains us as the sea screams out;
the female in the middle passage,
you endured.
we endured through you.
us endured. endured.

In the soul of my art, I embrace
the world that is you
as we giant step across our earth;
the sea again
again the sea unites us
as we couple with the land
and the stars of our ancestors
ancestor stars.
black universe. sky.
embrace

* * *

THE NARRATIVE
OF THE BLACK MAGICIANS

Fast fly the faces through our blood-years,
faces fly by the windows of the moon
and pass the sons of the slaves standing
on the shores of home.
time in their faces stops. and dances stilled
by the chained-sea whose sounds bring with
it memories out of our private and collective past.
The sea contains the tightness of our dreams;
contains conversations under the ships'
floor-prisons:
touchless hands, I lay beside you,
lips part in fever,
and the receding drums
telling of a new death.

Faces peer up into the rocking darkness:
this is the ocean that birthed us newly;
but the chained-sea is hostile,
as white madnesses clink in children's dreams.
roll on Jordan to no end.
These faces live to appear on the land that became
theirs by their blood,
made ours by our blood.
these faces appear in swampy places bundled
in motherless callings,
appear on the slave blocks, sold into ugliness,
shaped into ugliness by the white touch.

Their appearances flicker above the plotting fires—
they plan night-death to pale monsters.
faces mute. the fire-sun burns visions
into his eyes. in his black hands blood burns.

Eastward their faces turn, morning eyes strain
for the horizon.
these faces slither under cabin doors and see
themselves in strange cities.
they mouth that language awkwardly in an eastern
blueness.
faces under the timeless sky. their sky.
made by them. made for them.

These faces catch scottsboro freights north,
sing blues for the river gods,
turn up strange in memphis, dallas, chicago,
kansas city . . .
hammered steel out of those mountains,
laid their lives down in spite of themselves
as steel killed them in narrow tunnels.
they laughed with John Henry,
and played spy with Harriet Tubman,
and strong ones mostly.

These faces pour out of slavetime
into the subways of fear,
jockey for life between grey crushing mountains
and the 42nd street movies.
See these faces. they saw their best
killed in bleak winters, and their homes
upheaved by the progress-blood-drinking-machines.

Faces that flew pass the president's coffin,
who saw their own leaders busy at morning
betrayals. who, in spite, managed to love.

Child faces, blackly playing on those backstreet's
are children of gods and the Lion.
faces charged with change; these faces turn
from the west, turn inward eyes on themselves,
control the black cosmos, are gods.
dancing faces making the Earth live
in green blackness.
our bones are in this land.
It must be our's in the living.

Ancestor faces form on the film of our brains.
form our contours out of deep wails of saxes.
form in the voice of Malcolm.
form child. form in the rush of war.
form child. form in the taking of life.
form child. form in the sun's explosion
and in the avenging waves.
form child. form child. form child. form
form in the prison of america.
form child. form your image of men
and women tearing into the open,
tearing out the wombed deadness;
and face the form of our love in the final
clasping and embrace;
form your face out of the Earth;
form your face with searing waves of sound,
as beyond the wall there is a painful calm.

                                    Spring—1965
                                    a painful season

* * *

Malcolm X—An Autobiography

I am the Seventh Son of the Son
who was also the Seventh.
I have drunk deep of the waters of my ancestors
have travelled the soul's journey towards cosmic harmony
the Seventh Son.
Have walked slick avenues
and seen grown men, fall, to die in a blue doom
of death and ancestral agony,
have seen old men glide, shadowless, feet barely
touching the pavements.

I sprung out of the Midwestern plains
the bleak michigan landscape, the black blues of Kansas
city, the kiss-me-nights.
out of the bleak Michigan landscape wearing the slave name—
Malcolm Little.
Saw a brief vision in Lansing, when I was seven, and in
my mother's womb heard the beast cry of death,
a landscape on which white robed figures ride, and my
Garvey father silhouetted against the night-fire, gun in hand
form outlined against a panorama of violence.

Out of the Midwestern bleakness, I sprang, pushed eastward,
past shack on country nigger shack, across the wilderness
of North America.

I hustler. I pimp. I unfulfilled black man
bursting with destiny.
New York city Slim called me Big Red,
and there was no escape, close nights of the smell of death.

315

Pimp. hustler. The day fills these rooms.
I am talking about New York. Harlem.
talking about the neon madness.
talking about ghetto eyes and nights
about death protruding across the room. Small's paradise.
talking about cigarette butts, and rooms smelly with white
sex flesh, and dank sheets, and being on the run.

talking about cocaine illusions, about stealing and selling.
talking about these New York cops who smell of blood and
     money.
I am Big Red, tiger vicious, Big Red, bad nigger, will kill.

But there is rhythm here. It's own special substance:
I hear Billie sing, no good man, and dig Prez, wearing the
     Zoot
suit of life—the porkpie hat tilted at the correct angle.
through the Harlem smoke of beer and whiskey, I understand
     the
mystery of the signifying monkey,
in a blue haze of inspiration, I reach to the totality of Being.
I am at the center of a swirl of events. War and death.
rhythm. hot women. I think life a commodity bargained for
across the bar in Small's.
I perceive the echoes of Bird and there is a gnawing in the
     maw
of my emotions.
and then there is jail. America is the world's greatest jailer,
and we all in jails. black spirits contained like magnificent
birds of wonder. I now understand my father urged on by the
ghost of Garvey,
and see a small brown man standing in a corner. The cell.
     cold.
dank. The light around him vibrates. Am I crazy? But to
     under-
stand is to submit to a more perfect will, a more perfect order.
To understand is to surrender the imperfect self
For a more perfect self.

Allah formed brown man, I follow
and shake within the very depth of my most imperfect being,
and I bear witness to the Message of Allah
and I bear witness—all praise is due Allah!

Hart Leroi Bibbs

SPLIT STANDARD

Black man straddling the unbalanced scale,
torn by injustice and pushed by the law;
thereby, himself for and against
one short step forwards
against the hideously long one backwards
against vested constitutionality
his own victim and his own executioner.
The cook cooking himself
with liberals and *toms,*
the bourgeois civil servants
of traitors genes-color caste
whose complexes of oedipus
do not feel the brotherhood in blackness
nor of blood.
Do not yet let them feel—
not the bold meanings of death.

* * *

"LIBERALISSIMO"

Hey! That's the wrong goal post, traitor;
the catcher is now throwing strikes to pitchers.
even so is this freedom
you must say lackadaisical—
the non-action of liberalism
which assesses price-gold friendships
to inflated green dollar prejudices.
Bitter-walking, multi-paved paths
of concrete enviousness
and treachery
and plain-old-bill-tom ignorant
ass blockers of drop kicks.
Can I afford friendship?
I yours or yours mine
when we are both able to dance a jig—
the yard arm and the swan song
is thirty pieces of silver.

DIRGE FOR J. A. ROGERS

Deadly certain, death takes its time,
what time death takes—hoping
and hoping on and hoping
on into immortality
on the thru-way urge to build
perpetual monuments, presaging
the self and this irresistability:
man is no tibbit for worms.
In the regressive vault backwards,
past the search of seeking out
the quality forms—
those great leaps which dared greet love
and openly did defy tradition
by wrenching precedent from the past,
here, death must make man his mystique
and set himself up as the first known god
that man may vent his panache on it;
that man must read—no—investigate
his own bubble to verify
that he prick his own thought.
Since traditions trade by stealth, at night,
customs neither are worthwhile
and the long search, traveling back
then is no testimonal of a last supper
but a compiling of constitution—
nature guaranteeing manhood.
Yes, manhood, the foamy cushion of life
on which the granite blow of truth rests;
impeachable, inviolable and unparalleled immortal.

this force facing danger,
this factual grope for the thread end
on the other side of the needle's eye;
to catch a dangling end off the spool
of infinity.
to catch the circle of immortality reclaimed.
Is there such a thing in sorrow which is more full?
Then his present plaint might have been
had it been done another way
but across the dissatisfactions of all beginning life
stands a colossus of news—
a bearer of good and bad
but a colossus there of high cult facts.

Rolland Snellings

SUNRISE!!

*(for El-Hajj Malik El-Shabazz
and the Afro-American Nation)*

In the Void, in the Storm, in the Wastelands of our hearts—
    a cry is heard.
In our dreams, in the wind, in the sweatpangs of the night—
    a call is heard.
This Cry, this Call is the Song of the Race—through the
    years,
through the Veil, from the Lash that captured our humanity,
from the Mark that's slashed upon our bosoms in this land:
    the Mark of Cain.
SING to the Void! SING to the Voices in the Song of the
    Race—
in this land we will rise, we will rise—
as the Pyramids of Africa rise to find the Fathers of the
    Sphinx.
We will rise as a pine tree, tall and proud, rises under bloody
Southern skies to kiss the moon.
SING of our Race! SING out our Destiny
to your sons, to your warrior sons—in the ghettoes, on the
    tenant farms,
in the swelling cities by the Western Sea.
SING with your soul! SING of the Sun!—SUNRISE
swelling in our hearts, surging in our blood—as the mighty
    Mississippi
rushes to the sea.
WE are the New! WE are the Rivers of the Spring breaking
    through
the cold, white ice of Dying Winter.

WE—with the Sky, with the Soil, with the roaring of the
Sea—
    are the New!
SUNRISE: Voices of the Song of the Race.
SUNRISE: Voices of the Sting of the Lash.
WE are the New! We will resurrect the earth and flood
every heart of Man with our Light!

MISSISSIPPI CONCERTO

*(for Mary Lee Lane
and the Southern Black people)*

Upon the seas of Crumbling Servitude
blow the swift, eternal Winds of Change.
Above the tramp of frenzied fascist jackboots
flows the fountainhead of Human Hope.
Earth abides! Love abides! Naked Beauty sings!
Life abides! Joy abides! The people, the people
march into the bleeding hills of Dawn.
Fear slithers out upon the brooding soil.
Listen: the Voice, the Call, the Ancient Drumbeats
intensify the blowtorch of my heart.
We-earth! We-sky! We-Golden Sunrise!—
 We abide!
Silently we feed on jackboots;
Absorb, like sand, the racist blood-storm;
Defy the Rope, the Gun, the Alabaster Plague.
Roll on, roll on, gentle Red Earth;
I kiss your breast, your eyes, your hair—
 the magic night.
And vow before your throne with solemn heartache
to taste again your lips, reclaim your Song.

* * *

THE SONG OF FIRE

(for Africa, Asia, Latin &
Afro-America—the Wretched of the Earth)

Tears that weep for shattered Sunday schools
  are lost
like diamonds leaving ebon hands among the dark
  South African sands:
  lost-lost . . . and never found!
Save your tears! Save your anguished cries!
Save your prayers to barren, silent skies!
  Wait! Wait awhile!
For soon, the Dawn will come to man once more—
and Buddha's eyes will smile from burning
  saffron robes and charred pagodas—
  Shango
will shout his rumbling song to
  joyous Congo tom-toms . . . in the night
  Allah
will send his flaming sword a 'whistling
  through the "chosen land" . . . and bellow
  Free-dom! Free-dom!: here comes the Rising Sun!
  And HERE:
my twenty-million, tortured, chosen children—
  your day will come!

II

When it comes—like a tropic, summer storm:
the earth will shake as Calvary at crimson sunset!
Blood will stain the moon; snuff out the stars!

Blood will clog the wheels of mighty Juggernaut
and send him crashing from his Atom Throne!
BLOOD will wash your pain away!
    (Fire!)
Bright red flames! Burnt, charred death,
    grinning skulls,
    rolling eyes, and mad-mad
    cries to mute Madonnas!
    (Fire!)
will scorch the "Lonely Crowd" with Death's embrace
    like Mushrooms Suns . . . in mutant Hiroshima!
    (Fire!)
will vindicate the blues; sanctify the earth;
resurrect the mangled Jesus from . . . the Nordic
    lynch-tree!
    (Fire!)
will cauterize the Racist Plague!

III

Here I stand—at 25, dark . . . and lonely for my Mother's
    womb.
An angry, fiery man—awaiting nature's call
    to act out
my deadly hour upon the western stage. "All
    fall down!"
exclaimed the anguished poet. He is right! "All
    fall down!"
And so, we will all fall down, someday!
But to start anew—the Old must fade away,
or burn . . . or . . . crumble in the savage wind.
Therefore: the hordes that plundered Rome
were bringing in a new age—
and the Hun . . . became a Herald of the Dawn!
So, hush now—my wooly-headed lambs:
    Dry your eyes!
Lift your withered hearts; throw your chains away,
    and wait for:
    . . . the smell of BRIMSTONE!

* * *

EARTH

*(for Mrs. Mary Bethune and the
African and Afro-American women)*

Where are the warriors, the young men?
Who guards the women's quarters—the burnt-haired
women's quarters—
and hears their broken sobbing in the night?
To endure, to remain—like the red earth—strong and fecund.
Your coppery, chocolate, ebony warm-skin scoured . . . and
    toughened
      by the arid wind.
The wrinkles in your eyes, your smile, your frowning fore-
    heads
are the Stars within your Crown, my women.
Cares come and go; dreams fade away; sons are lost
on lonely battlefields . . . severed by the Nordic Meataxe.
Men are broken . . . babble . . . lift their bloody genitals
upon the tainted altar of the Snow Queen.
Her frigid, sterile smile is a tribute to the vengeance
    of her Caesars.
Where, then, is Spartacus, is Attila, is Hannibal?
Who thunders, now, upon those Seven Hills?
They are gone . . . and . . . *only you remain!*
You whose Womb has warmed the European hills and made
    the Pale Snows tawny.
Pagan Spain, sunny France, Italy and the fabled Grecian Isles
are drenched by the Sunlight of your smile:
    Mother of the World!

Fecund, Beating Heart!
Enduring Earth!:
Only you remain!
Where are the warriors, the young men?
Who guards the women's quarters? . . .

Carol Freeman

Christmas morning i

Christmas morning i
got up before the others and
ran
naked across the plank
floor into the front
room to see grandmama
sewing a new
button on my last year
ragdoll.

* * *

i saw them lynch

i saw them lynch festus whiteside and
all the limp white women with lymphatic greasy eyelids came
to watch silent silent in the dusty burning noon
shifting noiselessly from heavy foot to heavy
foot licking beast lips showing beast teeth in
anticipation of the feast
and they all plodded forward after the
lynching to grab and snatch the choice
pieces, rending them with their bloody teeth crunching on
   his hollow bones.

* * *

when my uncle willie saw

when
my uncle willie saw
aunt mimmies new baby he
look at his big cracked black hands the thick
pink nails split then
he looked at black mimmie with her gold teeth flashing and
he look at the baby
then
later on he brag to everybody how he
got indin blood from his grand mama
thenwhen
my uncle willie and aunt tee mimmie had
nother baby he
look at auntee then he
look out the window he
look at the midwife who smiling a little
shaking her head a little
and he say it albinodentyall member us get albinirs on mah
cudin Tim side?
Aunt tee she grinsome then she laugh then she say willie-
sherrif merriweather
say of this a boy if ah names him merriweather he gon give
you fi' dollars?
then!
i seen uncle willie cry some.

Kirk Hall

song of tom

up in the sky
over my head
came the
shriek of
a spirit
saying
    come
        fly
come fly
with me
but
boss
you been
good
to me
    come
        fly
come fly
with me
and my
wife and
kids is
near here
somewhere
    come
        fly
come fly
with me
and boss

where can
i
wear clothes
like these
and live in
a house
like this
    come
        fly
come fly
with me
and where
can i get
food like
i
get here
    come
        fly
come fly
with me
and
how else
could i
get the
others
to
look up
to
me
and . . . .

wig

most royal
affluent
advertisement
a
vote of
confidence
sophisticated
display of
ignorance
sign of
uncalculated
shame
and
despair

* * *

impressions

cool-slick-fly—
a whole generation of
mistaken identities
march by
a whole generation of unidentified persons
who fear the uncertainty of truth
who know the sheer hypocrisy of their lives
who have sold themselves to the Sandman!

* * *

illusions

rev. chickenwing
in his
pulpit
with two
six-guns on
his side
deacon goodguy
and
honest trustee
at the doors
with
thompsons
the senior choir
making
cocktails
no
more
toms

Edward S. Spriggs

WE WAITING ON YOU

witch doctor
come uptown
come tennis-shoed
come sucking on a short neck
come holding onto a tit in mt morris pk
come lick sweet on some caldonia's ears
(where ever you find them)
come hear what black rose hymns
into the altar of our afro'd ears
what makes us follow her way uptown
come tell us the truth aint never been
in the "truth" or across the street either
do sukey jumps or the boogaloo but come on
turkey us cats into hero bones
shoot your shit from starless roof
spread magic substances
pour it on our hymnals
on our tenement radiator pulse
candle the interior of our mammy'swomb
fatten it with roots of sassafras
witch doctor come up here
make it with overcoat and shades on
into the dark exploding black flag bombs
(net contents: teenless manyear harlem sixes)
come with black flag bombs
with fumigating action killing *them*
where you see *them* kill *them* where *they* hide
but make it last long
make it last strong

warchild wants to TCB
wants some action uptown
we waiting on you

* * *

For the TRUTH

(because it is necessary)

in the tea rooms
of our revolution
we blatantly debate
our knowledge of world revolts
—our anxious ears only half-listened
to the songs of the martinique
who sings in muffled tones
from beneath a mechanized tombstone
built by the pulp of greedy merchants
who got stoned on the juices of our servitude
& who write prefaces to our "negritude"

from the tea rooms
of our revolution we emerge
to pamphleteer
the anticipatory designs
of our dead
& exiled poets
—without sanctions
from our unsuspecting brothers
whose death we so naively plot
(we engage in a hypothetical revolt
against a not-so-hypothetical enemy

what kind of man are you
black revolutionary, so-called?

what kind of man are you trying to be
ultra-hip-revolutionary-nationalist-
quasi-strategist-ego-centric-phony
intellectual romantic black prima donna child
—screaming, "revolution means change . . ."
never finishing the sentence
or the thought
talking about "para-military"
strategy and techniques
publicizing a so-called underground program
wearing your military garb
as if you never heard of camouflage
so in love with intrigue
you have no thoughts
about the post-revolution life
that the total destruction
you talk about assumes . . .

you leave me quite confused
brother
i don't know who the enemy is
anymore
perhaps it is me, myself, because
i have these thoughts
in the tea rooms of our revolution.

* * *

Every Harlem Face is

AFROMANISM Surviving

Is Bakuba memory
(from Lumumba's region)
Is Apollo memory
(from Malcolm's region)
Is Bambara memory
(from Nkrumah's region—
The cia'll get him too)

Cleaved cubic planes hard
Ly remembering what it is
This jointtenancyincommon
(not mere ly words) this
Source of power keeping on
Keeping our past present

& indelible in ourselves
In our blood in our genes
In our sons on our faces
In our minds in our lives

Sharing this equilibrium—
Our faces in these aspects
Our being Afro Beings as we are
Our Afromanity survives it does
Like in our life and future
Here—we will never forget

my beige mom

is
georgia grown
georgia bruised
tall
strong-boned
beige beauty
was
afroamerican
in the twenties
turned "negro"
in the forties
proud "american"
in the sixties
will
die a christian
in california
tall, strong-boned
beige & bruised
i
took her strength
in thirty-four
now with love i
lay it at the
third world's door

* * *

sassafras memories

now i find my arms
relaxed, my legs gone
only sassafras memories
rest weightlessly

I WORKED FOR THIS MUCH
FREEDOM . . .
like the boy scout
oath of my tenderfoot days
when religion was
"thou shall not want"
& i thot "wanting is natural"
ly natural like flying
june bugs on a string

i've known this labor before
yes, the moment gives
me shoulders again

i've even forgotten how to cry
like a child   and i want to
feeling the blueness of sky
on my tight face—
     there are no walls now
     no ceiling behind my ears
midnite mo-jos jerk me
into your crescent back
i tumble like a dolphin
in familiar waters . . .

why should i remember her
now, the little girl
with the cotton candy
and me on the ferris wheel
and the smell of sassafras
in the air
and what we did
in the cellar of Shiloh
Baptist Church?

Henry Dumas

mosaic harlem

what news from the bottle?
    rats shedding hair in ice
    nodding veins filled with snow
    blackeyed peas, grits, red rice
through the broken glass I hear a breaking age
what song do we gurgle?

what news from the bottom?
    Jesus learning judo
    I scratch giant lice and ghetto
    fleas in the gutter of my mind
the sucking boll weevil converts to blood
when will the mosquito fear the rage under sweat?

what view from the bottle?
    cats pawing at cotton ideas
    the roach in the milk
    crawls safely to the nipple
why is green not black, brown, tan, only pain?
this hombre is a tiger rose star of sneaky david

what news from the bureau?
    a mole stoking coal in wine-steam and no gas
    building baby foundations from lamb-bone
    pray in Chinese, farting in English
I hear a black drum roaring up a green lion on yellow silk
come to kill the keeper of our cage

what news from James' bastard bible?
    al-Mahdi kneels in the mosque,
    Melchizedek, Moses, Marcus, Muhammad, Malcolm!
    marshalling words, mobilizing swords
the message is mixed and masticated with Martin
the good news of the gospel is crossing a crescent

what they do at the bottom?
    went to the cop and he took my pot
    the law giveth and the law taketh away
    I can neither pee nor blow
they will rope Mary and take pussy for my bail
I will remember, I will recall, bottoms up, I cop

what news from the black bastille?
    ram of god busting up shit
    unicorning the wolf, panthering the fox
    the old shepherd is himself lost
the ram will not stop, what news from the bottom?
the east!   the west!   and the top!

knock on wood

i go out to totem street
    we play
    neon monster
        and watusi feet

killer sharks chasin behind
    we play hide
    siren!
        and out-run cops
they catch
    willie
    and me
        splittin over fence
they knock
    in willie's head
    hole
they kick me watusi
    down
        for dead
like yesterday
    runnin feet in my brain
    won't stop willie lookin blood
        beggin me
cut off blackjack pain

so whenever you see me comin
    crazy watusi
        you call me watusi
i keep a wooden willie
    blade and bone outa that fence

a high willie da conqueror
    listen! up there he talkin
wooden willie got all the sense

i go out to siren street
    don't play no more
me and willie beat a certain beat
    aimin wood carvin shadows

sometimes i knock on wood
    with fist
me and willie play *togetherin*
    and we don't miss

cuttin down to size

me and tuko go down to the jew
to cop some vines
the jew say "yas boise, vat can i do for youse?"
me and tuko dont say nothin right away, see?
we checkin all the clothes and prices

the jew, he smilin and sawin his neck with a tape
"you vant nice suit, pants, shirt, boise?"
me and tuko walk around
the jew, he got a nigger flunkey workin in the back
we catch the nigger's eye, nigger drop his head

tuko tell the jew he wear size 30 pants 36 coat
now the jew is measurin tuko's legs, thighs, waist
he tape tuko's arm, sayin "Oh my," next tuko's throat
he rubbin tuko on the ass and when he pass me he wink
"big shoulders" he say lookin at tuko's crotch
i watch this motherfucker now, i got him measured

the flunkey is gettin tuko's size
the jew grinnin at me "you next boise"
i reach in my pocket, my thumb on my blade
"vat size you vant, pants, shirt?"
i say to tuko "i dont 'low no faggots touch me"

the nigger comes back showin the vines to tuko
the jew followin me with the tape:
like they do when they lynch a blackman
only this time he start measurin near my balls
but 'fore he touch me, my blade is cuttin tape!

then like lightenin me and tuko move together
i see his fist bustin the nigger's lips
the jew is reachin under the counter!
my blade is comin upwards past the jew's hips

me and tuko dont go downtown no more
we layin low, playin things cool
the jew died, they holdin the nigger on a stool
me and tuko dont say much, we read papers
goddam! who taught jews how to lynch niggers?

Reginald Lockett

THIS POEM FOR BLACK WOMEN

HEEEYYYSOOUUL
SISS-TERS
Your deepest concern for
us,
blackmen.
You . . . the fairest of the
fair
You, symbol of
eternal love
Love us, for all eternity
and eternity

Your love. . . .
is strength,
truth
in the deepest pit of my
heart
BLACKWOMENOFTHE
WORLD,IHEREDECLARE
MYIMMORTALLOVE
FORYOUALL.

DEATH OF THE
MOONSHINE SUPERMEN

Circular star, glowing
bright helplessly in
blackest sky
despair not
for the supreme
enemy
of
the
world, your
silvery light will render no
protection for them,
the creation
of
YACUB, who
made them in the
freezing caves
of the north.
Shine on-shine on 'em—as you
have
in   the
past,
of which they will
come
to
be   a
part
of

as if they are
joints
of
bones
bleached white in
blazing napalm sun.

DIE BLACK PERVERT

You sit there, sissified,
and brag about the
    T
    R
    I
    P
        TO
            E
                U
                    R
                        O
                            P
                                E
You are to take this summer
    To   t
        S   u
                d
                    y
        Beethoven,
                    and Chopin
        mozart.

You have gone
    T
    h
    r
    o
    u
    g
    h The same old ritual,

running blindly
>Through
>>a
>>T-maze,

and become a conditioned

>>>>>FAGGOT—

Carrying on Chuck's tradition
>and
getting an everlasting nut,
Splat, Splat, Splaaaaat

Odaro (Barbara Jones, slave name)

ALAFIA

I am writing at the request of
Larry Neal, Ed Spriggs and Harold Foster
Who seem to think that you
Might be interested in my
Poetry

They tell me that you will
Soon be publishing an Anthology
And that you were interested
In New Young Black Writers
I would appreciate it if you
Would consider some of my
Work

I am sending you all of the
Poetry that I think you
Might dig

The Brothers said that you
Might want to know something
About me also

I think my poetry will help
You in that area

I am 20 years Black, born in
Harlem
Poverty's little girl
Black Woman, Queen of the World

S. E. Anderson

SOUL-SMILES

For The S. O. U. L.
(Sisters Organized for Unity and Liberation)

let me look and see love's
earth-spirit's glow
grow in my sister's smiles

I be moved by ebony's
snow capped teeth
ready to speak in the name
of blackness
ready to grimace in
the struggle for freedomblack
ready to place a soft kiss
upon a sable warrior's lips
ready to breathe
freedombreath

my sister's smiles
are the sharpening
of agonyblades
hidden fomentingly
for years within
getting poised to
scream out: cut out
the festering of the
sore which is called:
dream

my sister's smiles
are the egyptian

medicine masters'
surgery mending
severed sable minds

let me look and see love's
earth-spirit's glow
grow in my sister's smiles
once she knows it is
in her to be of me,
I know she knows:
for warmth and soul
simmer around my heart
and mind melting me
into her
love: midnight love
melting her into me
love: natural obsidian love
        etching soul-smiles
        upon my sister's sepia face

* * *

THE SOUND OF
AFROAMERICAN HISTORY CHAPT I

the history of blacklife is put down in the motions
of mouths and black hands with fingering lips
and puckered ravenfingers bluesing the air of
today and eeking out the workgrunts getting down
to earth the nittygritty i mean they mean:
you dig and if you don't don't you worry pretty
momma we all feel dat way anyway and sister
it's a pity whitey done this to us but I love you
and my history says whitey ain't shit and should
be flushed but poppa and momma may have the 'ligion
but god don't mean a thing baby when you got no bread
or a bed and a bad head blinding you with blackblues
of gospel bashing out of bigblack sisters' lips
spiritually into the bop and now the avantgarde jazz
of a hard shepp and blackblues looking over hunched
hardworked shoulders into the sepia polyrythmic soil:
lord lord we done come far and still ain't nowhere near
even with long nappy hair and talk of rev'lution . . .
jumpin with my bro. you know out there in dolphyland
or baby maybe into that sun-ra shit/beautiful but bars
are 8 & 12 like dinah and luther king diggin malcolm
shinin in my front door sweet momma keeping kisses for
my high with fontella takin care of much business in the
                    rhythm of the blues

THE SOUND OF
AFROAMERICAN HISTORY CHAPT II

smith at the organ is like an anvil being
struck in time at a bach fugue at riverside
and riverside jazzsides are testimonials to other
organjazzers still leaping in black minds every day
is billy holiday: god blessin the chile dat got his
own silver and song for my fathers: du bois vesey
cinquez and garvey with ears soulfully singing from
sound of blues and rhythm of mary wells and martha
soloin with her vital vandellas subtly sayin:
remember the danger of heartbreak ahead if you are
givin more than you can get: that's why there was dancin
in the streets of ghettoes where daily black ears hear
james brown singing from somewhere on a lonely
cottonwhite plantation leaving impressions upon your mind
making you writhe to 'tunji and afrosounds that allow odetta
    to
meet makeba in a groovy thing that we call together and very
soulclean like mcclean and parker catchin hell in new orleans
back in the twenties when domino was not a theory but fat
    and
ragtime meant ragged black musicians creating the blues and
weaving a history that is so uptight and out of sight—our
black sight—that we are not hip to its beauty and weaponlike
use against the mindless monster of the european snows who
muffled jungle drums with j.c.'s holy hands and put us here
misplaced with ecumenical chants which became agonyhar-
    mony
becoming furious bitter rising up sounds

Clarence Franklin

DEATH OF DAYS AND
NIGHTS OF LIFE

For Olabumi and Roi

Beautiful, BLACK womanhood;
reaching inward to open the soul and
show the shape of life.

Finding sometimes substance, finding
always something concrete and valuable.
never finding what is known as death

But only, the other side of life,
which though black and dark; really is
beautiful, black and forever so......

VISIONS . . . LEADERS . . .

Flickering-sputtering-speaking-stuttering-strutting . . .
and we musn't forget presidents laughter—
HA! HA! my fellow friends; ask not what you can do . . .
You have begged and begged, and oh so hard!
for a beginning; and now you have an ending. . . .
do you go OUT or OUT or IN???????

SHAKY LEADERS . . .

LEADER OF WHAT? DOUBTS AND FEARS?
half-assed men dropping tears on forgotten relics of another
age;
But listen; listen, softly comes the sage of WISDOM,
FEARLESSNESS,
and above all LOVE........nothing up my sleeve....
except my arm and hand filled with money and LOVE and
CHAOS
AND LOVE and DOMINANCE and LOVE and unfortunately ORDER and LOVE.
But also secret desires such as still being tied to the
umbilical cord of the man!

PARASITICAL LEADERS . . .

Seen through other eyes one looks,
and then one dies;
Piece by piece of SAME black skin,
that skinned and skinned and skinned again;

DAMN! it never ends!!
    except when the skin is yours.......
    P.S. You gets what you pay for;
        or what you have coming . . . . .

* * *

TWO DREAMS
(for m.l.k.'s one)

I dreamed that the sky was tight and
grey-streaked, and the cosmic pistol was cocked and the
finger was squeezing. . . . squeezing. . . . and suddenly,
there was a clap of thunder, a flash of lightning,
and a million liquid bullets were shot into the heart of
the city and everything was wet and running,
  like open wounds.
  I dreamed of a million black hands
linked like a chain, surrounding the world;
squeezing . . . squeezing . . . another shot heard around the
  world.
and then, the destruction of, poverty, bobby bakerie,
hypocrisy, kennedy, servility, rockerfellerie, idolatry,
johnsonie, and leaving just a chain;
  of victory!!!!

Jay Wright

THE END OF ETHNIC DREAM

Cigarettes in my mouth
to puncture blisters in my brain.
My bass a fine piece of furniture.
My fingers soft, too soft to rattle
rafters in second-rate halls.
The harmonies I could never learn
stick in Ayler's screams.
An African chant chokes us. My image shot.

If you look off over the Hudson,
the dark cooperatives spit at the dinghys
floating up the night.
        A young boy pisses
on lovers rolling against each other
under a trackless el.
    This could have been my town,
with light strings that could stand a tempo.
        Now,
        it's the end
        of an ethnic dream.
I've grown intellectual,
go on accumulating furniture and books,
damning literature, writing "for myself,"
calculating the possibilities that someone
will love me, or sleep with me.
Eighteen year-old girls come back from the Southern
leers and make me cry.
        Here, there are
        coffee shops, bars,
        natural tonsorial parlors,

plays, streets,
pamphlets, days, sun,
heat, love, anger,
politics, days, and sun.

Here, we shoot off
every day to new horizons,
coffee shops, bars,
natural tonsorial parlors,
plays, streets,
pamphlets, days, sun,
heat, love, anger,
politics, days, and sun.
It is the end of an ethnic dream.
My bass a fine piece of furniture.
My brain blistered.

* * *

THE FRIGHTENED LOVER'S SLEEP

to Alice

I keep thinking that there is
someone lying beside me,
watching my nightmares,
breathing but not moving,
not touching me, letting
me sweat in whatever
fits she shouldn't know.
It is raining outside,
or must soon start;
the quiet evening breathes
like a fish expecting
an unthwartable wave.
Now, an echo of people
starts in the streets.
Some horn frogs the night,
a presentiment of movement
that, even in sleep,
I couldn't suspend.
I go on in this daze of supposition,
the garble of what I defend
in this half-sleep
like the clutter of hopeless ghettos.
Should someone, listening out there,
knock though the unfinished
phrasing of my autonomous whispers
she would be gone, gone in silence,
leaving me to whatever dangers they present.

And I should be left
in this amazed posture,
regretting the touch my dreams
have driven her from.

Yusuf Rahman

TRANSCENDENTAL BLUES
TRANSCENDENTAL BLUES

                    WEEP weep weep
in B R O K E N bluebones
of shattered fancies
                fall
                    ing bluely
bluely bluely blue-as-blue-can-be-ly
COME WITH ME IF YOU WANT TO GO TO KANSAS CITY
splattering to ashes
sounding louder than ALLAH's song
enclosing the bluefool in delusion
A no-nosed bluefool in darkness cannot smell light
A no-tongued bluefool in disorder cannot taste order
A blind bluefool in heat of hate cannot see love
                        see SUNDAY KINDA LOVE
Love
love love
lovelovelovelove
love love
Love your magic spell is everywhere
A no-nerved bluefool cannot feel peace
A deaf&dumb bluefool dying a thousand death at once can
    not hear life
A wailing-wailing failing fire
dances like a million ulcers demon-SCREAMING
in the hue-less womb
                of the subdued
                        vain new brain

but unsubdued
of the bluefool brimed full
         of un-new Hamlet-like confusion
Wisdom hides —
         visionless eyes of selfish souls seek
Red rhythms of devotion
                    ALL GOD'S CHILLUN GOT
RHYTHM red rhythms of devotion are induced by love's blue
    melody
Devotion's ministers fire pride's pyre &light night
BLUEMAN
BLUEMAN BLUEMAN BLUEMAN
transcending his bluefooldom
suffering bluehoney sounds
SWEATING sweating sweating blood
wounds redder redder   round & round round &redder
    redder &round
with passionate imagination of true knowledge
past the anthill-life
         where ape-ish
    strife-bound
         yellow-spined aphid men
poison brothers in human society
& crawl strife riddled concrete bottoms of skyscraper seas
                              a radical world of
unqualified objectives
         rolling rolling round &round
                         into OBLIVION
    past new dimensions of expanded consciousness
in &out of millions &millions &billions &trillions &eternities
    of aeons&aeons
into a new
         WHAT'S NEW
into a new peaceful & blissful Jesus-like hue
Nirvana in infinite Tao-blue
smelling eternal ALHOMDULLILAH!
A Gnostic frog-eyed owl
quilted by boneyards bitter blacknight

SOMEWHERE OVER A COSMIC RAINBOW
                              cuts a great hog
on a mute trumpet emanating BLUE soultalk
                                        Soul talking!
                                        Soul talking!
                                        Soul talking!
Could be Pops Armstrong a black Mack-the-knife
              strut strut strutting with some bar-b-q
Could be Fats Navarro love-ing his FAT GIRL   yes FAT GIRL
       LOVE IS A MANY SPLENDOR THING
Love
love love
lovelovelovelove
love love
Love your magic spell is everywhere

Could be clownprince Dizzy
              Ooh-bop-she-bam-a-klookla-mopping salt peanuts
       yes SALT PEANUTS on the A-TRAIN
Could be Miles ahead chasing the Bird
       to dig WHAT IS THIS THING CALLED LOVE
Could be LOVE IS A MANY SPLENDOR THING
Could be Clifford in brown study high as the cosmos
       discovering mysterioso spring-joy beauty of Delilah
on a Parisian thoroughfare
But Fats & Clifford are dead
So have they all died many deaths
But death dont mean a thing
if you've really got that swing
Ah! Could be ALLAH
But that riff is so stiff it dont mean a thing
cause ALLAH is everything swinging

BLACK WOMAN
BLACK WOMAN
BLACK WOMAN
A billion billion billion stars burning in my flesh
A billion billion drums beating in my soul
BLACK WOMAN

BLACK WOMAN
BLACK WOMAN
Sweet sweet sweetness humming humming humming in my
    sugar
Bitter bit her bitterness humming humming humming in my
    lemon
BLACK WOMAN
BLACK WOMAN
BLACK WOMAN
singing singing soil beneath bare feet
for me to kiss without becoming dirty
BLACK WOMAN
BLACK WOMAN
BLACK WOMAN
from you comes a symphony of food
to instrument my flesh &soul
BLACK WOMAN
BLACK WOMAN
BLACK WOMAN
when I probe to define beauty
my heart's dictionary thumps your melody
BLACK WOMAN
BLACK WOMAN
BLACK WOMAN
when for love chapel-in-me dings
there you are before dawn's dong
BLACK WOMAN
BLACK WOMAN
BLACK WOMAN
you are my life because you are life
naturally black &beautiful
LOVE ME EBONY LADY
YES! I see blue-crystal teardrops
            burning scars on your soul's cheeks
Your tears splash acidly in my stomach of reality
Outraged
my rivers raging Raging RAGING with your pain bleed like
    elderly ulcers

LOVE ME EBONY LADY
LOVE ME EBONY LADY
LOVE ME EBONY LADY
&listen to my silent scream of do-or-die action
White maggots will not christian-missionary your diamonds
  away
                            again
White maggots will not military your babies down dead
                            again
White maggots will not mercinary your fertile Nile to ache
  with pus
        again
MY spears shall rain
I-cant-give-them-anything-but-drops-of-hate
erasing them
exterminating them
so humanity can have a clear slate
Just keep me constant
                        ebony lady
LOVE ME EBONY LADY
LOVE ME EBONY LADY

Rudy Bee Graham

A LYNCHING   FOR SKIP JAMES

. . . they may get better
but they'll never be well
we know
     the dying
     a museum death
     the funeral homes
     of no rhythm
     in the music
     no breathing
     on the canvasses
we have seen
the unseeing steel
blue eyes on the rockets
the money-green gazes
from the subways

flag uniforms on parochial
killers wiping us out

from the kitchens we have felt
the cold seeping from the pale
shadows they make
along the walls
(as economic as death)

from classrooms on the streets
we have heard the silence
of their words calling us
out of life to their Snowdom

374

in grave-school-yards we have known them
using Time as a weapon
defending deaths they have coffined
in colors tones and sentences

We have danced in the tree-grey static
of their glances
and they have stolen us
into their catacombs
cleaning up.

You sang to me of the trenches
in your eyes the humanless years
have wrenched you through
and yet too wise for bitterness you
sound more like a human
than anyone

And I would murder the walking
shrouds that have hammered the cry
in your throat with their too deep
an ignorance of unfeeling ears
                they cannot feel
                they have no soul
and you have made your misery
music they have not heard
they cannot hear
                the humanity
                in the chords
                of the whines
                in the moans
        they cannot hear

And I would electocute
the phantoms who slit
warm throats with stainless steel
eyes looking away
to pluto

And I would gas the ghosts
who strangle us with mercantile facts
and neckties of a futile civilization
We are the children of Carthage
and we are singing
the only songs

in our blood the only prophecies
of man kind to come

and from the kitchens we can see
       god with his
       broken neck
       hanging
       from the
       moon
       that waits
       over the western road
       like a gangrene
       destination

       and sometimes
       the soul-fingered cloud
       in your voice
       closes his deathray eyes
       and cuts him down.

* * *

LEARNING TO DANCE

                yesterday
            out the window
                snow
        took
        the music
        from the room
    came more
    all at once
    but today
    in the morning
    weariness
                the piano player
                stumbles over his hesitations
                and stands up again
                with more and more steam
                until his wind blows the score
                out the window
    the dancer
    comes in out
    of the snow

    and in her wet shoes
    slides a kiss over to the cheeks
    of the piano player

                who plays
                she takes off
                her shoes

and they make
the morning
over

out of the reach
of yesterday's music
stolen by the snow
without a score
and the teacher
brings her body
into the doorway
with the music
in her hands
                takes off her clothes
                in front of the mirror and
                dances the dance
                of the music
                to the snow
                in the morning
                and the room
                of the night before
and the smile
in the swaying
of the reflection
told the piano player
as he finished the music
her body ashed for
smelling like the smile
of the walk through the streets
of night snow
we are only
the movements we make
and his fingers
told this to the girl
who had taken off her clothes
and laid them on the piano

Lefty Sims

AN ANGELS PRAYER

Send me O' Allah as a
Rampaging fire, to consume, your
Enemy, as I Praise your Name.

Turning myself to thee, Palms
upwards Arms outstretched facing
Eastwards, I seek only your Command.

O! Originator of the Heavens
and the Earth, I am of those Born
to die, My Desire is to kill a
Devil.

I hate Evil, and am pledged
to destroy Evil, snarer of Men,
emanating, from that Hellish Abode.

"Use me Allah" I be your
Guided Missile, your Delayed-
Action Bomb; I long to Explode.

Chance me, to get my finger
around a Devil's Neck, in
a Vise-like Grip.

My hand a Sword, my
fist a sledgehammer; as I
break down and Cut asunder his
Aider.

My Head a Bulldozer, that
I may Crash through their walls of
Oppression, Leveling their Cities.

We must have freedom Justice
and Equality for all. 400yrs of
mistreatment, has scared thy seed.

Silence his tongue, and Blighten his
Cold blue eyes, that he never, ably
Plot Destruction of thy first Creation
Devil cast a Block of confusion. Keeping
one Brother, divided from the other, the while,
pretending to be a true Brother
I can hardly hold myself in check
so I ask you dear Allah, please
give me the right of way.
Deem, I, your sword of Vengeance
to repay this Crafty Devil, according
to his murdering, Deceitful, lying
ways.
Command me, and I would
destroy him hastily, as the Poison
Issue is about to consume your
World.
This Mass Evil Grieves me so
that I yearn to wander the City's
streets, in hunt for a devil's
approach.
Oh Allah Strengthen my Chest
to repel a thousand bullets, to
live a moment in Glory before even.
I die.
Let me adorn my neck with
the skulls of Devils, Let me lie
in wait for them in their corner
of the Path.
Alhah-u Akbar, Allah-u Akbar
(Allah is the Greatest) Al Hamd-
ulallah.

Lebert Bethune

A JUJU OF MY OWN

To make a Juju of my own
For I was tired of strange ghosts
Whose cool bones
Lived on the green furnace of my blood
Was always my destiny
So she warned me—my grandmother,
And now and now
When I kindle again her small eyes with their quick
lights
Darting ancient love into my infancy
And when I break through to her easy voice
That voice like the pliant red clay she baked
She sings the only lullaby she sang me

'Me no care for Bakra whip
Me no care fe fum-fum
Come Juju come'

So I am fashioning this thing
My own Juju
Out of her life and our desire
Out of an old black love
I am baking my destiny to a lullaby—

"Me no care fe Bakra whip
Me no care fe fum-fum
Come Juju come . . ."

HARLEM FREEZE FRAME

On the corner—116th and Lenox
all in brown down to his kickers,
and leaning on a post like some gaudy warrior
spear planted, patient eyes searching the veldt

This gleaming wrinkled blunthead old sweet-daddy
smiles a grim smile
as he hears a voice of Harlem scream
"WE ALL SUPPOSED TO BE DEAD BUT
WE AINT"
And his slow strut moves him on again.

* * *

BLUE TANGANYIKA

Here its like that . . .
   atmosphere of surprise
   hot sudden rain
   the pulse of things
   swings at different pace
   fruit riper
   putrifying quicker
   (a sharper carcass marks all death in heat
   you wander at dusk and
   this turn in the path
   meets green eyes
   of a jackal
   disappearing into bush—
Now—sweet singing

BWAGAMOYO*

Safari to Bwagamoyo
Safari to Bwagamoyo
For a lost son of Africa
Black sun, blue dust
On the way to Bwagamoyo
May eyes catch meanings in tears . . .

Bwagamoyo—beginning and end.

Myself, coming in love
The path to my destination
A jumble of holes
Red clay black
Slim hipped bridges
Swaying above dry gullies
The way to this place
Brings back old terrors . . .

Bwagamoyo—crush your heart for all is lost now.

What drawn out journey
What endless coffle
What sharp-toothed rivers to cross
What rust-bruised
Blistered flesh and soul
(While dhows like cradles on the tide)
Could flay this meaning there . . .

* *Bwagamoyo* was an ancient collection point for slaves on the Tanganyikan coast. The word Bwagamoyo carries the four meanings italicized.

Bwagamoyo—throw off melancholy the terrible march is
ended.

And now to come
Again to this beginning
Oceans crossed
Quick beaked birds endured
To come anew to meaning
The brown earth
Fat blue winds
Small children roasting fish
Black sun

Bwagamoyo—lay down your heart here on the coast of your
homeland

Yusef Iman

SHOW ME LORD SHOW ME

The Lord is my shepherd and I do want.
So show me Lord, show me.
Show me how to get the culture I had.
Show me Lord, show me.
What is the language I use to speak, Lord.
Show me Lord, show me.
How to get my people free.
Show me Lord, show me.
How to get rid of fear, Lord.
Show me Lord, show me.
How to get my people together, Lord.
Show me Lord, show me.
To make them stop killing themselves.
Show me Lord, show me.
To make them start loving themselves.
Show me Lord, show me.
To make them unify themselves, Lord.
Show me Lord, show me.
Show me Lord, show me.
Show me Lord, show me.
Show me Lord, show me.
Lord I'm waiting.

* * *

LOVE YOUR ENEMY

Brought here in slave ships and pitched over board.
Love your enemy.
Language taken away, culture taken away.
Love your enemy.
Work from sun up to sun down.
Love your enemy.
Work for no pay.
Love your enemy.
Last hired, first fired.
Love your enemy.
Rape your mother.
Love your enemy.
Lynch your father.
Love your enemy.
Bomb your churches.
Love your enemy.
Kill your children.
Love your enemy.
Force to fight his wars.
Love your enemy.
Pay the highest rent.
Love your enemy.
Sell you rotten foods.
Love your enemy.
Sell dope to your children.
Love your enemy.
Forced to live in the slums.
Love your enemy.

Dilapidated schools.
Love your enemy.
Puts you in jail.
Love your enemy.
Bitten by dogs.
Love your enemy.
Water hose you down.
Love your enemy.
　　Love.
　　Love.
　　Love.
　　Love.
　　Love.
　　Love, for everybody else.
But when will we love ourselves?

Norman Jordan

BLACK WARRIOR

At night while
whitey sleeps
the heat of a
thousand African fires
burns across my chest

I hear the beat
of a war drum
dancing from a distant
land
dancing across a mighty
water
telling me to strike

Enchanted by this
wild call
I hurl a brick through
a store front window
and disappear.

* * *

SINNER

I got high
last night
alone
I had an urge to
express myself

So I started talking
to the Bible
and it kept telling
me to Die.

* * *

THE SACRIFICE

The price of
milk has
gone up again
and the baby
is drinking more
Hell,
I guess I'll
have to give up
cigarettes
and blow my
chances
of catching lung
cancer
what the fuck
you can't have
everything.

Stanley Crouch

BLACKIE THINKS OF HIS BROTHERS

They rode north
funky & uneducated
to live
& let themselves rest:

I come here
ghuddammit
to make my way,
lazy or not,
to own myself
open the touch
of my fingers

The southern twang covers
my language & I embarrass
others
I never work
but that is
of others' choice

No one knows my virtues
yet tears split
my flesh &
I say I sweat . . .
Fats Waller added
                    up everything
when the joint was jumpin
"Don't give yo
right name no
No NO"

BLACKIE speaks on campus: a valentine for vachel
lindsay

Jambangle
and a black body
sways in the wind
flies sup it and the sun ignores it.
Unless your neck is metal
leave.
Jambangle

Cornets & pianos now mirror the corrosions
of the soul, rusted in sweat
"get your pig feet beer & gin
there's plenty in the kitchen"
Stomp holes in floors horny
for dancing sweating legs & feet
Throw off oppressors
with wet belly rolls
and slit throats over dice on alley hankerchiefs
wishing for snake flags to carry
and battle medals to wear.
Let Bessie explain it:
Songs do not leave
only bones & bodies do.
Pity, the battalions of
bullet-proof coons did not come.

But came the depression
and niggers didn't know the diffrence
except the lyricism was longer
more niggers tore up clothes

sang psalms & collapsed
Daddy Grace was in the making
but Garvey was gone
& Alabama bled more black,
up the map

Years passed and Benny made money:
white niggers squealed in Carnegie's Hall,
who also made money.

Niggers suffocated in cement deserts
lost lives, exploded in blood
hugged gor-bellied bitches,
each squeezed tit misery's symbol.
Artie Shaw, also, made money.

But America is not maudlin
only clothes changed
more heads were combed
and lotions halted ashiness:
minds melted in America,
seeking the great white way.
Dropping drawls in college.

Garvey was forgotten
but now wore zoot suits
supported by Bigger Thomas
and black bastards in bop glasses
who wore goats' beards
and bowed to the East.

Around then, sent east, got guns
and dog tags
knew no one bowed our way
shot europeans who peed in jacob's face
and another menace was yellow (closer
to us, but also shot at)
BUT JOHN WAYNE WON THE WAR

and we took our purple hearts,
to the unemployment office

The fifties were cool
fewer niggers carried knives
more bought cadillacs
and conked their hair
McNeeley was a messiah
with a tenor full of fonky niggers
motel money and stuffed toilets

We chased yellow girls
and waited.

Desegregation became a fad
coons wore business suits
sucked butts
but did not pick their noses
& spoke, with egalitarian accents

Why so many mulattos leave Boston?

... And here, I am not lyrical enough
to declaim our losses & dead lovers
except to say
the lyricism of tender,
nigger, men
and sweet negresses
is still stepped on
as babies slide
from black sex boxes
and are measured
by our bearded white uncle
in a loud triple colored strip-ped suit
who loves us, blushing
Fuck you and your mama too

Frederick J. Bryant, Jr.

NOTHING LOVELY AS A TREE

Tenacious foilage; burgundy
rust, jaundice, sea-sick green.
Yonder breaks one more fantasy.
Scowered and white or paling,
jutted or slicing elementally,
a frozen hydra, one way or another.

Trees are niggerish.

Creativity felled, standing
backless, rooted for the
gleaned wintry texts to learn
other naked truthes, and . . .
every spring seems a twin,
subtle differences unseen
yet,
every one simpler than before.

* * *

BLACK ORPHEUS

One hears and sees
    heard and saw
One feels and feeling
    felt and feels
Hearing said feeling felt
    touching seen
Holding sees heard feeling
    has felt feels
The hears saw felt feeling
    heard saw touching
The hearing holding one one
    said saw sees has
And no one feels and feeling
    felt and feels
And no one hearing holding
    the and the
        to never know and scream

Sam Cornish

PROMENADE

a little house with a broken stair
watches me in a curving narrow street
facing another house in the shadow
of another house in the shade
of another house in the shadow
of an abandoned school
the door is opened
ready to speak
its paint hangs like peeling flesh
its rooftop looks sadly down
with melting artful tar
the door is opened and wooden steps
remind me
of a suspended tongue
my feet turn with a will of their own
walking toward that opened mouth
inside discovering
a house is only an opened womb
where unborn children raise a bottle
to the lips
two windows stuffed with bible pages
a cake of ice beneath the sink
clean glasses beneath the table
rolling in the dust
outside a one armed man
is chopping wood
all of this street
opened the eyes to smoke
rising from tar barrels
along the street where
houses are opened wombs

* * *

TURK

"nothing crumbles, you leave it alone
feet like stumps unconcerned move with open
eyes. The skull finds influences."

S.C.

i have darker hair
settling on my face tough
hung in my pants i live

there is no space
to move do not come
too close i am a private
me

time is what i have
while you draw your pay i sleep
inside of you

your words and concern
project you instead
of me

have you ever seen
with your eyes

Clarence Reed

THE INVADERS

Harlem. Where once I trailed the rivers edge
And listened to her sing
Cut my feet on the rocks down there
And heard voices tinkle on glass
Where the night smiled so sadly sweet and
Hung the moon against her
Magically, without strings

Where the day, heaped with yellow
slapped playfully down on lovely black things
That laughed and sang too
And saved the night for tears
(My ashey legs sweat and shimmer in the sun)

Little boy, why did you drink the sunlight
And wrap yourself in dark
And chew hot pavement tar
And shoot ducks to smoke in a corncob pipe?
(Is over the bridge still to Grandma's house)
And "your mother don't wear no draws"
Little boy
Fucking, or trying to, behind the stairs
on the roof
In the house when nobody's home

Snatch an apple and run, little boy
Didn't you know tomorrow would come
And the night
        Little boy . . .

Stupid little black bastard!
The beasts swung your way even then
Hot breathed and filthy
Reeking of shit

They came one by one
And gathered-looking sideways—and
Muttering low
(Greasy-lipped preachers-traitors to Orisha—
Called hogs
And the most beautiful Sisters shouted on—
    Too late

The beasts went their separate ways
Clanged their horny armor and
Came violently one against the other
Rending tearing, slithering in blood, leaving a
Trail of pus
And turning they came again
And again . . .
    Till all was done . . . .

The moon weptblood and the river stopped
Dry things rustled
And the wind sang dirges thru the night
And day
Limping. Silently. The beasts went on their way.

* * *

MY BROTHER AND ME

I saw him there riddled
With needle holes
His alcohol-drenched brain
As limp and soggy as his
Life-battered body . . .

He was greasy and tired
And too confused to die—
He just sat there on the stoop
Trying to remember thru the miasma
The green years of hope and youth
        And not quite making it .

Too heavy the turgid festered hand
Of an alien hostile land—
Too thick the scars
Of being put upon . . .
Too many trips down the gold coast
River
Sold by professional nigger gentlemen . . .

How much I love him
For he is me and I is he
And we refuse to die
Backed against the wall
Of our own shortcomings
And have yet magic, black as me
To move us through the night . . .

* * *

IN A HARLEM
STORE FRONT CHURCH

Forever let there be shouting Sisters,
"Oh yes"
Shouting joyous exalting shouts
"Yes Lord!"
Voices massed, husky-throated, buxom
Brown sisters shouting,
Oh praise be life and living
Oh dead don't squirm
They mourn for you too with glad heart
That you have lived
Sprung from their loins
Shimmering blue-black in the sun,
Sucked in life, spit out joy,
Laughed to manhood,
Shouted in hell,
Went down to death with a
      rhapsodic moan
Oh, shout, Sisters, shout
Sing me along with clapping hands
And heal my heart
Echoing tamborines in my soul
"Oh yes Lord"
There is no more to God than you
Giver,
Sustainer
Joyous Sister shouting..........

HARLEM '67

This is the night
This is the day
This is the onliness
Sulking streets
Raging hearts
    This is Harlem
    This is love

Why do we meet here
Why do we love
Ugliness clutches us like
A whore
Why do we meet here
Why do we love
When love is death
And we know we must die
Here
Because we are in Harlem
Because we love

Strong people and weak
We are here
Drenched in blackness
And tears
    Why are we here
    Why do we reach
    Why do we die

    Why do we seek
    Where do we come from

Where do we go
Have we forgot
Tell if you know
If you know
Please tell me . . .
I know that Harlem
Is mysterious everywhere
  Our dominion
    our dominion
      our dominion
Is what?

Albert E. Haynes, Jr.

ECLIPSE

I

Open mouthed statues built with
marble speak.
And in the darkness, in the
open-ness of their
mouths, speaks of caves and mines
and ghettos.

Marble statues with open
mouths speak of flesh eating man.

Speaks of black blood flowing slowly,
draining useful energy.

Speaks over the brilliant bleeding bruises
of asphalt chapped lips
Speaks of his dreams
formed within
by the slow inertia of infinite numbers,
blended, crawling on black heaven; black harlem
questing for a soft lap
to place his body.

Speaks of his night song.

Open mouthed statues are autumn leaves
in flight.

II

while a single leaf falls to the ground;
Black Autumn leaves,
while I look at the ground and the dead leaf
dies and hardens and dies carved and veined.
Black Autumn leaves,
while I pause in the face of a sainted marble
church; watching saints and christ talk to people,
from any given feature chosen by
the people's joy and anger at the aged
or newly born.
Black Autumn leaves, falls, kissing
the black diamond emerging from
the African rock fault.

III

Within the skin and bone of the Black animal passenger
whose travels have ceased, cover the ocean bottom, please
whose passage has ceased in the Black animal
stalking life (orisha, save me!)
sining to the soul that walks below the decks
stalking life
in the water on a dead mannequin,
lurking in the waves
face downward in the grain, stalking eternal death,
hugely, on the night-land, on the wetland,
below the sun cover, below sun-sails, (Allah!)
within the incoming night, and the rising
waves, walking tall, Black
from the distant beaches and cliffs
inside my parents. Spear—
Map of my soul, AFRICA

IV

The blues were composed in the middle passages
of autumn, in a frail tossing ship.
Rough waves splashed at the hulls of ships,
that sail toward my shores,
packed on parted waves.

The ships of autumn passing scratch against
a slate blackboard.
The ships of autumn passing fade
past the rims of the eyes, like aging
autumn leaves do in winter, into marble
statues of saints and heroes. (Malcolm! Garvey!
Into fading mottled statues of saints and
heroes. Nat Turner, Denmark Vesey!
Into the fading mottled blues.
Into the million spots of sky, from a crumbling world
floating downward to the sea,
while autumn passes above the slate
searching for a clearing in the cosmos of a
crumbling world,
floating on currents, in fantastic numbers;
overlaying vital parts, and bringing fear and
suffocating mixture, and searching for a
clearing in the maw of this heavy overlay
from the spattered blood of a million exploding black sprouts.
praises due to the five per cent.

V

Through the night-land and in the air
and on the black passenger singing to the soul
that walks below the deckline seeking life;
and in the night-time of autumn passing,
injured:
blood drips down on the slate.
Blood spots.
And on the heart of the tiny dead mannequin that
floats between the roots and the slate
blood spots, and hardens.

VI

The ship of autumn passes within the darkness of the
silver screen.
Within the passion of hiroshima.
Passes the sewer hub, in the recesses of the
ghetto. Dead men

Blessed are the fruit of the millions dead
in the fall of darkness.
Blessed is the fruit of the wound. But more
Blessed is the explosion of the fruit, and the
falling, dark-red
tiredness that had no pity for black-uncle-Tom
night-sweat.

VII

Praises due to Black Power seekers
Night time is autumn passing,
hush now, while I walk on by.

Black spittle dots the earth.
Dried ejaculation.
Open mouthed, cameo faced, slightly dull,
like a waxed penny, is the face of the moon.
The marble statue proclaims
the shades of darkness absolute king of night bliss.
And the moon is a bright life sadly deployed
to make men mad.
The Black marble statue speaks with
teeth and jaws of stone
about hot stars on a plate full of shimmering
jelly flesh;
eschewing grits, and dripping drooling saliva
in his ravenous hunger for just one continent on
the earth, Africa!

Lorenzo Thomas

ONION BUCKET

All silence says music will follow
No one acts under any compulsion
Your story so striking and remain unspoken
Floods in the mind. Each one trying now
To instigate the flutter of light in your
Ear. The voice needling the flashy token
Your presence in some room disguised
As the summer of the leaves. Hilltops
Held by the soft words of the running
Wind. What lie do you need more than this
The normal passion. And each thing says
Destroy one another or die. Like a natural
Introducing here on this plane to Europe
The natural. A piece of furniture, smell
Taste some connection to your earth and
"Realize" nothing more than you need
Another view nothing more than you need yourself
Or that is beautiful. Or your luck that speaks.
Lifting its shoulders out the language
Of the streets. Above. The sky worried
Into its own song. Solid rhythm. She stays
Too close for a letter, scared of a telegram
The finger drum express. Impatient blues.
Anxious blues. Her chemical song loud and
Bright in his dimension. This is the world.
The vegetables are walking.

TWELVE GATES

Face it. The stars have their own lives and care
They are forced into it by your other eye and
Opposite side of your thoughts. Who takes sides
The world quite as fashionable as liars imagined

A picture of one fragile girl in an avalanche
Of the kimono required for their soft trade.
Who is so daring at first to draw lines in the sky
Dingy with this neglected daylight. Opened fan.
Life itself is such a simple thing and we need it

Then here come the music again. And we need that too
People asking each other. The invention of reason.
And those who own nothing what of those walking around
Without land, without cash value, properties. Without

Nothing in their name. Whose destinies
Are not marked or marked down. What of
The ones who are meant to rise in the world
By their names. Whose names are not known.
These worlds are lost in a minute only a gem
Of substance remaining. The necessity to change the form.
These streets clothed in an atmosphere of ash and care—
Less emotion. Who are these persons roll their shoulders

Outside the window in starlight and streetlight
Each young man there reminds the girl of someone
These are the last words I send you for awhile.
Written across her fan. Her open eye all flame and
You can feel it take shape in your eye. The lines.

Sufficient confusion calls for a song and
The figure with how many sides. Holler.
Once to the ocean. Sing it for the woman
Whose hands open and deliver the "dream"

Arousing itself from the day's laborer walking
These streets back from the edge of the river
Deep into town. Traffic. Your voice plays across
The street on the curb right into my open hand

Gaston Neal

TODAY

the tone of my life takes
the future as a growl mingled
with the groan of the past
however, the growl must be
hidden, because the jungles of
the past have gone. . . .
deflowered by napalm
shot down carrying white refrigerators
murdered bringing the liberators charisma, in a
hall full of my black people. . . .
So you see, the warrior, must look
like the old woman.
the warrior must stand straight in
the dark
we must whisper to each other, and
dare to tell. . . . .
we must get our own together
with the revelation of the truth or
the pain of death
then the outer circles of strange allegiances
the slow tedious math of power will begin
to creep into our shoulders. . . .
the child of years from me
the eyes of a grandfather days from me
will know this strange word
freedom. . . . .

PERSONAL JIHAD

THE SEED OF MY DAY BEGINS
AS THE TORTUOUS NIGHT ENDS
THE COMMON BIRDS GRAY SHRILL
INTERRUPTS THE FLUSHING OF A MORNING PEE

IT IS THE EYES OF A DOG
THE SOFT EYES
LOCKED IN TOO LONG, IN SOME CRAMPED YARD
WITH THE DIRT OF HIS ASS
CLUTCHING VIOLENTLY THE SOFT
OF SOMEBODY'S WARM

I REGARD THIS DAY, AS EVERY
LOSER WOULD
AND I NEED A GOD,
A BLACK GOD, TO GIVE ME
THE INSIDIOUS STRENGTH, THE CALM
SOFTNESS, TO WAYLAY FEAR

AS THE MORNING SEED GROWS
THE BLUE OF THE SKY MINGLES
WITH THE TWISTED BLACK FEATURES
OF WINTER TREES
AND SILENCE LOSES ITS CLUTCHES
ON A BEGINNING DAY

AND I SIT HERE AWARE OF
THE PAIN AND URGENCY
THAT I
MUST ATTAIN DISCIPLINE
FOR BROTHERHOOD AND UNITY
SOFTLY, SAY IT NOW

SAY IT NOW—
DOWN IN THE SOUL————————DISCIPLINE

SAY IT SOUL BROTHERS
SAY IT SOUL BROTHERS
DISCIPLINE........

L. Goodwin

"THE DAY A DANCER LEARNED TO SING OF DREAMLESS ESCAPADES"

When this ancient, wallpapered melody
wears off,
What, my fair and humble home,
will your restless fingers snap to,
After the noisy, taciturn, tableclothed
harmonies and incongruent proletariet love
                                    legends?
You know what I'm hinting at,
The criss-crossed panacea, and long,
                                    long,
                                    long
distance phone calls.
And would a flexible, young and receptive
expectation be there?
Close between C sharps, and serious minded
A flats,
if we sung to each other,
And if we needed someone?
Here in the middle of my fossilized soul,
sits a paronoic dancer pleading
to an invalid audience that floors are
out to get him.
Yet the satin, gold curtain of my un-
protected heart,
                    gazes upon him in awe,
and casts over-simplified shadows that
break the homogenuity of his external
coordination.

416

Curiously, cautious, the repetitious
dancer just
shrugs his painted shoulder and swears
there are no such things as
DREAMs.

Ray Johnson

WALKING EAST ON 125th STREET
(SPRING 1959)

Walking east on 125th street
Listening to the barbaric yawps of Daddy Graces true
  believers
Walking on the gaudiest street in the world
Walking and watching the grey boys buying love
from brown biege and black tricking girls
Walking and seeing the pimps look at the love slain romeos
  with a hip sneer
Walking and hearing the black man on the step ladder his
  face a Ivory Coast mask crooning words of hate
Walking through the feverish crowd which shouts back "thats
  right man" dreaming of tidal rivers of blood
Walking past the Apollo where black minstrels sing
endless of lost love stolen love love for sale and
no love at all

Walking abreast of battalions of domestic workers and their
stockboy escorts who are glad for winter so their overcoats
  can cover the runaway erections
Walking in a 3 for 1 bar watching the partying crowds drink
down the national debt
Walking past the jew stores with the 1000 year guarantees
  on collapsible items
Walking away from off duty cops still looking like cops
  running the badge game down chisling chump change&
  free pussy
Walking near the boarded up post office covered with signs
  announcing the coming to Harlem of the oriental looking
  messiah

Walking out of the old Apollo bar where the shamen glide
in full majesty and glory except when the bar clock strikes
the closing hour and only the empty scented rooms await
where they cry and wipe away the tears with the soiled
lioncloth
Walking down where the central stomps overhead
Walking warily next to the lowdown bars with uniformed
policeman standing guard
     nothing but Stacker Lees in side whooping it up a per-
     mament convention of the (ill stick mah shank in
     your mother fuggin heart just to watch yuh die) razor
     switchblade nickle plated 32 lye throwing bottle break-
     ing baseball batting fist fighting goodtime fingerpop-
     pin ladies and gentlemen
Walking fast by the changing store signs Bodega & Carnercia
country
Walking underneath the jive moses memorial the triboro
bridge
Walking to the edge of the river i remove everything except
my chastity belt and keep on strolling
Walking down on the bottom of the east river scaring the
catfish
Walking lazily by the mafia boys in hip concrete bennies
doing a swinging tarantella
Walking with a orange peelin my ass a condom in my mouth
Walking.

Bob Bennett

"It is time for action"

It is time for action.

> Loud revolutionary action.
> Action that turns things upside down
> Action that stirs my bleeding heart.

Action that's gonna mean something for a *change*.

> (And when I say change, I mean change, brother.)
> I don't mean this bullshit we been thankin'
> the president, the senators, congressmen,
> little bobeep, jack horner, santa claus, jack frost,
> and any other whitey who would listen

Dig here!

I heard a preacher.
One of Sweet Jesus' preachers say

> (On TV by the way)

Lord, we ain't where we wanna be
> we ain't where we oughtta be
> we ain't where we gonna be
But thank God, we ain't where we was.

That's a footwashed Baptist lie and he knows it.

The devils are closer to pullin' an out & out genocide now
Than they have been since we got off the boat

That's right
   I'm talkin' out & out genocide
   Out & Out

Not this clandestine shit he's foolin' y'all with now

Yeah man, Right now
   In Viet Nam and
   In your home town

Viet Nam is almost funny, man
   Really funny.
   (I cry about it often)

Here he's got a double genocide goin'
   You and the VietNamese
The funny part is that he's got you killin'
   each other
     (Think about it)

(Bear with me while I clear this lump from my throat.
No wonder you punks won't throw the shackles off your
   colonialized minds.
But in the words of an ancient black revolutionary who
   wouldn't have fried his hair for all the back home preachers
   in Georgia.
   The truth shall set you free)

As far as your home town is concerned
Well, you remember last summer's riots
   Last summer's riot,   HuH
   Last summer's riot won't squat, won't turd, won't shit
Next summer the man is gonna do his best to do his best to
   wip you *out* . . .
   Yeah, my man
   OUT & OUT.

So you chumps, you punks, you faggots
   who ain't movin' yet

PLEASE!! get your mind together and be
    my main, my man, my brother . . . . . my brother
    (And that says a lot)
It's our *only* chance to survive.

    And so

It's time for action.

    Loud revolutionary action
    Action that turns things upside down
    Action that stirs my bleeding heart
Action that's gonna *mean* something for a change

Now if that's going in circles . . . it's about time.

Bob Bennett

(Title)

The girl with the Afro.
    without words speaks of black and blues and boogaloo
    without a note of music   there is rhythm

The girl with the natural
    Without words speaks of black and soul feeling
        GLAD TO BE BLACK
    And *mine* for itself
    (Makes me feel good)

The girl with the Afro
    Without words says she loves our mother
    And our mother's children
    (She is my sister: I am her brother)
    Without romance there is love

Ahmed Legraham Alhamisi

UHURU

uhuru (freedom. now. swahili. east african lango)
COROLYN WILLIAMS &
SHARON RHAE CHEATHAM: Natural Leaders For Our
  People
pome written for carolyne & sharon after being bombed out
  of my mind
from "THEIR" natural LOOK

as sun blinds
beauty kills so many people nowadays
just count the number of BROthers in Viet nam. or
Ala BAM. spelled in dumb teachers. & students. housed in
  DURfee. an
ins ti tu tion that screw dem for orgasm
For Rhae
BLACK PRINCESS of the day &
                    CAROL. the creator. in my
  mind all the way
MUSIKmusikMMMUUUsikMUSIKMUSIKMUSIK
  MUSIKMUSIKmusikmusikmusikMUSIKmusikkk
you have taken up
the ole folks burden. sent
forth a stronger breed POWpow. powpowpow. crackcrack
  crack. CRASHCRASH.
BOOM. BOOMBOOMBOOMBOOMBOOM. tearing down
  the Master's need. with buildings of BLK minds. the east
  african language
                Hujambo Bwana Nigger. Binti
Nigger. Bibi Nigger. YALL NIGGERS.

424

(go forth baby. & let yr beauty
          shine. & shine & shine

Repeat this day in all the days to come
Blow my mind. aaaaaahhhyyee
AAAAAAhhhyyee
aaaahh HHYYYYEEEEEeeeee
aaAAAAAHHHHHHYYYYYEEEE
EEEEeeeee. & i'm free
thur the blowing. THEIR
bodies   ———   —————
POW POW POW POW
POWPOWPOWPOWPOWPOW
                         POWPOW
POWPOW POWPOWPOW POW
                      POWPOW
kill the mothers. turn off their life. thur
math. & science as formes of arrows. frome the swift bow of
   geronimo. & they are dead thur the shooting. the powing.

Use the man. PRO TAG O RAS. the theorem. & take short
   cuts
from their lives. KILL KILL KILL
cause Flood to flow in the streets of BLACK HISTORY
            POW POW POWpowpowpowpowpowpow
                    powpowpowpowpowpowpow
snatch Rotten Berg's RedWhite&Blue mind from Jewish
   Faith. housed in
hidden memories of conSINtrayShun Camps & paint the
   real image Red. &
let the bouzhie niggers drown from the inner flow of a
   dying art, as boss
culture.
"WHY DONCHA BE NICE NIGGER. SHOOT HOLES
   IN AFRO TARGETS. THROW INSULTS AT
   NATURAL GALS. TEACH LAUGHTER AS A
   WEAPON. BE NICE. APE THE WHITE MAN. GIVE
   BIRTH TO BLACK DEATH.S. RAPE THEIR LIFE.

CUT THE NIGGERS THROATS & LET THE BLOOD
SPELL CULTURE. FREEDOM. "D' MOCRE SEE."
————A MER DER CA
yeah. be nice. &
when the evening mist
rises above the riverside
& the splindling asters fall lightly
under distant skies
think of me
             but dont stay long.
POW POW POW
POWPOWPOWPOWPOWPOW
POW POWPOWPOW
POWPOWPOW POW POW. KILL. KILL
KILL. the real enemies
inspire artists to paint flowing
blood from human robuts
peeping from behind parked thots in 2 eleven. force the
     sculptor
to cut minds on the band saw buzzzbuzzzbuzzzzzzbuzzzzzzz
KEEP THE POWER ON buzzzzzzzzzzzzzzzzzzzzzzzzzzzzzzz
                                    zzzzzzzzzzzzzzzz
zzzzzzzzzzzzzzzzzaahhyyyeeeeeee
KEEP YOUR FINGER ON THE TRIGGER powpowpow
     powpowpowpowpowpowwwwww
tumble the walls on christian thots.
rush baby & wrestle life from hunkys. &
kill the teachers thats against yr
life. yr beautiful black life. let blood flow
from the rooms. oh let the blood flow. oh
let the mothers blood flow. let thar
be screams & screams & more screams. then no screams
hipping us to our success. oh let thar be colored screams. pale
     screams. all screams. let thar be screams. screams. screams.
     screams. hipping screams.

peace now. peace. from Roberts Williams' dictionary. peace.
     peace of mind. & a piece of whitey's . . .

but be nice. &
THINK OF ME
under distant skies
when the evening mist
rises above the riverside &
the splindling asters fall
lightly
powpow powwwwwpowwwwpowwwpowpowpowpowpowpow
   powpowpowpowpowwwwwwwwwwwwwwww
shoot all the niggers. just line 'um up & mo 'em down with
   chine guns.
tactactactactactactactactactactactactacwith t.v. the president.
skulls. the constitution. george wallace. helmets on skull faces.
   the
draft. the lies. false histories. baseball games played in bars.
   arguments
at UNITY MEETINGS on special nights
from bodies of black power advocates with newer forms of
   integration.
        burn-it-down-build-it-up capitalist clothed in ujambo
jambo gani salaam kwaheri. pure colors dripping red semen
   on open sores
underneath chalk minds of boozhie niggers. with venom.
   drip drip dripping
dripping dripping dripping
DUCK SISTERS. don't git hit. yet. either way you die.

POME. FOR WEIRD. HEARTS. & ALL

you mothers

The bearded "TEACH" : walking. pissing thots. on church-
coated stools.
disguised as minds.
Anonymous voices: ha. ha. thats robert in the future . . . heh
heh . . .
they. black eyes. nappy-headed. grey minds. damn fools
that they are. have been taught
their death. frome split lips. of pimps
(Dr. White Folks. Mrs. Whitey
House. The Dean of American Forces. THE AMERICAN
DREAM. & nigger scene
exposing grey matters
of the bone. carved in voices. words. "good mornings."
"i have nothing against coloured people . . ." & we are
taught this vision thur white light
black might. in the night. & with
so much grace. this light. this w. & b. (INTEGRATED)
light. wind
ing itself skillfully in our minds. causing black
people to turn to themselves.
like dead & tired faces
hanging frome windows. piercing shadows frome light
come plex sion niggers. in blackest of ghettoes. considered
sane by intelligent tests. causing other creations:
the ofay. fat. punk. forced
into a double-vested vine on Lin-
wood. or

the bastard with the pokadot mind crying
"help me bros."

Damn! hearts are weird.

There's no love in these voices. anoymous voices.
resting in little minds. doomed
for dying. unless hip. teachers. teach them their
beauty. & the rulers. their death. No. it's
not hate to love yourself. only
love. baby. only love. for
life. our life. cause
their life. is our death. yr.
death. if logic is your
    mother.
    father. or
    lover.

D. L. Graham

the west ridge is menthol-cool

the west ridge is an old ridge—
a cold dying place,
tired waves swirl beneath
the green torch lady
and death rides the stark gray water-birds

down by the river a cross burns
in perverted truth—
spreading its inverted light,
casting ragged shadows.
as cladded men dance jim crow jigs
amidst children standing
like small tents.

the grain has withered on its stalks—
and drooped with the oleanders—
in a mush–brown–wet–rot
pale bodies writhe in ecstasy—
unmindful of the blood-caked-mud upon their
    skins—
while their bastard children cower in corners
and pray for purity to the nadinola gods—

the sands are shifting'
the wind is cold today and
there's likely to be hell tomorrow for
the green lady holds only embers

all around, brothers are balled
like ebony chains

whispering truths in a black hue
the black exodus is on . . .
we are going to "step-all the way up" and out of
this menthol scented lie . . .
the cry—"uhuru"

A Portrait of Johnny Doller

LADY, LADY
WHY DO YOU HOLLER
AIN'T NOBODY SAW YOUR
JOHNNY DOLLER

I. Piss
        aint never smelled sweet
johnny whispered and
                        walked away
walked away tired of
greasy pillow cases
and dirty house coats
and manny fat again
beggin   again
—johnny don't go—

                    Screaming from the window wont
                    bring your johnny back

Hey brother can i help you
hed say to some
piece for a price
and
judy would shake
her beauty
if the face was pale
enough

                    Pacing   wont
                    bring him back

II. Though times are hard
    i saw johnny at the Era
    drinking hundred pipers
    thru a straw
    no more pimp talk/ talks
    about guns pineapples 'n
    white cherries busted loose
    for his brother   torn
    from his television set
                             torn
    by a shotgun blast

                         Crying wont bring him back

    Nobody remembers that i
    turned somersaults and
    bled under the moon
    johnny said/ then
    sing a song brother
    sing a song about
    a thirteen year old
    who died in the streets
    sing/ cause you do that best

                         Pacing 'cross the floor
                         Wont bring your johnny
                         back

* * *

the clown

                    i wake up
                and hells around me
            mamma threw a bottle and it
              burst against the wall

            god i ll never forget mammas voice

        —get on back to your filthy whore—

                sisters in the amen corner
            her frail body is un-sprung tight

              —your aint my daddy—
                    she says

                ka-bamn . . . a bottle crashes
                thru the picture window
                and splinters chain-react
                crash tingle klank/
                the ceiling light catches
            an-acrobat-clown-contortionist
            in multi-poses of duck-jump
                    duck-turn

    DUCK DUCK FIVE THROWS FOR A QUARTER
                    . . . .
        DUCK YOU WIN DUCK YOU LOSE

434

blood spurts & splatters
to partly lead
        partly follow
the clown to an open door
beyond the light . . .
        beyond my vision

Victor Hernandez Cruz

O.K.

O.K.
you scat taking
simple ass
OPEN UP HIS HEAD / OPEN UP HIS HEAD
put your eyes in his head
till he sees the red dripping from his sisters
eyes till he sees snotty gringo machines
with his name on it
like a funeral
till he sees death
his name hanging on some door
his brains chewed like juicy fruit
                              dreams
of working for the Palmolive Peet Company
shattered
            industrial men rattle their false teeth
across golf courses of america
                        make your way
                        make your way
thru all the rigid & cold negatives
cement & steel structures with teeth full
of blood
        dripping/raining like lies
                        behind the lips
& inside the mouth of simple / torpid & stupid beings
without culture
        O.K. YOU HEAD HANGING / SWINE SMELLER
open up your head/ open up your head.

* * *

white powder!

in the dark corners of buildings
where politicians & their grey men
wont be caught dead
                    are the new arms
smacking themselves heads
                    the chinese
eyes/the red spots of the eyes/have
stories/lean back on pissed dried mattress
open up or melt at the corner
                    the nails
run thru the body scratching out need
now run up / smooth
                    burn the shit some
more he said/ it aint ready
                    who said when
the city sleeps/pass the last project/
exchange a deck/bars full of secrets/eyes
follow pool balls/almost falling to the
ground
          in the dark corners
          where brothers wait the hours
walking up & down with sweet soda/wiping
sweat/water spilling/
                    the trey bags are
so empty/tongues lick the paper/slowly
moving/
          but missing the light
          missing the light
          & there is so much to see
                              like
gringos & their grey men laughing.

Jacques Wakefield

"We exist living dead"

We exist living dead. The death of
living dead. The now death in our minds,
brothers.
The destruction of ourselves with the
help of.
from having life, beautiful and free,
children free and beautiful life of love.
Then the disillusionment, the search.
searching, not finding.
now the manifest of stone hearts and minds.
the lost,
the lost of beautiful hearts and minds.
Melt this death.
Help me, I'll help you.
please, lets flow with life love beautiful free and happy.
and die for real . . . .

Jacques Wakefield

".... days prior to"

.... days prior to: Two Brothers killing
each other. Stomping, cutting, cursing
each other. Mutherfucking each other.
not knowing common thing with each
other.
Brothers really dig each other.
damn Other cause Brothers to Mutherfuck
each other.
Brothers really dig
each other. So riots are boss outlets.

"Oh shit a riot!"

"Oh shit a riot!"
"Get A.J. Lesters!" Pink Pants...20.00 knit.
"Oh shit gonna get me some gator tops."
"WATCH OUT THE BLUECOATS ARE COMING!"
"Shit man get the match to this shoe!"
"They killed Martin Luther King."
 "THAT'S RIGHT"
 "UH, HUH"
 "DAMN RIGHT"
Hey, why don't y'all get some jew'ry stores.
 "I'M DOWN"
"COME ON!" They killed Martin Luther thingabob"

Kuwasi Balagon

Children of the Cosmos

Nothing out there that I didn't already see. A dump, an
overpopulated
dump. Nine million people looking through through trash;
fanning
maggots and flies, looking over scraps, that are in the end only
scraps. Piecing together broken chinaware, partly together
with come.

A Joker sits at his desk, looks up at the clock, takes a sip of
coffee;
looks at two stacks of paper on the right and left sides of
the desk.
Moves the ones on the left side one by one to the right
side, and the
ones on the right side, one by one to the left side. The ones
the
manikin is not quite sure about; he places in the middle.
Does'nt
know what in the fuck hes doing. He looks up at the clock,
makes an
uglier face, takes a sip of coffee, looks around at the dolls,
speaks
to the dolls, to all of the dolls. Speaks to the bags, hi! doll,
placed there to make sure that the office doesn't look like a
house
of ill repute, and then begins to reverse the procedure.
Nothing out there I didn't see already, nothing.

Curb your dog signs, stop signs, nickel and dime faces on
the subway,

an not so abstract jew. Circus barkers almost, incompletes,
    ill working
and complete here with us.

You and I make a complete spirit to deal with realities, while
    the
others flash and fan illusions about. It's us the children of the
Cosmos to grab the concrete, it's up to us to live complete
    lives.
Life is up to the 100% alive. Two in one spirit in meadows
    and fresh
green forests, with only the sound of youthful spring in our
    midst.

Children of the Cosmos never say goodbye, only minor
    interruptions
appear like small forevers. Only time when we must com-
    municate with
the vibrations of desperate souls, and then it's morning again,
    and
the sun steps out from hiding, and our world glistens. Spec-
    trums flash
and fade, streaks of purple and orange shot with soulasphere.
    Our
voices ripple and prance, our bodies glow like stars and melt;
transformed and reformed into compressed constellations
    that will
continue to continue. Yet we are only children of the Cosmos.

Within the illusions of one of their nights, they will peer into
the brightness of the darkness that surrounds them, and read
    the codes
of all of the children of the universe. The dump will last as
    the light
of a flash bulb, and those that produced it will move their
    last paper,
take their last sip of coffee, and make their last ugly face.
And we will be children no more.

Kuwasi Balagon

If You Love Them, Wouldn't You Like To See Them Better Off?

What do you see in a tired ole water-logged crackers face?
In soggy eyes that are surrounded by thick vomit flowing
   downward toward a clothes hanger holding a white shirt,
   flowered tie, jacket and pants, with a wallet with pictures
   of other crackers in OD green and numbered along the
   sides.
Might makes right, he made that law
Doesn't he look dead, gotta feel dead, would be better off
   dead.
   Look into his soggy blue eyes with love for the poor
sickly, tired, toothless beast
Kill him for his own good, roll his head with love
If you cannot hate.
But roll his head
Disrupt, disrupt
Everything that disturbs you
throw lit cigarettes in trash cans, turn underground
cattle cars into terror and even death machines
Put tense filled hands to use, Disrupt!!

Ole Mrs. Assbucket
Counterpart of Mr. Assbucket
tired ole wicked which, fresh out of a graveyard
and placed together like Frankenstein, a nonfunctional
robot, never could have babies only little gadgets
   Who could hate poor ole Mrs. Assbucket or Mr. Ass-
      bucket?
See some silly putty that dosn't bounce, just goes flop

443

Disrupt, disrupt terrorize
Take a cop's gun and shoot him, drag a john into an alley
kicking him until his flesh and clothes become like a
      cracked tile floor, piss on that motherfucker
It's all a thing of mind over matter
You don't mind—crackers don't matter
Disrupt

John Q. Average American
Ain't no good, not some good, some bad
Ain't 50-50, 75-25, ain't 90-100 ain't 99-100
Ain't no John Brown Society, there's a John Birch Society
      Throw a manhole cover on him as he come out with his
        Con Ed
overalls, run him down on country roads, take ole light
bulbs fill them with lye and water and use his face for
a dart board
      Anytime you kill him, anywhere you kill him, it's self
        defense
      Walk into Macy's with a time bomb, walk out leaving it
under some racks
      Watch corned beef fly out the window
Disrupt! Disrupt!
Disrupt their lives, take their lives
They're doing it to yours
Better off dead, if you love them
Wouldn't you like to see them better off?

Kuwasi Balagon

Untitle

Beating hearts
Untidily wrapped in raw flesh, nestled in the rain on highways
somewheres between here and there
Beating heart snatched out of so-called lovers chests
Having the same sound of a fot bag when passing cars run
over it
on the road to Bowie or D.C. or New York
Dig blood and water and a green WAKE UP WAKE UP
as I tell you of a merry christmas
Back in "54"
Push aside rat tails and baited traps of goose livers. Wooden-
toothed
fartbusters. Bullshitters. Elastic assholes.
Wipe the stains from your minds
The skid marks of clowns gingerly guzzling down week old
gold fish
water belching behind the fish licking their jaws full of gold
fish shit from nasty gaps of rusted nails
Push it aside, push the bullshit aside
Of Madame Caboo's faces of driftwood
And Kotex chewers and jack-in-the-boxes who pop out of
nowhwere and
gulp down bloody pussy rags
Push them from your world and repent to the only God
you can justly
call your own
For nothing can be made up for
Take control of your life and live black man
Lash the sounds of "you're going too fast too far" up money

hungry sellouts ass 'til their kidneys hang like hounds ears
from the sides of their heads
Go as far as you can go until it's oh, so far
Try to go too damn far, make it a point every day to get
    out of hand
Your fate isn't to submit to the flintstones
Of living in a circus, jumping through hoops, of living in a
    circus
where the beast has the whip and the chair
Get out of hand and on america's flabby ass
Get out of hand, wipe away the skid marks of oppression and
degradation
Get matches and gas in hand and get out of hand
Get the adominable snowman off the earth
Turn law by outlaws and rich get richer an poor get poorer
    order
upside down from the streets to the courts
Until your life is in your hands

Bobb Hamilton

"Brother Harlem Bedford Watts Tells Mr. Charlie Where Its At"

Man, your whole history
Ain't been nothing but a hustle;
You're a three card melly[1]
Mother fucker.
You've even run the shell
And pea game[2] on your own family.
I wouldn't trust you
As far as I could throw
a turd of
Gnat shit!
Let me run down
Just a little
       of my
Case against you
Chuck!
When you set your
Feet in our house,
Our troubles begun—
Yeah, we had our family fights,
But it took you
         to put
Shit in the game.

[1] Three card melly is culluaese for three card mente, a con game with two black jacks and a red queen which are shuffled and layed on the table for the "sucker" to pick out the queen which has been palmed during the shuffle and replaced with a duplicate of one of the jacks.

[2] The shell and pea game uses three walnut shells. A pea is placed under one and the "sucker" picks the one its under. The con man has taken the pea between his fingers while moving the shells around the table.

We thought you was sick
You looked so white and
Hairy, and we taken you
In like a brother
"Poor thing," we said,

"He looks like one of our ghosts.

Look at his pinched up nose

And his little narrow

Pink lips. And that hair is a gas.

A lotta little brown

And blond strings

Hanging out of his head

His god must be poor

And don't have no wool-er else

Awfully stingy."
And whilst we was
Wining and dining you.
And trying to put some Soul
In your poor pale frame.
You was casting
Your greedy gray eyes
Around, lusting after our
Shining black women, and
Our gold and silver
Yeah, and you even licked
Your fuzzy chops at your
Black beceped men!
You was scheming man.

Before we knewed it good,
We were took over.
Next thing we knowed
Ya'll had a squabble
Amongst yourselves
And divided up the whole
Country.
Old leopold run his
Cut like a game preserve
Chopping off hands and
Feets, plucking out eyeballs
Snatching off ears-He was
Swinging—
And when he got tired
He went home
Put on some silk drawers
Laid up in a
Big Belgian bed
Blew a fart and
Died.
The pope says he
Went to heaven.
Jeez man!
How dumb do you
Sombitches think we are?
What happened to
Your god's justice?
Speaking of justice
Your god is a fink
He let his own son get
Lynched over there in
Jerusalem Land.
If Shango had made
It with Mary,
He wouldn't a ever
Let his son
Lay in a stable
With all that

Oxshit and straw
Now man,
Mary woulda been
Set up in
The finest compound
With servants and good meals
And lots of
Palm wine!
And if Pontius Pilate
Had touched him,
His ass woulda popped
Like a motor boat
All the way back to
Rome!
And you got the nerve
To tell me, "that was noble."
You a jive cat
Charlie boy.
You paid off some
Rib picking Baptist Nigger preacher to
Go around telling us
To love you
            everytime
You kick our ass.
Let him do his Head—rag hop somewhere else
Cause if you ever kick me
You will make a
Dot and a dash
For footprints, cause you'll have
One peg and one shoe!
Help you fight in
Viet Nam?
Man, them's my folks
you fucking with over there,
Viet Cong
            or
Hong Kong
They is colored,

And I hope cuzz
Knocks a hole
In your ass
Big as the
Grand Canyon!
Man you been taking
One big piss
On me for
Four hundred years
And them
Calling me
Nasty!
Hell no
I ain't going
Nowhere!!

Bobb Hamilton

Poem To A Nigger Cop

Hey there poleece
Black skin in blue mask
You really gonna uphold the law?
What you gonna do when you see
Your Mama
    Running down 125th street with
A t.v. set tied up in a bandana trying to catch a train to
    Springfield Gardens?
    You mean to tell me you gonna
Bang your own mother?
    Bang! Bang!
I can see you now grinning
    A big black no nuts nigger
On channel number 5
Your teeth rolling across the screen
Like undotted dice
    Talking about how you "uphelt
    De Law."
While Mr. Charlie sticks his white
    Finger up your ass
And pins a little gold medal on your
    Chest!
And then you'll bust out into soft shoe shuffle
    While a background chorus sings
"God Bless America,"
With an Irish accent.

Fiction

Henry Dumas

FON

FROM THE SKY. A fragment of black rock about the size
of a fist, sailing, sailing. . . . CRAACK! The rear windshield
breaks.

Nillmon snaps his head to the rearview mirror, wheeling
the car off the road.

"Goddammit!" He leaps from the car, leaving the door
open. He examines the break, whirls around and scans the
evening countryside with squinting eyes.

The distant mooing of cattle blends with the sharp yap
of a dog.

And then he catches a movement.

Through the trees behind him—past a large billboard with
the picture of Uncle Sam saying *I Want You*, over and
down a rocky incline, toward a final rise at the top of the
levee—Nillmon thinks he sees several pairs of legs scurrying
away.

"Niggers!" He steps back to the car, leans across the seat,
jerks open the glove compartment, snatches up a pistol lying
between a half-bottle of whiskey and a stick of dynamite, and
crosses the torn asphalt in four quick strides. Pieces of pavement scatter beneath his feet. The road is in disuse except
for an occasional car and a few cattle crossings.

He runs toward a path by the billboard. As he loses sight
of the point in the distance where he thinks the figures
disappeared, he runs faster. He reaches the beams supporting
the billboard. The area behind the sign is a large network of
angled shafts and platforms. He follows the path, stooping
his shoulders and grunting. He lurches through an opening,

twisting his way from the entanglement of wooden beams. He curses. Then he slows his pace, realizing that he's chasing children.

He slips the pistol in his belt. He clears his throat and spits at the long edge of the billboard's fading shadow. Then he resumes his march up the hill.

He looks over the countryside. No niggers running. Across a thin stretch of young cotton three shacks lean back on their shadows, and the shadows, bending at every bank and growth of the land, poke at the muddy inlet of a Mississippi tributary. The only movements are the lazy wag of tattered clothes on the back porch of one shack, the minute shifts of what looks like chickens scratching in a bare yard, the illusory tilt of a cross barely gleaming on top of a tiny wooden church far away, and the fragmentary lines of black smoke climbing lazily but steadily higher and higher. Nill-mon peers. He thinks he sees a figure rocking slowly back and forth on the porch of the third shack. Probably an old granny. A cowbell jangles in the distance, and from the shacks Nillmon thinks he hears an angry voice rise and fall amidst a scurry of noises, and then trail off in a series of loud whacks and screams. He tries to locate that shack. He is about to descend.

He smothers a strange impulse to laugh and spits down the incline, jerking his eyes toward the road, over the levee cotton and through the trees.

Then he snaps his neck back toward the road for a second look.

It is not the slow motion of the car door swinging to the uneven idle of the motor that catches his eye. Nor the slight movement of leaves and branches.

Somebody is watching him.

A silhouette sits at the back of the billboard. The slow dangle of a bare leg is the only motion. The mesh of beams looks like a web. The billboard is empty except for the lone figure.

"Goddammit!" He snatches out the pistol. "Git down!"

The shadows in the trees waver and merge like a field of tall reeds marching gently under the steady touch of the wind. Nillmon wipes his mouth with his sleeve.

"Nigger, can't you hear?"

The figure, almost liquid in his giant movements, begins a slow descent, swinging across a shaft of sunlight like an acrobat. He drops to the ground and stands. A muscular black youth. Bands of fading light make imperfect angles and spears across his red shirt and black arms.

"Who else is up there?"

"My brother."

Nillmon attempts to approach the figure. The youth is standing with the weight of his body on one leg. Nillmon stops in front of him and searches for signs of resistance. The youth holds his head level, but his eyes glare outward, always away from the eyes of the white man, as if they were protecting some secret. Nillmon searches the billboard and trees. The nigger is a half-wit.

"All right, move!"

The tall youth slides into motion on the path made by children. But he carefully steps around the beams, over a few rocks, and proceeds toward the road.

"Black boy, I'm goin to see you put every piece of that glass back in place."

Nillmon watches the rear of the figure moving down the path, and he feels a rush of blood to his head when he thinks of the bullet going right through the dark head.

"I didn't break it," the youth says without turning around or slowing his pace.

"Nigger, you in trouble," says Nillmon. They reach the car. The youth is looking straight ahead. "Aside from gettin your ass beat, and payin for that glass, you goin to jail. Git in."

The youth turns slowly—as if in some fearful trance—and

is about to look squarely at the other man, but instead he rivets his eyes on the white man's neck.

"Boy, what's your name?" Nillmon asks.

Cowbells sound up the road. The youth shifts his weight, wets his lips, and looks off. Far, far down the road, cows gather at a fence and a voice yells, a dog barks, and then the cattle neck into the crossing, and some are mooing.

"Fon."

"Goddammit, Fon what?"

The sun has almost fallen. The shadow of the car bounces nervously. Then it stops.

"Al*fonso*."

Nillmon squeezes the pistol butt. This boy ain't no half-wit. Nillmon knows he is going to break him now. The nigger is trying to act bad. Maybe he'd break him later. Maybe Gus and Ed would want a piece of him. He looks at the youth and he can't decide whether he is bad or not. He hates to see a fool-headed nigger get it. No fun in it. He sees a thin line of smoke coming from the back seat of his car. Sniffing and leaning, he sees that his back seat, where the black stone landed, is smouldering.

"Set fire to it, too, eh?" He moves toward Fon.

He swings his foot upward, aiming for Fon's rear. Seeming to anticipate the move, Fon, without moving his legs, twists his back and avoids the blow, which strikes the air.

"Nobody *threw* that rock from there," Fon says.

Nillmon, half-stunned, finding himself kicking the air when what he wanted to kick was so plain, wipes his mouth in a nervous sling of his arm, and while the sleeve is passing over his face he tries to see if he holds a pistol, feels himself squeezing it and emptying it. But he can't. It is all too easy. This Fon nigger ain't scared. He knows now he has a nigger that needs a thorough job. Nillmon smiles and spits on the gravel in front of Fon. "Git in."

Fon moves around the car, opens the door, and slowly

gets in, closing his door carefully and firmly. Nillmon slams his and jerks the car forward. The car picks up speed. Nillmon grips the steering wheel until the blood is cut off from his hands. A thin line of smoke issues from the rear window.

"Yesss, nigger, think you can count them pieces of glass with the tip of your tongue?" Fon is silent. Nillmon relaxes his grip and looks at him from the corner of his eye. "What the hell you niggers doin up on that sign chunkin at cars anyway?"

A cattle crossing. The car, slowing, slowing . . .

"Teachin my brother how to shoot his arrows."

. . . and the car stops.

Nillmon feels himself lunging toward Fon, pushing him out of the car with his foot, and blasting his body till it swells and bleeds black blood like that Huntsville nigger they got last year. . . . He was deputy sheriff then. Hell, if he hadn't been implicated in that case he would still be on down there in Huntsville. That goddamn Federal Agent even suggested that he and Gus lay low till things got under control. The nigger civil rights groups were kicking up so much dust that an honest white citizen in the state couldn't see straight half the time. But it wasn't like that up here in Columbia County. He lowers his foot on the gas and the noisy engine stirs the cattle.

Fon seems to watch the rising humps of the cattle. They pass in quick strides. A brown-skinned boy, about twelve, hollers and whistles and a dog is barking at the heels of a straying heifer.

"You teachin your brother how to chunk at white folks? How long do you expect your brother to live, actin on what you say?"

"I'll take care of him."

Nillmon feels himself laughing, but his anger rises over it. "You 'bout a bad nigger, ain't you?"

The straying cow, a large black and white with a swinging udder, turns and heads toward the car.

Nillmon spits out the window. The cows are mooing, their bells are banging.

"Hurry up, boy. Git them heifers outa my way!"

The stray cow lopes nervously back to the line, followed by the dog. Nillmon scans the field for the last cow. A hot wave seizes him, and he gives in to the urge to chuckle under his breath. He looks back at the broken glass on the rear seat. He does not see the rock now, only a haze of smoke in the car.

Suddenly, Fon, his movements like those of a mechanic testing a loose door handle, opens his door, slides out, closes the door firmly and quietly, and walks across the road toward the levee which bends around a clump of trees and past the billboard.

Nillmon, dazed by the sudden movement of the car, aims the pistol at the last cow, but the car rolls over a heap of cow manure and he submits to the urge to curse all dead niggers, but he doesn't say anything then. Through the rearview mirror he sees that the sun is gone and the levee is a thin line hiding the river inlet, and on the road a dog is chasing the car, and in the field the cows are mooing and their bells are banging.

Only shadows fall in front of him now. The shadows in the trees are going over the hill with the cattle, and he sees a light far ahead in the road.

Suddenly he slows the car, leaps out and looks over the countryside. "I shoulda taught that sombitch a lesson," he mutters to himself. When he puts the pistol back in the glove compartment, he brings out the bottle and takes a long drink.

After about three miles on the flat straight road, the light becomes a filling station. Nillmon runs in. An old man with one leg is wiping his hands on greasy rags. "And just whar you been last two weeks? Drunk?"

Nillmon hardly looks at the old man, but breaks through the door leading to the rear of the store which is part of a series of rooms. The top of the house looms in the back. "Where's Gus, Pop?" he asks the old man. "A nigger just about ready to git hisself gutted."

"What nigger?" Pop asks, throwing the rags in the corner. "What's his name?"

Nillmon moves toward the house as the old man hollers, "Gus! Get out here!"

Before Nillmon can ascend a long row of rickety wooden steps up to a screened porch, a figure appears in the screenless doorway. Girlish laughter rises and falls, and the figure, struggling with arms around his waist, yells, "What the hell you want?"

"It's me, Gus." Nillmon approaches.

"Who?"

"Goddammit, it's me." He doesn't advance anymore. "A nigger just bricked my car. I'm goin to get him."

As if Nillmon had spoken something he had been waiting for, Gus, a short wiry man of about thirty years, freezes. He pushes the retreating arms away from his body, tosses his left hand in the air as a signal, and begins a slow deliberate descent. Nillmon turns and walks past the old man.

"Call Sheriff Vacy."

"Where's this nigger?" Gus asks. His words are clear and precise.

"Out at Canebrake. . . . A nigger named Alfonso, a big black sucker."

The figure of a blonde girl stands now in the doorway at the top of the steps. She straightens out her clothing. Pop limps toward her. "I'm goin call Vacy," he mutters. "Gus, I'm callin Vacy, you hear?"

"Yeah," Nillmon hollers, "and tell him we're pickin up Ed Frickerson."

"Naw we ain't." Gus examines Nillmon's pistol. They both take drinks from the bottle and slam the doors.

"Where's the nigger at?" asks the old man, limping out with a bundle of oily rags. "I'm callin everybody."

"Canebrake . . . nigger name Alfonso. . . ."

"Canebrake?"

"You comin?"

"There ain't no niggers livin in them shacks."

Gus looks at the bottle, clears his throat and takes a long swallow. He hands it to Nillmon who finishes it.

"There is now, and there's gonna be one less come sunup."

"Them Canebrake shacks is haunted, I'm tellin you. Niggers ain't live in them since the flood back in . . . you 'member, Gus?" the old man says, limping toward the car. Then he whispers, "The time the nigger woman put hoodoo on Vacy's papa . . ."

"Shut up Pop!"

The old man mumbles.

Nillmon races the motor and jerks the old car off in a cloud of dust. Down the road, just before they turn off, Nillmon flings his arm out the window and the bottle crashes on the road.

They pick up Ed Frickerson about ten miles later at a town café. They get another bottle and circle the town picking up two younger men. Then Nillmon aims the car down the road toward the levee. The faint red crown of the sun is the only thing left of day.

"Vacy's over in Huntsville," says Ed Frickerson. He is ruddy-faced, thick-necked, round-nosed, with a permanent smile wrinkling down his whiskered face.

"I'm the goddamn deputy, ain't I, Gus?" says Nillmon, spitting out the window.

"I want to see the nigger that'll chunk a brick at a white man," says Gus. He has the pistol in his belt and is patting the stick of dynamite steadily in his left hand. "Gus wants to see that boy."

The car moves fast. The men pass the bottle around.

Nillmon describes the last party he attended in Huntsville. They all listen, devouring with fear and a dark relish the exaggerated details that pour out of Nillmon. They all tremble inside as the car turns off onto a dirt road along the levee. All except Gus.

Nillmon drives the car within a few feet of the first shack. The lights illuminate every weather-worn line in the warping boards.

"Alfonso!" Nillmon shouts, standing near the broken step.

There is a silence over the whole night.

The car stalls and cuts off. Gus jumps out of the car, walks up on the porch, pushes once, twice, on the rickety door which falls as if the light from the headlights had struck it. Dust travels across the plane of light like legions of insects. The shack is empty.

The car backs out and then spins out of its own dust. At the second shack they find the same thing. Nillmon snatches up the oily rags. The two younger men light them and hurl them in and under the shack.

"Where'd this nigger chunk that rock from?" asks Gus. He lights up a cigarette. The car races down the road.

Nillmon spits out the window. "Back up the road by that signboard." He feels his hands tighten around the steering wheel.

"Lights down the road," says Ed Frickerson.

"Hell, I know niggers live up here cause I saw about five or six herdin cows."

"What this nigger look like?"

"Like any nigger. Had a nasty tongue. I gotta get me some of him."

They reach the third shack. The outline of the second shack a quarter-mile down the road slowly rises in the flames that leap out of its windows. "Ain't that a crowd of niggers in front of that church over yonder?" asks Ed Frickerson.

Nillmon does not look. The headlights of the car strike

the doorway of the third shack. A figure stands illuminated there, his hands behind his back as if he is contemplating the situation. It is Fon.

"All right, boy!" shouts Nillmon. "I'm back to settle that business 'tween us."

Gus is out of the car, advancing toward Fon in rapid strides. He holds the pistol in his right hand and the empty bottle in the other. Fon steps off the steps before Gus reaches the shack, and heads toward Nillmon, who is now standing right in front of the headlights. Lighted rags fly through the night.

The other men surround Fon. All of a sudden a series of flashes comes from the area of the church. It practically blinds Nillmon. Gus aims the pistol at Fon's head. They shove Fon into the rear between the two younger men. Gus sits in front. Ed Frickerson, who is sitting behind Nillmon, has collected pieces of glass in an oily rag and tosses the mass in Fon's lap. The bright light continues to shine and the men instinctively turn away. Nillmon slows as he approaches the structure which seems like an old church. "What you niggers think you're doin out here?" Ed Frickerson asks Fon.

"Those are my brothers," says Fon.

"What I want to know," says Nillmon, "is who threw that rock."

"It came from the sky."

Gus whirls and strikes at Fon with the bottle, which breaks on the door frame and the glass falls in Fon's lap. "You *are* a smart nigger." He jabs the bottle neck at Fon, and the sharp edges dig deeply into Fon's side.

Nillmon slows the car in front of a column of black people. They murmur and stare inside the car.

"Keep goin!" shouts Gus.

Suddenly they see Fon inside, and a cheer leaps up from them such as the white men have never heard. A sound of distance and presence, a shaking in the air which comes from that invisible song, that body of memory, ancient. A long sustained roar from the bottom of the land, rising, rising. . . .

"Move out!" shouts Gus.

The car jerks forward and the light from the church follows it far, far in the distance. . . .

The headlights strike the billboard. The sign is old and worn. They shove Fon from the car and push him beneath the wooden structure. The night crowds in around the sharp line of the car's headlights. They make torches with the rags.

"All right nigger, git on your knees." Gus wraps his bloody fist in a rag.

Fon—slumped slightly, his right hand touching the ground lightly by his right knee—does not blink in the direct light of the headlights. Nor does he look in the faces of the men around him. They are lighting torches and threatening him. Only Nillmon speaks to him. Fon watches the trees and the long shadows of the beams.

"Boy, what you mean, that rock come from the sky? I thought you said your brother chunked it."

"My brother shoots only arrows."

"Goddammit, you gonna let your brother go, while you go to Hell?" asks Ed Frickerson.

"I'm not *goin* to Hell," says Fon.

Ed Frickerson stuffs the dynamite in Fon's rear pocket. Gus lights the last torch.

Nillmon seems confused. He eyes Fon. This nigger still ain't broke.

"Nigger, you mighty popular, eh? You know how to pray?"

"Prayer is for people who want help," says Fon.

A torch is pushed near Fon's feet.

"Where's your goddamn brother now?"

Fon does not answer right away, but seems to watch the flickering of the shadows from the torches. High in the heavens now, a star comes into view from the clouds. A thin glow from a hidden moon peeps ominously from a horizon of clouds.

"My brother is in the trees somewhere, now."

Gus slaps Fon. One of the lights of the car goes out. Something has broken it. A puff of blue smoke sails away from the dying light. One of the torches falls, and Nillmon, standing next to Fon, thinks he hears a man's voice moan. "Gimme the pistol." Nillmon turns to see Gus—the pistol falling from his hand—stumbling, clutching an arrow which has completely pierced his neck. Suddenly the other light explodes, and the only light is the darting flame from the dying torches on the ground. Nillmon leaps to where he thinks he saw the pistol fall. . . .

But as he leaps he finds that he is falling, grabbing a sharp pain in his neck.

Silence.

In the distance a dog barks and Fon hears the faint sound of a cowbell. He clutches his side and walks deliberately over to each torch, stomps it out with bare feet. He thinks, *that was mighty close. But it is better this way. To have looked at them would have been too much. Four centuries of black eyes burning into four weak white men . . . would've set the whole earth on fire. Not yet,* he thinks, *not yet.* . . . He turns toward the levee where a light in the night reaches out to him and to the great distance between him and the far blinking of the stars. The light from the church reaches out almost to him. They are expecting him back. . . . When the tower is finished. . . . One more black stone. He will be able to see how to walk back. A fragment of the night, kicking, kicking, at the gnawing teeth of the earth.

C. H. Fuller, Jr.

A LOVE SONG FOR SEVEN
LITTLE BOYS CALLED; SAM

THE SEVEN had been confined, since the first grade, to their own special section of the class. This year, as expected, their teacher, Miss Arnold, had seated them in the rear near the door. It was close to the lavatory, but otherwise it was the worse spot in the third grade. They were all eight years old, except for Reuben, who was eight-and-a-half. He sat at his desk, staring at Miss Arnold's wide nose, and recalling that his mother had promised a surprise for his birthday, *if* he got an "A" in Spelling. He didn't like his mother's surprises, or Miss Arnold. His mother always surprised him with clothes, and his teacher always complained about the way he dressed. But he did wish he was nine. When you're nine, you're bigger, and nobody messed with you; like the white boys did every afternoon.

He bet if he and his friends were all nine, the white kids would leave them alone. Not that the seven of them couldn't fight. Stevie, Billy, Allen, Francis, Harold, and Kenny were the best fighters he'd ever seen. It was just that *every day* they had to fight, and Reuben was sick of it. The bell in the Ingram Elementary School rang, and its only black pupils, seven little boys, picked up their schoolbags, and started outside into the afternoon chill.

No one talked to them. Even Miss Arnold, the lone colored teacher in the school, shunned them, except for the two times she complained about the way they talked.

Reuben watched her now, crossing the street against the
light, holding the hands of two little white boys. She never
took his hand—he wouldn't let her either! If she didn't like
them, he didn't like her. The seven of them waited at the
corner, and sprinted across on the traffic lady's signal. Reuben
sucked in a deep breath, and pivoted around. The daily
trouble was just about to begin, and he wondered why, when
they stopped the buses in the first grade, they didn't send
them to a school in their own neighborhood.

"Hey Sams! Hey look 'et all the little black Sams!" A group
of five second-graders shot past them, their schoolbags swinging, their white faces, red with excitement.

"Your mother's a Sam!" It was Billy. He always talked
about people's mothers. Reuben didn't like that stuff, and
if they played the "dozens" with him, somebody was gonna'
get hurt.

"Your mother's a black dog," one yelled.

"When I catch you, I'ma' punch you in the mouth, hear?
I don't play that stuff, boy!"

"Awwww, shut up, blackie! Old black Billy, and ole black
joe, must be niggers, 'cause they run so slow!"

"Old black Sams! Seven old black Sams!"

The white kids continued to run. When they reached the
corner, they turned and headed west, but not before Allen
picked up a stone, and threw it. It hit the boy on the leg;
he stopped momentarily, looked at the bruise it had made,
then kept going when he realized Allen was almost on top
of him.

It was the same everyday. Reuben had gotten used to it.
There were three blocks of enemy territory. Every afternoon,
the older white boys would send the little white boys darting
past them, shouting "Sam," "blackie" or "nigger." Then,
after the first block, they would meet a group of the older
boys, who'd blame them for chasing the little boys, and after
a fight, the seven of them would be chased home. Reuben
hated it.

The white kids had been doing it every day for a month. He didn't understand white people. They sit next to you in school, and beat you up on the way home. They can't be trusted. Once they passed the graveyard they would be safe. Black people lived on the other side of those graves, and the white boys never chased them that far. "Over there, they wouldn' mess with me," Reuben thought, preparing himself for what would happen when they reached the next corner. "Billy! Billy Mayfield!" It was Miss Arnold. Reuben recognized the weak, scratchy voice. Her hard, black face was staring at Billy. She was a witch.

"Yes, Miss Arnold?"

"What did you say to those boys?"

"I didn' say nothin'!"

"I heard you! You want me to send a note to your mother?"

"He had no business callin' me nigger! My name ain't no nigger!"

"Billy, sticks and stones may break my bones, but names will never harm me! You ought to be glad you can go to school with different kinds of people."

"My name ain't nigger—Mom told me to let nobody call me that!"

"Well, we'll see what your mother has to say!"

"I didn' do nothin'!"

"Goodbye, Billy."

"I didn' do nothin'!—and my mother ain't gonna' do nothin' to me either! 'cause my name ain't no nigger!"

"Why they kept you kids in the school I'll never know—" She mumbled something else, but they didn't hear her. Harold Davis called her a black bitch behind her back. She disappeared into a store. "She don't never say nothin' to them," Reuben said, aware that this had a great deal to do with why he disliked her.

"My father said, she's prejudice," Harold Davis said, leaping out in front of them.

"What's that," Kenny asked.

"You don't know nothin' Kenny! My mother said only white people are prejudice. 'Cause white people don't like black people—and she said only white people do prejudice. I know all about that," Stevie put in.

"Well, Miss Arnold ain't white!" Kenny looked around at them. They were all silent for a moment.

"My father said, some colored people do it too, but white people do it all the time," Harold Davis said authoritatively. It satisfied Reuben. Harold Davis knew everything.

"Hey! What took you Sambos so long? You scared or something?" Reuben looked up at the corner and wanted to cry. There were a dozen white boys blocking the sidewalk, and swinging their schoolbags in a preparatory challenge. Reuben tried to slow down, and even wished he could leave his friends and run home, but he didn't do either. There was an attraction in this daily meeting. Something compelling in twisted expressions of the white boys made him want to take every opportunity to smash the ugliness from their faces. The sight of their hate for him made him angry. No one had a right to look at him that way! There was a moment of stillness. Suddenly everyone was moving. Harold was the first to run. He charged into the boy at the head of the gang, his schoolbag aimed at the white boy's head. Reuben felt himself running. Billy was screaming like an Indian, and swinging his fists at everything in his path. Everyone was yelling, and at one point, Reuben heard Francis crying, and knew his friend had been angered sufficiently enough to want to kill. Reuben ran straight at a blond-haired boy with large freckles, and bucked teeth. The boy made the mistake of charging forward, and when fear suddenly gripped him, trying to run away. He had already knocked down two boys, as he tried to get out of Reuben's way. Reuben instinctively followed through the escape path the white boy had made, swinging at the boy who was hollering hysterically. When he was through, Reuben turned around and kicked someone in the leg, and felt a schoolbag smash into his own face. It shocked him for a moment, and someone else punched him in the stomach before he had a chance to grab at one boy's hair and try to pull it out. Someone struck him with a stone on the hand, and he watched, horrified, as the skin curled up in a twisted black ball, and black flesh suddenly spurted red. He kicked his assailant, saw Francis spit on a red-haired boy's coat, and heard Harold screaming. They had knocked Harold down! One boy was leaning over him, and casually punching him in the face! An instant later, he and Kenny were pushing and kicking people off Harold and helping him up. Reuben punched someone in the nose, and watched another boy examine the sudden rush of blood before cursing him. They had almost made it. Kenny and Harold were already running, and the others were far ahead. Once they got started, the white boys could never catch them. The seven of them ran like the wind. Reuben, as he bolted away from the white gang, hadn't run far when Billy screamed "WATCH OUT, REUBEN!"

He tried to dodge what was behind him, and as he turned, he heard it. His coat was tearing. His three-month-old coat was being ripped by a sandy-haired white boy with a jagged can. Reuben swung, just as the boy turned and ran. He started after him but realized he would be running into the charging gang. He'd get the boy later, he thought, angry enough to cry. He turned and joined his friends in the one-block sprint to the graveyard. They crossed the street and stopped.

"You tore my coat! I'm a' git you for that!" He was staring at the boy.

"Why don'tcha come here and git me, blackie?"

"You black nigger!"

"You wait! I'm a' beat your ass!" He said the curse word softly, afraid someone his mother knew might hear him.

"Awwww, go on home, blackie! We can get you tomorrow!"

"You better run, Sambo!"

"Your mother better run," Billy shouted. They started home.

Reuben was worried. Not simply because of his torn coat. His mother's outrage was predictable, but the thought had just occurred to him, that if they didn't stop those white boys they'd be chased home for the rest of their lives. He didn't tell the others but it scared him, and he wished magically the white boys would disappear. If he had a machine gun, he bet they would leave him alone. But he didn't have one. He had a right to go home in peace. Why didn't they let him? His father had said, white people always bother Negro people, and when he had asked him why, he recalled his father saying, 'cause Negro people don't fight back! He and his friends fought back every day, and still got chased. His father had missed something. He said goodbye to his friends, and went into his house.

"Reuben, that you?"

"Yeah."

"What's the matter?" He didn't answer his mother. Instead, he took off his coat in the vestibule and placed it over his arm with the torn portion folded in, where she couldn't see it. "Reuben, what are you doing?"

"Nothin'!" He walked into the kitchen with his hands in his pockets.

"Mom, I don't wanna' go to that school no more."

"What?" His mother turned away from the sink and put potatoes on the stove, then wiped her hands on her green apron. "What's the matter, Reuben?"

"Them white boys is always fightin'."

She looked at him for a moment. "Reuben, what happened to your coat?"

"Nothin'."

"Reuben!" She grabbed the coat from his arm. "What?"
"I didn't do it, Mom! That white boy tore it!"
"Reuben, you let some boy tear your coat? What is wrong
with you?" She shook him. Reuben was crying.
"It wasn't my fault, Mom! I couldn't help it! They chased
us!" He heard his mother say, 'Damnit,' something she never
said unless she was upset.
"What you let them chase you for?"
"They do it every day!"
"Well, can't you fight? Hit 'em back when they hit you!"
"It's too many."
"Go someplace! Go someplace before I whip you! Your
father spends good money for a coat, and you let somebody
tear it up? Go ahead, Reuben! Just go before I give you a
beating! Wait 'til your father gets home. Get outta' my
sight!"
"It wasn't my fault. It wasn't!" He went to his room, and
slammed the door. For a moment he stood there, so angry
he wanted to tear the door from its hinges. He couldn't help
it if they chased him everyday! He had tried to be friendly
like his mother had told him, but they didn't want to be
friends. All they wanted to do was fight, and call names. Now,
they even had his own family against him, and he hated
them for it. If only he was bigger, stronger. It wasn't his
fault! It wasn't! He fell across his bed in tears.
When he heard his father, he sat up on the bed. He was
sure his mother was going to tell. She couldn't keep a secret,
no matter what.
"Reuben! Reuben, come here!" He went downstairs crying. "What's this about lettin' some boy tear your coat?"
"They wanna' fight all the time, Daddy, an' call us names!"
"Who? What did they call you?"
"Them white boys—they called me nigger!"
"And what did you do?"
"I punched one in the nose, and bloodied his face!"

"I tol' you not to let him go to that damn school, Willa Mae! I told you! He don't need to go to no white school—and as long as he does, I want them to keep their damn hands off him! I'm sick of it! Reuben, don't come in here agin' with your clothes ripped up. You figure out somethin' to make them leave you alone, you hear? I'm not playin' either. Now eat your dinner!" Reuben ran to the kitchen.

"It's not his fault," his father said. "It's them damn white kids, Willa Mae! You think they'd have better sense than to teach that shit to their kids! Goddamn white people! No! You wanted him in there, and he's gonna' stay! Reuben's got to learn that you don't let people walk over you! If we take him out, he'll be runnin' all his life. Once he beats them, they'll leave him alone—I'm not gonna walk him from school, and neither are you!"

Reuben didn't eat much dinner, and when he went to bed, he lay there for a long time, trying to figure out something that would stop the fighting. He considered himself lucky. His father didn't whip him. Maybe Pop understood it wasn't his fault. He watched the white boys on his ceiling. They were standing in a gang, and the sandy-haired boy was out front, threatening him with another tin can. He cursed at Reuben, and Reuben swung at him, and the boy's face disappeared only to be replaced by an entire group that looked just like him. He pulled his blanket over his head. He had to think of something. It came to him, just before he fell asleep. When he took a final glance at the ceiling, the white boys were gone.

The following day, just before the bell sounded the end of the school, Miss Arnold spoke to the class. There was something hanging from her nose, and it annoyed Reuben that this woman, behind her big desk, could scold them, when she didn't have sense enough to blow her own nose. But she wouldn't bother him anymore, after today. Everything was going to change today.

"Now, children, someone told me that the white boys were fighting their colored friends. Is that true?"

"Yeah, teacher. That punk called me 'nigger'!" Billy stood and pointed to the blond-haired kid.

"I didn't!"

"You did—and I'm a' get you."

"I didn't!"

"I'm sure he didn't mean it, Billy. You didn't mean what you called Billy, did you, Gavin?"

"Nooooo, Miss Arnold!"

"OOOO, you liar!"

"Billy, sit down!"

"I'm a' gitcha', hear? I don't take that stuff!"

"Sit down!" She shook her head.

When the bell rang, the seven of them bolted from the room. Reuben had told them his plan on the way to school, and they rushed from the class to execute it. It was going to be over—today. Miss Arnold came out of the building with two little white boys, as she always did. When she approached Reuben, she waved a warning finger at him. He waited until she had crossed the street, and with Billy and Harold Davis, followed behind her. Allen, Stevie, Francis and Kenny were out of sight now, and it was a part of the plan for the three of them to stay close to Miss Arnold.

"Hey, Sammy! Hey, black Sams!"

"Little black Sambo!" The little kids sprinted past them. Billy started to shout something but decided against it when Miss Arnold turned around and stared at him.

"Billy, remember, sticks and stones."

"Yes, Miss Arnold."

Reuben looked at her and laughed. She was a part of the plan, and didn't know it. She'd take them to the corner, and not only get an opportunity to see the boys waiting for them, but help, by her presence, to frighten them. The white boys were already gathering on the corner. "Hey, Miss Arnold!

Look at them boys! See what I tol' you? All they wanna'
do is fight, and call us names!"

The woman looked up suddenly, and her expression told
Reuben that she was not only shocked, but afraid as well.
The white boys were blocking the sidewalk, this time in a
large circle. The first two boys held up tin cans menacingly.
Miss Arnold was speechless, and when she did open her
mouth, she stuttered.

"You boys! You boys—what—what are you doing there? I
don't want any fighting. Go home! You heard me! Go home
before I report you." Several white boys backed up.

"You Sams is scared, aintcha'?"

"They gotta' go home wif' the teacher!"

"Did you boys hear me? I said go home!"

"Awww shut up!"

"Who said that? Who said it?—what grade—?"

"Black Miss Arnold, like a dirty carmel! Black Miss Arnold
like a dirty carmel!"

"We don't want no black teacher!" One boy leaped away
from the crowd his hands on his hips. "Go back where you
came from!"

Reuben was glad they'd hurt her. She stood in front of
them, her mouth wide open, her eyes large and glassy. It
serves her right, he thought. He was the first to run. While
the white boys' attention was on Miss Arnold, Reuben, Billy
and Harold charged, striking the first blow at the boy who
stood with his hands on his hips. The sudden attack came as
a surprise to the boys, and for a while they retreated. Harold
was whooping like an Indian, and punching a tall, skinny
boy in the back until the boy collided with a parked car,
and skinned his face on the fender. The white boys didn't run
far. Halfway up the block they scattered in every direction,
running on stoops and hiding in doorways. Allen, Francis,
Stevie and Kenny had been waiting for them, and the first
white boy who approached them was slammed in the face

with a rock. Reuben's plan worked, and he started swinging at them as they raced back trying to dodge stones. He grabbed one boy by the collar, and tripped him to the ground, kicking him in the leg. Another boy he garroted, and out the corner of his eye saw Harold pin a red-haired boy against a wall. He punched the boy he had tripped in the side, and ran by Harold, and slapped the red-haired boy in the face. It would end today, he was sure of it. The boy he slapped started crying, just as he saw the kid who had torn his coat. He noticed, momentarily, a panorama of screaming, crying white boys, running everywhere, and Stevie's foot going high in the air, and a fat boy running with his hands over his head, and no one chasing him. He sprinted after the sandy-haired boy, who, when he saw Reuben, started screaming "he didn't mean it." Reuben caught him at the corner right in front of Miss Arnold, and knocked him down. The boy was hysterical—screaming, kicking, and at one point, Reuben thought he might faint.

"I'm a' tear your coat!"

"I didn't mean it. I'm sorry, Reuben! I'm sorry! Please! I didn't—"

Reuben punched him once and stood. It had just occurred to him that the boy was deathly afraid, and for the first time since he had been in the Ingram School, a white boy had used his name. They were beaten. Reuben walked back to his friends.

"Did you tear his coat?"

"Nawwww."

"Why not? I'd a' tore his coat and bloodied his nose, man." Billy stuck his chest out.

"Man, I beat the piss outta' one guy," Allen said.

They turned around when they reached the graveyard. The white boys were going home in two's and three's. There were no names being shouted, no one throwing stones. Reuben knew why he felt good, but he wasn't sure why he

suddenly liked his friends so much. They seemed different
now. Stronger. Taller.

Miss Arnold was still on the corner, staring at them. Reuben didn't feel sorry for her. She hadn't shared in their
victory, and tomorrow she'd punish them. He didn't understand her. At least the white boys had what they believed was
a reason for disliking them.

But what about Miss Arnold? She was the same color as
he was. Maybe she wanted to be white? The thought made
him laugh. They put their arms around each other's shoulders,
and started home.

"We're rough. We're tough. We black boys don't take no
stuff!"

From that day on, they didn't.

Julia Fields

NOT YOUR SINGING,
DANCING SPADE

IT WAS ridiculous to have an issue of such an insipidly written magazine in the apartment, he knew. Nevertheless, he picked it up again and began to read the article written about himself. The audacity of it, and the incredible and insane arrogance it suggested, made him feel helpless against the terrible tide of consciousness so established and so knowledgeable to him and to his people. His brains were sealed, signed for and delivered, just as his body would have been in the previous century.

He focused his eyes and finished the article, his black hands and black eyes drooping wearily over the side of the plush gold sofa. Then he lay down upon it, keeping his shoes on. It was not very comforting at all.

The article stated clearly that his childhood dream had been to pursue and to possess a "blonde goddess," that he could never be happy without her. It made fun of a black entertainer he had dated. It said he paid her to give him his "freedom." There was no picture of her. But there was a listing and pictures of national and international ladies with fair hair to whom he had been linked romantically at one time or another.

There was a picture of him with his wife—his wife bright and grinning, and his teeth matching her fairness kilometer for kilometer. His hair was falling into his eyes. It always seemed to be fallen into his eyes, whenever he was playing

479

golf, or driving, or dancing, or singing. And he always had to toss his head, give his neck a quick snappy jerk in order to keep his tumbling hair neat. It always got into his eyes. He bent over to light a cigarette. The hair fell into his eyes. He used his free hand to brush it back, knowing that it would tumble into his eyes again.

His wife entered the room. She was very, very white. He had asked her to stay out of the sun. And the black maid entered with a tray of beverages. The children liked the maid and his wife liked the maid. He hated her. She was almost as black as himself, and her hair was short. He always felt like singing an old down-home blues whenever he saw her . . . "I don't want no woman if her hair ain't no longer'n mine; she ain't nothing but trouble and keep you worried all the time." But no matter how much hatred he showed towards her, the woman was always kind and serene; yet, there was the very faintest hint of laughter and incredible mockery in her eyes when she looked at him. He knew the look. He himself had given it to others many times. He remembered the party in Greenwich Village, the interracial party with all the loud music and the loud dancing, which belonged to a younger time than now.

There was a colored girl there, he was told, but all the girls looked of the same race because there was not the brightest lighting. Still he thought that he would know a "Sapphire" if he saw one. The girl's white date had laughed at him for saying this, and slapped him on the back. He had felt so clever, so able to take "it," so "free," so optimistic, so "in," and that was when he knew that he could make it if he chose to make it in the big world of the American dream. And this world, as he knew it, was not white. It was a gray world with room in it for all the people. He felt so "in" that he almost blessed Emma Lazarus.

A group of them were laughingly trying to sing a foolish ditty with dirty words. They were all so happy and drunk.

And there was a girl whose hands kept going to her temple and down behind her ears with long locks of hair which she pushed over her shoulder. Then she would toss her hair, or attempt to, but the long hair barely moved. The long strands did not move freely. They seemed waxen, stuck around her face like fetters. His hands went to his own head in sudden derision, and stuck in the Dixie Peach. The girl swung her head again and caught his eyes. He looked into her eyes as deeply as he could, and his bitterness spilled like a white sizzle across to her in mockery and despair and a tender, compassionate hatred.

The boy who had slapped him on the back moved toward the girl, caught her by the hand and began to dance with her, his hips swaying, brutally ungraceful in mock-Negro.

He went to the window. Dawn was moving up to the river and over the roofs. It was time for him to go. He knew that he would never go to another party with a Negro. No matter what color the Negro was—they were all embarrassing. He might go if he were the only one. Only if he were.

He knew that his wife somehow resulted from this promise which he had made to himself a long time ago at the Village party. He had come a long way. His name, his picture, his life, were on the lips and the life-sized posters of the world. Subway bums, whores and dogs could lean against his photograph in most of the world's swinging cities. And he was very wealthy. He had his own entourage of jesters and the best hairdresser in the world—one who kept him well stocked with the best pomade.

The article in the magazine shouldn't have bothered him so much, he told himself. It wasn't the first time, nor would it be the last. He had to pay the price. They were requiring it of him, and he had to make it. He had to keep making it. It was too late to stop. Where would he go? There was no place elsewhere but down. Down to scorn. Back, slowly, but certainly, to a world which had become alien, black, strange and nameless. The wolves would chew him black.

Back to black indeed. Never. What did it matter? The whites had begun their assaults late; the blacks had berated him all his life. "Black bastard. Black bastard. Bad hair." "Boy, get a brush." And comparisons: "Almost Bunky's color." "No, not quite as black as Bunky." "Child, I couldn't see nuthin' but eyes and teeth." "I like him, sure, but my daddy would kill me if I married a man that black." "Child, I wouldn't want to mess up my children with that color." He was recalling the words of parents, relatives and lovers. His yellow mother. His jet-black father who was his mother's footstool. His mother's freckles. Her rituals with Black and White ointment. Her "straight" nose. He hated his flat nose. All of his pictures were in profile. Except the one in the magazine. In that one, all of his black faults were on view. In that picture, the heat had turned the expensive pomade on his hair to plain and simple shining grease. Ah, chicken-eaters of the world, unite. You have nothing to lose except your shame.

He began to dress, immaculately as always, for there was, his agent had said, a chance to make another million. Melanin and millions. Millions and melanin.

Numbly, he moved about the dressing room, larger than his parents' living room had been.

Mutely, he dressed. Dejectedly, he faced himself in the mirror. Silently, the green gall of self-revulsion passed through his psyche and soul. Swiftly, he recalled the chance to make a million and the wife who would spend it on furs, jewels, fun, cosmetics and servants. And the whole world would see what black bastards with millions and melanin could do. Yes, they would.

The agent's smooth voice, on the phone, reassured him about the million. There was nothing to reassure him about himself. Nothing. Nothing.

Down the stairs, voices were shrill suddenly. His little girl was sobbing. He heard the maid say, "Be quiet. You'll wake up your mama."

"But Cathy said my daddy's a nigger monkey."

"What do you care what Cathy says?"

"And Daddy puts gasoline in his hair to make it nice like her daddy's hair. Isn't Daddy's hair nice?"

"Of course it's nice. That little sickly Cathy with those strings hanging 'round her face. Don't pay her no attention. She's just jealous because your daddy's got the original beauty."

"The what?"

"The first, best beauty in the world. Black. Your daddy's a pretty man. That's why everybody likes him. Where've you seen Cathy's daddy's pictures? Not nearly's many places as your daddy. Your daddy is a beautiful man."

"Is he?"

"Yes. Of course he don't know how pretty he is. Anyhow, it's easy to be pale. Like milk. It ain't got nothing in it. Like vanilla ice cream. See? Now take any other flavor. Take chocolate. Milk with cocoa. You love chocolate malt, don't you?"

"Yes."

"Take strawberry. Any ice cream. It's nothing as just plain milk. What goes in makes it beautiful. It can be decorated, but by itself, it lacks a lot. Your daddy was born decorated. Born a pretty king. Born beautiful. Don't believe Cathy. She's dumb."

"Born beautiful. Daddy was born beautiful. That silly Cathy. She's a dumb one. My Daddy is pretty. I always thought so."

"Yes, I always thought so, too."

Numbly, he stood there. He had to listen. The annihilated searching, seeking to be. Terror. Who had first given assumption and such supreme arrogance to the captives? He knew she had read the article which had denied her existence. A black female. The race and sex which, according to them, could never move him to love, to cherish, to desire. *Caldonia, Caldonia, what makes your big head so hard?*

He remembered his boyhood. And all the lyrics which laughed at and lamented black womanhood. Blackness. Black manhood. Black childhood. Black.

They had made the world for him, had set all the traps. He had been born to it. The horror of blackness. They had outdone themselves. They had outdone him. And it was not meant that he should ever be saved. He must believe. And they could assume postures and lies. And they could believe in his self-hatred. And they could rest comfortably, believing that he believed, and continue their believing.

They were so arrogant, so stupefied by history and circumstances that they could accept any incredible thing they said about him. Terror. Who was the bondsman? Who was the freed man? He knew.

Life began to flow again. His blood sang vital and red. Freedom. Power, even. Yes, I *am* beautiful. Born black. Born with no lack. Decorated. Born decorated.

At the foot of the stairs, he could hear the maid again, angrily muttering. With dancer's feet, he moved nearer. Nearer to hear, nearer to self, to recovery.

"Lies, lies, lies. Sometimes we have to lie to make it. Even to live. We got to lie to ourselves, to our friends and to our enemies. To those we love and to those we hates. If they so smart they ain't got to b'lieve us."

He saw her throw the movie magazine clear down his long, sumptuous living room. And he heard his little daughter laughing as she went to get the magazine.

"Here. Put it in the trash can."

"But it's got Daddy's picture. Daddy's picture's in it."

"Your daddy's picture's everywhere. Besides, that's not a good picture of him. Some fool took it. Here." The child obeyed.

"Arrogant, uppity folks'll believe anything. Let 'em pay. And pay. White bastards."

"What? What?" The child questioned.

"Nothing. Go on to the playroom until I call you for lunch. I got to vacuum up this room."

Then he was there standing in the beautiful, luxurious room facing the black woman with the short hair.

"Humph," he heard her say as she turned to push a low, red, incredulously plush and ridiculously expensive chair aside for her vacuuming.

"Here, let me be of service," he said.

"Never mind."

"Let me!" he said again, and gently pushed her aside.

"Humph," she said again. But he got a glimpse of her face, which had years of anger and defiance and hope written in chicken-scratch wrinkles and crows' feet. And there was the mockery he always saw there. And yet, a kindness, a laughter which was very sweet and strong. And the barest hint of tears in the eyes, tears like monuments to despair.

When he replaced the chairs and kissed his wife and child, he said his goodbye to the black woman and sang a snatch of his latest recording as he walked to the elevator. He felt light—weightless and yet strong and pretty. "I feel pretty," he thought. Well, not that kind of pretty, he mocked himself. But it was surprising that he sang, for he had promised himself that he was only an entertainer, that he wasn't your singing, dancing spade, that he, a professional only, wouldn't be caught dead, drunk or straitlaced, singing off the stage or away from the T.V. cameras, or dancing like some ham-hocking jigaboo.

Nevertheless, his chauffeur smiled happily when he cut a step from his latest musical sensation as he entered the limousine with the sacrilegious words, "I feel pretty," floating, cakewalking from his lips.

Jean Wheeler Smith

THAT SHE WOULD
DANCE NO MORE

Ossie Lee came into the café to drink some beer. He had
worked hard today. It had rained too much to do any plowing—couldn't put a tractor out in that Delta land when it
was wet. The rich, loose top soil was so deep that a tractor
would sink down in it. So his boss man had made him dig
ditches all day, ditches that led nowhere. The man had only
required the work of him in order to keep him busy. And
Ossie Lee had had to dig the ditches. There wasn't much else
he could do. He lived on the man's place, in his house, owed
him money.

But Ossie Lee set aside his thoughts. He wouldn't worry
about all that now. Just sit here and rest a while, spend the
dollar he had in his pocket for some beer, and wait on his
friends from the other plantations to come around. "Miss
Lula, bring me a quart of Falstaff and some skins."

Miss Lula came over to the table. She was a big woman,
not yet old, maybe forty-nine. She called everybody "baby."
"How you doing, baby? Look like you been working hard.
Got that mud all over your clothes, in your hair. A good-
looking man like you ought to take better care of himself.
You still young—how old are you, 'bout thirty-five?"

"I'm thirty-eight, Miss Lula."

Miss Lula raised her voice so that the rest of the people
in the café could enjoy the exchange. "Well, you sure don't
look a day over thirty-five. Maybe 'cause you still got a good

486

body, strong, not all broke down like a lot of the men around here. And I always did like the way you held yourself. You know, like couldn't nobody walk over you." Miss Lula was smiling; she was pleased to be able to speak so well of him. Maybe he'd feel a little better now.

Ossie Lee appreciated her effort and replied in kind. "Well, Miss Lula, I always liked the way you carried yourself, too. It took some doing to keep the café open without even a man to help you. You a pretty good old lady, even if you are getting fat from your own cooking."

She feinted a slap at his head for this little insult and then resumed her businesslike air. "I got to see what Jimmie Lee and them want over at the bar. I'll bring you your Falstaff soon's I take care of them. I got some good neckbones cooked in the back. You want to try some?"

"No, Miss Lula, I ate at Mama's already. Just bring me the beer."

Ossie Lee put his foot up on the next chair and looked around to see who was there. It had taken him a while to get used to the darkness. The only light came from the Schlitz beer signs, with the luxuriously dressed brown girls, and from the music box which commanded one end of the small café. Nobody was there that he knew. Well, he'd just wait. Nothing else to do. No reason to go home.

There were two girls sitting over in the corner of the café. He had not seen them before, but they looked like they might be sisters. The smaller girl was very pretty. She was black and so thin that you felt you could see everything that was happening within her, the movement of every muscle, the angle of every bone. He liked the way she looked. He figured that they were from up on Mr. Mills' place. He had heard that Mills had brought in a new family up there.

Miss Lula returned to his table. "Here, baby, here's your Falstaff." She noticed Ossie Lee's feet in her chair. Her lips tightened. "Now, why you want to mess up my chairs, putting your feet on them? Come on and do right. Always wanting me to keep this place but you-all won't help me to keep it up. You thirty-eight years old, had a house of your own, you know how to treat other people's things."

Ossie Lee was offended, but he took his feet down. He couldn't afford to get her mad with him. Miss Lula had a shotgun back there that she would put to anybody.

Seeing that she had put Ossie Lee in his place, she resumed her friendly manner. She said, "I guess you pretty lonesome now since your wife left you. I never did know what happened. What did happen?"

"Nothing much. She was messing around James Edward —you know him, he live down on Mr. Henderson's place— and I wasn't going to have that. Everytime I told her about it she tried to get smart with me. So I'd just have to whip her. She musta got tired of that. One day she went down the road to the store and just kept walking. Didn't even take her clothes."

"Yeah, well where is she now?"

"She sent three bus tickets for the children. The tickets were to Memphis. I guess that's where she is now."

Miss Lula stood quietly at the table for a moment. Then she directed his attention across the room. "You see those two girls over there in the corner? They just come over to this county. Come from up in Tallahatchie County a week ago. Some nice girls, too, named Minnie Pearl and Johnnie Mae. The thin little black one with the yellow dress on, Minnie Pearl, she loves to dance. Why don't you put a quarter in the music box. She'll dance for you."

Ossie Lee looked at the thirty cents he had left from his dollar. He weighed the value of spending it now on the little black girl against the possibility that later he might get somebody to match it and buy another quart of beer. He didn't know anything about the girl. But she did look nice. She was a pretty girl. He hadn't been getting much satisfaction from drinking beer, or from doing anything else, lately. Seemed like no matter what he did, he couldn't get satisfied. The disappointments of his life weighed heavily on him.

In fact, Ossie Lee had, for the sake of his sanity, accepted his life situation. He had yielded to it long ago, at the age of eight. The acceptance of his life style had been irrevocably forced upon him the night they came to take him.

That night they called Ossie Lee's father to the door. They were two. "Jesse, come here. Want to talk to you bout that smart-acting boy of yours."

His father turned to his mother. "Get them in the back, Sarah Mae." She hurried the children, ranging in age from eighteen years to three months, into the back of the two-room house. His father went to the front door, forced a smile to his face. "How y'all this evening?"

"We fine, Jesse. Only thing wrong with us is that boy of yours, Ossie Lee. He let one of my chickens get run over this morning. Send him out here. Got to teach him a lesson. He got to learn to take care of property, else he ain't never going to be a good hand."

Ossie Lee saw his father's shoulders drop. "Well, sir, Mr. Perry, I knew he been running too much, ain't got good sense yet. But he still young. I give him a good whipping tonight. He do better."

"No, Jesse, I think I ought to take care of this myself. He going to be working for me thirty, forty years; he got to learn how to take care of my things."

Realizing that he was in trouble, Ossie Lee slipped over to where his mother had gathered the smallest children. Perry, ignoring Ossie Lee's father, walked straight through the house and into the back. He had a long cotton sack on his arm. "Sarah Mae, give me the boy." Ossie Lee's arms went around his mother's waist. She folded him into her skirt, pressed him to her. She pleaded with the boss man, "Please, sir, don't take him off. He just a baby. Just made eight years. We take care he don't do nothing like that no more. Spare him this one time. He just a baby."

Perry did not bother to respond. Ossie Lee looked up at his mother and over to his father for help. Neither his father nor his mother could look back into his face. He began to cry, "No, Mama, don't let him take me. Mama, Daddy, Mama." In support of him, the other children set to crying. Perry seemed not to hear or to see any of them. He leaned over to Ossie Lee, pulled him from his mother and, despite the boy's kicking and struggling, forced him into the cotton sack. As Perry moved toward the door, no one offered resistance.

Ossie Lee cried hard. He knew that they must have heard him. Were they going to let this man take him away? Why didn't they run after him and pull the sack from his hands? Mama, Daddy, you always took care of me. Where are you?

Perry carried the boy out in the sack and handed him to the other man, who had been waiting in the truck. He cranked up the truck and drove away. No one came even to the porch to see in what direction their boy had been taken. As the truck moved away, Ossie Lee came to understand that his people could neither refuse to let him be taken, nor even demand the knowledge of where he would be taken. Understanding this, he himself ceased to struggle against so obviously powerful a force. His kicking subsided, his crying ceased, his muscles relaxed. He merely waited to see what they would do to him.

After riding about ten minutes, the truck stopped. Ossie Lee was pulled from the truck and emptied from the sack onto the ground. They had come to the muddy river where Ossie Lee had fished only a few days earlier. The white men stood over him. Perry said, "Boy, you been mighty careless lately, letting that chicken get run over. Don't seem like you want to be a good hand, do it?"

Ossie Lee's immediate reaction was to defend himself, to

assert that he had been watching the chickens as best he could but that there had just been too many of them, that he couldn't have kept up with all those chickens. But then he checked himself; he admitted that nothing he said would matter to these powerful men, that it was their show and not his. Accordingly he replied, "That's right, sir, look like I ain't able to be no good hand."

Perry went on. "You got to learn to take care of property. That's what's wrong with you colored people now. You don't know how to take care of nothing. I'm going to give you this whipping so you'll watch after them chickens from now on. Get your britches down."

For the last time, Ossie Lee's self revolted "No, not my clothes; you can't make me take off my clothes. Daddy don't even do that. No!"

Perry stood over him. "You not going to do what I tell you? Well, I'll take them off for you." And, ignoring the last willful act that Ossie Lee was to perform in his lifetime, the white man tore off his britches and began to whip him with a corded rope.

Perry whipped him until he got tired and then the other man whipped him. They kept it up for about thirty minutes. It hurt badly and Ossie Lee cried, but he didn't really care anymore. When they finished, they shouted some words at him and left him lying by the river at which he used to play. Ossie Lee waited until they left and gathered strength to clothe himself and return home.

In another half-hour he made it home. His parents were waiting for him, in the same positions they had held when earlier they had allowed him to be carried off. His father stood by the door, alone. His mother sat in the back room. Only the smallest children looked into his face as he opened the door and entered the dimly lit house. At his arrival, the family went back to its normal activities. His mother gave the baby to Carrie, the seven-year-old, and set about cooking some bread for supper. The older children went out to get water and wood for the next morning. The little children began to harass one another.

Ossie Lee said nothing. He went over to his space on the bed which he shared with three brothers and lay down and buried his face in the quilt. His only effort was not to think, not to assess the situation which, an hour ago, had been thrust upon him. Soon after he had laid down, his mother called him to supper. She handed him two tin plates with biscuits and molasses. "Here, take your Daddy his supper too." Ossie Lee walked to the front and gave his father his supper. He sat down on the floor next to his father and began to eat. His father leaned over, took the boy's head in his hand, and gently shook him. "You alright, boy?"

"Yessir, I'm alright."

"That's just the way things is, you know."

"Yessir, I know."

The remainder of Ossie Lee's life followed the order established that night. He did carefully what he was told, never more, never less. Along with the other children, he tended the animals and chopped and picked the cotton. And when each year, after the cotton had been "laid by," it came to be revival time, he too went to the mourner's bench and got religion. When he was big enough, he was told to start driving a tractor; this he did and continued to do for the rest of his life. He learned to drink whiskey and to go with women. At some point he married and brought forth three children to share the life which had devastated him.

Through it all, there was something in him which refused the final admission that he was dirt under white folks' feet and that he deserved the dehumanization that they meted out to him. Yet he could not reject it; he felt too old to leave home and start over again. And, since his father had died and his older brothers had left for Chicago, he had to stay on the place and do the man's work so that his mother and the children would have a house to live in and something to eat. Thus, being able neither to accept nor to reject his life, Ossie Lee had constantly to buffer himself against it.

But lately things had been going badly. More closely, each week, dissatisfaction had approached his consciousness. And he no longer had the means to push it back. He still found comfort in the church and release in fighting and drinking with his friends. But not like before. Now it was hard work to "get happy." Ossie Lee had grown weary in the defense of himself.

After he had finished his beer, Miss Lula came back over to his table. She encouraged him further about the girl sitting across the room. "Go on and put your little quarter in the music box. Ain't going to do you no good sitting there." Ossie Lee looked across at the girl once more. He did like the way she looked. Under Miss Lula's prodding, Ossie Lee walked across the small room to the glowing, big bellied music box and deposited his quarter. He turned his head toward the girls. "Y'all want to come choose some records? Come get the music you want and dance for me." The girls conferred with one another for a minute and then came over to where he stood. They looked to be about twenty years old. Ossie Lee studied the little black one. She looked clean, had a pretty face. As he watched her, she looked from the music box to him, assessing her new arena of activity. Her sister asked him his name, where he lived, and all that. She said nothing, only kept time to the music until her sister would be ready to dance.

When the music burst from the music box the two girls joined hands and danced together. They danced lithely, gracefully. To Ossie Lee the little black girl, so thin in her loosely fitting yellow dress, looked especially graceful. His senses followed her and were refreshed. He followed her so closely that, for the while that she danced for him, he was able to push away the disturbing consciousness of his life.

As she danced, he relaxed and leaned back on the music box to watch her. When the music ended, the girls went back to their seats, laughing and talking, breathless from their dancing.

Later, someone fed more coins to the music box. This time it sent forth blues music. Slow, pounding, insightful music, about loving and living. Ossie walked quickly over to the girl in order to reach her before anyone else. When he brought her to him to dance it was as he had expected. Her body fitted itself to him, fitted itself and then relaxed into him. As they moved slowly with the music he pulled her still closer, drinking in the ease with which she lived and moved. They danced for an immeasurable time.

When finally they sat to rest, neither spoke. He remained beside her for several minutes and, finding no words, stood up and walked over to where some friends were lounging against the far wall. They received him without comment. He too leaned against the wall, propping himself with his booted foot. He inquired of them, "That little girl got a man round here?"

One of the men answered, "No, don't think so. She ain't been here but a few weeks. And ain't none of us hit on her yet. We just been watching her. Miss Lula watches her pretty close. Miss Lula really likes that girl. Ain't let us get next to her. Say we don't mean her no good. She likes for us all to dance and have fun, but she don't want you to take that girl nowhere." Ossie Lee grunted something in acknowledgement and walked away from them. He kept walking, through the door and on to his mother's house.

His life thereafter was centered around evenings at the café. His days assumed a strange proportion. The mornings went quickly; he easily did his plowing, ran his boss man's errands, and carried the other hands home from the field to eat dinner. He was eager to make the day go by so that evening would come. But then, after dinner, when the evening was indeed near, time seemed to stand still. Every task took forever. The cotton rows seemed to be miles longer than they had been in the morning. It seemed that evening would never come. When finally the work day ended, Ossie Lee would go home and, so that he could savor every aspect of being with her, he would force himself to change his clothes in a leisurely manner and to walk slowly up the road to the café.

When, one evening, he directed her from the dance floor to the door of the café, she followed him outside. He motioned to her to get into his '56 Ford. As he cranked up the car, he turned to her. "We're going to get your things. I want to marry you. You can stay with me and Mama this week and next Saturday we'll marry. I'll get you a house soon as I can."

The girl turned to face him. "What about your wife?"

"She's gone. She knew what she was doing when she left. Do you want to marry, or don't you?"

She said, yes, she would marry.

Ossie Lee drove to her mother's three-room house. Some of the children were sitting on the sagging porch, trying to fight off the mosquitoes and to get some cool air. She went in, spoke a few words to her mother and her sisters, and gathered her things to go with him. Her mother came to the porch to see them off. As the girl climbed back into the car her mother called to her, "You know you can always come back home."

At Ossie Lee's home the girl was well received. His mother was glad to have another woman around to help in the field and to see after the children. The children liked her at once. She played with them yet took them seriously. And she danced with them, even with the baby who couldn't walk.

In the evenings, Ossie Lee took her to the café. When he told Miss Lula that they were to marry, she shook her head. She sat down at the table with them and took the girl's hand in hers. She said, "Baby, I don't know how to say this, but I don't think you should marry. It's too much in you for you to go off with some man now. I wish you wouldn't do it. I'm a old lady. I seen a lot of pretty black girls. But you got something special. Don't throw it away. I know you got to live and you got to help your mama. Well, it ain't enough work here for two, but I'll give you a job here in my café if you'll just stay on with your mama."

The girl understood. She answered simply, "I think the best thing is for me to go with Ossie Lee."

The older woman turned to him. "You a good man alright, Ossie. But you don't mean this girl no good. You ought to let her stay home. Let her stay out where she can dance."

Ossie Lee chose to take her words lightly. He laughed. "You better get away from here, talking like that. Me and Minnie Pearl going to marry on Sunday. And everybody is invited to the wedding, down at Pilgrim's Rest."

Miss Lula turned back to the girl. "Remember, baby, if anything happen, you got a friend here."

The girl smiled. "Thanks, Miss Lula, I'll remember. And— I'll be alright."

They married on Sunday.

Later in the week, Ossie Lee saw his boss man about getting a house for them to live in. The man told him where he could have one, but he said it might have to be cleaned up some. Then Ossie Lee and his wife went to look at the house. It was an old, wooden, two-room house with a tin roof. Because of its age, the whole building leaned to one side. It was filled to the ceiling with hay.

Ossie Lee was slapped again by the circumstances of his life. He sat down on the broken steps and leaned his back against the wooden roof support. "That bastard expects folks to live in a place that he won't use for nothing better than hay. I don't know. Sometimes I just don't know."

His girl stood on the porch, between him and the door of the house. She said to him, "That's alright. We'll fix it up. Come on, let's go up to the café for a while."

"No, I don't want to go to the café. I don't want to go nowhere."

He walked away from the shack, his head down and his arms dangling loosely. She followed him to his mother's house. Ossie Lee came into the house, stepping over children and around beds and ducking electrical wires. He laid across the bed. She laid down next to him and tried to make him feel better.

"You'll see. It will be nice. We'll get the hay out, put in some windows, buy some curtains from the ten-cent store." He just lay there.

When he tired of the noises of the house, he sat up on the bed. "Come on, let's get out of here."

As they walked slowly up to the café, she tried to take his hand, but he shook his loose. He didn't want her hand. She couldn't help. Nothing could help, nothing could remove the fact of that hay-filled shack to which he would take his wife.

They entered the café and took seats at a table in the middle of the room. She looked around the room for her sister. Recognizing her in the back, she went over to talk with her. Soon someone put a dime in the music box and the two girls began to dance. Ossie Lee watched his girl. She danced with the same ease and enjoyment that she always had. But he could not come out to her. He could no longer lose himself in her dancing. He was held too tightly to the hay-filled shack, too closely to all the meaningless ditches he had dug. As he sat immobile in the chair, he grew angry. How could she dance like that when she had just seen that place? What kind of a fool was she to think that there was anything to be happy about, any place on earth to relax! As he watched her, his anger grew still more and his muscles stiffened. He pulled himself up and went outside to get some air. He sat down on the steps, rested his head on the wall, and looked out into the darkness.

A big hand descended on his shoulder. It was his cousin, Willie C. Willie C. was a tall, thin, brown-skinned man, with most of his teeth missing. He and Ossie had grown up together. He leaned his dirty, sweating face to within inches of Ossie Lee's. "Hey, Ossie Lee, I ain't seen you out by yourself in a long time, not since you got that little black girl from up on Mr. Mills' place. I got some old corn whiskey out in the car. Jake and Fats, they out there now drinking it all up. Come on, drink some with us, before it's all gone." He pulled at Ossie Lee's shoulder.

Ossie Lee said, "Alright, man, let's go."

They went around back of the café to where the other two men were standing. Ossie Lee helped them to finish off the pint of whiskey which they passed around. He drank quickly, thanked them, and left.

He went back around into the café and took the seat he had had earlier in the evening. His girl was at the table, laughing and talking with her sister about finding her a husband. They tried to include him in the talk, but he only grunted. When the music started, the girls once more got up to dance. She asked him, "You want to dance?" When he did not answer, she went off with her sister.

Again he watched her move and his anger swelled. He could not permit her to dance like that, not today, not in the face of that hay-filled shack. Ossie Lee held himself in his seat for as long as he could, by looking the other way, by talking to people at the next table. But he could not ignore the pounding of the music. He could not negate the sound of her laughter as she danced. He rose from his chair, walked over to his beautiful black girl and slapped her to the floor. She got back to her feet but was too stunned to hit back at him. Again he hit her, now in her stomach. She doubled over in pain.

The other people who had been dancing moved back from the couple. Only the girl's sister pushed her way over to her, screaming at Ossie Lee to stop hitting her sister. She enclosed her sister in her arms and stared back at Ossie Lee, who was readying to fight her, too. As he approached them, he was stopped by the sound of a gunshot.

The crowd moved aside for Miss Lula. She placed the barrel of the gun into his side. Her face was tightly drawn, her eyes shining, her arms holding steadily to the gun. "Ossie Lee, don't you touch that girl again in my place. If you got something to settle, take her home. But as long as she is anywhere near where I am, you can't hurt her. Now get out of here."

He turned to the girl, "You coming with me?"

She nodded yes. The two walked away from the café back to his mother's house.

At home they silently prepared for bed. The thin, black girl slipped into bed beside her husband. He took her in his arms. For hours he caressed her, aroused her, loved her. He worked with her until he felt sure that he had given her a baby, a baby which would weigh her down and destroy her balance so that she would dance no more.

Ronald L. Fair

LIFE WITH RED TOP

RED TOP and I share a two-room apartment out here in Nothing. We've lived here for two years and will probably stay put until they raise the rent or until a highway comes through or some kind of urban renewal. It's a nice place if you like old, obsolete buildings and substandard living. We used to have a cat here about a year ago but the rats chased him away. We used to wash walls and windows and sweep the place once in a while, too, but it just gets that way again, so what's the use.

I remember how it looked when we moved in and how we put Black Flag down all around the rooms every night before we went to bed until the people in the other apartments complained that we were disturbing the equal distribution of roaches and threatened to kick us out of here if we didn't accept our share of the bastards and stop trying to be such aristocrats. We live in a democracy out here and we didn't want to make enemies of our neighbors so we accepted our quota and learned to live with them. We haven't learned to eat them yet. We eat just about everything else, but not these slimy little companions.

Red Top is my roommate and quite obviously he's a Negro. He has a real name but I've forgotten it. I guess he's what you'd call a handsome man; about eight inches over five feet, 175 pounds, a head full of nappy red hair, gray eyes that slant upward slightly and practically no beard at all. He manages to stay in pretty good shape for his age and he's quite popular. He never has to buy any—he says.

I should be half so lucky. My checks might go a lot

farther if I didn't have to pass a little around among the ladies' lingerie lounges and at supermarkets for that occasional loaf of bread or bottle of wine from time to time. I get most it back—in time I'll get it all back from them. People like Red Top and sometimes they come by to visit and bring little things for us.

Red Top gets out more than I do. Sometimes he stays out all day. Once they locked him up for two weeks as a material witness in a murder trial. I thought he was dead. It seemed like a logical assumption to me. He didn't come home so he must have been dead. I was a little disappointed when he finally returned because I had already cashed his check and spent most of it. He was disturbed about this. He was angry with me. He's a pretty vicious guy sometimes. I had to get a job to pay him back—two weeks he made me work just for money, and then he made me pay the rent myself.

We understand each other, though; and the arrangement works pretty good most of the time.

Red Top is not a native of the city. Is anybody? He was born on a farm; the son of a sharecropper who was the son of a sharecropper who was the son of a slave—the son of a white man's slave; the son of a son of a bitch. He got a chance to break away from home during the big war when he was drafted into the army as a cook and after he had helped free the rest of the world he came back home to become a modern-day slave in the great U.S.A.

He fought the old ways for a while, joining every group that promised him equality and freedom, but always ended up being investigated by the Feds for membership in a subversive organization. Any damn organization with letters is Communist-inspired; and any movement to correct an existing deformity is Communist-inspired and any outspoken critic of the "Good Old American Way" (whatever the hell that is) is stamped and sealed Communistic. And Red Top was one of the hottest Communistic non-Communists in the U.S.A.

They shook him up so he was afraid to sign his name on a

pledge card in church. He was smart, aggressive and on the way up, good job and all, but he wanted to charge out in front of the ranks carrying the flag of the cause and he did, and when he looked around for the rest of the troops they were miles behind him and nobody was near to defend him when they pulled the flag away and cut him up in little pieces and left him for dead—and left him dead, spiritually without substance, without soul—DEAD.

He drifted around the country for a few years after that, sleeping where he could and living from time to time, but dying away a little more every day.

We bumped into each other one day outside the Cut-Rate Liquor Store. We were both standing outside waiting for one of the guys to come out with a bottle of wine and let us have a taste when three little punks appeared with a basket of bottles they had collected throughout the neighborhood and brought to the store to cash in for the grand deposit. When the kids came out I took their basket and started to amass my own personal fortune. Red Top followed me down the alley. We struck up a conversation, joined forces and spent the afternoon talking about Nothing and the effect it has on the rest of the city and searching for bottles.

The kids had stripped the alleys clean—we could find only a half-dozen bottles; scarcely enough for a bottle and a loaf of bread. When we got back to the store there was a pop truck parked at the curb. The driver and his helper were inside restocking the place when we hit on the idea to take the empties right off the truck. "You get the bottles and I'll watch these cats," Red Top said, and I began unloading the truck. As I'd take a case off the truck I'd hurry around to the side of the building and hide it among the boxes piled there. I got twenty cases of empties before Red Top alerted me.

After the truck left we carried the cases down the alley and stacked them where they'd be safe for a while and then returned to the store with enough bottles for two pints of wine. We turned in a few others at the grocery store and got bologna and bread. The idea to buy food was Red Top's. I wanted to drink it all up but he's the kind of guy who has to take care of his stomach since it's all fouled up. I sort of felt he had the right idea, but it was a strange feeling to spend money for food instead of begging for it—buy what you want and beg for what you need; that's been our philosophy out here for generations. It's always worked. Why should I suddenly have to buy food when it's out there if you stand long enough and put it on real strong for some good-natured chump?

We've got all kinds of do-gooders walking around just praying to find somebody begging for a meal. But they always have to give you a lecture, the bastards. It's not enough that you say "Thank you." Hell no! They want some assurance that you're not going to buy wine. They want to ease their conscience because they can't stand the sight of you and though they want to take you to a restaurant and buy a dinner for you, it's just too much to ask that they should have to socialize with you. They're feeding you and that's enough they keep telling themselves; so they say it just before they drop the money in your hand (Of course they drop it. You think they want to touch *your* hand?) and it always sounds the same way: "Now you're sure you won't use this to buy yourself a drink?" Or they say: "Now get something to eat."

And you stand there smiling and lying and agreeing to anything they say so they'll let go of the change and drop it into your crummy black hand and you can take off and get some bread and cheese or bologna or a cup of coffee and most of all a pint of something that's really drinkable.

They don't give you that much, though, just nickels and dimes—just small change to help ease their conscience.

Once in a while they'll try to proposition you, too, like the cat who asked me to go to bed with his sister so he could watch us. She was a nut about Negroes—she was a nut about men—and he was another kind of nut who was nuts about her being nuts about Negroes. It takes all kinds. . . . And then there was the old lady about nine hundred years old and the little fairy (he's always around; he's a safety valve for some of us) and all kinds of weird people.

So Red Top and I got along pretty good. We got on relief about the same time and moved into this crummy place and have been here ever since. At first I used to go out and find odd jobs but that got to be too laborious and I decided to just stay home. Sometimes I write. Sometimes I read. Most of the time I get drunk—that's making sense out of life.

Red Top worked for a while but the Welfare Officer caught up with him and was taking fifty per cent of his pay as a kickback and Red Top said to hell with him, why should the white man get rich off him? He quit the job and now just takes it easy like me and has a little hustle going at night down the street in one of the houses; he sort of sees to it that the girls are properly protected before, during and after. I think that's why he never has to buy it. He says it's not true but I know it is—he's not that good. Nobody is. Everybody has to pay. Sooner or later everybody has to pay.

It's sort of a quiet life we lead here; no television or radio to distract us from our thoughts and dreams and drinks. For a long time we had a rather interesting schedule for the first week of the money—what with money being plentiful and dwindling away to absolutely nothing by the middle of the month. Beginning with Monday as the first day to find out what had taken place over the weekend, we'd start out at Marovitz's grocery store, standing in front of the meat counter listening to the women relate their long narratives about Susan's kitchenette whippin' (this applies strictly to adults fighting, not children), to Sam's encounter with the Book, who never pays on time, all the way to Big P. bailing a couple of his girls out of jail.

"And, Mr. Marovitz, you should have seed her when she came runnin' out of her room. Why . . . she had blood all over her and not a stitch of clothes on—not even—well, just not a stitch."

Mr. Marovitz' eyes would light up and he would be lost to the story and not see the children stealing sweets. For that matter, he wouldn't even see me and Red Top stealing.

"Well, I sure saw that woman," a lady interrupted. "She bust right into my place and begged me to help her. And all the time my husband, the damn fool, he just standing there smilin' like some stupid ass—he just smilin' and lookin'. I gave her my housecoat and told her I didn't want no blood on it and I wanted it back."

We'd hang around there until we found where they were holding the inquest. That's right, the inquest. Monday without an inquest would have been like Monday without daylight, it would have been like Monday without breathing. We had to have an inquest because somebody always got killed over the weekend, either by car or knife or gun or heroin or a policeman or falling from a window . . . Anything but suicide.

We don't do that. We leave suicide for white people because they're fragile and can't take it. Suicide is for the whites because they've got everything. Suicide is for the whites because they don't have anything.

So, by Monday morning, the weekend of drinking had caught up with us and it was a pleasure to sit in a quiet funeral parlor and smell the flowers and listen to the witnesses lie, everybody blaming the dead man or woman. The flowers were always pretty. We got to love this time of the week; the clean floors, the high ceilings, the beautiful flower arrangements, the various scents filling the room. We got so we enjoyed the damn places so much we started stopping by in the evenings during the middle of the week to see if there was a wake going on—the Black Pat and Mike paying our respects to the bereaved family. If we were lucky and

didn't look too bad, they might invite us by for a drink afterwards. We had some swinging wakes; sometimes Red Top
would make out with the cat's wife or aunt or cousin or
maybe even his brother. I never made out with anyone; but,
then, I never do, so that's not too important.

After leaving the inquest on this first day of the first week
of the month, our checks in our pockets, we'd go back to
Mr. Marovitz' store, cash our checks, bring the food accounts
up to date and head for the hottest spot on the street—
Herb's Barber Shop. Everybody was there. They loved the
place. The guys in show business staying at the hotel used
the shop as their conversation corner during the day. A few
of the policy runners, with their little books, would stop in
between deliveries on their runs and joke with the rest of
the sitters sitting around, living and reliving the weekend
before they cut out to start back to the hustle.

Herb was about forty—he's always been about forty, except he's losing his hair now and can no longer stand in
front of the mirror combing and pushing his pomp—and used
to be a little on the heavy side before he started playing golf;
like everybody started playing golf at about the same time
because the money got big for all of them at about the same
time and the courses began to open up (a couple of them,
anyway) and take Negroes in on a large scale. Herb was
happy, smooth, dapper and everyone loved him. He had a
memory like an elephant and could recall vividly incidents
that happened when he first came to the city at the age of
nine. He knew everybody and didn't seem to be impressed
with status one way or the other. Oh, he respected authority
and was pleased when someone who grew up with him made
the big time, but it didn't really move him. He just liked
people and didn't give a damn where they come from or
what line they were in so long as they conducted themselves
like gentlemen when they were in his establishment.

Herb had a barber working with him back a few years ago

—well, before that he had three barbers working there, but that was during the war when things were really good—and the cat couldn't leave the bottle alone. Herb wouldn't let his barber drink in the shop so you'd see the cat cut a while, talk a while, cut a while and then step outside and around the corner to a place where he stashed his pint and then come tipping sheepishly back to his customer making some excuse about not being able to get his throat cleared.

Herb would cut his eyes at him and the message would be delivered without words. Herb would never have said anything in front of the customers. The cat used to get so stoned that by five o'clock he couldn't cut another head and Herb would tell him to go home. He'd come back the next morning apologizing and promising never to do it again. And always Herb would forgive him.

Things went on like that for a year until Herb finally had to let him go and the cat went up and down the street telling everybody what a rotten bastard Herb was for kicking him out after the way he had run the shop so efficiently for him and all and the way he used to stay late and see to it that Herb would get away for business and how tight Herb was for not giving him what he was really worth, but instead all he gave him was a kick in the ass. You know, people believed this guy—some of them actually believed him. It's convenient to believe only what you want to believe.

Sometimes a singer who had made it up the ladder to one of the big clubs downtown would come in and tell stories of things that had happened to him in Detroit and New York and Philadelphia and San Francisco and everyone would sit quietly through each tale and then prime him for another. Black Jack kept us posted on who had hit the numbers and for how much and Slick and Mr. P. would argue about who had the best girls. Cats would come in selling hot shoes and shirts and socks and jackets and coats and furs and cufflinks and all kinds of good buys.

Sometimes Red Top and I would buy, but mostly we'd just look the crap over and pass it on to the next cat who would look it over and pass it on to the next who would look it over. And somebody was always stopping in to put the quiet touch on Herb. They'd come in and whisper something in his ear, he'd nod and run his hand in his pocket and bring out the right amount. He had a knack for bringing out just what the guy had asked for and no more and he would nonchalantly slide it into the cat's hand with his left hand while his right hand kept cutting and cutting and cutting.

And the slick-'em-back boys would sit under the dryers with their scalps tingling and their inner souls bursting with anticipation, the longing for the waves to be meticulously set by the barber who has grown to be barber-beautician with the advent of the new hair-straightening operation called "The Process." Now the whole world can have straight hair.

We'd get our monthly haircut and sit around for another hour or two soaking up the stories and then we'd cut out for Jake's Lounge and sit for a while drinking whiskey and beer and then drop by the Cut-Rate Liquor Store for the stockpile of wine; take the blood home and hide it from ourselves and then take off for the street with a pint in the back pocket, off for the big street, stopping in alleys from time to time to taste. . . . Up and down the street, one side and the other, pinching butts, joking, making out, trying to make out (but you've always got to pay) the best we knew how and sharing a wine with the cats who didn't have any because they'd have some sooner or later and we damn sure wanted to be on the list when they started paying back.

And as always we'd get damn good and drunk and end up with some of the reserve supply gone and a babe in the bed who's still drunk. She had to be drunk when you woke up or it didn't seem real. If you got one who was as sober as you the next morning you didn't trust her; you just knew she had taken all of the blood and hid it some place while you were stoned. You'd wake her up and kick her out of your bed and start Tuesday off with a tall glass of ice-cold water; trying to activate the high and get it going again without drinking any of your blood. It never worked, though, so you'd have to start in again in order to remain stable and steady.

Larry Neal

SINNER MAN WHERE YOU
GONNA RUN TO?

"Could there be a man in whose mind and consciousness all hopes and inhibitions of the last two thousand years have died? A man speaking our language, dressing and behaving as we do, and yet living on a completely different plane? A man who would be the return of ancient man, pre-Christian man . . . ?"
RICHARD WRIGHT in The Outsider

No ONE SEES the Appointed Ones on the David Susskind show. They do not talk about how the "brothers will burn down 125th St." The Appointed Ones are too busy taking care of business—t. c. b. baby; that's where it's at. T. C. B. I mean the A. P. O's are together. And let me tell you something else: I discovered that when the Appointed Ones meet one another, say on a subway, or in a crowd, at a party, anything, they always recognize each other. It's kind of weird. They can feel each other's vibrations. If they be in a crowded room, they can feel the vibrations—the force of that person in the room. Inevitably, their eyes will meet. They will nod. And that's all. And they go back to what they've been doing. And without looking to see, each can tell when the other has gone. They're the most beautiful guerilla unit on the planet. Just the sheer force of their will and soul-force, and things happen. These are the highest, most pure type. They are total physically and spiritually: and they have worked themselves up into the highest chambers of the white man's power, and are even now working juju on him.

I mean, they be working juju on the "Man" so tough, they make him fuck up his plans. He be jamming up his foreign policy, and his domestic tranquillity, and he don't even know why. He be making the world hate his ass. And he don't know why. At least, if he knows, he will not allow himself to see it. For the chief weakness of these men are their illusions, and their supreme arrogance before a world of black faces. Even when he kills, and viciously so, he wants to be loved. So when the world spits at his cardboard kindness, he begs to be loved, to be understood. Even as he murders you, he pleads for understanding. And deadly children that they are, they weep in confusion, because the world does not see that they are kind and peace-loving children.

So, the A. P. O's, spiritually in league with Universal Black Brotherhood, be working super juju on them—fuck up his thinking. Make them cause chaos themselves. Make him harm his white self. And he be so dumb and soulless he don't even see. That is why he continues to destroy the spiritual world with one hand; and with the other, wipes his ass with a bloody olive branch.

"The monster's eyes are watery colorless. With endless space beyond. The thing inhabits the voids of reason. Its function was as a horrible nothingness. As absence of feeling of thought, of compassion. Out between the stars where life does not exist. This beast is the twisted thing a man would be alone . . . without his human soul."

"Sinner man where you gonna run to,
  where you gonna run to judgment day?"

I left Reverend Worth and his deacons. And they were happy. I had done a good job on their legal papers. On the road, in the darkness, I thought about them. *Who* was their God? How did they see Him? What made them pray to Him so fervently? And for *what* were they praying? Was it for forgiveness? If so, what was the nature of their sins? Was it for understanding, as they stumbled through the white light of confusion?

Reverend G. K. Worth, smiling like Rex Ingram in *Green Pastures*, smiling benevolently like DE LAWD. Who would want to hurt such gentle people? It was a painful question. Because it is clear that there are many ready to crush them just for that gentleness. And for this reason, some of us have to descend into the Blackness and protect them by all the means at our disposal. So that that very gentleness would some day flower into bright sun-colors, blooming and singing in the universe. It is so awful—the pain. And the irony of it all is that the Appointed Ones will be the last ones to be loved. After chaos, someone will remember them as an afterthought. The last ones to be loved.

Even though we have acted out of love for them—for those who would or could not help themselves. Even though —even though we are nothing without them, and they without us—we would be vilified, scorned by our own for disturbing a false peace. And paying those kinds of dues is all part of the same tune.

The thick night and the swamp smell moved within me disturbing the argument. Occasionally something splashed in the darkness. The tree winds and the dog barks seemed linked somewhere in the distance. A narrow bumpy road, and there were no signs marking the way. Somehow, I had turned off the main highway. I stopped the car, and took out the road map. It was little help. I saw nothing that gave me direction. I could hear what sounded like whistling, way, way, off into the swamp, more, and then silence. The wind would rise out of the swamp, and it would be difficult to hear the

whistling anyway. But when I did hear it, it was very distinct, lonely; it would rise; then fall into the womb of the
darkness, beautiful and piercing. I looked down the road as
far as I could see, and there was nothing there. Then I saw
him standing at a kind of bend in the road; beyond him
thick brushes, and a criss-crossing entanglement of trees and
vines. And the whistling was clear now and rhythmic. I just
sat there for awhile looking at him. He waved his hand.

"Hey man, hey! You know where the highway is?" No
answer. "I say, brother, you know where the road is?" Still
no answer. He walked to the car and motioned for me to
follow. Instead of taking the bend, he turned into the trees
and vines. He was about thirty yards in front of me; he
seemed to fade in the darkness and appear again.

"Hey man, this car can't get in there!" He stopped, turned
around, and came back.

"Get out the car, then."

"Just tell me where the highway is, man."

"I know you. And I know what you have done. And what
you will do before it's over, nigger." Yeah, it was just that
direct. That was when I first realized that the Appointed
Ones recognized each other. But it frightened me then. I
didn't want to understand it. I remembered the .38 in the
glove compartment, but did not reach for it. He simply
smiled.

"What are you talking about, man?"

"Nigger, don't pull that shit on me. I ain't dumb. I
guards the roads. And I knows a lot—"

"Where *is* the main highway?" I wanted to change the
subject.

"Oh that. Don't worry about that now. Don't worry. That
can wait."

"What can wait?"

"*That*. Your business, nigger, can wait. There be more
them than you can handle by yourself, anyway."

I knew that he did not know the plan. But he acted as if he knew it. I believed that only Carlton knew it. How would this country-looking black boy know it? And I am weak. Something ancient and sacred moved between me and him linking us together in a design of rhythm and night. The trees did their dance; and the whistling and dog barks commingled in the night—the rolling, undulating tug of history.

"Git out the car, brother." I obeyed. He began walking again deeper into the swamp, again the whistling. Then I heard something that sounded like hands clapping. It was rhythmical; and was beginning to augment itself to the whistling, which was becoming more and more shrill. The clapping. Suddenly, there was brightness as the lights from shacks were turned on. A large crowd, black men, women, and children, stood in a circle, in the center of which was a cross. But it was inverted. Around the cross was a kind of pit, raggedly cut out of the red earth.

The whistling was reaching an intense pitch; a kind of scream which blended into the clapping. Then the feet. Stomping against the ground. It was more of a shuffling than a stomping. It sent dust swirling in the night.

Then the Spirit began moving through it. Through the whistling, shuffling, and clapping. The first person it grabbed was a little girl, very thin, very black who danced around the edges of the circle, spinning and frenetically jerking herself like an epileptic. The others, her family, urged her on, shouting, intensifying the energy.

"Go on, child!"

"Have mercy, Spirit!"

"Owweee!"

"Feel the Spirit!"

"Yeeess, Sweet Spirit!"

"Owweee, Father!"

"Feel the Spirit, child! Feel the Spirit!!!"

"Oh, my baby, my baaaby!"

"Get it, child. Yes, God-Almighty so powerful!"
"God is good!"
"God is love!"
"God is pain!"
The child was dancing more powerfully now; the words seizing her body along with the energy of the rhythm, and throwing her with the force of hundreds of years of pain and death. She was dancing to the after-beat, the beat slightly behind or underneath the main one. Perfectly now. Precise. Spinning. Jerking. Somersaulting and occasionally rolling on the ground. Sometimes the child twisted in pain, a shout punching its way out of the frail body. No one moved to help her. Often, someone would slap his hands on the earth before her. But no one touched her. They just clapped and continued that stomping-foot-shuffle—the feet in one rhythm, the whistling and clapping in another, but total.

Then a young boy caught it. The Spirit riding him, throwing him into the air somersaulting, back flips, around the girl again and again. And fear rode my insides. And the rhythms rushed within me also. I moved with it—the Spirit of Obatala
. . . Yemaya . . . Shango . . . Oshun . . . Allah . . . Siva
. . . *Ba nla oka Yemowa! Orisha, wu mi ni 'budo ibi re l'orisha ka 'le!!!* The words pulled at my tongue, urging themselves up from the collective depths of my history. Visionary demons. Swirls of songs. Rivers. Streams. Old women peering over a baby near warm tropical springs where naked black women bathed. Drum nights. Fire nights. Ships flanking the shores. Chains. The smell of human flesh packed together. Song on song, song on song, singing off the layers of pale lies. Pulled at me. Pulled at the Word in my soul. *And would I ever live to reclaim my own?*

He appeared as if to calm us. Appeared in the midst of the most frightening moan I have ever heard. And I wept. And the moan rising into the rhythm, splintering somewhere in space and time; and in that moment, everything was everything that it could be; all that ever was existed in that moment, preserved within it were all of life's opposites; and everything danced with the night rolling, rolling through a cosmos of pain and suffering. How puny we are against the Gods within us. And He appeared among us as if to calm us, to begin the Act. The moan subsided as he spoke:

"Brothers and Sisters, we been brought across wide seas. We done seen children weepin' and moanin'. And the images of our Fathers broken and scattered to the Wind. Yes, I will tell it as I does every year. Seen the blood and heard the horror. No, my children, we are not strangers to blood. Yes, I will tell you. Seen them come tearin' and killin'. And yes, my children, we have prayed to their god; a god who has forgotten us. . . . Have seen things unspeakable before these children; but things they yet must know. Yes. And have believed, yes.

"For Nadi in the first year on the big boat . . . killed four white mens. . . . Was cut into pieces and eaten by the sharks and by the sea."

"Yes, we affirm, he is with us," they answered.

"For Baba Oyeluwa, great warrior who destroyed one of the big boats, escaped only to die by the hands of one his own."

"Yes, we affirm his presence."

"For Sekou who killed the Captain, and was himself caught and killed. May he be remembered."

"Yes, we remember."

"For Kwame, child of Saturday, wise priest, his head cut off defending his wives and children."

"Yes, we affirm he is with us."

"For Obafumi, great hunter, and a guardian of the tribes."

"Yes, we remember him."

"For Ezekiel Jones whose plan failed when he was betrayed by Mr. Jones's houseboy. May he be remembered."

"We will remember him, O Father."

"For Sarah Faulkner who refused Mister Faulkner and

was split and pulled apart by two field horses. Her body dragged through the fields, and her guts spilling out of her vessel of creation."

"We remember her, and proclaim that she is with us."

"For all of the Nameless in the Motherland, and under the oceans; and those who died fightin' for the Spirit. For all of those by the devil and his children. For the wars upon wars, achin' bodies piled on the fields. For the Living and Dead, and for those about to be born. Let us remember them and affirm their eternal presence among us."

"We remember and affirm. Let the words make it so."

"Let us recall that we are the few remaining of the old; the bearers of a great secret; appointed by the Spirit to vindicate the Ancestors. I am merely your servant, elected by you to continue. . . . And I trust, yes trust, children, that I have served you well. . . ."

"The words have been spoken. The deeds told. The Wind and Trees have heard them. And the Ancestors have made their presence known. You have served us well, Father."

He turned then in the direction of the inverted cross. As if it was a cue, several young men began drenching it in oil. The pit around it was filled with dry timbers. These were also drenched in oil. He was then given a large brass vase. He held it high above his head. Then the moan started up again, building, building slowly while he poured the libations. And the song . . . an old song . . . old and familiar poured out of him. The moan continued, screaming through the trees; and we whirled through time.

And then I saw them bringing him. He was young, strongly built. His hands were tied behind his back. And he struggled. They held. He screamed and squirmed as the horror leaped in his eyes: "NIGGERS! NIGGERS! NIGGERS! NIGGERS! NIGEEEERS!!!! WHAT ARE YOU NIGGERS DOING? LORD DON'T LET THEM DO IT! DON'T LET THEM KILL ME! PLEASE DON'T LET THEM, GOD! PLEASE DON'T LET THEM!

The fire made his face glow redly as the saliva hung from

his lips. The trees danced in the wind. The moan stopped. Everything fell into silence. And the white man was silent also. It was much too large for him to understand. They dragged him to his cross, and stripped him naked. A young man came forth and whispered something to him, inaudible. And he seemed to relax a little. Just a little. The man was drained of everything now. He was ready to die. They tied him to his cross. Others came forth to help bind him. They poured the oil over him, again drenching the cross and the timbers in the pit. It was light. The flames exploded in the darkness, sucking at the wind which fed them. And he screamed, a white piercing scream of death; the swamp enveloped it, the darkness swallowing the scream and the light from the flames. We watched in silence. The stump burned. And when the fire died down, it was rekindled. It was so simple, yet so . . . yet so . . . .

Finally, nothing of him remained. Nothing. The Father carefully gathered up his ashes; and then very carefully scooped them into a black urn. The moan was continued, softly now. And they wept for him and his people. They wept for themselves. For the Act would vindicate only part of his sins. They were humble enough to realize this. They were humble enough to realize that they were dealing with unknowns.

The boy walked slowly toward me. Led me to the car. Walking through the swamp, neither of us spoke. When we reached my car, he gave me the directions I needed.

"You think you can find your way now?"

"Yeah, I think so."

"You on the right track now—straight ahead."

"Thank you, Brother. Thanks for the help."

"Anytime, Brother, anytime . . ."

Charlie Cobb

AIN'T THAT A GROOVE

Reply to whitey taken from words of black Atlanta DJ:
    "It ain't the size of the ship
    that makes the wave
    it's
    the
Just about where we at.
    motion of the ocean."
Question: *How to spread the revolution—or need of one?*
    What, where, how who to say this to?
    We know/accept, that we got to struggle. Understand I
hope, that our heart, our life—our struggle, is of black people.
Lou Rawls on Radio: "I'm in a world of trouble . . . playin
double." Indeed, we is. It's got to stop. Let every black,
packed, on every block; bent in every field, get into *his* thing.
But, make it against the man.
    (Understand, that We, are a people!
    Our work and responsibility is meeting the needs of our
people. Black People. Know, that in this white man's country, talking as a black and gearing yourself to meeting the
needs of black people, is revolutionary in itself.)

On the question, though: Communications has to reach
Blacks. Its thrust cannot be within the framework of white
America. It's to call for action—to talk of struggle against
the white man. To destroy white oppression. The tools for
what we say, have to be accessible.

Some tools:
Our natural forms such as the oral tradition, song, dance,

519

play, rhythm, RACE (maybe we begin by suggesting that we all dig ourselves in the mirror—it's permanent). Other tools are those vehicles that reach us most effectively: Sound, the record, radio. The SNCC Atlanta project often goes to a playground with a sound truck, to play records. While there are some political ends in mind, these ends do not negate the actual record—the sound—itself as an integral part of the effort to communicate. The effectiveness of whatever we might have to say, is always dependent on our link to the active tones of the community. And, we all got a minute for the latest sound.

Black people got to take to their streets. If the brother is gonna hang on the corner, let it be a threat to the man downtown who thinks he owns that corner. Suppose we presented a play. People jam, block, the streets in order to watch or participate. That the play is written for the community, and aimed at their experiences. Suppose this happening on a number of blocks at the same time, to the point where it forces a confrontation between the community and "white power." Depending on the preparation and understanding of the people, the nature of this confrontation would range from a backing away, to a stand to hold the streets against this "white power."

The streets become a threat to "white power."

Streets and sidewalks can pose political threats.

Magnolia Street twists through the heart of one of Atlanta's northwest ghettoes. Its tenement houses swell and sag in the summer heat. Families are crowded in from the roofs to the basements. They are owned by the whiteman, and a few Negroes aspiring to "white power."

Lillie Mae Blackchild, age ten, her father somewhere—anywhere but home—mother on welfare supporting her eight children is out to see if she can hire out as a maid. Playspace is the sidewalk cement, as Lillie Mae has been warned of the dangers of the streets. She chalks out hopscotch blocks, and gathers her friends, keeping an eye on her baby sister whom it's her responsibility to watch.

ENTER: Organizer who pauses and watches.

Lillie Mae: Hey, Nitty Gritty, when you gonna play some Record?

ORGANIZER: Hey there, your mama home?

L.M.: She went to see 'bout work. She doan like to stay home when it's hot. You hop scotch?

O: Yeah, but different.

L.M.: How you do it?

O: I'll show you. (He bends down, taking chalk from L.M., scratches out the number in the first square, and writes FREEDOM NOW.) That's where we begin.

L.M.: Howcome?

O: FREEDOM NOW's a good place to begin. You know what it means?

L.M. Freedom Ride, right?

O: If you promise to ask your mama what it means, we'll talk about it after that. O.K.?

L.M.: O.K.

(Organizer sticks a few Black Power and Black Panther stickers in the last square of the hopscotch area.) Ask her about these too. We always want to try and get here. (He gives her a couple more stickers.) Got to go. Give your mama these. I'm Lester.

L.M.: My name is Lillie Mae.

(L.M. is now showing stickers and pointing at the hopscotch area to her friends. "Freedom," "Black Power," "Black Panthercat" is heard aloud.)

A simple communications tool: Chalk and playing for a while with some kids.

We shouldn't be afraid to mark up buildings. Use anything from a paintbrush to a Magic Marker. Folk scrawl

"shit" or "fuck" or so-and-so loves/digs/wants to make it
with, so-and-so. The key thing here is that there is a natural
focus against objects (that need tearing down anyway—or
at least need to be taken over). "Shit" scrawled on a wall gets
an idea, a feeling, across. Can we begin to put the words of
the struggle on walls? Are our words legitimate enough for
folks to keep the words in sight?

I live not too far from a bus stop at Wynnwood Street.
About five feet from the ground is a sign. It asks in orange
letters against a blue background, "NEED HELP?" The
rest of the 5′ by 8′ sign is space. I got somethin to say in
that space. You have too . . .

II

4 July.   Atlanta Stadium.   Energy, Music, Motion. Twenty
thousand blacks erupting into a finger popping of dance and
rhythms.

> "You don't mind if i do the
> Boogaloo?"
> WELL, ALL RIGHT

feels so groovey
     HEY
Ain't that a groove.

Only James Brown—"the hardest-working man in show
business." Soulful wrenching, "gonna jerk it out, baby." Black
motion. A dozen kids spill over onto the top of the dugout.

White cops scramble after them. Their rhythm is "order."
Their motion is ugly, brutal, and disjointed. They move as in
fear of a black voodoo.

> "It's just the boogaloo"

feels so groovey
     hey
Ain't that a groove.

The kids spin off. Up the stadium stairs. Into the shadows.
Into a larger motion. O.K., everybody now: Ain't that a
groove.

There was the potential for a most "happening" politics. There was something that we needed. Nothing we've ever said has taken on that kind of collective, yet personal, relevancy. We've got to be able to elicit that kind of responsive energy.

III

HARLEM: (Sweltering night. The scene is set on a spot of sidewalk between Teddy's Shanty and 126th Street. Seventh Avenue is alive with squeals and rattles of cars. Music blares out from a next-door record shop. A couple of black teenagers are hangin-out in front of the Shanty. One holds a small package; a cop comes up.)

WHITECOP: What you got there, boy?

1st guy: for my mama "I got you—   hey!hey!hey!hey!

WHITECOP: Let's see it

1st guy: Why you wanna mess with me? What I done?

      "Neighbor, neighbor

2nd guy: Put the boogaloo on him don't worry bout what

                                                    goes on

(Music from the records swell. Street motion begins to take on the rhthms of the music. A young black boy semi-dancing past the scene, bumps into WHITECOP, who turns, hand streaking for his pistol. The other two guys, who had been more and more getting into the rhthms of the music, freeze for an instant).

FROM SOMEWHERE: Split!

(Someone from behind the cop knocks him in the head. He is knocked out. The teens involved are long gone. Heard somewhere: "We all look alike anyway." Laughter. The street life continues as every hot, Harlem night. WHITECOP'S partner—a Negro cop—returns from his pick-up of a pay off by the local numbers man. He is seen pocketing the money.)

      "People get ready
      there's a
      train

                    a
                    commin
don't need no ticket you just get on board."
(Somewhere, the boogaloo goes on.)
   Whitecop jacked up is a real reason for doing the boogaloo.
Look at us: dance, sing, and swing. Black rythyms. Watch
out now (I'm into *my* thing).
or participant. We must explore this it seems.
   Nina Simone in her singing of "Sinnerman," goes into a
long chant:
     "Power, give me Power"
Twenty-two million black people in the United States need
to back her up. There is an energy—a power—expressed.
MUSIC of twenty-two-million Black souls.
   Play James Brown on a Black block anywhere.
   Play it loud. No matter what folks are doing, his sound
gets included. People can dig our leaflets, but it's not the
same. Not the same. . . .
   Black singers, Black music, or co-options thereof, have been
used for the most irrelevant or
teenage friends, with the Local Mothers Against Rock and
Roll.
Let's use it.
Our sound.
Out beat.
Against the problem of the Local White Motha-fuckers.

Drama

Jimmy Garrett

WE OWN THE NIGHT

A Play of Blackness

Characters

JOHNNY	DOCTOR
LIL'T	TWO BLACK YOUTHS
MOTHER	TWO BODIES
BILLY JOE	

We Own The Night
We are unfair
And unfair
We are black magicians
Black arts we make
in black labs of the heart

The fair are fair
And deathly white

The day will not save them
And we own the night
                    —LEROI JONES

The scene is an alley way, dark dirty, dingy. A large trashcan sits stage right, next to a red brick building. The entire rear of stage right is a line of buildings shaded and faded, red or brown brick or graying white wooden frames. A dim yellow light sits above the building closest to the front of the stage.

527

*To the left of the stage is a tall white picket fence, also grey-
ing. To the right of the stage front, around the trashcan, are
wastepapers, balled up. Next to the trashcan is a broom, leaning against the building. At the very rear of stage left lies a
dead body; a black youth. In the center rear of the stage is
another body, a white man, dressed in a policeman's uniform.*

*The lighting should be that which gives an effect of dim-
ness, not darkness though it is night, of muted light, of
soft shadows, of a kind of gray dinginess.*

*The time is that of the present and that of death and
dying.*

*From offstage there is the sound of gunfire, in short bursts,
then in a long sustained burst, followed by high shrilling
sirens. Then more gunfire.*

FROM OFFSTAGE: Johnny's been shot! Help me!

SECOND VOICE: Is he hurt bad?

FIRST VOICE: Yeah. Get a doctor, Billy Joe.

SECOND VOICE: Okay. I'll try to find his mother, too.

FIRST VOICE: To hell with his mother. Get a doctor, damnit.
We'll be in the alley behind Central Street.

*Two young black men enter from stage left as if from
behind the fence. One, tall and thin with fine black features,
is being crutched by the other, who is small-statured, and has
a high-brown face. They move toward the building at stage
right.*

LIL'T: Come on, Johnny, sit here. (*He props* JOHNNY *up
against the building in front of the trashcan.* JOHNNY *is
clutching his left side, where his shirt is covered with
blood. He is holding a pistol in his right hand.*)

JOHNNY (*Breathing heavily*): Lil'T . . . Lil'T . . . Bad . . .
Mother . . . fuckin' . . . cops. (*Clutches* LIL'T) . . . Caught
us from behind . . .

LIL'T: They won't fuck with nobody else. I blew 'em away.

JOHNNY: Good . . . Good . . . (*grimaces, then clutches* LIL'T)
Lil'T, find Mama.

LIL'T: Cool it, Johnny. Don't talk, brother. (*He touches the wound.*) You're bleedin' like hell. The doctor'll be here in a little while.

JOHNNY: No . . . find Mama . . . Tell her . . . Stay away. Tell her stay home. Ain't no . . . women here . . . Tell her . . . Lil'T.

LIL'T: Don't worry, Johnny. I'll keep your mother away. She knows we got a war to fight in this alley. She knows we're kickin' the white man's ass.

JOHNNY: Naw, man . . . She ain't . . . She ain't . . . no good . . . that way . . . keep her away. She thinks too much of the white man. Man, keep her away . . . til we win . . . then she'll understand, Not now . . . Not yet . . . (*He nods his head from side to side.*)

LIL'T: She can't stop us, Johnny. Nobody can. The white man can't. Your mama can't. Nobody. We're destroying the white man. There's wars like this in every big city . . . Harlem, Detroit, Chicago . . . all over California. Everywhere. We've held off these white mother fuckers for three days.

JOHNNY: Yeah . . . If we can keep pushin . . . we'll win . . . we'll . . . win. Keep Mama away . . . Keep her away . . . 'til we win. I'm scared. I can't fight the white man and her, too. (*He clutches his sides and grimaces.*)

LIL'T: Cool it, brother . . . You the leader, Johnny. You ain't scared of nothing, everybody knows that. You're smart. You know how to fuck with whitey. You fight too hard to be scared of a woman.

JOHNNY: You don't know. Lil'T. You don't know . . .

LIL'T: What you mean, I don't know? I've known you for three days . . . Three days of fire. I know how you fight . . .

JOHNNY: No. You don't know. On the street. In the alley, I'm a fighter. But in my Mama's house I ain't nothin.

LIL'T: What you mean?

JOHNNY: She's too strong. She about killed my Daddy. Made

a nigger out of him. She loves the white man . . . She'll take me home.

LIL'T: Home. This is home. This alley and those bodies. That's home. I'm your brother and you're my brother and we live and fight in alleys. This is home. And we'll win against the white man.

JOHNNY: We're brothers, 'T, but Mama believes the white man's God. (*He lapses into silence, nodding his head from side to side.*)

LIL'T: Cool it, Johnny. Don't be so uptight. Where's that fucking doctor?

VOICE OFFSTAGE: Go for soul! (*turns his head toward stage left and rises. A short, stocky, black-faced young man enters. A rifle hangs loosely at his shoulder.*)

LIL'T: Where's that doctor, Billy Joe?

BILLY JOE: I got him. I found him hiding at his home. Come on in the alley, Doc. A lil' dirt won't hurt you. (*DOCTOR enters, crouching low moving slowly, passes BILLY JOE toward LIL'T, who is standing. He looks around as if expecting to be shot. He is a light-complexioned Negro in his late forties, dressed in an expensive-looking grey suit. LIL'T goes over and jerks him forward. (BILLY JOE leaves.)*)

LIL'T: Come on, Doc. We ain't got no time to be jiving. Johnny's bleeding bad.

DOCTOR (*standing above JOHNNY*): I don't . . . I don't know what I can do.

LIL'T (*raises his gun*): Man, you'd better do something quick. (*DOC leans over JOHNNY and kneels.*)

DOCTOR: That boy rushed me so quick I didn't get a chance to get my tools. I just stuffed what I could in my pockets (*The DOCTOR presses the area where JOHNNY is bleeding.*) That's a bad wound.

JOHNNY: Aw. (*He slides away from the DOCTOR.*) Be cool, man.

DOCTOR: Be still Boy, or you'll bleed to death. (*Two black boys rush on stage from the right, one carrying a pistol, the other a rifle.*)

FIRST BOY: Lil'T. (*He stops to catch his breath.*) The cops've broken through the barricade on Vernon.

LIL'T: Which barricade? What happened?

SECOND BOY: The one on Vernon . . . The cops come in buses, five of 'em.

FIRST BOY: Yeah, looked like bout fifty cops a bus. The cats saw all them cops, an' ran.

LIL'T: Where'd the cats go? Up to the park?

FIRST BOY: Yeah, they set up another barricade.

SECOND BOY: We got to think of something or them cops'll break that 'un, too. We came to get Johnny. He'll know what to do.

LIL'T: He can't move. He got shot lil' while ago. (*The two boys turn to go over to Johnny, but are held up by* LIL'T.) Naw, man, don't bother him . . . He's been hurt bad. Wait til the doc's finished.

FIRST BOY: Man. We can't wait. (*They rush over to* JOHNNY). (*The first boy kneels in front of the* DOCTOR, *the other stands behind him.* JOHNNY *rolls his head around.*) Johnny, Johnny. Wake up brother. Hey, what's wrong?

DOCTOR: I gave him something to kill the pain.

SECOND BOY (*kneeling, grabs* JOHNNY *by the arm*): Aw, fuck. Wake up, Johnny.

LIL'T: Whyn't you cats leave him alone? (*moving over to the group*)

JOHNNY: Oh. Oh. (*waking*) What. Wha . . . Lil'T. Lil'T.

LIL'T (*kneeling*): It's all right, Johnny, These cats . . .

FIRST BOY: Look, Johnny. We know you hurt but we need your help, man. Them cops're rushing the barricades in busses. Hundreds of cops.

SECOND BOY: Man. We got to stop them buses or they'll wipe us out. Cats ran from Vernon. They're all the way down

the park now. Got another barricade goin'. But it won't
hold long!

DOCTOR (*as* JOHNNY *sits up, listening*): Wait a second. I'll
be through with this bandage in a minute.

JOHNNY (*to* DOCTOR): Yeah, yeah. Look here. Throw broken
glass in the streets. Then pour gasoline up and down the
street for a block or so. If the glass don't stop 'em, plant
cats in places so they can hide with fire bombs. An' when
the busses get in the middle of that gasoline, chunk them
bombs under 'em.

FIRST BOY: Roasted cops!

SECOND BOY: Wow! Oh, man . . outta sight. Outta sight!
Come on. Let's go. We'll get 'em. Go for soul. Thanks,
Johnny. You're a heavy cat. (*They exit.*) Go for Soul!

DOCTOR: Boy, if you don't be still, you'll bleed to death.

LIL'T: He's right, man. Ain't no use in you cuttin' out on a
humbug. You blowin' too much soul. (BILLY JOE *enters.*)

BILLY JOE (*to* LIL'T): I saw Johnny's mother down at the
barricade.

LIL'T (*takes* BILLY JOE *to the side of stage left*): She's not
coming here, is she?

BILLY JOE: Yeah, man. I told her to come. I thought Johnny
might die. I thought his mother should . . .

JOHNNY: Lil'T . . . Get this dude off me.

DOCTOR (*turning to face* LIL'T): I'm just patching him. He's
restless.

LIL'T: It's okay Johnny. Take it easy Doc. (*back to* BILLY
JOE). Look man . . . we got to keep his old lady away
. . . she's a bitch. Johnny don't want her around. Go keep
her away.

BILLY JOE: But. She's his mother . . .

LIL'T: I don't give a shit. Keep her out of here. Go on!
(*pushes* BILLY JOE)

BILLY JOE: Okay man. (*He rushes out.* LIL'T *turns toward*
JOHNNY *and the* DOCTOR.)

FROM OFFSTAGE: Look out son. You nearly knocked me down. Where's my son at? Where's Johnny at?

BILLY JOE: You can't come in. Lil'T says you got to stay out . . . (JOHNNY'S MOTHER *enters, backing* BILLY JOE *into the alley. She is an imposingly large black woman, wearing a simple dress of floral design and flat shoes. She never smiles.*)

MOTHER: Boy, don't you mess with me. Where is my son at? (*As she speaks,* LIL'T *turns. He is blocking* JOHNNY *from his* MOTHER'S *view.*)

BILLY JOE: I don't know where the dude is. (*realizes he is in the alley and stops.*)

LIL'T (*walking toward them*): I told you to keep her out.

BILLY JOE: I . . .

MOTHER: Johnny! (*She rushes over to* JOHNNY *and kneels pushing the* DOCTOR *out of the way.* BILLY JOE *shrugs his shoulders and leaves.*)

JOHNNY: Mama. Mama. Go back home.

DOCTOR: Don't shake him women! He's been shot. He's bleeding inside.

MOTHER: My son. He's my son. (*She speaks loudly but does not sob.*) You the doctor? Will he be alright?

LIL'T (*clutching the woman by the shoulders and trying to lift her*): He's alright. Come on now. Billy Joe'll take you home.

MOTHER (*jerking loose*): Naw. Let me go. Who are you? Why'd my son get hurt like this. You're the cause of it.

LIL'T: He got shot by a white cop.

JOHNNY: Go way, Mama. 'T, get her out of here.

MOTHER: Don't you talk to me like that. You bad boys. Sinning. And this is what you get. (*points at* JOHNNY'S *wound*)

LIL'T: Ain't nobody sinning but the white man. Now he's payin' for it.

MOTHER: Johnny layin' there bleedin' and the white man's payin' Help me doctor. Help me take him to the hospital.

JOHNNY: Mama leave me alone.

LIL'T: Johnny ain't goin' to no white man's hospital. Them motherfuckers would just let him die.

MOTHER: Don't you curse white people like that. Doctor help me.

DOCTOR (looks up at LIL'T who has lifted the gun): No. We shouldn't move him. I've slowed the flow but he's still bleeding internally. He'll die if he moves around too much.

MOTHER: But he can't stay here in this alley. Oh, Lord help me what can I do?

DOCTOR: I've got to get that bullet out quick. I'll go back to the office and get my case.

LIL'T: Okay Doc. Billy Joe can take you and make sure you get back. Billy Joe? (DOCTOR rises. BILLY JOE enters.) Take the doctor back to get his stuff.

BILLY JOE: Okay, come on, Doc. (*They leave.*)

MOTHER: Is it bad Son? Is it bad? Oh Lord. What can I do? I need strength.

JOHNNY: Mama, don't pray. It don't do no good.

MOTHER: I told you to stay home. Out here fightin' the police. Burnin' down white folks' businesses. I'm ashamed of you. God knows why you're doin this.

JOHNNY: I'm bein' a man. A black man. And I don't need a white man's God to help me.

MOTHER: What you say? What you say bout God?

JOHNNY: Forget it.

MOTHER: Where'd you learn all that stuff. (*She rises and turns to* LIL'T.) Did you teach him this sacrilege?

JOHNNY: Nobody taught me.

LIL'T: He's a leader. He knows how to fuck with whitey.

MOTHER (*to* LIL'T): Boy, can't you talk without cursin'. Don't no child like you need to talk that way. (*to* JOHNNY) Your daddy's a man, and he don't curse.

JOHNNY: Where is he Mama?

MOTHER: He's at home where you should be stead of out here in this alley.

JOHNNY: Is he hidin' Mama?

MOTHER: Naw he ain't hidin'. He's just stayin' close to his home.

LIL'T: While his woman's out on the street. Bullshit. A man don't need to hide. Can't. He'd be out here fightin'.

MOTHER: You're wrong, boy. God knows you're wrong. You out here breakin laws. Killin'. Look at what you've done. (*She points at the bodies lying on the stage.*)

LIL'T: People die when they face the white man. Better to die like a man, bringing the white man to his knees than hidin' at home under a woman's skirt.

MOTHER: My husband ain't no sinner. He don't break no laws. He works hard . . . He don't bother nobody. He . . .

JOHNNY: He's still a nigger.

LIL'T: He believes what the white man says.

MOTHER: You don't know him. You don't know what he believes.

LIL'T: Be a good nigger, work hard, pray, kiss ass, and you'll make it.

MOTHER: How do you know? How do you know?

JOHNNY: I know, Mama.

MOTHER: I'm gonna take you home. Away from this sin.

JOHNNY: Don't bother me Mama.

MOTHER: I brought you into the world. I clothed and fed you. And now you don't want me to touch you? I'm taking you home. (*She tries to lift* JOHNNY. LIL'T *rushes over and grabs her by the shoulder pulling her away.*)

MOTHER: Let me go (*breaks away from his grip*) Don't put your hands on me again

LIL'T: Well you leave Johnny alone. Can't you understand? He's a man. He's a leader. He's my brother. We're gonna stay here in this alley and fight the white man together. Right Johnny?

JOHNNY: Yeah, brother.

MOTHER: You ain't no leader, boy. You ain't even got no mind. (*turns to* LIL'T) He's got the mind. A dirty mind. Why don't you leave him alone? He's just a boy. He didn't know about hatin' and killin' til he started running with you.

LIL'T: Killin' ain't no dirty thing to do to a white man.

MOTHER (*rising*): Murder ain't never been clean.

LIL'T: Except when the white man did it, right?

LIL'T: I'm a man. The white man is the devil.

MOTHER: I ain't speakin' of the white man as you call it. He ain't done me no harm.

LIL'T: He beat you and raped you. He made a whore out of you and a punk out of your man.

MOTHER: Naw. The white man ain't done nothing to me. But I don't know you. Where are your folks?

LIL'T: My mother and father are dead. They died the first day fightin' the cops. My brother's in jail. My sister's somewhere fightin' or dyin! My home is this alley and Johnny is my brother. This is where I live or die.

MOTHER: You don't have nothin left. You don't feel nothin'. You ain't found god. You don't have love.

LIL'T: That God you pray to is a lie. A punk. The last dick the whiteman's got to put in you.

MOTHER: You see Johnny. He's got no heart. He's got no love.

LIL'T: Love! Love! Everybody knows that love ain't enough for the white man. He don't understand love. You got to kill him. Love! Ass suckin' love. Askin' him for forgiveness when he's done wrong. Lettin' him shoot you in the back while you're on your knees prayin' to his God.

MOTHER: Jesus said . . .

LIL'T: Another punk . . .

MOTHER: Jesus said love those who are spiteful of . . .

LIL'T: Strokin' his rod, cleanin' his shit . . .

MOTHER: Forgive those who do harm . . .

LIL'T: Blowin' up black children in Churches . . . Beatin' pregnant women . . .

MOTHER: We must pray to God for salvat . . .

LIL'T: Kill that motherfucker! Cut out his heart and stuff it down his throat. Bury him in his own shit.

MOTHER (*quietly, slowly*) I will not strike out at white men. They have been good to me. Fed my son. Gave me shelter when there was no work for my husband. Gave me a job so I could care for my family. White men have done me no harm. Only niggers like you trying to take my son away and lead him to sin.

LIL'T: The white man gave you a job and took away your husband's balls. You have the money and your husbands a tramp in his own home. Ain't that right Johnny?

MOTHER (*to* JOHNNY. *She speaks quietly at first then building to the end.*) Johnny. Son. In god's name, you know how I love you and your daddy. How I've worked and slaved for you all. And you know how white folk's have always helped us. They're smart. They know whats right and what ain't. We got to trust in them. They're good. They run the whole world don't they. How come you're out here killin' white men. I don't understand. Livin' in this filth. Crawlin' around alleys bleedin' to death. You call yourselves men. Don't no men act like that. The white man don't crawl around, cussin' and stealin'! You ought to be actin' like the white man stead of tryin' to kill him.

JOHNNY (*tries to rise*): Mama . . .

LIL'T: Sit still Johnny. You'll start bleedin'.

JOHNNY: I'm already bleedin'. (*tries to rise. He gets to his knees and stops, breathing heavily.* LIL'T *starts toward him, then stops.*)

MOTHER: Don't try to get up, Son.

JOHNNY: Just stay away . . . I'll make it . . . I should try to be a white man, huh? White as snow. White as death.

Don't you wish I was white Mama Clean and white like
toilet paper

MOTHER: Johnny . . .

JOHNNY: (*starts to rise from his knees. He is holding the
pistol with one hand and clutching his side with the
other.*) And Daddy. Don't you wish he was white too
Daddy's smarter I thought he was. He had to decide
between bein a white-man and bein nothin' and he decided to be nothin!

MOTHER: Sit down Johnny, you're bleedin!

JOHNNY: So I'm bleedin'. Its a blood comin' from a black
body shot by a white cop. Or don't that matter

MOTHER: You were doing wrong.

JOHNNY: The white man decides whats wrong. The white
man's right no matter what he's done. Right Mama. I'm
wrong from the time I was born. You love the white man.
And I kill the white man.

MOTHER: You made yourself into a criminal.

JOHNNY: My name is criminal. I steal and kill. I am black
and that is my greatest crime. And I am proud of that
crime.

MOTHER: I didn't raise you to be no criminal.

JOHNNY: You raised me to be white, but it didn't work. The
white man is my enemy. I wait in alleys to stab him in
the back or cut his throat.

MOTHER: But that is heathen.

JOHNNY: I have been a heathen for three days. He has for
three hundred years. But I am not guilty. I feel passion
when I kill, love. He don't give a shit for nobody. He kills
efficiently. I kill passionately. He is your God and I have
sworn to kill God. Can't you understand, Mama We're
gonna build a whole new thing after this. After we destroy
the white man. Black people don't want to kill. We want
to live. But we have to kill first. We have to kill in order
to win.

MOTHER: But you can't win. They've got guns and bombs. (*loud explosion. They all stop—startled*) God. What is it?

JOHNNY: It's the police busses, they got to the police busses.

LIL'T: Blow them motherfuckers away! I'll go see. (*He leaves stage right. As soon as he is out of sight a second explosion roars. He rushes back on stage jumping wildly.*) Boom! Man, Johnny, you should see that scene.

JOHNNY: Are they gettin' to 'em?

LIL'T: Go in for soul. Gimme five brother. (*He extends his open palm to* JOHNNY *who takes his bloody left hand away from his side and slaps* LIL'T'S *palm.*)

JOHNNY: See See mama We're winnin'. (*dabbing his side*)

MOTHER (*quietly*) I don't see nothing boy 'cept you lost your mind. There's nothin' I can do with you.

(*a third explosion*)

LIL'T (*rushes up to* JOHNNY *and spins him around seemingly not remembering that* JOHNNY *has been shot*) Forget her, Johnny. She's too old. (*JOHNNY spins around with* LIL'T, *stumbling, but trying to acquiesce to the dance.*) This is judgment day, and we're the judges. Mother fuck the police. Mother fuck the white man. (*JOHNNY is stumbling, holding the gun and clutching his side.*)

JOHNNY: And motherfuck Daddy and Mama and all them house niggers. Death to the house niggers.

(*a fourth explosion.* JOHNNY *tries to dance and falls to his knees.*) It's all over for the white man, huh, 'T

LIL'T: You damn right. (*He picks up his rifle.*) I'm goin' out to the barricade. I ain't gonna stay and wait for that doctor no more. We got a war to fight.

JOHNNY: Okay, brother, be cool.

LIL'T (*walks up to* JOHNNY *who is breathing very heavily while his body falters*): I hope you don't die, brother . . . But you know how death is. Its over with. Ain't no more after that. Gimme five. (*He extends his hand.* JOHNNY *slaps it with his last expression of strength.* LIL.'T *wipes the blood on to his shirt, and leaves, not looking back.*)

JOHNNY: Mama . . .

MOTHER: You ain't my son. I don't know you. You rejoice when you kill white people and don't even feel sympathy for each other when you dying. That boy did more toward killin' you than any white man but you love him.

(JOHNNY *falls forward, bracing himself by his elbow.*)

JOHNNY: Mama . . .

MOTHER: Don't Mama me. I don't care about that no more. You steal and kill and curse God. You call yourselves criminals and feel no remorse. You hide in alleys cuttin' throats. You blow up buses and burn down property. That boy left here knowin' you'd die and he was smilin'. I don't understand. He'll probably be dead himself in a few minutes. I just can't see it. I know you're wrong. The white people wouldn't never do those things. You must be wrong. I don't understand. But they'll know. They'll understand. They'll make it right. They'll explain it to me. They'll show me the way. I trust in them. Ain't no nigger never been right. (*She turns slowly and walks toward stage left.*) And never will be right.

JOHNNY (*points the gun at her back*): We're . . . new men, Mama . . . Not niggers. Black men. (*He fires at her back. She stops still, then begins to turn.* JOHNNY *fires again and she stumbles forward and slumps to the stage.* JOHNNY *looks at her for a moment, then falls away. There is a loud explosion followed by gunfire.*)

Curtain

Marvin E. Jackmon

FLOWERS FOR THE TRASHMAN

A One-Act Drama

THIS PLAY IS DEDICATED TO MY PARENTS.
SOMETIMES LOVE IS IMPOSSIBLE
—LIFE WON'T STAND FOR IT.

—MEJ

Characters

JOE SIMMONS—Negro college student
WES—his hoodlum friend
YOUNG NEGRO PAROLEE
MIDDLE-AGED, BOURGEOIS WHITE MAN
JAILER

SETTING: *Jail cell is barred. Bench runs length of back wall. The audience views the action through bars except in Scene Two, when Joe is in phone booth.*
The time is the present, 1 A.M.
(At rise, we see the white man gripping the bars madly and shouting.)

MAN: Damnit, I wanna make a phone call. Jailer! By god, you better let me outta here. I'm not guilty, I'm not guilty, I tell you. (*Pause.*) Jailer! I didn't do anything. I tell you I didn't do anything. You won't get away with this, Jailer. I know my constitutional rights—I pay my taxes. Believe me, I know some very important people

around here; somebody's going to pay, that's for sure—
somebody's going to pay for this. (*Frustrated.*) Jailer.
Where's the damn jailer around here? Where is he? Jailer!

(*He stands defeated. The* JAILER *enters with* WES *and* JOE:
dressed in sport attire: WES *in hip style,* JOE *in collegiate.
Their clothing is disheveled;* WES *has bandage over left
temple.*)

JAILER: (*When boys are seated. Playfully*): Now what's all
the noise about, Mister? Hell, I didn't tell you to get
arrested—it's not my fault, so just take it easy, all right?
I'm only the jailer, I can't do anything.

MAN: You can allow me to make a phone call; by God, you
can do that. I'm no criminal, I'm a respectable citizen. I
don't belong here, here with these—

JAILER: Of course, of course you can make a phone call. I
told you you could make one, soon as I got a break.

MAN: Well, Jesus Christ, you told me that two hours ago.
You think a person can wait forever? Seems like I been in
this damn cell for two centuries.

JAILER: Well, I was busy taking care of those two jerks.
(WES *gives him the finger.*) Better watch that, sonny,
you're in enough trouble as it is, fighting an officer. Who
in the hell do you niggers think you are?

WES: (*Nasty.*):Yo mama!

JOE: Wes, be cool, man.

JAILER: Better watch your mouth, boy. Say something else
smart and I'll—

WES: (*Attempting to rise, but restrained by* JOE.): And you'll
what, you'll what, goddamit?

JOE: (*Pulling* WES *down.*): Wes, c'mon, sit down. Sit down,
man. Be cool, Wes, just be cool.

JAILER: (*To* WHITE MAN.): C'mon, Mister, let's make that
phone call. (*They exit stage left.*)

JOE: Man, you jive too much.

WES: Ah, Joe, damn that cat.

JOE: Just be cool, man. All right?

WES: (*Laughing*): I'm cool, baby. Gimme some slack—just a teaspoon fulla slack.

JOE: (*Relaxed.*): Go to hell. Wes. (*pause*) Wes, why you wanna call that cop a motherfucker?

WES: Joe, don't bug me about that mess. Hell, you saw they damn near ran over us. Think I was gonna stand up there and smile? You must be a damn fool.

JOE: But you didn't have to call 'em no motherfucker.

WES: What else is they, Joe? Huh? What else is they?

JOE: (*Disgusted.*): I shoulda kept ma ass at the pad. You're nothing but a hang up, I swear.

WES: (*Teasingly.*): Ah, man.

JOE: Ah, man, my ass—you a hang up.

WES: But that was a pretty boss dance, wasn't it?

JOE: It was all right—wasn't no big thing. Damn sh'o wasn't worth going to jail for.

WES: I agree wit ya on that. (*brief silence*)

JOE: Man, I can't stand no jail. I can't stand it. (*stands*) I'm gettin' outta here. I'm not gonna stay in this funky, piss-ass jail. (*smiling*) I'm gonna call ma old man.

WES: (*Shocked.*): You ganna what?

JOE: (*with emphasis*): I'm gonna call ma old man.

WES: You're jivin. (*laughs*) You got to be jivin'.

JOE: (*Pacing the floor.*): I ain't jivin'—I'm not jivin' a pound. Wait 'til that white cat comes back.

WES: (*Leaning back with hands on knees.*): And what in the hell makes you think yo old man's gonna come down here an git yo black ass out?

JOE: Damn you, Wes. The bastard better come git me, he better. . . .

WES: (*Giggling.*): He ain't better do nothing. Y'all ain't said not two words ta each other in seven months—an he gonna git off some coins fa yo ass?

JOE: (*Sitting.*): I ain't worried 'bout all that. He'll come down.

He will—bet ya he will.

WES: An Skippy's a punk too, ain't he?

JOE: I don't know what Skippy is, but I'm gonna call'm soon as that gray dude comes back.

WES: Yeah, all right. (*laughs*) It'll be a rainy day in hell before old sick-ass Simmons git down to this jail.

JOE: We'll see.

WES: (*playfully*): When he kicked you out, didn't he say he didn't never wanna see you no mo'?

JOE (*bugged*): Naw, he didn't say that. You know he didn't want me to leave.

WES: Sho, sho . . .

JOE: He didn't think I'd really jam, that's all. He thought if he told me to make it, I might change. You know that cat digs me: son going to college an all that stuff.

WES: Yeah, he digs ya—digs the hell outta ya. Now go call him up.

JOE: I am. (*pause*) Shit, you the main damn reason he told me to make it: comin' round there with all them skunky broads; bringing me all that damn weed—you know people can smell that stuff a mile away.

WES: Ah, that wasn't it. Y'all didn't never say nothin' ta each other, that's the reason.

JOE: Hell, we ain't never said nothin' to each other, that ain't no big thing. (*Sharply.*) Did you ever talk to your old man?

WES: Nigger, I done told you a million times I ain't never ever seen ma old man. I don't even know that the som'bitch looks like. Ma mama used to jive me bout 'm all the time. (*Pause.* WES *thinks back to his childhood.*) When I was real little, I say, "Mama, what Daddy look like?" One time she say, "Oh, he tall an light, got good hair," and stuff like that. Then another time I say, "Mama, what daddy look like?" Then she say, "Boy, why you keep askin' me bout that nigger? He big, black an funky—looks like 40 miles of bad road. Now don't ask me no mo foolish questions 'bout that no-count nigger. Go on to the store an get me a pound of hamburger meat an hurry on back here."

JOE: Boy, yo old lady is cold-blooded.

WES: Yeah, she somethin' else, man. (*pause*) But, Joe, I swear, didn't nobody stay in that pad but you an yo old man and I ain't heard y'all never say "shit" to each other; sometimes y'all didn't even say "hi." That old weak sucker'll probably have a heart attack if you call him an tell him you in jail.

JOE: I don't care. He better come git me out.

WES: And just what is you gonna do if he don't come git you?

JOE: Stay my ass in this damn jail an look like a damn fool.

WES: That's what I thought. (*silence*) Joe, I ain't jivin', you got the coldest old man in the world; he's outta sight: who ever heard of a nigger down in the ghetto selling flowers?

JOE: Wes, there's a lotta damn things you ain't heard about, and never will hear about less you git yaself together.

WES (*hurt*): Now you tryin' ta say I'm dumb, huh, man?

JOE: Naw, baby, I ain't callin' you dumb. I'm just tellin' it like it is: you jive too much. You always talkin' 'bout my old man, what the fuck did yo old man do—what did he do?

WES: I don't know. But I bet he wasn't no goddam flower man. (*lights cigarette*)

JOE: What did he do? For all you know, he could've sheveled shit.

WES: (*slightly angry*): Maybe he did. I don't know and I don't really give a rusty fuck—he ain't never did nothin' fa me. But, I bet anything he didn't go round sellin' no goddam flowers. Yo old man must think he white or somethin': Niggers don't know nothin' 'bout no flowers. Nothin' 'cept roses is red an violets is blue.

JOE: Go to hell, Wes. Git off ma old man's back.

WES: What's wrong, you in love with 'm or somethin'?

JOE: That's not it. I'm just tired of people talkin' 'bout'm—includin' yo black ass.

WES (*with mock affection*): Ah, Joey, who's been talkin' 'bout yo' old man? Hell, I can't help it if he sells flowers.

JOE: (*rising and going to bars. Bitterly.*) Ain't nobody asked you to help it, nigger.

WES: Now you pissed-off. I don't give a damn. (*pause.* JOE *ignores* WES. *He stands at the bars thinking to himself.*) Man, it sho was some boss soul-sisters at the dance, wasn't it? (JOE *ignores him.*) Did you see that chick I was hittin' on from L.A.? Boy, she was a stone fox, no bullshit about it. I rapped on that broad two thousand, man. But she busted me cold-blooded: told me my money wasn't big enough. She was right, cause I ain't had no coins, you know that. (*pause*) Yo' old chick, Irma, was at the dance, man. Did you see her? (JOE *says nothing.*) She come buggin' me 'bout you; she say, "Where's old cool Joe at? He still goin ta that school? You tell him I said he's a chicken-shit nigger." (JOE *gives* WES *a disgusted look.*) She still pissed off cause you quit her. I don't blame you for quittin' her, man. All that broad do is run her mouth. Wish I had me some goddam wine, man. White port and lemon juice be outta sight. (WES *sings.*)

White port.
White port an lemon juice—
White port.
Make you feel so good—
Yeah.
White port.
White port an lemon juice—
Yeah . . .

JOE: (*turning suddenly to* WES): Why-don't-you-shut-yo-goddam MOUTH! (WES *is stunned.*)

WES: Fuck you, Joe, I can sing. This is a free motherfuckin country.

JOE: Yeah, that's why you in jail, ain't it—cause this is a free goddam country.

WES: So what, you in jail, too.

JOE: (*pacing the floor*): I'm not gonna be here too much longer—bet ya that.

WES: Yeah, okay, you ain't gonna be here.

JOE (*passing in front of* WES): Wes, I would tell you something, nigger, but you'd probably laugh. Hell, in a way, it's funny.

WES: What, Joe? Tell me. I won't laugh. (*giggles*) Somethin' 'bout yo' old man?

JOE: (*walking away from* WES): Ah, fuck it, man.

WES: (*attempting to look serious*): Go on, man, tell me.

JOE: (*now standing near* WES): Well—you know—last week I was down at Pearl's Café eatin' dinner. I don't know how come you weren't with me. You were in the pool hall or somewhere. Anyway, you heard about that broad, Sugarlump dyin'?

WES: Yeah. Overdose?

JOE (*sitting*): Yeah, well, anyway, you know, the waitress was collectin' money to buy the broad some flowers.

WES: Ah, hell, what happened?

JOE: Well, let me tell you, goddamnit. Anyway, I was sittin' there eatin' some turkey wings or ham hocks or some shit, so this cat beside me asks the waitress who's she gonna buy the flowers from—

WES: Oh, Lord, run it on down.

JOE: Be cool, nigger. The waitress said she didn't know. So this black nigger say, "Well, baby, whatever you do, I sho' hope you don't get 'em from that nigger Simmons: that nigger ain't shit. Naw, don't deal wit him—you can't depend on him. I sees him walkin' round in that shop like he 'bout half dead. Naw, baby, don't spend no coins wit that nigger—run on uptown to the white man an git ya some decent flowers."

WES (*with restrained laughter*): He said yo ole man wasn't shit, huh?

JOE (*bitter*): Goddam right, said he wasn't shit. Then the fuckin' waitress said, "Oh, don't worry, honey, I don't do no business with that nigger no mo'; he used ta be all right—that was 'fore his wife left 'm. Now you tell that nigger you want some flowers delivered at ten in the mornin' an they liable ta not be delivered til ten that evenin'. Naw, I don't spend no money wit him—you can't depend on no nigger, you know that. Sometimes this white man up on 14th Street gives me a pretty good deal on flowers—I 'spect I'll go see him."

WES (*sympathetic*): Boy, that's cold, that sho' is cold.

JOE: You ain't jivin'. I didn't know what to do. They were tellin' the truth, most of it was the truth, anyway. But it sho' did hurt.

WES: Did they know who you was?

JOE: Hell, naw!

WES: You shoulda told 'em. I wish it was me. They wouldn't got away with that shit. I'da jumped off that stool (*he stands*): "Do you motherfuckers know who ya talkin' about? Goddamnit, Mr. Simmons is ma old man, an I don't preciate nobody talkin' 'bout 'm—y'all hipped ta that? You say somethin' else bout 'm an I'll wipe the fuckin' floor wit yo asses. I dare ya ta say somethin' else bout 'm. An' on second thought, I ain't even gonna pay for this goddam food." Yeah, that's what ya shoulda ran down to 'em (*he sits*).

JOE: I should've done somethin'. I just sat there. I couldn't eat any more. But what was I gonna say? Shit, they weren't lyin'. (*pause*) I don't know, man. Ma old man kicked me out an' all that, and we don't speak to each other, but when they said that 'bout 'm—I don't know— I wanted to be with him. I don't know why, they were tellin' the truth: he ain't nothin' no more, never was nothin' far as I'm concerned, but I wanted to be with him.

WES: I know how you feel, man. (*lights cigarette*) Want one?

JOE: Naw. (*bitter*) You know, it's a goddamn shame for a father and son to be like us. I feel kind of sorry for the dude: sixty years old; ma old lady left him; all his damn children against him; one son in prison; his daughter's on the block. What's he got to live for, huh, Wes? Gimme a cigarette, shit.

WES (*handing him a cigarette*): Well, he had ya, Joe. That old cat digs ya, man. He ran a whole bunch of stuff down to me one day I was at ya pad waitin' fa ya ta come from school. Said, ya got a lotta sense, man. But he didn't know what was wrong with ya; couldn't figure ya out; didn't know how come ya didn't never have nothing ta say to him; said he was proud of ya for goin' ta school and not turning out like old Frank: spendin' half his life behind bars. But, he said ya just didn't have no respect for 'm an he couldn't tolerate it.

JOE (*leaning against wall*): That sucker. Sounds just like him: always talking about respect—respect, my black ass. Shit, if somebody told you all your life, ever since you could remember, they was gonna do this for you and do that for you—and they didn't ever do it—they talked a bunch of trash all the goddamn time—after a while you just play freeze out on them. You know what I mean?

WES: Yeah, I know, man.

JOE: I don't hate him, man. Hell, I wanna love 'm—cause he's ma old man. Everybody wants to love their old man, ain't that right. (WES *nods.*) But I don't have no feelings for that man. I want to have some, but I don't. So much time's gone by—so much has happened to keep us apart. It's too late, man.

WES: You really think so, Joe? Y'all maybe could still bury the hatchet or somethin'.

JOE: I don't know. Maybe it is, an maybe it ain't, I don't know. Maybe'll go see the cat when we get out—if we get out.

WES: If we git out! Don't be talkin' that shit—we better get out 'fore I git mad.

JOE: Well, baby, you know how the man is.

WES: Yeah, an' I know how I am, too. I don't stand fa too much bullshit from nobody—not even the goddam white man. But you ought ta to see you old man, though. Wish the fuck I could see mine—I wouldn't even know where ta start lookin'.

JOE: I don't know, I might go see him. Maybe it ain't too late.

WES: Hell, man, you livin', ain't ya—then it ain't too late. Least you know where ya old man's at.

JOE: Yeah, I see what ya mean. I guess sometimes—sometimes we feel a certain way and just don't wanna change—we're scared, I guess. Life is a bitch.

WES: It's a motherfucker, Joe, a motherfucker.

(*The* JAILER *and* WHITE MAN *return.*)

JOE (*rising and going to the bars*): Say, I'd like to make a phone call.

JAILER: Would you, now? Well, I'll be damn. Who you gonna call, the NAACP?

JOE: I'd like ta call my father.

JAILER: Oh, he wants to call his father. Come on.

JOE (*turning to* WES): Later, Wes.

WES (*smiling*): Yeah, later, Joe. (JOE *and* JAILER *exit.* WES *stretches out on the bench. The* WHITE MAN *is standing at stage right corner of cell, near the bars.*)

Lights down on the scene.

SCENE 2

Time is same. The cell is blacked out. We see JOE *standing in phone booth down stage left.*

JOE: What you mean you not coming down? Why? Why you ain't coming down? (*pause*) Ah, what're you talkin' 'bout, I'm no better'n Frank? Didn't I tell you it wasn't my fault, didn't I say that? Ah, ain't nothin' wrong with

Wes. Naw it isn't. I told you they damn near ran over us. He should've called 'em somethin'. What? What do you mean, you know how we boys are? Are you gonna come git me out? (*pause*) Why should you? Why *shouldn't* you? I'm your son, ain't I? Well, that's why. (*pause*) Ahhhhhh . . . Man, you better come get me outta this place. You're not? (*pause*) Call Mamma? You must be losin' your mind. You gettin' old, man. Yeah, you must be losin' your mind. You must be. Mama's two hundred miles away. I'm askin' you. Mama's down there tryin' to be a daddy and a mama—taking care of your kids. You know she doesn't have no money. (*pause*) Man, please, please don't say nothin' to me 'bout respect. Cause it don't mean nothin' to me. Naw, it don't mean nothin'. Don't worry if I'm goin' to make it or not. I'll make it all right—I made it this far without your help. I don't appreciate what you've done for me? What have you done for me? Well, your best wasn't good enough. Respect? I know about respect. I know all I need to know about it. What's it got you? (*pause*) Hell, man, don't nobody respect you. Naw they don't. Not anymore. I do know what I'm talkin' about, yes, I do. I know 'cause I heard niggers talkin' about you. Don't make no difference who it was. Naw it doesn't, not if they were tellin' the truth. Man, stop talkin' all that trash. Are you gonna come get me out? (*pause*) You ain't, huh? Okay, okay. (*long pause*) Ahhhhh . . . Man, you ain't shit. That's right—you're not shit— no, not a goddam thing. Ah, go to hell; just take a merry ride to hell. . . . (JOE *slams phone into booth and goes off stage left.*)
Lights down on the scene.

SCENE 3

At rise, JOE is standing in center of cell. WES is seated, just coming out of his slumber. The WHITE MAN is standing quietly at stage right corner of cell, near the bars; he *is watching* JOE, *whose anger and disappointment have not subsided.*

WES (*laughing*): Yo old man comin'?

JOE (*slumping on the bench next to* WES): Naw, man, he wouldn't come get me out—the black-ass nigger.

WES (*pointing to* WHITE MAN): Say, baby, watch yo mouth, you see Charlie standin' over dare.

JOE (*violent*): Wes, damn Charlie. Charlie ain't nothin'. He ain't nothin' but a goddam nigger, too.

WES (*laughing*): Cool it, Joe.

JOE: Cool it! Cool it, my motherfuckin' ass. That's all niggers do is be cool, be cool. Motherfuck a "be cool." I gotta be cool 'cause some dizzy-ass white man's standing over, looking like a goddamn fool?

WES: Joe, light'n up. That man ain't done nothin' to you.

MAN (*attempting to communicate*): Yes, yes, that's right, son, I haven't done anything to you.

JOE (*enraged, he rushes toward the* WHITE MAN): What the fuck's wrong wit you, you blue-eyed devil? You done everythin' to me, man. Every goddam thing in the books: slavery, murder, castration, starvation, frustration, humiliation—everything—you (*points finger in man's face*)—you done to me. Don't talk that bullshit 'bout you ain't done nothin' to me. Standin' in that corner like you innocent. You guilty, motherfucker! You hipped ta that—you guilty —just as guilty as my black ass is gonna be when I see the judge. Standin' in that corner ain't gonna help ya one damn bit. (WES *forces* JOE *to sit down.*)

WES: C'mon, Joe, give the cat some slack, man. (JOE *sits for a moment, then rushes after the man once more.*)

JOE: You scared of us niggers, Charlie? Why you scared? You made me, baby. Think on that. You made me. I'm your creation. You defined me, told me my limits, my possibilities. Yeah, everythin' I believe in: God, the devil,

democracy, all that bullshit, you gave to me, gave to me
outta the kindness of your heart.
WES (*calling* JOE): Joe, c'mon. Freeze on the dude, man.
JOE (*ignoring* WES): What're ya thinkin', Charlie? C'mon,
tell me what's on your feeble mind. Go on, don't be shy,
run it on down to me, Mister White Man. (*pause.* JOE
*paces the floor for a moment. Then, as if he had a sudden
thought, continues*) I know what's on his mind. You
wanna git home to yo little white wife and yo little white
kiddies in yo little white house—ain't that right, Mister
White Man? You don't dig integration after all, do you,
Mister White Man. (JOE *turns from the white man and
heads for the bench. Still not satisfied, he challenges the
white man.*) Now, motherfucker, if you don't like what I
said, then jump in my chest—just jump right down in my
chest. (*Finally,* JOE *sits.*)
WES: Cool it, Joe. Cool it, baby.
JOE (*slumping against wall*): Fuck a "be cool," fuck a "be
cool."
WES: Man, you the craziest nigger in the world. You been
readin' too many books. You better light'n up.
(*The* JAILER *enters with a shabbily dressed young Negro.
The* JAILER *stares curiously for a moment, then exits. The*
NEGRO *sits on* WES' *right;* JOE *is on his left.*)
WES: What's goin on, brother?
NEGRO (*slumping against wall and scratching his head*):
Nothin', Blood, nothin'.
WES: What'd ya git busted fa?
NEGRO: Ah, man, they tryin' ta say I snatched this white
bitch's purse.
WES (*smiling*): But you didn't do it?
NEGRO: Hell naw, man. I'm on parole. I don't be snatchin'
no goddamn purses.
JOE (*coming out of depression*): Ah, nigger, you know you
snatched that purse, stop lyin'.

NEGRO (*to* WES): Blood, who is that square lookin' mother-fucker? He git busted wit you?

WES: Yeah, this is ma old square pardner. (*slaps* JOE *on the knee*)

NEGRO (*to* JOE): Look, Blood, like I say, I don't be snatchin' no goddamn purses—and I don't be bullshitin' too much, either.

WES: You have to excuse him, brother, he didn't mean no harm.

NEGRO: Yeah, okay. (*pause*) Gotta smoke, man? (WES *gives him a cigarette.*) What'd y'all git busted fa?

WES: Ah, we got into a little fight with some jive cops. We was comin' from the dance.

NEGRO: Yeah. That's cold, Blood. I jammed up by the dance; didn't go in; didn't have no coins.

WES: We laid dead an got some half-price tickets.

NEGRO: That's cool. (*pause*) Blood, if they pin this shit on me, it's all over.

WES: How long you been out, brother?

NEGRO: 'Bout four months.

JOE (*interested*): Say, where'd you do time at?

NEGRO: What?

JOE: Where'd you do time at?

NEGRO: Soledad. Why you wanna know?

JOE: No shit, you was in Soledad?

WES: He got a brother down there.

NEGRO: Yeah. I was in North.

JOE: My brother's in North. You might know 'm.

NEGRO: What's his name?

JOE: Frank. Frank Simmons.

NEGRO: Simmons! Frank Simmons not yo brother?

JOE: Yes he is, he's my brother, 'lease that's what ma mama told me. You know 'm, huh?

NEGRO: Ah, man, sho', I know 'm. You not his brother? (JOE *nods.*) I'll be goddamn. Shit, yeah, I know Frank. Used to sit in his house an listen ta sides. Frank's somethin' else. Boy, that dude don't care 'bout nobody, nothin'. Is you the one send 'm all them books 'bout the Negro—I mean 'bout the black man—Frank say it ain't no such thing as a Negro. He's a crazy dude, man. You the one send 'm them books?

JOE: Yeah, that's me.

NEGRO (*shaking his head in remembrance*): That nigger talked about you a lot. Don't you go to college?

JOE: Yeah, when I can make it.

NEGRO: Man, what the fuck you doin' in here?

JOE: You know how the man is.

NEGRO: Yeah, he's a som'bitch all right.

JOE: Plus, I have a friend who likes to fuck up all the time. (JOE *playfully elbows* WES *in the side.*)

WES: Say, baby, light'n up on me—gimme some slack.

JOE: Wes, I'd whip yo ass, if you wasn't bigger than me.

NEGRO: Man, is you tryin ta be a writer or somethin' like that?

JOE: Yeah, somethin' like that.

WES: He ain't shit.

JOE: Go to hell, Wes.

NEGRO: Frank showed us some stuff you wrote, it was in a magazine.

JOE (*smiling*): Oh, yeah?

NEGRO: Yeah, it reminded me of some of that stuff that blood cat—what's his name, that little ugly dude—Boldin?

WES: Man, you mean James Baldwin?

NEGRO: Yeah, that's his name, Baldwin—you write like him. You dig that cat?

JOE (*shrugging his shoulders*): Yeah, I think he's pretty cool; he's honest. He's a writer that wants to be a man; that's what I want to be, a man . . .

NEGRO: I know what ya mean. But I dig 'm cause he's a soul brother. But ain't that cat a fag?

JOE: I don't know, man.

WES: Yeah, he's a fag.

JOE: And just how in the hell do you know what he is, Wes? You been in bed wit 'm?

WES: Ah, man, you know that cat's a fag.

JOE: And so goddam what if he is? Jesus could've been a fag.

NEGRO: Blood, you sho' is cold, gettin' down on J.C. like that.

JOE (*laughing*): Well, he could've been—all them damn disciples he had.

WES: Shut up, Joe, you fulla shit.

JOE (*still laughing*): Bet ya old J.C. really had a gay time spreadin' the gospel.

NEGRO: Blood, you crazier'n yo' brother. (*pause*) But Frank really cracked me up when he got ta runnin' down yo' old man.

WES: Oh, Lord.

JOE: What'd Frank say 'bout 'm?

NEGRO: Blood, he was sho' down on that dude. Talkin' 'bout yo' old man an dem flowers he be sellin'.

WES: Yeah, he's a old flower man—ain't that cold?

JOE: Fuck you, Wes.

NEGRO: You know, we all had different names for our fathers —didn't hardly none of us dig our fathers, sho' was cold— but Frank gave your old man the coldest name of all.

WES: What'd he call'm, what'd he call 'm, man?

NEGRO (*laughing*): The Trashman. (JOE *shakes his head hopelessly.*)

WES (*also laughing*): The Trashman! Lord have mercy.

NEGRO: Yeah, that's what he called 'm. Frank is somethin' else.

WES (*still laughing*): The Trashman! Naw, naw, he didn't call him that.

NEGRO: Frank say, ever since he could remember yo' old man ain't talked nothin' but trash. He say that's reason yo' old lady put 'm down: she got tired of listenin' to his trash. Boy, we used to crack up—goddamn . . .

JOE (*smiling, but slightly disgusted*): I don't know what to
say 'bout ma brother.

WES: The Trashman, The Trashman! That's cold, that's too
cold.

JOE: Go to hell, Wes.

WES: When's he gittin out, Joe?

JOE: When he's paid his dues and yo mama's paid hers!

WES (*standing and pointing his finger at* JOE): Man, you
cool that shit 'bout ma old lady, all right?

NEGRO: Boy, you dudes somethin' else.

JOE: You light'n up on my old man (*The* JAILER *enters
slowly, but with an urgent and serious air.*)

JAILER (*unlocking the door*): Mr. Simmons?

JOE (*rising*): Yeah?

JAILER: Please come with me. (JOE *leaves cell.*)

WES (*to* JAILER): Don't whip 'm too hard. (JAILER *ignores*
WES. *They exit.*)

  Lights down on the scene.

SCENE 4

  JOE *is being brought back into cell. He is very grave and
  solemn. The* JAILER *locks him in but doesn't leave. Instead, he stands, curiously watching.*

WES (*as* JOE *comes toward the bench*): Say, man, what hit
you? What's wrong, Joe, what happened?

JOE (*slumping on bench*): The cat had a heart attack, Wes.
He's dead . . . dead, man . . .

WES: Who! Your father?

NEGRO: You jivin—when?

JOE: He was coming to get me, Wes. (*The* JAILER *exits
slowly.*)

WES: Man, that's cold. (*pause*) I'm sorry, man. (JOE *rises
and, with hands in pockets, goes to bars;* WES *follows him.*)
Your old man acted like he was sick all the time, Joe.
But I didn't know he had a bad heart or nothin' like that.

JOE (*gripping bars*): I didn't either, Wes. (*pause*) There's
so goddamn much I didn't know 'bout 'm—so goddamn
much. I don't know why we couldn't ever talk. I don't
know. (*pause*) We could've said somethin' to each other,
something. We didn't talk about nothin', man—the president, Cuba, integration, nothin'. How could we be so far
apart, Wes? So far apart and yet so close—so close together.
How come I didn't git to know him, Wes? He was a man,
wasn't he? I was his son—what kept us apart? (*pause*)
And he was coming to get me, Wes. Ain't that cold, he
was coming to get me.

WES: Yeah, that's cold, Joe.

JOE: Think we'll get out in the mornin'?

WES: Probably so, Joe.

JOE: Hell, we didn't do nothin'.

WES: I know, Joe.

JOE: They damn near ran over us, Wes.

WES: I know, man.

JOE: I gotta start doin' somethin', man.

WES: Yeah, Joe.

JOE: I gotta start doin' somethin'. The old man'd go for
that. Wouldn't he, Wes?

WES: Sho' he would, Joe.

JOE: I wanna talk to ma sons, Wes. Know what I mean?

WES: Yeah, man, I dig ya.

JOE: That's why I gotta start doin' somethin'—I wanna talk
to ma sons.

WES: C'mon, let's sit down, Joe. (*They turn to sit.*)

Curtain

Charles Patterson

BLACK-ICE

A *Play in One Act*

Characters

GREEN   YARGO
J.D.   MARTHA
CONGRESSMAN

The scene is the basement of a deserted house near the water-
front. The time is the present.
Enter three men, one of whom is tied and gagged.

GREEN: Put him in that chair over there, J.D.
J.D.: Come on, little Congressman. (*He shoves him into the*
  chair)
GREEN: Don't be so rough, J.D.
J.D.: He's going to die, anyway.
GREEN: You cut his throat then, like you did those two cops.
J.D.: You know that was an accident!
GREEN: Yeah, an accident that could have blew the project!
J.D.: Well, we didn't blow!
GREEN: It isn't over yet.
J.D.: You're just a worrier, Green.
GREEN: Aren't you? You were ordered not to kill on this
  project.
J.D.: It was an accident!
GREEN: All right, it was an accident. I wonder what's delaying
  Yargo and Martha. They should've been here by now.

559

J.D.: Green, do you think they will let Chambers go in exchange for the Congressman?

GREEN: I don't know, J.D.

J.D.: Let's assume they don't, and we kill him. What happens then?

GREEN: Only Yargo can answer that question.

J.D.: Maybe I did blow the project. I shouldn't have killed those two cops. It was a stupid thing to do. But they wouldn't listen to me and I lost my head. Green, they thought I was joking!

GREEN: Easy, brother. Easy.

J.D. (*He begins to pace*): I can't help it, Green. I've never killed anyone before. What's keeping Martha and Yargo? They should have been here by now. You think something went wrong?

GREEN: They'll be here, take it easy. Why don't you go upstairs and watch for Martha and Yargo.

J.D.: Yeah. I'll do that. (*The* CONGRESSMAN *begins to moan.*) He's coming to. Think we should give him another shot?

GREEN: Naw, he's had too much already.

J.D.: Every time I look at him, I begin to wonder if his people will exchange him for Chambers.

GREEN: The answer to your question and the weight it carries, I have no desire to answer. The responsibility is too great.

J.D.: I think you can carry it.

GREEN: Go upstairs, J.D. (J.D. *exits.*)

GREEN (*turning to face the* CONGRESSMAN): You butcher! You dog of a butcher! I know they won't exchange Chambers for you. My brother will die this day. My brother will die this day! We can't save him. But this project isn't a failure. We have you, butcher! Your death should step up the pace of the revolution. Another page will be written, and we will have entered yet one more phase. Everything from your woman to your dog will be taken! (J.D. *enters, very excited.*)

J.D.: Martha and Yargo are coming!

GREEN: Stop shouting. I can hear you. Are they all right?

J.D.: As far as I can tell. I didn't see anyone following them.

GREEN: It's what you don't see that sometimes kills you.

J.D.: We're safe, we got away didn't we! You sound like a a tragedy that hasn't happened.

GREEN: We only have three hours! It's that close.

J.D.: Just a few moments ago, you told me to be easy. (YARGO *and* MARTHA *enter.*)

YARGO: J.D., take that gag out of his mouth and untie him.

J.D.: But he'll know who we are.

YARGO (*motions with his hand*): Martha, would you get us something to drink? (MARTHA *exits.*) Green, I told you to stay close to J.D. I didn't want any killing on this project.

GREEN: It couldn't be avoided.

CONGRESSMAN: What is the meaning of this? (*rising from his chair*)

YARGO: Sit down!

CONGRESSMAN: Who do you think you are? You can't treat me like a . . .

YARGO: J.D. (*motions*)

J.D. (*Grabbing the* CONGRESSMAN *he slams him in the chair.*): Now, stay there!

CONGRESSMAN: Who are you? What do you want with me? I'm a Congressman! You can't kidnap an official of the government! Are you mad! You murdered two policemen in cold blood. Before you go any farther, you'd better release me.

YARGO: Shut up!

CONGRESSMAN: Are you all crazy? What do you want with me? The penalty for kidnapping in this state is death. You can't possibly get away with this. Think of what you're doing.

YARGO: Do you know who John Chambers is? I'm sure you do.

CONGRESSMAN: The terrorist! The fanatical Black Nationalist! He's going to be hanged for attempting to overthrow the government. Are you . . . (*hysterically*) . . . you're his . . . his . . . let me go! (*He runs for the door.*) Help!

YARGO: J.D. (J.D. *and* GREEN *subdue and tie the* CONGRESSMAN *to the chair.*)

CONGRESSMAN: You can't do this to me. Please let me go. I'll see to it that you get off very lightly.

YARGO: You're not in a bargaining position, Congressman.

MARTHA (*entering with some drinks*): You should be leaving soon.

YARGO: Green and I can handle things at the ship. I'm leaving J.D. here with you.

MARTHA: Are you sure that captain can be trusted?

YARGO: We have no choice, and very little time. For the money we're paying him, I doubt if he'll turn us in. Besides, he's a brother.

MARTHA: All black men are not your brothers. Trusting him could prove fatal. Are you sure of him, Yargo?

YARGO: No! And I'm not sure they'll release John in exchange for him! That's why we've got to get out of the country. The ship is our best bet. Green and I are going down to the docks to pay the captain the remainder of the money. The captain is a brother and I don't think he will betray us.

MARTHA: Are you sure, Yargo?

YARGO: Goddamnit, Martha, I don't know! Green, go and start the car. (GREEN *exits.*) I'm sorry, I shouldn't have screamed at you.

MARTHA: It's just that I don't trust that captain. Yargo, let's use the alternate plan.

YARGO: It's too late.

MARTHA: Please, Yargo! (*begins to cry*) Please, Yargo!

YARGO: Martha, get a hold of yourself. Don't worry . . . things will turn out . . .

MARTHA (*throwing her arms around him*): Be careful!

YARGO: I will . . . I will. J.D., guard him well. (*exits*)

J.D.: Things have gone as planned, Martha, don't upset yourself.

MARTHA: I wish I were as confident as you, J.D. I feel somehow that my fear is not imaginary. I'm a woman. Look, J.D., take the other car and follow them.

J.D.: Martha, you know I can't do that!

MARTHA: J.D., you take that other car and follow them; if that captain betrays them, you kill him!

J.D.: Martha, Yargo gave me a direct order. You want me to disobey an order? Let's assume I did what you say. What would happen to me if something should go wrong here? Yargo would kill me and I would deserve to die. You're asking the impossible, Martha.

MARTHA: If you don't go, I'll tell Yargo you made advances toward me. I swear it, J.D.

J.D.: That's a vicious thing to say, Martha.

MARTHA: You're wasting time, J.D.

J.D.: I'll go.

MARTHA: I'm sorry I have to do this to you, J.D.

J.D.: I'll try to understand, if I live through this. (*He exits.*)

MARTHA: I've always imagined Congressmen as being very cruel and hard. You're a very poor example of the eagle.

CONGRESSMAN: You're all mad! You don't know what you're doing.

MARTHA: Then we're not responsible for our actions, are we?

CONGRESSMAN: Why are you doing this? Surely not because of one man? They won't release him, you know.

MARTHA: Then you'll die.

CONGRESSMAN: Killing me will not solve your problem. It will only serve those whose purpose is to see white and black at each other's throats. Think woman, think of what you're doing. You can save them. One phone call and you can prevent untold bloodshed.

MARTHA: Are you afraid to die, Congressman?

CONGRESSMAN: You're damn right I am!

MARTHA: Chambers doesn't want to die, either. Thousands of black people didn't want to die; but your people killed them just the same.

CONGRESSMAN: Hate! Hate. You can't think beyond your hatred!

MARTHA: Must I love my enemy? Hate myself.

CONGRESSMAN: It is more human to love even your enemy.

MARTHA: You take that idle brain philosophy and shove it up your red ass!

CONGRESSMAN: You're insane!

MARTHA (*She walks over to him and pistol-whips him.*): You, the prince of thieves call *me* insane! You who cheated the world and robbed and murdered in the name of a God —hell! Call me insane! You, who butchered half the world. Call me insane! You degenerate bastard!

CONGRESSMAN: You'll be caught and hanged! The lot of you! Listen to me. If you love your man, save him. Let me go and I assure you that I will do everything in my power to save him.

MARTHA: Which includes sending him to jail for the rest of his life. And what about J.D. and Green? Do they receive the same treatment?

CONGRESSMAN: That needn't happen if you free me. All of you will go free.

MARTHA: How can you promise that? You're just a Congressman.

CONGRESSMAN: You'd be surprised at the power a Congressman has. We run this country.

MARTHA: You needn't convince me that you do. But you don't have anything to offer me to betray myself. You can't buy me! I'm not for sale!

CONGRESSMAN: You're a fool!

MARTHA: Yes, a fool in love with freedom! (*There is a noise on the floor above and* MARTHA *turns to listen.*) Who's there? Yargo? J.D.? Whoever it is, better sound out!

J.D. (*He enters the basement and is seen to be bleeding from many wounds.*): Martha, help me!

MARTHA (*rushing to him*): J.D., what happened? What did they do to you! Where's Yargo . . . Green! What happened to them?

J.D.: They were waiting for them . . . so many cops . . . the captain sold us out. He sold us out! They didn't have a chance. They just kept shooting. They were dead and they kept shooting! But I got the captain . . . Martha, I got him! (*falling on his face*)

MARTHA: Yargo!

J.D.: Martha, help me . . . I've got to kill him. Please, Martha, help me! (*starts dragging himself toward the terrified* CON-GRESSMAN) Martha, I've got to kill him! (*dies*)

MARTHA (*Sobbing, she cradles J.D. in her arms*): Oh, J.D. Yargo! Green! (*rising, she faces the* CONGRESSMAN.)

CONGRESSMAN: I'll say that they forced you into this! All right? I'll fix everything! You'll see! Please don't kill me!

MARTHA (*She raises the gun and fires, then walks toward him.*): You didn't die very well!

Curtain

Ronald Drayton

NOTES FROM A SAVAGE GOD

Characters

PEOPLE (*heard offstage*)
BOY
MAN (*offstage*)
HARRY (*heard offstage*)
JOE (*heard offstage*)

There is a very small room with nothing but a bed, one chair, a closet, cigarette butts and ashes on the chair and floor. A lonely young man is sitting on the bed. There is one light over the bed. This room has a prison atmosphere, air of destitution, hopelessness and defeat.

The man is a young Negro, wearing tight, light pants and a blue buttoned-down shirt. Offstage, someone singing a lonely, far-gone, but beautiful blues. ("See-See-Rider") The young man leans on the bed, looks around his dingy room. He grabs his pillow in moments of flight and fear, hearing the noises and other voices with an air of bewilderment, forlornness, and despair. The protagonist is really talking to the room. The people offstage begin to shout at the singer.

PEOPLE: Shut up . . . Goddamnit . . . Get some sleep . . . Shut up . . . That motherfucker is always singing. (*The noises stop; there is silence.*)

BOY: Oh God, how did I get here? I did, I git here, one moment, how I get here? (*A man walks by the room, his walking accentuated; you hear noises—he is farting; he stops for a while, laughs to himself.* BOY *quivers in his bed.*)

MAN (*knocks on his door*): Close your door, man, somebody will come in. (BOY *runs to close the door which is ajar.*)

MAN: "Is that you, Jim? . . . Jim, Jim?" (BOY *doesn't answer*) Hey, open the door, let me see who you are.

BOY: I can't find the key.

MAN: (MAN *laughs*) You don't need a key to open the door. (BOY *doesn't answer*)

MAN: Alright, keep the door closed, or somebody will come in. (MAN *laughs to himself; one hears the flushing of the toilet, dangling of the keys, opening of a door.* BOY *quivers, lights a cigarette and breathes; he feels his chest, his face, his body, sort of an investigation of himself.*)

BOY: I feel diseased. Well, I have reached bottom, the bottom everybody talks about, but nobody knows what bottom is until it's reached . . . Well ain't this a bitch? (*One hears the swallowing of spit*) My castle . . . My new home . . . My little house by the seashore . . . My terrace overflowing New York sadness. (*in anguish*) I would do anything to get out of here—turn tricks, sell myself, my mother, father, daughter, child, life, suck, blues, anything—anything (*a wine bottle drops, laughter*) to get out of here. I can't have any more fits of depression, it makes me look bad. I have to always look as though I'm in love. It gives the impression to the rest of the world that I'm happy . . . I am Happy . . . (*He looks around the room.*) . . . Fuck it . . . If only my friends could see me . . . Friends, lovers, even Professor Polsaki . . . My sojourn with college, a good year of bourgeois aspiration . . . If anybody could see me . . . It would make everything seem right, everything . . . Last night (*he laughs, someone coughs, tubercular sounds.*) I walked around New York as though I was a mad man, through the village five times, forty-second, fourth, Harlem

. . . I couldn't stop. I walked and walked and didn't know where I was going, who I was looking for, mother, God, an unforgotten lover, but I walked. The lights glared, tenements sucked me in, the ground swallowed my debris, I felt in another world, but not part of it, I walked, walked and walked. (*He grabs his seater, falls on the bed, moans, groans. The people outside his small room and window are laughing, screaming.*) Some people seem to be having fun . . . they laughed . . . they joke . . . by God, they even seem to be happy with each other . . . that's a futile chore . . . How can you find happiness in each other? You are a notorious liar, I am a notorious liar—where is truth? (*He moves his hands as though he is erasing something.*) How can anybody find happiness? All I see in front of me is how *you* can make me feel good. It's the price worth paying (*laughs to himself*). That's probably why I go from bedroom to bedroom, hoping in that moment of utter joy, I will find my beloved—and what I find is the desire for another bedroom. Only songwriters and poets talk of love. I would murder all of them just to smash that illusion. There is no love and God is dead . . . I haven't eaten all day, I have to go to the bathroom . . . but not that dirty room, filth on the toilets, shit in the lights and the strangers in the corners. No, I won't go . . . I'll die right here, my self-appointed prison. (*He urinates in his room. You hear two men in the background, talking.*)

HARRY: Hey Joe, man, come on in here, let's talk.

JOE: No, I'm tired . . . I want to get some sleep.

HARRY: Oh! man, I need somebody to talk to.

JOE: Talk to the walls, motherfucker.

HARRY (*His voice fades out.*): Oh, Joe . . . . (BOY *begins to laugh, mimics what he has just heard.*)

BOY: 'It's me, It's me, please come to the door, please come to the door, I would like to talk, I have no one to talk to. For godsakes, I know talk is meaningless because I never say what's bothering me' . . . ha! ha!

VOICE (*offstage*): Shut Up! (BOY, *on his bed, lights a cigarette.*)

BOY: Fuck Youuuuuu. . . . (*One hears a few verses of songs sung by a drunkard fraternity "Johnny Comes Marching Home," "God Bless America." "Should Old Acquaintance Be Forgot."*)

BOY: If I had some money, I'd go to the bathhouse and freak off, or find some drunkard whore and drag her to the nearest hallway. That's all I have to do to complete it . . . the crime has been done . . . another note to my list as the accomplice to my suicide . . . and the murderer to anyone who touches me . . . only through crime can I find who I am . . . gun in hand . . . murder in my throat . . . death on my breath . . . blood on my shoes . . . my identity is shaped by the very fragments of my disorder (*He searches his room in agony.*) . . . you see, we are all murderers, there are those who walk with their heads up high . . . others buy shades to hide their deeds . . . fancy clothes to cover the filth . . . Tall cathedrals and sky-scraping monuments to give the effect that mankind has reached maturity . . . Bull Shit, Bull Shit, Hell, Shit, Hell. One murder would liberate me (*He falls in his urine, lost and confused.*) Why do I have these thoughts? Where do they come from, for Godsakes . . . Oh, God . . . how many times I have called on you and you didn't answer . . . Oh, God, Please, please . . . (*Someone knocks on the door.*)

MAN: Hey, kid, it's me again. Open up, everybody is sleeping . . . Ah, come on . . . (*The boy drags in his urine to the door. He opens up. The lights go out. The man is silhouetted.*) That's right.

Curtain

Ronald Drayton

NOCTURNE ON THE RHINE

Characters

PRIEST
THIEF

The scene takes place in a jail cell, which is constructed as though it were out of shape, grosteque. The priest comes in to give the last spiritual rites to a thief before he is executed. PRIEST *has a cross that is quite large.* THIEF *looks very despondent.*

PRIEST: (*enters saying to the faceless guard who is dressed completely in black*). Thank you. (*The guard nods his head.*)

PRIEST: Hello, young man, how do you feel? (THIEF *says nothing.*) I feel fine . . . I know it's a stupid question, asking you how you feel . . . before they . . . but I'm interested in you . . . (THIEF *says nothing.* PRIEST *walks around.*) Well . . . this is a dirty, filthy, dingy cell. Do you think so? (THIEF *says nothing.*) Well, I guess I'll have to tell the Warden to keep it cleaner, yeah, I'll tell him. . . . Well, I heard they are . . . aren't they? (THIEF *very despondent*)

THIEF: The walls are green

PRIEST: No, they're yellow

THIEF: No, they're green

PRIEST: I said they're yellow

570

THIEF: I mean they're green

PRIEST: They're yellow with blue roses

THIEF: They're green with red roses

PRIEST: O.K. I'm not going to argue with you . . . Let it be. . . . green walls with red roses. Fine . . . you're a good chap . . . old man.

THIEF: Why are you here?

PRIEST: To save your soul from the Devil, my lost sinner.

THIEF: Ha, Ha, Ha, that was a juicy joke.

PRIEST (*very concerned*): You're about to die in another hour, and I want your soul to go to Heaven.

THIEF: (*raises his hands high and begins to scream*): Rr,rrr, rrr,rrr,rrr,rrr

PRIEST (*begins to scream*): Rrr,rrr,rrr,rrr,rrr

THIEF: My soul is going, it's going it's going, going going, it's gone with the wind.

PRIEST: No, with the ocean.

THIEF: No, with the wind, clouds, Sun, Moon, earth, atmosphere of Mars.

PRIEST: No, the ocean, the waves, the boats, Green Grass on my Father's grave.

THIEF: You're going to tell me, where my soul is going. You fool, I should know where my soul is going, I have lived with it for 27 years. If I don't know where my soul is going who does?

PRIEST (*very reverently*): God!

THIEF: Oh yes, God. Yes, Great God! Help me please, I's trembling, trembling. I'm so afraid. God, I know you're up there, I can feel him . . . His breath twinkles under my toes. I can feel him looking down at me . . . Hy Buddy.

PRIEST (*makes the sign to God*): Hi, Friend, How have you been? I haven't talked to you for a long time. . . . I have been interested in getting some money, so I could build an altar for the prisoners. I think they should have some place to pray before we kill them for their awful crimes.

Don't you think so Give me an answer . . . oh, come on, just a little answer.

THIEF: An answer?

PRIEST: sh, sh, we must keep quiet. God will give us and answer . . . sh . . . sh . . . .

THIEF (*in whisper*): But an answer?

PRIEST: Let us sit down here and wait, in quiet, peace, tranquility. (*A bell rings.*) PRIEST: (*is very elated.*) Did you hear the answer . . . the answer . . . its here its here, Great God Almighty. . . . Money should be coming from the heavens. . . . Do you see it Its coming . . . coming . . . coming.

THIEF: That was the bell for us to get some grub. Fool

PRIEST: It was the bell from the temple of St. Peter in Rome I feel it . . . do you?

THIEF (*acts like a bell*) (*like a bell*): Ding,dong,ding,dong, ding,dong,ding,dong,ding,dong,ding,dong.

PRIEST (*does the same*): Ding, dong, ding, dong, ding, dong, ding, dong, ding, dong. (*pauses*) What's the matter with you?

THIEF: Ding, dong, ding, dong, ding, dong, I'm a bell from the temple of St. Matthew's in France. Ding dong, Monsieur, ding, dong, ding, dong, bonjour.

PRIEST: You hypocrite. (THIEF *suddenly falls on his knees.*) PRIEST: (*making sign of the cross.*) Oh, Father, Holy Ghost, bless this man . . . forgive him for his past sins and let him enter the pearly white gates of Heaven. He is the child of God who didn't know what he was doing.

THIEF: I knew damned well what I was doing.

PRIEST: Oh, Father forgive him, please.

THIEF: Father, don't forgive me. . . .

PRIEST: Oh Lord. . . .

THIEF: I knew damned well what I was doing. I needed to build a hospital for my home town. Everybody was dying in the mines and the government wouldn't give us the money for the hospital so I took it. There . . . If that stupid Guard didn't bother me, he would be living today in his warm, comfortable house, but instead his rotting soul is on the mountains.

PRIEST: Father forgive him

THIEF: Father, forgive you . . .

PRIEST: You think I'm a sinner like you. I'm not a sinner. I'm a man of God . . . of God, of God.

PRIEST: Of God

THIEF: Of Christ

PRIEST: Of God

THIEF: Of Christ

THIEF: There is no God, only Christ. He was a carpenter, simple, kind and warm, who walked among the masses, felt their sufferings, scorned their enemies. He moved through the universe with a love and compassion in his heart, blessed the sick, the weak and died to prove to the world that his love was the greatest of love . . . I remember the story of Mary Magdeline, who was a wretched whore. Christ first looked at her and said I love you still.

PRIEST (*makes the sign of the cross*): Blessed be his soul. . . . God bless his soul. . . . Bless his soul. Forgive him, he doesn't know what he is doing. . . . Bless his soul (*He says some Latin.*) Bless his soul. (*The guard, dressed in black, comes and gets* THIEF.)

THIEF: NOCTURNE ON THE RHINE . . . I'm ready. (*They take him out.*)

PRIEST (*still on his knees*): Bless his soul . . . (*He says it in Latin.*) yes, yes. Blessed, Blessed. (*One hears one loud shot.*) NOCTURNE ON THE RHINE? Well, another dead sinner gone to the Devil. Terrible . . . terrible . . . terrible . . . I have to go over to this other sinner and save his soul. How many more do I have today? Let me see . . . all . . . Great GoGoa Monga!

Blackout

LeRoi Jones

MADHEART

A Morality Play

Characters

BLACK MAN (*late twenties Early thirties*)

BLACK WOMAN (*twenties, with soft natural hair, caught up in gaylay*)

MOTHER (*Black woman in fifties, business suit, red wig, tipsy*)

SISTER (*Black woman in twenties, mod style clothes, blonde wig*)

DEVIL LADY (*Female with elaborately carved white devil mask*)

DEVIL LADY: You need pain. (*coming out of shadows with neon torch, honky-tonk calliope music*) You need pain, ol nigger devil, pure pain, to clarify your desire.

BLACK MAN: (*turns slowly to look at her. raises his arms. straight out, parallel to the floor, then swiftly above his head, then wide open in the traditional gesture of peace*): God is not the devil. Rain is not fire nor snow, or old women dying in hallways.

DEVIL LADY: There is peace.

BLACK MAN: There is no peace.

DEVIL LADY: There is beauty.

BLACK MAN: None that you would know about.

DEVIL LADY: There is horror.

BLACK MAN: There is horror. There is . . . (*pause, as if to cry or precipitate a rush of words which does not come*) only horror. Only stupidity. (*rising to point at her*) Your stale pussy weeps paper roses.

DEVIL LADY: And horror.

BLACK MAN: Why aren't you dead? Why aren't you a deader thing than nothing is?

DEVIL LADY: I am dead and can never die.

BLACK MAN: You will die only when I kill you. I raise my hand to strike. (*pulling out sword*) I raise my hand to strike. Strike. Strike. (*waving the sword, and leaping great leap*) Bitch devil in the whistling bowels of the wind. Blind snow creature.

A fanfare of drums. Loud, dissonant horns. The action freezes. The lights dim slowly, on the frozen scene. The ACTORS *fixed. The music rises. Lights are completely off. Then a flash. On. On. Off. Off. As if it was an SOS signal. Then the music changes, to a slow insinuating, nasty blues. Rock. Rock. Voices offstage begin to pick up the beat, and raise it to falsetto howl. Scream in the sensual moan.*

VOICES: Rock. Rock. Love. Me. Love. Me. Rock. Heaven. Heaven. Ecstasy. Ecstasy. Ooooahhhhummmmah-ah-ahoooooh. Let Love. Let Rock. Let Heaven. All love. All love, like rock . . .

Lights go up full. Silence. The action continues. The actors, from the freeze, come to life, but never repeat this initial action; as if in slow motion

BLACK MAN: Hear that?? Hear those wild cries. Souls on fire. Fire. Floods of flame. Hear that. Ol humanless bitch. Dead judge.

DEVIL LADY: I am the judge. I am the judge. (*She squats like old Chinese*) The judge. (*rolls on her back, with skirt raised, to show a cardboard image of Christ pasted over her pussy space. A cross in the background.*) My pussy

rules the world thru newspapers. My pussy radiates the
great heat. (*She rolls back and forth on the floor panting.*)

BLACK MAN: The great silence. Serenades of brutal snow. You
got a cave, lady?

VOICES: Blood. Snow. Dark cold cave. Illusion. Promises.
Hatred and Death. Snow. Death. Cold. Waves. Night.
Dead white. Sunless. Moonless. Forever. Always. Iceberg
Christians, pee in the ocean. Help us. We move. (*music
again, over all, the high beautiful falsetto of a fag. The tra-
ditional love song completely taking over*)

BLACK

(*Lights up, the* WHITE WOMAN *lies in the middle of the stage
with a spear, or many arrows stuck in her stomach and hole.
As the lights come up, the singing subsides to a low hum.*
THREE BLACK WOMEN *enter slowly* (MOTHER, SISTER, WOMAN),
humming now softly.

The BLACK MAN *is standing just a few feet away from the
skewered* WHITE WOMAN. HE *is gesturing with his hands, at
the prone figure, like* HE *is conjuring or hypnotizing.*)

BLACK MAN: You will always and forever, be dead, and be
dead, and always you will be the spirit of deadness, or the
cold stones of its promise. (*He takes up a huge wooden
stake and drives it suddenly into her heart, with a loud
thud as it penetrates the body, and crashes deep in the
floor.*) Beautiful. (*preoccupied and still unaware of the*
BLACK WOMEN) Beautiful. (*He makes to repeat his act, and
one of the women speaks*)

MOTHER: No. Mad man. Stop!

SISTER: She is old and knows. Her wisdom inherits the earth.
(*stepping forward suddenly at* DEVIL LADY) I love you. I
love the woman in my sleep. I cannot love death.

WOMAN: Perhaps we are intruding. (*The two women turn
and stare at her, and form a quick back-off circle to point
at her casually and turn their heads. The* WOMAN's *head is
wrapped in a modest headrag, and her natural hair cushions*

her face in a soft remark. Pointing) You want the whole thing.

BLACK MOTHER: You want the whole thing, baby. (*advancing*) The earth, the sky.

BLACK SISTER: You must leave what the womb leaves. The possibility of all creation.

BLACK MAN: The dead do not sing. Except through the sawdust lips of science fiction jigaboos, who were born, and disappeared, in a puff of silence at the foot of the Woolworth heir's cement condom.

DEVIL LADY: (*from the floor, moaning through her teeth, from beyond the grave. Let there be music, and setting, to indicate that these words come from behind the veil.*) OOOOOOOOAHHHHHHHH . . . My pussy throbs above the oceans, forcing weather into the world.

BLACK MAN: The cold.

BLACK MOTHER: The light and promise. (*from an ecstatic pose, suddenly turns into a barker, selling young black ass*) Uhyehhh. Eh? Step right up. Get your free ass. (*starts moving wiggle—suggestively*) Come on, fellahs—

BLACK SISTER: And free enterprise.

DEVIL LADY: Enter the prize. And I am the prize. And I am dead. And all my life is me. Flowing from my vast whole, entire civilizations.

BLACK WOMAN (*almost inadvertently*): That smell. I knew I'd caught it before.

BLACK MAN: Broom sticks thrust up there return embossed with zombie gold.

BLACK MOTHER: Out of the bowels of the sun. I slap around drunk up Lenox. Stumble down 125th into the poet who frowns at me, lost in my ways. You'd think that ol nigger was worth something.

BLACK SISTER (*dazed*): It's just . . . just . . . (*staggers toward the dead* WOMAN) . . . that I wanted to be something like her, that's all. (*weeps but tries to hold it*)

WOMAN: Yet she be a stone beast, ladies! A stone ugly pagan.
Israelites measure your beauty by what the filthy bitch
looks like, lying around like an old sore.
BLACK MAN: An old punctured sore with the pus rolled out.
SISTER (*falling to her knees. Screams.*): Aiiiieeeee . . . it could
be me, that figure on the floor. It could be me, and backward out of the newspaper dreams of my American life.
Out of the television enemas poured through my eyes out
of my mouth onto the floor of everybody's life. I hate so.
I am in love with my hatred. Yet I worship this beast on
the floor, because—
BLACK WOMAN: Because you have been taught to love her
by background music of sentimental movies. A woman's
mind must be stronger than that.
BLACK MAN: A black woman. (*throws his hands above his
head*) A black woman! Wouldn't that be something?
(*The dead* WHITE WOMAN's *body wiggles in a shudder and
releases, dead.*)
WOMAN (*Her voice goes up to high long sustained note.*):
I am black black and am the most beautiful thing on the
planet. Touch me if you dare. I am your soul.
MOTHER: What is wrong with the niggers, this time? I'm old
and I hump along under my wig. I'm dying of oldness. I'm
dying of the weight. The air is so heavy. (*taken by more
somber mood*) And dying all the time. Diseased. Broken.
Sucking air from dirty places. Your mother. Shit filthiness.
In a cheap mink. In a frozen roach funeral.
SISTER: Brazen bitch. You trying to steal my shit?
MOTHER: Make for the exit, child, before you bleed on somebody. (*They begin to have at each other. Breathing hard
and cursing. The* BLACK WOMAN *backs away, hands at her
mouth, terrified.*)
WOMAN: (*Coming close to the* MAN, *as the* WOMEN *begin to
fight in aggravated pantomimed silence. Clock gongs away,
maybe fifty times. Slow sudden insinuating drums, and*

brushes. The TWO WOMEN *fighting clutch each other and fight more stiffly, finally subsiding into a frozen posture.*) What do you want, black man? What can I give you? (*in a calm loving voice*) Is there a heart bigger than mine? Is there any flesh sweeter, any lips fatter and redder, any thighs more full of orgasms?

BLACK MAN (*leaning toward her*): Sweet pleasure. (*he touches her arm.*)

DEVIL LADY (*beginning to moan on the floor*): Ooooooooooo-ooooooaaaaaaaaaa. My white pussy is beating the air. My navel is raw and ready to be attached. I come back from the dead 'cause I wanna.

BLACK MAN: Oh, bullshit. Go back, for christsakes.

WOMAN: Christ was a pagan. A stumble bum in the Swedish baths of philosophy. (*The* TWO WOMEN *struggle suddenly on the floor. With violence and slobbering*)

TWO WOMEN: Fuckingbitch Fuckingbitch Fuckingbitch Fuckingbitch Fuckingbitch Fuckingbitch Fuckingbitch Fuckingbitch Fuckingbitch Fuckingbitch Fuckingbitch—

WOMAN: Thing on the floor, be still. I'm tired of your ignorant shamble. Let me be alone in the world with women and men, and your kind be still in the grave where you have fun. (DEVIL LADY *screams with throbbing thighs.* MOTHER *and* SISTER *begin crawling across the floor to the* DEVIL LADY. *She writhes and stiffens in death. The* MOTHER *whimpers, the* SISTER *gaga, and weeps and whines.*)

SISTER: My dead sister reflection. Television music. Soft lights and soft living among the buildings.

WOMAN: She went for luxury.

BLACK MAN: I used to see her in white discotheque boots and sailor pants. (*pointing to the crawling women*) This is the nightmare in all of our hearts. Our mothers and sisters groveling to white women, wanting to be white women, dead and hardly breathing on the floor. Look at our women dirtying themselves. (*runs and grabs wig off of* SISTER'S *head*) Take off filth. (*He throws it onto the dead* WOMAN'S *body*.) Take your animal fur, heathen. (*laughs*) Heathen. Heathen. I've made a new meaning. Let the audience think about themselves, and about their lives when they leave this happening. This black world of purest possibility. (*laughs*) All our lives we want to be alive. We scream for life.

WOMAN: Be alive, black man. Be alive, for me. For me, black man. (*kisses him*) And love me. Love, Me.

BLACK MAN: Women assemble around me. I'm gonna sing for you now, in my cool inimitable style. About my life. About my road, and where it's taking me now. Assemble, sweet black ladies, ignorant or true, and let me run down the game of life.

WOMAN: Get up, you other women, and listen to your man. This is no fattening insurance nigger graying around the temples. This is the soulforce of our day to day happening universe. A man.

SISTER: A man. Dammit. Dance. (*change*) Men. What do they do? Hang out. Niggermen. If I have to have a nigger-man, give me a faggot, anyday.

MOTHER (*laughing high voice and sweeping her hand*): Oh, chil', I know the kind you mean. Uhh, so sweet. I tell you. But . . . a white boy's better, daughter. Don't you forget it. Just as sof' and sweet as a pimple. (*spies* BLACK WOMAN *stil standing separate and looking confused, hands covering her ears*) Haha . . . (*hunching or trying to hunch* SISTER) Haaha, will you look at that simple bitch. My lan', chil', why don't you straighten up and get in the world?

SISTER: Yeh, Desideria, why don't you make up your mind?

BLACK MAN: What is this? (*To* BLACK WOMAN) What's all this mouth mouth action? Why don't these women act like women should? Why don't they act like Black Women? All this silly rapping and screaming on the floor. I should turn them over to the Black Arts and get their heads relined.

WOMAN: They've been tricked and gestured over. They hypnotized, that's all. White magic.

BLACK MAN: White Magic. Yes. (*raising his stake, suddenly*) Maybe this dead thing's fumes are sickening the air. I'll make sure it's dead. (*he strikes*)

SISTER (*screams as* BLACK MAN *stabs the* DEVIL LADY. *Grabs her heart as if the* MAN *had struck her.*): Oh God, you've killed me, Nigger.

BLACK MAN: What? (*wheels to look at her*)

WOMAN: You're killed if you are made in the dead thing's image, if the dead thing on the floor has your flesh, and your soul. If you are a cancerous growth. Sad thing.

SISTER: I'm killed and in horrible agony, and my own brother did it. (*staggering around stage. Finally falls in great over-dramatic climax*) My own bro . . . ther. (*falls*)

BLACK MAN: Oh, God! (*rushes over to her*) Is this child my sister?

WOMAN: No, get away from her. She is befouled.

BLACK MAN: But my own sister . . . I've killed her.

WOMAN: She's not even dead. She just thinks she has to die because that white woman died. She's sick.

BLACK MAN: (*stands over* SISTER, *pondering what the* WOMAN *has said*) Hmmmmmmm.

MOTHER: You've killed her. You've killed my baby. (*rushes over to* MAN *and starts beating him on the chest. She's weeping, loud and disconsolately.*) You've killed my own sweet innocent girl. My own sweet innocent girl . . . she never had a chance. She could'a been somebody.

WOMAN: Woman, you're crazy.

BLACK MAN: I killed my sister. (*mumbling*)

MOTHER: No, I'm not the crazy one. You all are crazy. Stuntin' like this. All that make believe. And you ki—led your own flesh. And this ol nappy head bitch agitated the whole shit. (*weeps*) My baby, she never had a chance. She never even got a chance to be nobody. Oh, God, why's my life so fucked up? And you, man, you killed your own sister. I hope that shit you talk's enough to satisfy you. Or that nappy head bitch.

WOMAN: Why don't you find out something before you show how long ignorance can claim a body? An old woman like you should be wise . . . but you not wise worth a mustard seed.

MOTHER: You talk to me with respect, whore . . . or I'll— (*threatening gesture*)

WOMAN: What? Or you'll beat me with your wig? You're streaked like the devil. And that pitiful daughter of yours is not even dead. But she'll act dead as long as she licks on that Devil Woman.

BLACK MAN: My mother, my sister, both . . . like television dollbabies, doing they ugly thing. To mean then, me, and what they have for me, what I be then, in spite my singing, and song, to stand there, or lay there, like they be, with the horizon blowing both ways, to change, God damn . . . and be a weight around my neck . . . a weight . . .

MOTHER: Well, leave us alone, murderer . . . punk ass murderer. Gimme a drink an' shut up. And drag that whore's mouth shut, too.

WOMAN: You shut up. And get back in your dead corner with the other rotting meat.

BLACK MAN: I've killed my sister. And now watch my mother defiled, thrown in a corner.

WOMAN: If she was your mother, she'd be black like you. She'd come at you to talk to you, about old south, and ladies under trees, and the soft wet kiss of her own love, how it made you fight through sperm to arrive on this planet whole . . . (*soft laugh*) . . . and beautiful.

BLACK MAN: Who're you . . . to talk so much . . . and to stand apart from this other jive? The lousy score's two to **one**, diddybops! (MOTHER *starts singing a sad dirge for the* *daughter, trailing around the body, throwing kisses at the still figures . . .)*

MOTHER: Yohoooooo, Yohoooooo, daw daw daw daw daw daw daw yodaw hoooodaw deee. All the beauty we missed. All the cool shit. All the sad drinking in crummy bars we missed. All the crissmating and crossbreeding and holy jive in the cellars and closets. The cool flirts in the ladies' meeting. The meeting of the ex-wives. All the Belafontes and Poitiers and hid unfamous nigger formers, hip still on their lawns, and corn and wine, and tippy drinks with green stuff with cherries and white cats and titles, all the television stuff, and tapdances, and the soft music, and stuff. All of it gone. Dead child, save me, or take me . . . *(She bows, kisses the two bodies.)* . . . or save me, take me with you . . . Daw daw doooodaw daw ding ding daw do do dooon . . . *(She trails sadly around the bodies.)*

BLACK MAN: This is horrible. Look at this.

WOMAN: It's what the devil's made. You know that. Why don't you stop pretending the world's a dream or puzzle. I'm real and whole . . . *(holds out her arms)* And yours, only, yours, but only as a man will you know that.

BLACK MAN: You are . . .

WOMAN: I'm the black woman. The one who disappeared. The sleep-walker. The one who runs through your dreams with your life and your seed. I am the black woman. The one you need. You know this. Now you must discover a way to get me back, Black Man. You and you alone, must get me. Or you'll never . . . Lord . . . be a man. My man. Never know your own life needs. You'll walk around white ladies breathing their stink, and lose your seed, your future to them.

BLACK MAN: I'll get you back. If I need to.

WOMAN *(laughs)*: You need to, baby . . . just look around you. You better get me back, if you know what's good for you . . . you better.

BLACK MAN *(Looking around at her squarely, he advances)*:

I better? . . (*a soft laugh*) Yes. Now is where we always are . . . that now . . . (*he wheels and suddenly slaps her crosswise, back and forth across the face.*)

WOMAN: Wha??? What . . . oh love . . . please . . . don't hit me. (*He hits her, slaps her again.*)

BLACK MAN: I want you woman, as a woman. Go down. (*He slaps again*) Go down, submit, submit . . . to love . . . and to man, now, forever.

WOMAN (*weeping, turning her head from side to side*): Please don't hit me . . . please . . . (*She bends.*) The years are so long, without you, man, I've waited . . . waited for you . . .

BLACK MAN: And I've waited.

WOMAN: I've seen you humbled, black man, seen you crawl for dogs and devils.

BLACK MAN: And I've seen you raped by savages and beasts, and bear bleach-shit children of apes.

WOMAN: You permitted it . . . you could . . . do nothing.

BLACK MAN: But now I can (*He slaps her . . . drags her to him, kissing her deeply on the lips.*) That shit is ended, woman, you with me, and the world is mine.

WOMAN: I . . . oh love, please stay with me . . .

BLACK MAN: Submit, for love.

WOMAN: I . . . I submit. (she *goes down, weeping*) I submit . . . for love . . . please love. (*The* MAN *sinks to his knees and embraces her, draws her with him up again. They both begin to cry and then laugh, laugh, wildly at everything and themselves.*)

BLACK MAN: You are my woman, now, forever. Black woman.

WOMAN: I am your woman, and you are the strongest of God. Fill me with your seed. (*They embrace.* MOTHER *is now crawling around on her knees*)

MOTHER: Tony Bennett, help us please. Beethoven, Peter Gunn . . . deliver us in our sterling silver headdress . . . oh please deliver us.

LeRoi Jones585

BLACK MAN: This is enough of this stuff. Get up, supposed-to-be-mother, and drag that supposed-to-be-sister up, too. This stuff is over and done. Get up or so help me, you die with the dead bitch you worship.

MOTHER: What I care? Batman won't love me without my yellowhead daughter. I'm too old for him or Robin. I can't paint soupcans, the junk I find is just junk, my babies stick in they eyes, I'm sick in the big world, and white shit zooms without me. I'm a good fuck and an intelligent woman . . . frankly . . . frankly . . . (*laughs. Turns to look at the* MAN) Fuck both of you stupid ass niggers . . . you'll never get no light . . . Daughter . . . Daughter . . . put on your wig and wake up dancing. The old Italian wants you to marry him.

BLACK MAN: Why won't these women listen? Why do they want to die?

WOMAN: The white one's fumes strangle their senses. The thing's not dead.

BLACK MAN: I've killed it. And death must come to the thing. I'll do it again. (*shouts*) Die, you bitch, and drag your mozarts into your nasty hole. Your mozarts stravinskys stupid white sculpture corny paintings deathfiddles, all your crawling jive, drag it in and down with you, your officebuildings blowup in your pussy, newspapers poison gases congolene brain stragglers devising ways to deal death to their people, your smiles, your logic, your brain, your intellectual death, go to a dead planet in some metal bullshit, dissolve, disappear, leave your address in the volcano, and turn into the horrible insects of a new planet . . . but leave. I am the new man of the earth, I command you . . . Command bullshit. (*He runs over and stomps the dead* WHITE WOMAN *in her face.*) This kinda command. (*He drags her over to the edge of the stage, and drops her off.*) Into the pit of deadchange, slide bitch slide. (*Smoke and light shoot up where she lands.*)

WOMAN: Yes. Yes . . .

MOTHER: You fool. You crazy thing . . . get out of here.

WOMAN: Why don't you listen . . . or die, old hag!

BLACK MAN (*grabs* MOTHER *by the arm, drags her over to the edge*): Look down in there, smell those fumes. That's ashy death, bitchmother, stinking filthy death. That's what you'll be. Smell it. Look at it!

MOTHER: You fool, you mess with the gods, and shit will belt you.

WOMAN: Listen, old woman, this is a man speaking, a black man. (MAN *shakes the* MOTHER *violently*).

BLACK MAN: Yes, you listen.

MOTHER: No, no . . . (*She pulls away . . . goes to* SISTER *who's now starting to turn over, fan and shake herself*) Get away . . . you've killed my daughter . . . you . . . what, she's still breathing??

WOMAN: I told you she was . . . "sick actress from Broome Street."

MOTHER: Oh, daughter . . . the Italian called you jest a while ago. Get up, pussycat, mama's worried so about you. You hungry? (*She pulls out a box lunch from her brassiere.*) You must be starved.

SISTER (*wakes up, looks around, senses the* DEVIL WOMAN *is missing, dead*): Where . . . where's she . . . ooh . . . Where's my body . . . my beautiful self? Where? What'd you do, you black niggers? What'd you do to me? Where'd you hide me? Where's my body? My beautiful perfumed hole?

MOTHER: The hairy nigger killed you, daughter, dropped you in a . . . pit.

SISTER: What! OOOOOOOOOO . . . (*horrible shriek*) OOOOOOOOOO . . . here . . . OOOOO . . . (*runs toward* BLACK MAN) You beast bastard . . . OOOOOOOO . . . Where'd you stick my body . . .

(MAN *grabs her and tosses her to the floor,* MOTHER *goes over to comfort her*)

MOTHER: Oh, please, pussycat . . . ain't you hungry a little bit? I saved some dinner for you. Eat something, pussycat, baby, don't aggravate yourself. You'll ruin your complexion. Don't let these niggers upset you.

SISTER: Oh, God, I know . . . he's killed me. He's dropped me in that pit. (*weeps unconsolably*)

WOMAN: Bitchfool.

SISTER: You jealous 'cause you ain't blonde like me, nigger. You shut up and get outta here with that nigger . . . You get outta here . . . get outta here. So help me I'll kill you . . . get outta here, get outta here, get outta here . . . (*screams, turns into mad raving creature, runs, puts wig back on head, pulls it down over her eyes, runs around stage screaming,* MOTHER *chasing her, trying to feed her from the box*)

MOTHER: Please . . . oh, please, baby . . . jest a little bit a greens, they's flavored with knuckles . . . oh, pussycat, please, you'll be alive agin . . . that nigger can't stop you . . . pussycat . . .

BLACK MAN (*Stunned, staring, tears coming to his eyes, the* WOMAN *comes to comfort him.*): What can I do . . .

WOMAN: Baby, baby . . .

BLACK MAN: My mother . . . and sister . . . crazy white things slobbering . . . God help me.

WOMAN: Oh, baby, you can't help it . . . you just can't help it.

(*The two women finally fall in the middle of the stage, holding each other, the older* WOMAN *feeding the* SISTER, *with a spoon, out of a small pot, some collard greens. The* SISTER *still sobs.*)

SISTER: OOOOOHhhhhhh God, God help me . . .

BLACK MAN: But this can't go, this stuff can't go. They'll die or help us, be black or white and dead. I'll save them or kill them. That's all. But not this shit . . . not this . . . horrible shit. (MAN *runs over and gets firehose, brings it back and turns it on the two women*) Now, let's start

again, women. Let's start again. We'll see what you get
. . . life . . . or death . . . we'll see . . . (*He sprays them
and they struggle until they fall out. Then the* MAN *and
* WOMAN *stand over the two on the floor.*)

WOMAN: You think there's any chance for them?? You really
think so??

BLACK MAN: They're my flesh. I'll do what I can. (*looks at
her*) We'll both try. All of us, black people.

Curtain

Ben Caldwell

PRAYER MEETING
OR, THE FIRST MILITANT MINISTER

one-act play.

Characters

BURGLAR
MINISTER

The time is the late Sixties. *Black-white trouble in a large U.S. city. The scene is Black. Someone is searching in this darkness with a flashlight. Talking to himself, angrily, in whispered tones. He bumps into an object and curses.*

BURGLAR: Damn! Where's a mother-fuckin' light switch? I can't find nothin' this way. Oh, here it is. (*He spots a lamp with his flashlight and turns it on. The scene is a bedroom, decorated in very expensive French Provincial. The room is semi-dark and eerie from just the light of the table lamp. He looks around appraisingly.*) Mmmmmmm. Looks nice. Oughta be a lotta good shit in here. (*He starts to search in dresser drawers, closets, under the bed, etc. He examines small items and places some, upon approval, into the small canvas bag he's carrying. On the dresser is a picture of a serious looking minister. He picks it up, looks at it, puts it face-down on the dresser.*) I shoulda known this was a preacher's pad. A nigger livin' like this, either a preacher, a politician, or a hustler Really ain't no difference

589

though. All of 'em got some kind of game to get your money! (*All the larger items he's selected, he places near the place of his entrance: a portable T.V., a clock-radio, several suits.*) Sho' is a lotta good shit in here! (*still placing items into the bag*) When you get home tonight, Rev., you gon' find you've been un-blessed. Oh, oh! Somebody's comin'! (*He hides behind the dresser at the sound of someone approaching.*)

MINISTER (*slowly coming, Singing and humming*): What a friend we have in Jeee-sus. Jesus Christ! How many times have I told Ellen 'bout leavin' these lights on! (*Enters the room and drops wearily to a position of prayer at the bedside. Talking to himself; not really praying; so much on his mind that he doesn't notice the disarray of the room. There is no sincerity in his words. It's as though he's rehearsing a role he plays, checking to hear if he sounds convincing in this role. He sounds tired.*) Thank God this day is over! Lord! What a trying, troublesome, day. Trying to console my people 'bout brother Jackson's death at the hands of that white po-liceman. I tried, Lord. I tried to keep them from the path of violence. I tried to show them where it was really brother Jackson's fault fo' provokin' that off'cer. There's a time for protest and a time for silence. They say the off'cer hit him a few times. Brother Jackson could've taken a *little* beatin'. It wouldn't be the first time he'd taken a beating. Now the people want to go downtown and raise hell, Lord. They talk of vengeance! We should leave such things in yo' hands. You said, Vengeance is Mine, Lord. (*pause; long sigh*) For the first time in all my years of delivering God's word they were unbelieving (*shaking his head in disbelief*) and beyond my control. What have I done wrong that has shaken their faith, Lord? (*He practices his most pitiful whine.*) I'm trying to show them the right way. Your way, Lord. But I am truly perplexed. The mayor said if I can't stop them there'll be trouble . . .

and more killing! What must I do, Lord? Tell me how I can save my people?

BURGLAR (*disgustedly*): Aw, man shut up and get up off your motherfuckin' knees! (*The minister is shocked. He looks around, fear all over his face.*)

MINISTER: My God! What? Who's that?! (BURGLAR *starts to come out of hiding and confront the minister with his arguments, man to man. He suddenly realizes that the minister believes he's been answered by God. The minister hides his trembling face in his hands. The* BURGLAR *decides to elaborate on this deception.*)

BURGLAR: What do you mean, who? Who the hell was you talkin' to? Didn't you expect to get an answer? (*The minister rises slowly from his kneeling position and stands frozen in the middle of the room.*) That's right! Get up off your knees! And stop trying to bullshit me! You ain't worried 'bout what's gon' happen to your people. You worried 'bout what's gon' happen to you if something happens to your people. You so sure that if they go up 'gainst the white man they gon' lose and whitey won't need *you* no more. Of if they go up 'gainst whitey and win, then they won't need you. Either way yo' game is messed up. So you want things to stay just as they are. You tell them to do nothin' but wait. Wait and turn the other cheek. No matter what whitey do, always turn the other cheek. As long as you keep them off the white folks you alright with the white folks. MY PEOPLE got to keep catchin' hell so you can live like this! YOU STOP PREACHING AND TEACHING MY PEOPLE THAT SHIT! You better stop or I'll reveal myself and put somethin' on your cheeks!

MINISTER (*nervous and excited*): Lord, Lord! Believe me. Those were not my motives. I was only trying to bring them along in your righteous way. Didn't you say that. . . .

BURGLAR: Don't tell me what I said, DAMNIT! How in the

hell you know I haven't changed my mind since then!
How you know how I feel 'bout that violence-vengeance
bullshit now? I haven't written anything since the Bible!

MINISTER: But my people can't win with violence.

BURGLAR: If you call what they doin' now, winnin', you the
dumbest m.f. ever tried to interpret my word. My people
can do anything if I am with them. I can do anything but
fail. Do you remember that line?

MINISTER: But there are men like the man who killed brother
Jackson who are hoping such a thing will happen. They'll
welcome the opportunity to come into the black community and kill up a lot of inno . . .

BURGLAR: So what! They got to bring some ass to get some
ass! I want my people to BE READY when they come.
The shit you preachin' gon' get MY PEOPLE hurt!

MINISTER: Lord, you keep saying 'my people.' Are black people
your 'chosen people?'

BURGLAR: You goddam right! and you and everybody else
better ack like it!

MINISTER: I, I, I can't accept that. . . .

BURGLAR: What! You questionin' me, man? I oughta come
out from here and . . .

MINISTER: I didn't mean that, Lord. I just thought. . . .

BURGLAR: Stop thinkin'. Especially for so many others. The
only thing you better think about is how to tell my people
the opposite of what you been tellin' them for so long. I
know what's best. I made *all* this shit up. Y'all messed up.
I'm tryin' to help straighten it out.

MINISTER: Give me the strength, Lord, and I will try to do
your bidding.

BURGLAR: Try? Man, you better. Ain't nobody afraid of dyin'
but you. And those like you who're so comfortable they've
forgot they're victims. It's time to put a stop to this shit.
Some of my people gon' have to die so the rest can live
in peace.

MINISTER: But . . .

BURGLAR: But nothing! Tomorrow you'll lead a protest march to end all protest marches. I don't want this to be no damned 'sing-along.' I said a *protest* march! You'll demand justice. And if you don't get justice you'll raise hell. I want brother Jackson's death avenged. You tell my people to be ready. Ready for what ever might come. Tell them I don't want no more cheek turnin'. Tell them I will be with them. (*gestures menacingly with his blackjack*) And if you don't tell them, you will be the first one to feel my . . . wrath. Now pray that you don't forget to do anythin' I've told you to do.

MINISTER: This is a heavy burden you place upon my shoulders, Lord.

BURGLAR: I feel like I'm takin' some of your burdens away. (*He is passing some of the larger items out the window.*)

MINISTER: But why? Why me, Lord?

BURGLAR: Because I feel like it should be you. You don't question that white man's judgment, don't you dare question mine!

MINISTER (*dropping to his knees*): Yes, Lord! Thank You, Jesus!

BURGLAR: And stop calling me Jesus! My name is God! (*MINISTER begins a fervent, mumbled prayer. While he is so occupied, the BURGLAR gathers all he has selected and exits. The MINISTER finishes his prayer, gets up from his knees. He goes to the night table, picks up the Bible. He leafs thru it till he finds the desired passage. He reads it aloud to himself.*) 'As I was with Moses, so I will be with thee; I will not fail thee, nor forsake thee.' (*more searching*) 'An eye for an eye; tooth for tooth; hand for hand; foot for foot.' (*He lays the Bible down, reaches into the drawer, takes out a revolver, checks it, places the Bible and gun atop the table. He walks to the dresser, stands before the mirror, and affects a pulpit pose.*)

MINISTER: Brothers and sisters, I had a talk with God last
night. He told me to tell you that the time has come to
put an end to this murder, suffering, oppression, exploitation to which the white man subjects us. The time has
come to put an end to the fear which, for so long, suppressed our actions. The time has come . . . (*Lights fade
out.*)

Curtain

Ed Bullins

HOW DO YOU DO

A Nonsense Drama

ALL THEIR FACES TURNED INTO THE LIGHTS AND YOU WORK ON
THEM BLACK NIGGER MAGIC, AND CLEANSE THEM AT HAVING SEEN
THE UGLINESS AND IF THE BEAUTIFUL SEE THEMSELVES, THEY
WILL LOVE THEMSELVES.

LeRoi Jones

The play was first performed at the Firehouse Repertory Theater
in San Francisco on August 5, 1965. It was produced by the San
Francisco Drama Circle and directed by Robert Hartman. The
sets were designed by Louie Gelwicks and Peter Rounds. Lights
by Verne Shreve.

Characters

PAUL, *the Image Maker*	Mack McCoy
DORA, *Stereotype*	Marie Bell
ROGER, *Stereotype*	Ray Ashby

*Scene: There must be music throughout rhythmic music of a
blues harmonica or guitar. A long, backless, rough bench is
at front stage; a lone, blinking spot focuses upon the bench.
As the play progresses, the white spot is alternated with
red, orange, green, blue—any color to suggest changes of
mood.*

*The two male players are young, but nearly out of their
youth; the matron is well-fleshed and attractive. Roger is*

595

shabbily dressed; Paul's clothes do not matter. The look and import of taste must be apparent in Dora's dress and mannerisms, except when she becomes excited.

The players are black.

When the curtain rises, Paul sits on one end of the bench. A Georgia chain-gang song plays, and the light is steady.

PAUL: I must make music today, poet music. I've sat here too long making nothing, and I know I've been born to make song. (*A figure appears from the wings. It dances in the shadows to a small plaintive melody, mingled with the blues, and Dora bumps and grinds into the light to the incongruous music. She stops behind the man, and when the music changes to barrel-house blues, she dances like a child around the bench.*) How shall I begin? Should I find the words first, or the melody? Should I suggest a theme?

DORA (*strutting in front of Paul like a streetwalker*): What are you doing? Are you talking to yourself, man? Why are you here alone?

PAUL: Who the hell are you?

DORA: I asked you first! If you're talking to yourself that means you're crazy. I think I'd better report you. (*She starts off, twisting her hips to the quickly-blinking light.*)

PAUL: GO TO HELL! (*DORA reaches the shadows and slows, then hesitates, and stops as she meets ROGER striding briskly toward the light.*)

ROGER: Why hello! Fancy meeting you here.

DORA (*taking Roger's arm and re-entering the light with him*): Fine, thank you. And you?

ROGER (*offers her a seat on the far end of the bench from Paul. He sits next to her and puts his arm around her waist*): Did I ask you how do you do? Oh, I guess it doesn't matter, now does it, old top? As you can see, I'm in wonderful shape. In face (*grimaces*), I'm marvelous. (*Paul sits silently, no longer outwardly brooding. He is ignored by the couple, and looks lost in thought.*)

DORA: Do I know you? I has assumed as much. That suit fits you so well. How much did it cost?

ROGER: One hundred-and-fifty dollars. One of my cheaper numbers. I have sixty-two of them. All exactly like this one. I only wear them on Wednesdays. They were made especially for me. I look so beautiful in my clothes.

DORA: You sho' does.

ROGER: It's nice that you know. You have a fine . . . uhhh . . . intellect.

DORA: I'm president of three clubs!

ROGER: Really!

DORA: And I have color TV!

ROGER: How grand!

DORA: How much do you make?

ROGER: I have a very good job. I'm classified very highly. I'm a G-OOOO. And my credit rating is magnificent.

DORA: How magnificent!

ROGER: Are you married?

DORA (*clutching between his legs*): Would it matter?

ROGER: How do you do?

DORA: Fine, thank you.

ROGER: Fancy meeting you here.

DORA: Yes, one turns up in such exotic surroundings. Especially when one is so cultured and refined.

ROGER: How obvious.

DORA: I have fifty-seven pairs of drawers.

ROGER: Tremendous! Tremendous!

DORA: I don't have my shoes reheeled.

ROGER: Reheeled?

DORA: Yes!

ROGER: I buy my socks by the box.

DORA: How ecstatic!

ROGER: How do you do?

DORA: I'm fine.

ROGER: I know that . . . ha, ha, ha.

PAUL (*not turning from his contemplative position*): OH, FUCK!

ROGER (*to Dora*): Did you fart?

DORA: I'm a lady.

ROGER: Oh, how could I have forgotten? I'm so refined that I sometimes forget the larger issues, you know.

DORA: Is that a British accent?

ROGER: French.

DORA: Sorbonne?

ROGER: Berlitz.

DORA: They're the most pretentious on the continent!

ROGER: How do you do?

DORA (*laying her head upon his shoulder, but only resting her hand on his leg*): I can positively hear the mandolins playing. It's as if we were floating down the Grand Canal in Venice. (*The offkey blues gives a funky squeal.*)

ROGER (*shoves* DORA *who takes a pratfall behind the bench*): Bitch! Get yo' greasy head off'a mah rags!

DORA (*looking up fom the floor*): I have a run in my hose, but I got twenty-eight mo' boxes.

ROGER (*inspecting his manicure*): I say there, old girl, the membrane in the cochlea on which is located the Organ of Corti . . . etc., etc., etc.

DORA: How true.

PAUL (*stands and walks over to* ROGER): Shut up!

ROGER (*looking down at* DORA): Did you say something, Sweetcake?

DORA (*rising and edging toward the bench*): Yes, I said I liked your gold tooth.

ROGER (*flashing his gold tooth and showing her the large diamond on his finger*): You do? What's your name, Honeychile?

DORA: Dora. What's yours?

ROGER: Roger.

DORA: Dodger?

ROGER: No, Stereotype.

DORA: My, my, Sugarpie, so am I.

ROGER: What?

DORA: Of the same breed.

ROGER (*looking at* PAUL's *back retreating to his seat*): Who's dat?

DORA: Just some ole nigger. Dirty, no count Southern boogie, probably.

ROGER: He must be here for some reason. (*calling to* PAUL *in the voice of a white man*) Hey, boy! (PAUL *glowers back at him.*) Yeah, you, fellah. Come down here! (PAUL *stands and saunters back to* ROGER.

The lights change color when PAUL *gets in position and continue to change throughout the play. The music also picks up in tempo, and in* PAUL's *longer speeches, a funeral dirge is played.*)

DORA: He's not a bad-looking chap when you get used to him, a bit coarse, but . . . hummph, probably couldn't pay my taxi fare to town.

ROGER: What's your name, boy?

PAUL: It's Paul.

ROGER: What are you hanging around here for? You're not of our class and quality.

PAUL: No, I'm not.

DORA: What do you do, Honey?

PAUL: I'm an image-maker.

DORA: How do you do?

ROGER: Fine, how are you?

DORA: Better, if the weather holds.

ROGER: How clever. Why didn't I think of that?

DORA: I'm in the society pages of *The Coloured Courier* every day. I'm a debutante.

ROGER: Your ole man did an excellent job shining my shoes dis' mornin'. Tipped the ole nigger a dollah. Some days when I feel good, I tip him two.

DORA: I'm the president of three clubs.

PAUL (*speaking as a lecturer*): Build into the black/white consciousnesses of the Western Judeo-Christian culture, the reality of the diabolical black socio-pathe that it has created.

ROGER: I pay fifty-two fifty for my shoes. I don't support my bastards. I drink forty per cent of the scotch imported in dis great country of my fantasies. I'll work for a white man, when I works. A black woman can't do anything fo' me 'cept lead me to a white one. I hate myself.

DORA: Mink and ermine . . . ohhh, chile . . . it's enough to give me an organism . . . besides poker. My husband ain't a man. He makes love to my brother.

PAUL: Know that man can philosophize himself into any and all positions to justify his greed for power and his cowardice.

ROGER: I can bullshit mah boss just like dat. 'You're one out of a thousand niggers, Roger Stereotype,' he says. 'Y'all sho' knows wha yo' talkin' 'bout, bossman, suh,' I tell him.

DORA: I haven't had an organism since I was beaten by my last white lover. He didn't know how to put a good nigger whuppin' on me like mah ole man usta, but I didn't have patience ta larn him.

PAUL: Tell your victim you are goin' to kill him but giggle, buckdance and break wind before you pull your razor.

DORA (*jumping slightly from her seat*): 'Scuse me.

ROGER: See bitch, I tole you you farted.

DORA: I'm a lady. You don't go 'round talkin' ta ya white bitch like dat.

ROGER: She's refined.

DORA: And me?

ROGERS (*turning to Paul*): Go on, man. Get on with your shit.

PAUL: Give the lady her say.

DORA (*brazen and free*): Yeah, you black mothafucker. How can you expect me to be a fictitious pile of shit when you ain't even man enough to be mah man. If you want to go for that mythical bullshit about the white goddess, then respect yourself by makin' your own dreams. Put a black goddess on her own pedestal beside that white one who's shittin' on your dumb black head as well as her white man's. Don't wait for a white cat to glorify me before you come sniffin' on round home, black sucker. (*pauses*) And another thing, fool. Start takin' care of your nine bastards that you got from showin' me how much man you was, and take me down to the Club on your arm. I've been a waitress enough times to know what fork to stir mah soup with. Yeah, instead of takin' your latest white girl, take me to Sardi's fo' cocktails, and see how you feel with a fine black woman on your arm.

ROGER (*singing girlishly*): I'm so fine. I have the finest rags on my behind.

PAUL (*resolutely, not getting through at all*): Know that evil is the inverse of good, that violence is the basis of power, that hate works to meet its own ends.

ROGER: That Jew boy I work fo' is no older den me. I could wheel 'n deal as good as him. I got mo' on the ball den dat square-ass mothafucker (*He feels* DORA's *thigh.*) Hey, baby, have ya seen mah new Cadillac?

DORA: Your boss drives a Volkswagen.

PAUL (*recollecting*): Should Jews . . . should Jews buy VW's?

ROGER: I's a boss nigger. I'm so hip I can't even talk. It ain't mah language anyway . . . dat's why I talk in an Oxfordian accent. Yawhl.

PAUL: Scratch your head, shuffle, pray to his gods until you decide what day you'll call Judgment.

DORA: I think it's just a shame that we Americans tolerate all those damned . . . pardon me . . . that isn't ladylike, is it? (ROGER *has his hand up her dress now.*) I think something should be done about Cuba, and Red China and the black Congolese. At least that's what my white boyfriend tells me in bed.

PAUL: Imitate him; become an alter-ego Superman, Lone

Ranger and Tarzan, in blackface, but really turn into the Shadow.

ROGER: Are you familiar with karate, chaps?

DORA: Mah white man can do seven pushups!

PAUL: Make him think that you don't know anything about language. That you can't logically think because you say: "I ain't never done no nothin' . . ." DESTROY HIS INSTITUTIONALIZED, STRUCTURED LOGIC THROUGH ILLOGIC . . . YAWHL! (PAUL *is tiring. The couple on the bench are in hot embrace but still speak their lines as if they were having an elocution lesson.*)

ROGER: I live in a hundred-thousand-dollar house, drive a nine-thousand-dollar car, am in debt for sixty thousand. I do well on ten thousand a year.

PAUL: Never let him know you have any brains.

DORA: Chile, that was the grooviest thing I ever fell into. I really, but I mean really, baby, dig all that action . . .

ROGER: We drank twenty fifths of White Label at Blue's last Sadee. Naw, I don't eat watermelon, fried chicken, and I don't know what chittlin's, hog maws and corn bread is, chile. I just don't think of it! . . . Oh Jesus! . . . It's all so unrefined. (ROGER *is becoming more effeminate;* DORA's *voice is turning husky.* PAUL's *speeches don't carry conviction.*)

DORA: You should try my beef stroganoff, darling.

ROGER: My tummy might tumble. (*They break their embrace.*)

DORA: No, it wouldn't, Sweetcake.

ROGER: I'm Ivy League, you know.

DORA: Yes, I was born in Georgia, but my parents left before I was born.

ROGER: You should just see my last golf score.

DORA: Why, of course I buy flesh-colored Maiden Forms.

ROGER: I'm the first one in my firm.

DORA: I sit next to the window where everyone can see me.

ROGER: How do you do?

DORA: Fine, how are you?

ROGER: Fine day, if it doesn't cloud up and shit.

DORA: Really!

PAUL: Don't rape his women, seduce them—you don't have to rape anybody—everyone wants to screw your black ass. RIGHT! (PAUL'S *voice is now a whisper, and* ROGER *feels his manhood returning.*)

ROGER: I wonder if that white bitch will say 'yeah' if I put a one-hundred-dollah bill on the table.

DORA: I've been to every white motel in town.

PAUL: Don't blow up all dat good technology (*cough, cough*) and them there institutions at your disposal. Infiltrate his technology with Ph.D's. (*The harmonica brays like a jackass and the lights flicker as never before.*)

DORA: Let's all turn white.

ROGER: I'm de best, 'cause I just know it. Don't need to go any further den dat. I can't git any better.

DORA: I got to per cents in school, and shit, dat's all I could do to pass. Nex' year I was pregnant.

ROGER: Read a book? Sheet! Ain't gonna be wastin' mah time readin' some fuckin' book. I read one once in school. Just sat up dere and finished it to see what it was all about. Found out dat readin' ain't shit. Ain't gonna be wastin' mah time.

PAUL: Kill him in the mind—the age of the body is done; imitate the State, it kills its questioners in the cerebrum. Become a guerrilla warrior of ideas.

ROGER (*speaking to* DORA): How bout lettin' me buy ya a drink, baby?

DORA: Where?

ROGER: Some little out-of-the-way place I know.

DORA: No!

ROGER: Why?

DORA: You got to take me some place where I can be seen.

PAUL: Sell illogic like he sells soap—his mind is tuned like yours to pick up any crap that comes along and sounds just as good as the other crap.

ROGER: Socratic irony without compassion is Fascism.

DORA: Sophist rhetoric without sympathy is salesmanship.

PAUL: Right, children. (*motioning them to leave*) Now go out and play, children. Go out and burn and turn and learn. Go spread the word.

ROGER: I can take you to the bar of the biggest white motel in the state.

DORA (*smoothing her dress and pulling up her stockings*): I'll be a knockout.

ROGER: All the white chicks will look at me.

DORA (*looking in a hand mirror*): I'm so fine.

ROGER (*standing, holding out his hand to* DORA): How do you do?

DORA: Fine, thank you.

ROGER: Qu'est que c'est?

DORA: Trés bien, merci.

ROGER: ARE YOU INDIAN?

DORA: My great grandfather told many tales . . .

ROGER: I have great empathy with the cause of human rights. But I'm so refined I can never get any farther than a white bar in spreading brotherhood.

DORA: You have great promise and proportions.

ROGER: How do you do? (*They leave the stage doing versions of the latest dances—the twist, swim, frug, etc.*)

PAUL: Fine day, thank you. (*He walks back to his end of the bench and sits.*) I must make music today, poet music. I know that I can make song. (*He seems inspired and begins singing.*) How do you do? Fine, thank you. And you? Trés bien, merci. Really! Fine day if it doesn't open up and swallow us. CAN'T SAY IF I SEE THE QUIET SUB-TLETY IN NO HOPE . . . How do you do . . . I have a gold tooth . . . etc., etc., etc.

Curtain

Joseph White

THE LEADER

A One-Act Play

Characters

REVEREND ABRAHAM LINCOLN BROWN, *a flamboyant Negro minister in his mid-forties, who conveys the impression of devoted self-love*
CORA, *a white woman, aged thirty-five, sophisticated, witty, intelligent*
JOHNSON P. JOHNSON, REVEREND BROWN'S *aide; a comical and exuberant man whose demeanor belies his competence*
MRS. ELIZABETH HARRIS *and*
MRS. GLADYS MAE SCOTT, *group representatives from the Negro community*
REPORTER, *man or woman; arbitrary characterization*
INTERCOM, *female voice*

SCENE 1

A modest business office equipped with several chairs, many books, a coatrack, and a desk on which there are two telephones, an intercom, books, and papers. Several paintings of Negroes adorn the walls, as well as a large mirror on wall stage center.

CORA (*perched on the desk top, legs crossed with shoes removed. She is smoking intermittently, between observing*

REV. BROWN *and referring to the papers in her hands.*): Okay, Hon, start with (*she reads*) 'and as I said to this audience . . .'

REV. BROWN (*paces floor, hands clasped behind him. Pomposity marks his vocal inflections.*): And as I said to this audience at the start of my address, this country, founded on the concept of equal and unallien—unalein—

CORA: Inalienable.

REV. BROWN: Yeah. Yeah. Inalienable . . . And as I said to this audience at the start of my address, this country, founded on the concept of equal and *inalienable* rights for all citizens is now a cesspool of immorality for the black man, in its blatant denial of his full equality. For him, the words 'my country 'tis of Thee, sweet land of liberty' hold no truth. For the twenty-two million black Americans, these lyrics mean:

My country 'tis not free,
it's a wasteland of hyprocrisy,
for thee I cry.
Land where my fathers died,
through history pushed aside.
Where? Where is freedom's ring?

CORA (*applauding*): Wonderful, darling. Those Negroes in Detroit will be hypnotized when they hear you spouting those glorious words.

REV. BROWN: You think so, huh, baby?

CORA (*slides off desk, struts back and forth, speaking rapidly*): They will be positively under your spell; mesmerized by your eloquence; completely overcome with emotion as you make them aware of their humanity.

REV. BROWN (*laughing*): In other words, they gon' *looove* them some Reverend Brown. (JOHNSON *appears at office doorway. Stands there unobserved*)

REV. BROWN: Mirror, mirror, on the wall, am I not the most powerful black man of them all? There are other leaders

whose names we know, but when Negroes want action
(*brief laugh*), they know where to go (*points to himself
Laughing uproariously,* CORA *and* REV. BROWN *lock arms
around each other.*)

CORA (*nestles against* REV. BROWN): My beautiful, beautiful
black leader. My white womanhood is yooooours *forever.*
(*They notice* JOHNSON.)

JOHNSON: They waitin' for you in the conference, Reverend.

REV. BROWN (*flamboyantly raises arm to check the time*):
Great balls o' fire. Is it four o'clock already? Well, lemme
get on in there and get this thing started. (JOHNSON *walks
to clothes rack and removes* REV. BROWN'S *coat. He holds
it as he puts his arm into it.* REV. BROWN *takes a long cigar
from his pocket, removes wrapping and plants it between
his teeth. Immediately,* JOHNSON *lights it.*) Be sure to get
some extra copies of my speech made and keep trying to
reach Hillary in New York. (*puffs of smoke surround*
JOHNSON, *and he begins to cough uncontrollably.*) I'm
gonna be here late tonight, I can see that now. (*snatches
papers from desk and turns to* CORA) Baby, I'm gon' be
here 'till six. You wanna pick me up 'round that time?

CORA: Okay, Hon, I'm going to have a nice dry martini and
then I'll stop back for you and we'll have dinner at my
place.

REV. BROWN: Make sure one martini don't lead to a whole
family of martinis, like they usually do. (*exits*)

(JOHNSON *shifts papers on desk, picks up one, reflects momentarily, then reaches for another, ignoring* CORA. *She
freshens her makeup in the mirror, then walks provocatively
across the office. She slips into her shoes and adjusts stock-
ing garter. She glances to see whether* JOHNSON *is watching
her.*)

CORA: Johnson, what do have against me?

JOHNSON (*raises his head slowly from the paper he is reading*): You white.

CORA: Well, I think you're being silly. Don't you know that race is theoretical? It's human character that counts.

JOHNSON (*angrily*): Broad, don't tell me nothin'. Go home! You always sittin' 'round here runnin' your mouth 'bout stuff you don't know a damn thing about! The Reverend can't even do his work, for you in his way all the time. You ain't foolin' me none! I know you a spy! I wish I could put your butt outa here for good. I tell the Reverend every day that you ain't worth his time, an' I'll keep tellin' him 'till he listens.

CORA: All I know is that Reverend Abraham Lincoln Brown is a man among men, a human pillar of strength. And I love him with every fiber of my soul.

JOHNSON: That ain't very much, 'cause I don't believe white folks got a soul.

CORA: And Negroes talk about white people being racists! You're worse than any Mississippi sheriff. (*takes her coat from the rack, slips into it*)

JOHNSON: You right. I admit I'm a racist. I don't like white people walkin' or ridin', slippin' or slidin' . . . (*becoming angered*) especially them ones like you, joining civil rights groups with they dresses up to they tails talkin' 'bout (*mimicking female voice*) I'm here to help the black man.

CORA: That's a horrible thing to say, and you know it.

JOHNSON: Don't say nothin' else to me. Git out!

CORA (*leaving*): I'll get out but I *will* be coming back because he needs me. You have his confidence, black people have his leadership, but don't you ever forget that it's me who has his love. (*slams doors as she leaves. Lights fade out quickly.*)

SCENE 2

Next morning, lights up, and REV. BROWN *is seated at his desk and speaking on the telephone.*

REV. BROWN (*clears his throat often, throughout conversation*): Uh-hum, why yes, Governor, I did see that mentioned in the newspaper this morning, but with all due respect to your suggestion, it is not a question of how much the demonstrations irritate the white community. It is the position of the National Freedom Association to continue demonstrations until racial discrimination is gone from the face of America. (*nods emphatically several times*) Absolutely, Governor. (*nods, clears throat*) And I might prevail upon you, sir, to assert the powers of your office to influence the people of the state to curb their attacks on our marchers. . . . By all means, Governor. I'd be in favor of such a panel. (*nods*) . . . within a week? Fine, sir . . . absolutely . . . good of you to call, Governor, and may God bless the righteousness of our ways. (*replaces receiver, and leans back in his chair, laughing.*) They *all* is scared of *this* black boy. (JOHNSON *enters, carrying several papers. He places them on the desk.* REVEREND BROWN *stands and begins pacing the floor.*) Johnson!

JOHNSON (*snaps to attention*): Yes, sir!

REV. BROWN: I wanna ask you some very, very important questions.

JOHNSON: Yes, sir!

REV. BROWN: Who's the most powerful, the most respected black man in America?

JOHNSON (*rapidly, as if rehearsed*): You is, Reverend Brown. (*emphasizing with head gestures*) You the most powerful black man in America! Everbody know that! Yes, sir! You the big chief black man in charge!

REV. BROWN (*laughs uproariously*): You ain' lyin', Johnson. I am the black man's Julius Caesar. (*clears throat*) With certain exceptions in our characters, of course . . . Johnson, the next question is gonna be a really hard one. (*spins around and stabs a finger at* JOHNSON, *who jumps back*) And you *really* got to be on the ball to answer this.

JOHNSON (*now grinning, nodding expectantly*): Go 'head, Reverend, see if I know.

REV. BROWN: All right, here I go . . . (*comic interpretation,*

singing the words) Who do the President of thee You-
nited States of America send for when black folks start
acting up?

JOHNSON (*breathless, immediate response*): He send for you!

REV. BROWN (*explodes into laughter*): Who do you say the
President of thee You-nited States send for? (*cups his ear.*)

JOHNSON (*with comical head bobs*): He send for Reverend
Abraham Lincoln Brown! That's who he send for when
black folks start actin' up. 'Cause he know who the most
powerful black man in America is!

REV. BROWN (*pounds* JOHNSON *on his back*): Johnson, my
boy, them words sound so goood to my ears I don't ever
wanna wash 'em no more.

JOHNSON (*his head bobbing vigorously*): Yes, sir. He send
for you.

REV. BROWN: Now, Johnson, for the last question. Why do he
send for Abe Brown?

JOHNSON (*quick reply*): 'Cause he know them black folks
can't wipe they behinds unless you there to tell 'em to!

REV. BROWN (*laughs approvingly*): Johnson, you all right; and
(*gets serious for the moment*) someday, when the good
Lord sees fit to put me out in the pasture, there can't be
no other logical choice but you to take over here.

JOHNSON (*feigned diffidence*): Oh . . . (*he laughs.*) . . . how
could anybody take your place, Reverend?

REV. BROWN (*as though he were standing before his congregation*): The good men of this earth die, but better men
come forth to take their place and carry out the good
deeds of the Lord Almighty.

JOHNSON: Yes, Reverend Brown, people all over America
know about your good deeds.

REV. BROWN: Not everybody, Johnson. And that's what me
and you got to talk about. . . . In order for a man to stay
in the minds of the people, he got to keep getting himself
in the news. We got to start a publicity campaign for me.
We got to make my name so well known that when

America thinks of black people and civil rights, the Reverend Abraham Lincoln Brown pop in they minds, automatic.

JOHNSON: I know what you mean . . . like when you think of Sears, you think of Roebuck, or when you think of hog maws, you think of chittlin's.

REV. BROWN (*clears throat*): Yeah. That's exactly what I mean. (*paces floor, hands clasped behind his back*)

JOHNSON: Well, Reverend, I think people already think of you when they think of hog maws—I mean, civil rights.

REV. BROWN: Yeah, but these young boys, these radicals, is messin' with my image. I got to show them that there's only one *official* black leader . . . and that's me. . . . We got to *engraaaave* the name Abe Brown on the mind of America.

JOHNSON (*emulates* REV. BROWN; *paces the floor*): Hmmmmm . . . . . (*They crisscross each other several times in deep concentration.* JOHNSON *stops, snaps his fingers.*) I got it! You could make a statement about United States involvement in Southeast Asia, or maybe you could write a book.

REV. BROWN (*unimpressed*): Naw. Everybody and their cousin got somethin' to say about American foreign policy . . . and it take too long to write a book. (*They continue to pace.*)

JOHNSON (*snaps fingers*): I got it!

REV. BROWN (*looks at* JOHNSON *hopefully*): What? What?

JOHNSON (*grinning*): I could try and get one of the national magazines to do an exclusive article about you, and you could tell the interviewer some things you've never said before . . . that oughta do it.

REV. BROWN (*reflectively*): We'll try it, but it ain't exactly what I had in mind.

JOHNSON: Okay. (INTERCOM *rings.*) In the meantime, I'll be thinkin' up some bettuh ideas. (*reaches for desk switch*) Yes?

INTERCOM: The ladies from Taylor, Mississippi, are here.

JOHNSON (*into* INTERCOM): Okay. I'll be right there. (*to* REV. BROWN) You got that three thirty appointment with these ladies, Reverend.

REV. BROWN: I feel like jaw-jucking with those Mississippi hens much as I feel like brushing my teeth with pepper. . . . Okay, show 'em in. (JOHNSON *exits*) (REV. BROWN *sits at his desk stiffly, adjusts his tie, and begins to write intently.*)

JOHNSON (*walks in, followed by the two ladies*): Reverend.

REV. BROWN (*stands, smiles broadly*): Ladies, how y'all do? (*walks around to front of desk, extends both hands in a warm clasp to one, then another*)

JOHNSON: This here is Mrs. Elizabeth Harris, and this is Mrs. Gladys Mae Scott.

REV. BROWN: How nice to see both of you.

MRS. HARRIS (*grinning*): It's *our* pleasure, Reverend.

MRS. SCOTT (*grinning*): Yaaaaaass.

REV. BROWN: Have some chairs.

MRS. HARRIS
MRS. SCOTT: } (*chorus*) Thank yuh.

REV. BROWN: Y'all care for coffee or tea?

MRS. HARRIS: Well, yaaaaass . . . . . coffee, please.

REV. BROWN: How 'bout you, Mrs. Scott?

MRS. SCOTT: I think I'd like some tea, please. (*quick laugh*)

REV. BROWN: Johnson, coffee and tea for the ladies. (JOHNSON *nods and exits.* REV. BROWN *returns to his chair.*) From what y'alls letter said, there's some *graaave* problems in your city. . . . Lemme see. (*bends over, looking for the letter in lower desk drawers*) I got your letter right here. . . . (*The ladies nudge each other and snicker.*) . . . Well, I can't find it right now, but tell me briefly what the situation is.

MRS. HARRIS: I guess Mrs. Scott oughta tell you, she's the best talker.

MRS. SCOTT (*quick laugh*): No, you go 'head, Mrs. Harris.

MRS. HARRIS: All right. Well, Reverend . . . people in Taylor
are scared. They are just as scared to vote in the 'lections
now as they was before the government passed the law
givin' them the right. They have been without political
power so long they don't realize that in a county where
we is the majority, we can begin to have some control
over our future. (MRS. SCOTT *nods affirmatively throughout.*
REV. BROWN *listens attentively, forming a bridge with his
fingers.*)

MRS. SCOTT: In the last election for sheriff . . . (JOHNSON
*enters with serving tray and serves the ladies. They ex-
change courtesies.*) Like I was saying, in the last election
we had for sheriff, only three per cent of the eligible
Negroes voted. If thirty per cent had turned out, we could
have a Negro sheriff. Now we stuck with one of the worst
crackers in the county for the next two years.

MRS. HARRIS: As we said to you in the letter, Reverend . . .
(REV. BROWN *suddenly alert, catches himself dozing; clears
throat; stiffens his posture.*) the election of a police commissioner and other city officials is three months away,
and we want *our* people to have some of the jobs.

MRS. SCOTT (*interjects*): When is *our* chance gon' come?

REV. BROWN (*cautions them with raised finger*): Our time
will come, for the Lord giveth and the Lord taketh away.

MRS. SCOTT (*reverently*): Well, the Lord been givin', (*em-
phatic and rapid*) and the white folks been takin' it away.

MRS. HARRIS (*sipping from her cup*): That's why we've come
to see you, Reverend. We thought you might have some
ideas to encourage our people to register and vote.

REV. BROWN: Has any of your community groups launched a
door-to-door campaign?

MRS. SCOTT: Well, not a community group 'zactly, but Helen
Chester and Annamay Smith was goin' door-to-door until
Helen's husband went on nights at the saw mill, and she
had to stay with the kids. (*looks to* MRS. HARRIS, *who*

acknowledges with supportive head bobs) And Annamay got into the last months of (*shyly*) the family way.

REV. BROWN (*clears throat*): I see. . . . Well, my suggestion is that you form a community group for just this purpose, giving the field teams specific areas to cover. (*looks at his watch*) That's the only way to reach each and every potential voter. (MRS. SCOTT *begins taking notes feverishly.*) You might also try sending letters throughout the nation, such as the Department of Justice, attorney general's office, uh—

MRS. HARRIS (*interrupts*): But we've tried them all. (*throws up her hands in exasperation*) We've tried everything.

MRS. SCOTT (*flustered*): She's right. Reverend. We've done everything we can. (*in rapid and frenzied succession, counting on her fingers*) We've been to see SNICK, FLICK, RICK, TICK, KOR, POOR, SNORE—

MRS. HARRIS (*places her hand on* MRS. SCOTT's *to silence her.* REV. BROWN *clutches his lapels, clears throat, and stares at the ceiling*): Well, Reverend, you see (*pauses*) well, what we really want (*pauses*) I mean, what our community wanted was (*pauses*) well, would you come down to our city and start a voter registration drive?

REV. BROWN (*His composure slipping, he straightens in his chair and lowers his head gradually*): By all means, Mrs. Harris. I'd be only too happy to do whatever I can for y'all. Howevah, (*pauses*) you should first exhaust all the local methods, and then if that doesn't work, well, the National Freedom Association will definitely enter (CORA *enters*) the situation.

CORA (*stumbles into the room, intoxicated, with her shoes under one arm*): Hon! Hey Hoooonnn! (*advances toward the two ladies*) Well, well, well! (*examines them closely*) Some blaaack, big-lip, flat-nose ladies from—don't tell me—from Downnnn South! (*hysterical laughter; she snatches* MRS. SCOTT's *hat*) And that beeeeautiful hair all fried and

fizzled! (MRS. SCOTT *spins around reaching for her hat.*
CORA *replaces it, covering* MRS. SCOTT'S *eyes. Straightening
the hat in anger* MRS. SCOTT *looks at* MRS. HARRIS, *and they
exchange looks of astonishment.*)

REV. BROWN (*clears throat and smiles*): Excuse me, ladies.
(*moves to restrain Cora, who darts across the office and
avoids him. She sits on the floor.*)

CORA (*singing*): Hon can't catch me. Hon can't catch me.
Wooweeee, your big black leader is chasing a white lady!

REV. BROWN (*loudly*): CORA! (*Apologetically, he turns to the
ladies and appeases them with a broad smile. He turns to
CORA and says calmly, but firmly.*) I've got some business
here and you must get up and leave right now. (*The two
ladies, heads together, begin whispering.* CORA *laughs uncontrollably. Office door opens.* JOHNSON *rushes in, wearing
hat and coat. He races straight for* CORA.)

JOHNSON: You stupid! ———

REV. BROWN: Johnson! . . . I'll handle this! (*turns to the
ladies*) Ladies, I'm sorry this happened. You bettuh leave
now. (*smiling*) I'll get in touch with y'all. (JOHNSON
*ushers them out hurriedly, as they whisper and look back
at the scene.*)

MRS. SCOTT (*The ladies exit, then the door opens and* MRS.
SCOTT *steps back inside, holding on to door knob. Abruptly,
she turns to the audience*): Don't tell me white folks ain't
crazy! (*closes door and exits*)

CORA: Where's the black ladies goin'? (*calling after them*)
Blaaaaaaaak laaaaaaaaadies!

REV. BROWN (*lifts* CORA *into chair*): There, now.

JOHNSON (*shouting*): Reverend, Reverend, I told you! I told
you she wasn't nothin' but trouble! What we gon' do
now? Time them women hit the street, everybody gon'
know 'bout this mess. You got to git rid of her, Reverend.

REV. BROWN (*Kneeling before* CORA, *he puts on her shoes.
He speaks with calm seriousness*): Johnson, I listen to

your advice when it's got to do with the affairs of this organization, but this is my *woman,* and I care about her more than I care about all the Negroes in the world! And the whole civil rights movement! (*pause*) I'll never git rid of her. (CORA *is oblivious to the conversation and hiccupping intermittently.*)

JOHNSON (*clasps his ears in disbelief*): Oh no, Reverend! You don't mean that. You can't mean that!

REV. BROWN (*stands and faces* JOHNSON): I've never been more truthful in my life. (*points to Cora*) This is where *my* heart is.

JOHNSON: But . . . but . . . what about those women? They gittin' away and you ain't helped them with their problems.

REV. BROWN (*annoyed*): I don't care about those women and their problems! . . . Don't stand there gaping! Get Cora some black coffee!

CORA (*points feebly at* JOHNSON): Thas right, you heard 'im.

JOHNSON (*exits slowly, as if his vitality has been siphoned*): Oh Reverend. Oh Reverend. (*lights fade out slowly*)

SCENE 3

The next morning, REV. BROWN *is seated at his desk, being interviewed by a reporter, who takes notes as* REV. BROWN *speaks.* JOHNSON *is seated to the rear of the reporter, so that only* REV. BROWN *sees him.* JOHNSON *gestures and coaches* REV. BROWN *occasionally during the interview.*

REPORTER: Reverend Brown, and is it also a fact that you have few or no interests outside of your total commitment to the civil rights movement?

REV. BROWN (*clears throat*): Hmmmm. Yes, that is an accurate statement. . . . I cannot indulge in the pleasantries of life while my brothers and sisters are being oppressed.

REPORTER: Do you attribute this dedication to your personal philosophy, or has it been stimulated by your religious background?

REV. BROWN (*pauses, angles his head, epitomizing his concept of how it looks to be sincere*): Young man, throughout my life, I have been a *strong* believer in these words of Edmund Burke: 'The only thing necessary for the triumph of evil is that good men do nothing'. (*relaxes and adjusts his tie*)

REPORTER: Very nice words, they are. (*Rather obviously, REV. BROWN looks at his watch.*) Sir, I'm curious to know who some of your close friends are.

REV. BROWN (*clears throat*): On this planet, those close to me number very few; namely, (*massages his chin and hesitates*) my sister, Olivia, and my trusted associate, (*points to JOHNSON*) Johnson P. Johnson, who, I might add, has been with me since I first became pastor of Holy Disciplines Baptist Church, in Rocky Mount, North Carolina. But, I reserve my intimate communication for the (*looks upward*) All-mighty.

REPORTER (*humbly*): Of course. Of course. (*pause*) Do you expect fruitful results from the protest in front of the Capitol next week?

REV. BROWN (*looking to JOHNSON, who nods his head*): I think it will point out to our legislators and to the nation at large that the black American has reached the end of his patience and will no longer mark time where full equality is concerned.

REPORTER: Rev. Brown, you say that the black American has reached the end of his patience? . . .

REV. BROWN (*forcefully*): Yes. I did say that.

REPORTER: Sir, are you saying that there is the possibility of widespread rioting?

REV. BROWN (*sees JOHNSON shaking his head frantically and takes his sign*): Well, I am simply saying this: the black American has reached a point of *no* return in his fight for civil rights. (*JOHNSON nods affirmatively, grins, and gives REV. BROWN the forefinger-and-thumb "o" of approval.*)

REPORTER (*moves to the edge of his chair*): Sir, I don't wish to belabor the point, but when you say the Negro has reached a point of no return, are you not saying in effect that rioting seems to be the logical recourse, if conditions in America do not improve? (REV. BROWN *considers the question momentarily, straightens in his chair, and prepares to answer.* JOHNSON *coughs loudly and rushes over to the* REPORTER, *patting him on his back, simultaneously raising him out of the chair and concluding the interview. While he does this, he says . . .*)

JOHNSON: Er—well, sure glad your magazine wanna do a story on the Reverend. We gon' be lookin' folwa'd to it. (*to* REV. BROWN) Ain't that right, Reverend Brown?

REV. BROWN (*quizzical expression*): Yes, of course.

REPORTER (*He takes the hint and places his notes into a folder.*) Reverend, I've taken enough time from your busy schedule. If I need further information, I'll call your office.

REV. BROWN (*stands and shakes the* REPORTER'S *hand*): It's been my pleasure. I'll been lookin' folward to the story in your *fine* magazine.

REPORTER: Good-bye, sir. And good luck to you.

REV. BROWN: Thank ya, and give my regards to Mel Clemens on your staff.

REPORTER: I certainly will. (*He is escorted to the door by* JOHNSON, *while* REV. BROWN *sits and reads newspaper.* JOHNSON *shakes the* REPORTER'S *hand, and they exchange good-bye's.* REPORTER *exits.*)

JOHNSON (*approaches* REV. BROWN, *first hesitantly, and then with a sense of urgency*): Reverend Brown, I'm worried.

REV. BROWN (*puts down newspaper, which he had been scanning*): Well, speak up, Johnson. You know you can talk to me.

JOHNSON (*quickly*): Well it's those two women. You *know* they're gon' run their mouth 'bout Cora bustin' in here.

REV. BROWN (*motions his indifference*): Oh, forget that busi-

ness. I got more important things on my mind. (*pause*)
But if you're worried 'bout it, then you take care of it.
(*continues reading his newspaper*)

JOHNSON: Well, I plan on calling them and reconcilin' the
whole thing.

REV. BROWN (*nods his head and continues to read, while*
JOHNSON *picks up paper from the floor and inspects the*
office briefly. Pause): Johnson . . . (*puts down paper*)

JOHNSON: Yes, sir.

REV. BROWN (*serious*): Sit down here a minute.

JOHNSON (*a quick servile smile. Sits*): Yes, sir?

REV. BROWN: Johnson, I wanna ask you some very, very important questions.

JOHNSON (*quickly*): Yes, sir! Youthemostpowerfulblackman-
inAmerica. Everybody know that. . . .

REV. BROWN (*laughs approvingly*): Naw . . . naw, Johnson.
Not them questions. This is about that publicity campaign we've been talkin' about.

JOHNSON (*elated*): You think of somethin' good, Reverend?

REV. BROWN (*pauses, takes out cigar from coat pocket and*
lights it. Poses first question to JOHNSON *by enunciating*
each word clearly to make his point): What would you
think of a man who climbed up a tree to rescue a cat?

JOHNSON (*puzzled, pauses*): What you gittin' at?

REV. BROWN (*impatient*): Just answer the question, Johnson!

JOHNSON (*contemplates answer*): Well, I'd think he was a
vary kind man who loved cats.

REV. BROWN (*considers the answer with several nods of the*
head): Hmmmmm . . . What would you think of a man
who jumped into a river to save someone who was drowning?

JOHNSON (*quickly*): I'd think he was brave.

REV. BROWN (*stops pacing, turns abruptly, and looks at* JOHN-
SON): Why?

JOHNSON: 'Cause I cain't swim!

REV. BROWN: This is no time for clownin'. (*pauses; begins to pace*) Tell me this, Johnson. What would you think of a man who burned himself to death to dramatize his feelings for a cause he believed in?

JOHNSON (*shakes head several times*): Personally, I'd think he was crazy . . . but I guess other people would think he reeeeally believed in that cause.

REV. BROWN (*speaks with unusual seriousness*): Well, Johnson . . . (*pauses*) I'm gonna burn myself up——

JOHNSON (*leaps from his chair, runs to* REV. BROWN, *shouting*) No Reverend—No! I won't let you do it! (*tearful*) Our people need you! Oh, Reverend. No!

REV. BROWN (*grinning*): Steady boy. I'm not gonna burn ah hair on my head. (*blows cigar smoke in* JOHNSON's *direction*)

JOHNSON (*takes out his handkerchief and wipes his eyes*): Well, why you say that, Reverend? Why you ever say somethin' like that? (*coughs from the smoke*)

REV. BROWN (*pacing floor*): Sit down, Johnson. (*pause*) You know our people won't let their leaders be like MacArthur or Eisenhower and fight battles from behind the lines; they want their leaders right up front, gittin' their heads busted—and then gittin' put in jail. Well, I got an idea that will make me the most famous black man in the history of the world. (*stops and speaks directly to* JOHNSON) Next week, when all those thousands of Negroes go protesting to Washington, well, I'm not gonna give my speech. (*shrewdly*) No. Instead, you gonna help set me on fire——

JOHNSON: What!

REV. BROWN: But, you gonna scream and shout and put out that fire before I git burned.

JOHNSON: Oh Reverend, why you got to do somethin' crazy like that?

REV. BROWN: It's all part of the game, Johnson.

JOHNSON: That ain't no game, playin' 'roun' with your life like that.

REV. BROWN: You worry too much, Johnson. I know what I'm doin'. After this, when I cut my toenails, it'll be in the news. (*exits*)

JOHNSON (*Gets up from his seat and paces in a confined area. Stops, looks up at the ceiling—long pause—and then shrugs his shoulders. Goes back to the desk and picks up phone receiver*): Yeah! (*authoritatively*) Git me Elizabeth Harris or (*he takes a card from his coat pocket and looks at it*) Gladys Mae Scott. They stayin' at the Regency. Yeah! (*Holding on to the receiver, he sings softly and performs an exaggerated dance step in place. His routine ends abruptly when party on other end responds.*) Uh—uh—Hello. To whom am I speaking to? (*pause*) Why, hello, Miz Harris. This is Mr. Johnson—Reverend Brown's assistant. Yes, dat's right. How you feelin' today? (*pause*) Good. (*pause*) Yes, well, Reverend Brown asked me to call y'all and offer his apologies for what happened yestiday. (*pause*) Terrible thing. (*pause*) Yes. The Reverend feels awfully bad 'bout it, and he gon' try to git down your way after the demonstration in Washington. (*pause*) Well, he'd sure appreciate it, 'cause a thing like that git out—well, you know how those newspapers exaggerate, and before you know it, they done made a mountain outa molehill. Well, all right— (CORA *enters, stage left.*)

CORA (*She is in high spirits and her tone of voice is musical*): Where is he? Where is my darling? Come out, come out, wherever you are.

JOHNSON (*cups his hand over the phone and motions frantically for* CORA *to leave. Speaks into receiver rapidly*): Thank ya for callin'. (*to the point of incoherence*) I meanitwasnicetalkin'toya (*slams down receiver. Addresses* CORA *with building anger.*) Woman! Git to your senses! Don't come bustin' in here carryin' on like a fool! This ain't no hangout for you, anyway. I told you a hundred times! Git out! You *see* the Reverend ain't here. (CORA *appears unaffected. She promenades slowly around the office, touching books,* REV. BROWN'S *chair, etc. She remains oblivious to* JOHNSON'S *remarks. Finally, she stops in front of the mirror and inspects her makeup.*)

JOHNSON (*calmed down*): Why you keep comin' here?

CORA (*flippantly*): Because I love him, you fool!

JOHNSON (*He stares at* CORA, *who continues to admire herself in the mirror. He rests his chin on his hand and reflects. He speaks softly*): You know, Cora, in all honesty, you a good lookin' woman. (CORA *is startled. She turns sharply and faces Johnson, as if paralyzed.*)

JOHNSON (*softly, with sincerity*): I've said some mean things to you, but I gotta admit you ain't as bad as I say.

CORA (*incredulous*): Well! To *what* do I owe *this*?

JOHNSON (*Keeping his distance, he fidgets with his hands*): I just been thinkin' that there ain't no point in us argin' and carryin' on.

CORA (*seriously*): You really mean that, Johnson? (JOHNSON *nods yes. A long and awkward pause, during which* CORA *combs her hair, occasionally looking at* JOHNSON, *who moves next to her. Another long pause, during which they face each other for a moment. Then* JOHNSON *walks over to and behind the desk, carelessly looking at some papers.* CORA *continues to comb her hair. Then she replaces the comb in her handbag and walks over to the front of the desk very slowly, placing her bag on top of the papers that* JOHNSON *is looking at. Pause. They stare at each other for an extended moment. Another pause. Then* CORA, *walking very slowly over to* JOHNSON, *begins to embrace him.*)

JOHNSON (*recoils immediately and at the same time shouts hysterically*): I KNEW IT! I KNEW IT! (*ranting and waving his arms*) YOU WASN'T NO DAMN GOOD! I KNEW YOU WASN'T NO DAMN GOOD! (*begin-*

ning to control himself, he laughs loudly.) I trapped you,
woman! I got you! You don't love him. You never loved
him. You anybody's woman. (*slow and deliberate, as* CORA
remains calm) Just wait 'till I tell Reverend Brown. Your
ass won't be around here no more! (*laughs. Pause* CORA
*picks up her handbag and walks to the door. She stops
and turns around.* JOHNSON *laughs at her.* CORA *mimics
his laughter and throws out her arm exuberantly. She slams
the door and exits. Lights fade out quickly.*)

SCENE 4

Before lights go up, JOHNSON *is heard offstage shouting
excitedly:* "Rev. Brown! Rev. Brown!" *Lights up.* REV.
BROWN *is at his desk reading a newspaper. When he
hears* JOHNSON *yelling his name, he looks up and shrugs.*

JOHNSON (*enters in a hurry*): Reverend Brown!

REV. BROWN: What you eat for breakfast? Grasshoppers?

JOHNSON (*slightly winded*): Reverend Brown. I got somethin'
important to tell you!

REV. BROWN: Nothing in the whole world is serious enough
to make a man open his mouth that wide so early in the
morning!

JOHNSON: It's accordin' to what he got to say!

REV. BROWN: Well, before you bust a gut, lemme hear it.

JOHNSON: Reverend, it ain't easy to come to you with somethin' like this—

REV. BROWN: (*indifferently*) Yeah?

JOHNSON: I hate I got to tell you—

REV. BROWN: If something's bothering you, let's talk about it.

JOHNSON: Reverend, I know how you feel about Cora, and
you know all along I've been tellin' you to git rid of her.

REV. BROWN (*displays irritation*): Is that all you gotta say?
You sound like an old broken record.

JOHNSON (*pauses*): Much as it hurts me to tell you this, I
got to for your own good.

REV. BROWN: If it's about me breakin' up with Cora, I don't wanna hear it.

JOHNSON (*with mounting excitement*): Reverend, you don't realize the seriousness of this situation. . . . Yestiday, in this office, I'm mindin' my own business, an' Cora, tried to . . . tried to . . . make love to me!

REV. BROWN (*suddenly enraged, he tosses the newspaper aside, stands and speaks loudly*) How *daaaaare* you! How *daaaaare* you come to me with a story like like . . . ANSWER ME!

JOHNSON (*stunned*): Reverend, it's the truth. She did try.

REV. BROWN (*throws up his hand in protest*): STOP! I don't believe it. You're lyin'. You're sayin' that because you never liked her. I'm *shocked* that you would stoop so low! Fabricatin' like that!

JOHNSON (*weakening*): But——but——

REV. BROWN (*roaring*): Don't you *but* me! . . . In all my years of association with you, I've never seen the snake in you come out like it is today! . . . Now, you stop that poison tongue, and I never wanna hear it again! (JOHNSON *is dismayed, appears completely overcome. Long pause.* REV. BROWN *paces floor with a stern expression on his face, while hands are clasped behind his back. Dumbfounded,* JOHNSON *stands in place with his mouth open, staring at* REV. BROWN. *After a pause,* JOHNSON *speaks. His voice is barely audible.*)

JOHNSON: Reverend Brown? . . . (REV. BROWN *does not reply.*) Reverend Brown? . . . I'm sorry 'bout what I told you. (REV. BROWN *still does not reply.*) I shouldn't have said it, Reverend . . . I don't know what got in me. (*shakes his head and looks at the floor. Softly*) I was wrong. (REV. BROWN *stops pacing, turns, and faces* JOHNSON. JOHNSON *raises his head and looks at* REV. BROWN.) I was wrong.

REV. BROWN (*approaches* JOHNSON *slowly, and, in a fatherly gesture, puts his arm around Johnson's shoulder. A short pause*): I understand. (*another short pause*) The trademark of a great man, in my mind, is one who can admit when he's wrong. And you have demonstrated that right here. You have demonstrated it. And I forgive you one hundred per cent. Give me your hand.

JOHNSON: (*Solemnly, he extends his hand. They shake.*)

REV. BROWN: Now let's forgit about this woman stuff and get down to business. (*He walks briskly to his desk and sits. He opens a lower desk drawer, removes and opens a large envelope.*)

JOHNSON (*appears preoccupied and unresponsive to* REV. BROWN's *sudden gush of energy. He looks down at the floor for several seconds; then he speaks restrainedly*): You still gon' through with this thing in Washington?

REV. BROWN: (*ebullient*) The more I think of it the more I can't wait to get down there! (*laughs*) Man, those news wires gonna be buzzin'. (*sorts through his papers, studying them with intent. He looks up at* JOHNSON, *who remains somber.*) Stop sulking like an old hen and come on over here. (JOHNSON *walks around desk to* REV. BROWN's *right.* REV. BROWN *points to papers on desk.* JOHNSON *bends over as* REV. BROWN *speaks.*) This here is Pennsylvania Avenue, in front of the White House.

JOHNSON: In front of all those people?

REV. BROWN: We ain't gon' be *there.* We gonna be in the park, 'cross the street, where this X is. Okay. (*claps his hands as he says the following word*) Now! (*waves a finger at* JOHNSON) Everything depends on you! (*points with pencil*) This is you and me. Looka here. (*gets up*) I'll show ya. (*motions* JOHNSON *to stage center and begins to instruct him.*) There some benches in this park. You'll be sittin' in the last one, which is about fifteen feet away from me. Get that chair over there and pull it over here. (JOHNSON *gets chair.*) Now sit down in it. (JOHNSON *sits.*) First we check to see if anybody's around. (*They look around.*) When we sure nobody ain't lookin', I'll pour the gas on my clothes. I'll lay down on the grass, you start yellin', and I'll light the match. As soon as you see fire and smoke, you run over and *smother* me with your coat. And don't stop yellin' the whole time! Understand?

JOHNSON: I understand, but—ah———

REV. BROWN (*interrupts*): Now, if the reporters ask any questions, like how come you was there to save me, you tell 'em you knew all the time I was gonna do it, but at the last minute you couldn't let me. (*returns to his desk, picks up several papers, and hands them to* JOHNSON, *as he speaks*) Now, we going down there next Wednesday and by that time have this stuff memorized and don't let it out of your sight.

JOHNSON (*takes papers and puts them in his inside coat pocket*): Yes, Reverend.

REV. BROWN (*looks at his watch*): Uh-oh! (*walks hurriedly to the coatrack.*) S'pose to meet Cora at ten o'clock. (*puts on coat*) I'll be back by two. (*exits*)

JOHNSON (*mimics* REV. BROWN'S *exit comically and with sarcasm. Looks at watch*): Uh-oh! (*walks hurriedly to coatrack*) S'pose to meet Cora at ten o'clock. (*puts on coat and looks into audience*) I'll be back by two, too! (*exits, while lights fade out quickly*)

SCENE 5

A *week later, in* REV. BROWN'S *office.* CORA *stuffs papers into* REV. BROWN'S *valise.* REV. BROWN *busies himself.*

CORA (*completing the punchline of a joke*): And so he says (*in a man's voice*) 'It's not the clothes—it's the pose!' (*They both laugh.*)

REV. BROWN (*laughing*): Cora, you and them dirty jokes! (*pause*) How much time I got till the plane leaves?

CORA (*looks at her watch*): Little over an hour.

REV. BROWN: Well, I better get a move on! (CORA *fastens the valise and brings it over to* REV. BROWN. *She places it on the floor. She removes his coat from the rack and holds it for him.*) When you come down to Washington in the morning don't you come bouncin' over to the hotel looking for me. I'll get in touch with you tomorrow night.

CORA: Of course, honey. I'll wait for your call. (CORA *helps him on with his coat.*)

JOHNSON (*enters*): You 'bout ready, Reverend?

REV. BROWN: In a couple minutes, Johnson. (JOHNSON *exits.*)

CORA: That man's been acting strange lately. When you get back, Abe, you ought to consider getting rid of him. A bright young man could do his job much better.

REV. BROWN: I could never find anybody as reliable and trustworthy as him, so I don't even think about anything like that. (*looks about the room*) Now, lemme see. Have I got everything? Yeah. Yeah. (*to* CORA) Don't forget what I told you. I'll try and call around nine.

CORA: Okay, honey. Tomorrow will be another big day in your life!

REV. BROWN: It just might be the biggest! (*picks up valise, kisses* CORA *on the cheek, walks to the mirror, and addresses it.*) Mirror, if I ain't now what I said I was before—I'm *gonna* be when I get back, so you better grow some more! (*exits. Lights fade out quickly.*)

SCENE 6

In the park in front of the White House. REV. BROWN *and* JOHNSON *stand there and look at the White House.* JOHNSON *carries shopping bag with gasoline can inside it. Inside his coat pocket is folded newspaper.*

REV. BROWN (*admiring*): That White House sure looks pretty! (*pause*) If I was white, I'd be sleeping there tonight!

JOHNSON (*slaps* REV. BROWN'S *back and laughs*): Well, you can forget about that.

REV. BROWN: I'll be so famous after today, ain't no tellin' where I'll be sleepin'.

JOHNSON: Reverend, is you sure you want to be famous (*holds up can of gasoline*) this bad?

REV. BROWN: You watch and see how much publicity I *git* from this!

JOHNSON (*shaking his head*): I don't see how you can do it. I know I couldn't, 'cause my heart pumps Kool-Aid. (REV. BROWN *laughs vigorously, until* JOHNSON *interrupts. He nudges* REV. BROWN, *looks over his own shoulder and says seriously*) Hey, Reverend. Hey, Reverend. Them people over there lookin' at us.

REV. BROWN (*clears throat and straightens up*): Come on. Let's go sit on that bench. (*They walk very casually to the bench and sit down.*) Take out your newspaper and open it up. (*They hide themselves behind the paper, each holding one side. They shake the paper nervously.*) I'm the one gon' burn myself, and you nervouser than me! (*Pause. They stop the shaking.*) They still lookin'?

JOHNSON (*pops his head over the paper. Turns his head and looks over his shoulder*): Reverend! I think they takin' pictures of us! (REV. BROWN *shakes the paper.*) Naw, 'scuse me, Reverend, they takin' the White House.

REV. BROWN (*puts the paper on the bench*): Okay. Let's get started. (*pause*) Now. Uh—you know what to do. The minute I light the match, you start screamin' and come runnin' over. Okay. Gimme the can. (JOHNSON *takes out the can and hands it to him.* REV. BROWN *stands up and looks to see whether they are being observed.*) Well, here goes. . . . (*He walks about ten feet away, pauses, looks at* JOHNSON, *and then raises the can.*) I sure hate messin' up my good clothes like this. (*He pours the gasoline liberally over himself. Then he lies down on his back on the grass. He reaches into his pocket and takes out a pack of matches. He lights the match.*) Okay, Johnson. Start screamin'.

JOHNSON (*screams*): HELP! HELP! (REV. BROWN *sets match to his clothing.*)

JOHNSON (*not quite as loud as before*): Help.

REV. BROWN (*screams in agony. Smoke is seen*): JOHNSON! JOHNSON!

(JOHNSON *stands up without much concern while* REV. BROWN *frantically slaps at the flames*): SCREAM, JOHNSON! SCREAM!

JOHNSON (*remains standing by bench. In a conversational tone*): I'm screamin', Reverend. I'm screamin'. (REV. BROWN'S *screams become fainter.* JOHNSON *walks over to him and looks down, while* REV. BROWN *rolls over and over, writhing.*)

REV. BROWN (*weakly*): Help me. Help me. (*rolls over on his stomach and bounces up and down.* JOHNSON *returns to bench and begins reading the newspaper.*)

REV. BROWN (*a short moan*): Ahhh! (JOHNSON *hears voices offstage. Looks up.*)

OFFSTAGE: (*many voices*) 'What is it?' 'What's going on?' 'What's happening over there?,' (*etc.*)

(JOHNSON *runs to* REV. BROWN. *Jumps up and down all around his body, yelping.* REV. BROWN *suddenly becomes motionless.* JOHNSON *quickly removes his coat and pounds the still figure.*)

CROWD (*enters in confusion. They surround the body. One man joins* JOHNSON *and pounds the form with his coat. Spoken individually and, at times, simultaneously*): 'Oh my God!' 'It's a man.' 'Somebody help him!' 'Quick!' 'Call an ambulance!' (*someone exits quickly*) 'He's burning!' (*A male voice says*) Stand back! Let me take a look at him. (*The crowd moves back in a semicircle. A long silence. The man comes out of the crowd. All eyes follow him.*) He's dead. (*another silence.* JOHNSON, *who has been unobserved up to this point, now comes forth slowly and walks away with his hands in his pockets. Exits. Lights fade out quickly. During transition,* JOHNSON *speaks before lights come up.*)

JOHNSON: Yes, this organization and the Negro people will miss—will *certainly* miss—the good Reverend Brown, who left this earth for a sacrifice for his people. (*ad libs until lights come up*)

SCENE 7

REV. BROWN'S *office.* JOHNSON *is seated behind the desk, smoking a big cigar. He is being interviewed by the* REPORTER.

REPORTER: And, finally, sir, as the new head of the National Freedom Association, do you plan on any changes in policy?

JOHNSON (*blowing smoke*): There will no immediate changes. Under Reverend Brown's direction, the Association made great progress.

REPORTER: Well, thank you, Mister Johnson. I think I have all I need.

JOHNSON (*They both rise. Pompously*): Oh! My pleasure! My door is always open to the press. (*They shake hands.*)

REPORTER (*gets ready to exit*): Good day, sir.

JOHNSON: Good day! And give my regards to your staff.

REPORTER: I certainly will. (JOHNSON *walks* REPORTER *to the door.* REPORTER *exits.*)

JOHNSON (*walks back to the mirror. Pause. With much animation, he addresses the mirror.*) Mirror, mirror, on the wall, noooooow who's the most powerful black man of them all?

Curtain

THE SUICIDE

Carol Freeman

A *one act play*

Characters

THE SUICIDE
THE WIFE
THE PREACHER
THE NEIGHBOR
THE COPS

The scene is a small cramped living bedroom in an apartment; against one wall on sawhorses and planks, a plain casket, draped with a lace tablecloth, at each end withered flowers in vases, and soda pop bottles. The room is very crowded, containing a double bed, some kitchen chairs. On the wall, directly over the casket, is a small carpet, with The Last Supper scene on it. Next to that is a calendar from the New Light Church with a fly-blown picture of a café au lait family, on their knees in a church pew, grinning ecstatically at the ceiling. Sounds of muted merriment from the street, below. In a room off the living room, comes the smell of frying chicken, and women's voices.

THE NEIGHBOR: What ah wants tuh know, is how he git daih in the first place. Frank ain' had no car, is he? Newspapers jus' say he jumped, nombah some thousan' jumped from the bridge, didn't hardly say much mo'.

WIFE: Ah tell ya how, mussa bummed him a ride, fum somebody,

NEIGHBOR: Got enny mo' in that showtneck?

WIFE: Take it all. Wine ain' what ah needs now, issen you got a cuppla' dollahs ah could have the loan of tell toomarrie mawning? Frank's momma gon' cum git the body then tuh ship back to loozana, en um gonna hit huh fuh leas' twenny bucks.

NEIGHBOR: Bitch, if ah had moe'n a kwarder you thank ah'd be settin heah? (*She fidgets nervously, and wipes her throat with a dishcloth.*) Damn! It's hot in heah, open up a winder or somethin', shit, ah got highblood pressuah an dis heat gonna mek me fain inna minit.

WIFE: Ef ya havin' hot flashes, go stand in front of the frigidaih and stick yo' haid inside, but ain gon open dese winders, evvy fly in ten miles, be done come in heah then. (*She speaks sourly.*) Frank, ya know Frank, he railly was a good man, 'cept readin' o-all them books, and drankin' so much wine done rumn him crazy. But he was good. (*She is silent, with her desire to explain to the neighbor how Frank had been.*) Ah mean, he didn't hit me, didn't take mah change, didn't cheat on me, welllll. . . . (*There is a knock at the door, loud, impatient. The women are silent.*)

WIFE: Wait uh minute, somebody at the do'. Jes' uh minute. (*She raises her voice to the door, and then stands up; a gaunt black woman, perhaps thirty, or forty. Her eyes are red, she has on a purple crêpe dress, with sequins and rhinestones down the front; the dress is too large, her hair is dyed an obvious red. She is graying. High-heel black shoes, and no stockings, her hands are blunt and coarse, the nails bitten to the quick, but painted a thick red. Going to the door, she stumbles on the coffin, stares at it a moment, then opens the door.*)

PREACHER: Mrs. Frank Jones?

WIFE: Yes, won't ya please come in, Revend.

(*enter the* PREACHER, *a very young, stocky black man in a dark suit, and white collar. He has on horned-rimmed glasses, and a black felt hat. Under one arm is tucked a large black Bible. He is a pompous man, recently out of divinity school. He speaks formal English, and, aware of his importance, gives himself airs. He enters, and stands in the middle of the crowded room, ill at ease.*)

PREACHER—(*extending his hand*): Harrumph! I am Reverend Theophilious Handee, your landlady told me of your misfortune, plus I read in the paper of your husband's untimely demise, and although neither you nor your husband were members of my congregation, I felt it my Christian duty to come to you in this time of need, and offer up a few prayers to the Lord for this unfortunate soul.

WIFE: Would you lak to rest yo' hat?

PREACHER: Indeed, indeed.

WIFE: Y'all kin set down on de bed ef you wants to, ain' got many chaihs 'cep them kitchen ones. (*The preacher sits gingerly on the edge of the bed with his hat in his hand. The woman is now uncertain what to do next; she walks over and lays her hand on the casket, hesitantly, with her back to the preacher. She turns suddenly.*)

WIFE: Y'all want to see Frank? Kin ef yu wants to, ah got the lid closed on count of the flies, but you kin look ef you wants to.

PREACHER: Don't mind if I do. (*He crosses over to the casket, the woman raises the lid, and they both stare intently at the body. The* NEIGHBOR *enters silently from the kitchen, her glass in her hand, and stands behind the* PREACHER *and peers at the body.*)

NEIGHBOR: Ummph, Ummph, ummph!

(*The* PREACHER *and the wife jump, startled. The* PREACHER *is really shook.*)

PREACHER (*his voice unnaturally high*): Good God, woman! Where did you come from?

NEIGHBOR (*her voice surly, and blurred*): Ah come from the

kitchen, where you thank ah come from? (*She finishes her drink.*) Where you come from?

WIFE: Ah, woman, hush! This here's the preacher.

NEIGHBOR: Hell, ah know what he is. (*She speaks petulantly. There is a silence; they stand uncomfortably with each other. The wife closes the coffin. Next door, suddenly, comes the sound of a record player, and Jimmy Reed, blaring out a blues song. The* NEIGHBOR *goes over and bangs on the wall.*) Turn that off! Turn that music off! We got dead folks in heah! (*A muffled voice through the wall yells 'Fuck you!' The* NEIGHBOR *turns to the wife.*) Who is that next do?

WIFE: Some ol' hoa, what's gonna git huh ass kicked tomorrow! (*She has raised her voice so that the woman next door can hear.*)

PREACHER: For goodness sakes! Please, Mrs. Jones! (*The* PREACHER *clears his throat and opens his Bible. There is a knock at the door, then a voice through the door*): Please don' kick my ass tomorrow, bitch! Come on out heah and kick it now, come on out!

WIFE (*screaming*): Ya gawdam right ah will! (*She grabs one of the soda pop bottles, empties the wilted flowers on the floor, and rushes offstage. Outside can be heard the two women screaming at each other, then the sounds of tussling. The* PREACHER *jumps from the bed, and stares at the* NEIGHBOR.)

PREACHER: Somebody should stop them, this is no way to hold a wake! If they don't stop I'm going home! This is indecent!

NEIGHBOR (*goes into the kitchen, and returns with a butcher knife*): Set down, preacher, Mrs. Jones be right back. Ah'll stop this shit. (*She leaves. Outside can be heard a full-scale battle, with screams, more curses. The* PREACHER *jumps over to the coffin and lifts the lid. He stares intently at the body, and returns to the bed. He opens his Bible, and reads something, then he goes to the door. Suddenly, from outside)*

WIFE: Aw, shit! That bitch done stabbed that hoa! (*screams*) Somebody call the ambulance! Call the cops! (*The PREACHER grabs his hat, and opens the door and steps out into the hall. Muted sounds from outside, then sirens, heavy steps on the stairs.*) Cops! heah the cops!

COP: Get back! Get back, let me through! All right what happened here? (*murmuring voices*) Hold it! One at a time. Reverend, what happened here?

PREACHER: Officer, I cannot tell you all the details. I was inside, with the body.

COP: What body? What the hell are you talking about?

PREACHER: Well, uh, uh, the body in there, in the casket. (*reenter the PREACHER, and the COP into the room.*)

COP: Jeesus, what's going on here?

PREACHER: Well, I was saying, Officer, I came over here to Mrs. Jones to help her mourn the passing of her husband, even though she nor her husband were members of my congregation. I was given to understand that she could not afford a church ceremony, and as the body was being shipped out tonight, for burial in the family plot in Louisiana, I . . .

COP: Hold it, Rev. (*He crosses to the door, and yells outside to another policeman.*) Hey Art! Come in here, you gotta see this! Nigger bitches fighting over a dead man! (*A SECOND COP enters, behind him is the WIFE. They close the door, the WIFE sits on the bed.*)

COP: All right, Rev. Tell it from the start. . . . Hold it, who is this woman? Is this the one that did the stabbing?

SECOND COP: Naw, she's out in the wagon. We're taking this one in, too, she started the whole thing.

WIFE: (*Her face is bruised, one eye is closing, her hair awry, her dress torn, she stands over the coffin. She yells angrily.*) Who opened dis coffin? Flies! The flies on Frank! Motha-

fuckas! You bastids! Told you to keep that lid closed!
Now the flies on him!

COP: Christ! Get her out of here! (*The* SECOND COP *grabs the*
WIFE *and hustles her out the door. She is still screaming.*)

WIFE: Let me go! Let me go, mothafucka!

SECOND COP: Oww! You go to jail for that, bitch! (*The door
closes. The* PREACHER *closes the coffin, and stands by it.
The* COP *walks over and opens it, and stares at the body.*)

PREACHER: Please close it, Officer. The flies. . . .

An Afterword

Larry Neal

AND SHINE SWAM ON

. . . Just then the Captain said, "Shine, Shine, save poor me
I'll give you more money than a nigger ever see."
Shine said to the Captain: "Money is good on land and on sea,
but the money on land is the money for me."
And Shine swam on . . .
Then the Captain's lily white daughter come up on deck,
She had her hands on her pussy and her dress around her neck.
She say, "Shine, Shine, save poor me,
I'll give you more pussy than a nigger ever see."
Shine, he say, "There's pussy on land and pussy on sea,
but the pussy on land is the pussy for me."
And Shine swam on . . .

The quote is taken from an urban "toast" called the
Titanic. It is part of the private mythology of Black America.
Its symbolism is direct and profound. Shine is US. We have
been below-deck stoking the ship's furnaces. Now the ship is
sinking, but where will we swim? This is the question that
the "New Breed" which James Brown sings about, asks.

We don't have all of the answers, but have attempted,
through the artistic and political work presented here, to confront our problems from what must be called a radical perspective. Therefore, most of the book can be read as if it
were a critical re-examination of Western political, social and
artistic values. It can be read also as a rejection of anything
that we feel is detrimental to our people. And it is almost
axiomatic that most of what the West considers important
endangers the more humane world we feel ours should be.

We have been, for the most part, talking about contemporary realities. We have not been talking about a return to some glorious African past. But we recognize the past—the total past. Many of us refuse to accept a truncated Negro history which cuts us off completely from our African ancestry. To do so is to accept the very racist assumptions which we abhor. Rather, we want to comprehend history totally, and understand the manifold ways in which contemporary problems are affected by it.

There is a tension within Black America. And it has its roots in the general history of the race. The manner in which we see this history determines how we act. How should we see this history? What should we feel about it? This is important to know, because the sense of how that history should be felt is what either unites or separates us.

For, how the thing is felt helps to determine how it is played. For example, the 1966 uprising in Watts is a case of feeling one's history in a particular way, and then acting it out in the most immediate manner possible. The emotions of the crowd have always played an integral role in the making of history.

Again, what separates a Malcolm X from a Roy Wilkins is a profound difference in what each believes the history of America to be. Finally, the success of one leader over another depends upon which one best understands and expresses the emotional realities of a given historical epoch. Hence, we feel a Malcolm in a way that a Roy Wilkins, a King, and a Whitney Young can never be felt. Because a Malcolm, finally, interprets the emotional history of his people better than the others.

There is a tension throughout our communities. The ghosts of that tension are Nat Turner, Martin Delaney, Booker T. Washington, Frederick Douglass, Malcolm X, Garvey, Monroe Trotter, DuBois, Fanon, and a whole panoply of mythical heroes from Br'er Rabbit to Shine. These ghosts have left us with some very heavy questions about the realities of life for black people in America.

The movement is now faced with a serious crisis. It has postulated a theory of Black Power; and that is good. But it has failed to evolve a workable ideology. That is, a workable concept—perhaps Black Power *is* it—which can encompass many of the diverse ideological tendencies existent in the black community. This concept would have to allow for separatists and revolutionaries; and it would have to take into consideration the realities of contemporary American power, both here and abroad. The militant wing of the movement has begun to deny the patriotic assumptions of the white and Negro establishment, but it has not supported that denial with a consistent theory of social change, one that must be rooted in the history of African-Americans.

Currently, there is a general lack of clarity about how to proceed. This lack of clarity is historical and is involved with what DuBois called the "double-consciousness":

. . . this sense of always looking at one's self through the eyes of others, of measuring one's soul by the tape of a world that looks on in amused contempt and pity. One ever feels his two-ness— an American, a Negro—two souls, two thoughts, two unreconciled strivings; two warring ideals in one dark body, whose dogged strength alone keeps it from being torn asunder.

The history of the American Negro is the history of this strife— this longing to attain self-conscious manhood, to merge his double-self into a better and truer self . . .

This statement is from *The Souls of Black Folk*, which was published in 1897. The double-consciousness still exists, and was even in existence prior to 1897.

Nat Turner, Denmark Vesey, and Gabriel Prosser attempted to destroy this double-consciousness in bloody revolt.

In 1852, a black physician named Martin Delaney published a book entitled, *The Destiny of the Colored Peoples*.

Delaney advocated repatriation—return to the Motherland (Africa). He believed that the United States would never fully grant black people freedom; and never would there be anything like "equal status with the white man."

Frederick Douglass, and many of the abolitionists, strongly believed in the "promise of America." But the double-consciousness and its resulting tension still exist. How else can we explain the existence of these same ideas in contemporary America? Why was Garvey so popular? Why is it that, in a community like Harlem, one finds a distinctly nationalistic element which is growing yearly, according to a recent article in *The New York Times?* And it is a contemporary nationalism, existing in varying degrees of sophistication; but all of its tendencies, from the Revolutionary Action Movement to the African Nationalist Pioneer Movement, are focused on questions not fully resolved by the established Negro leadership—questions which that leadership, at this stage of its development, is incapable of answering.

Therefore, the rebirth of the concept of Black Power opens old wounds. For the conflict between Booker T. Washington and W.E.B. DuBois was essentially over the question of power, over the relationship of that power to the status of Black America. The focus of the conflict between Washington and DuBois was education: What was the best means of educating black people? Should it be primarily university education, as advocated by DuBois; or one rooted in what Washington called "craft skills"? Since education functions in a society to enforce certain values, both men found it impossible to confine discussion simply to the nature of black education. It became a political question. It *is* a political question. Therefore, what was essentially being debated was the political status of over ten million people of African descent who, against their wills, were being forced to eke out an existence in the United States.

Queen Mother Moore once pointed out to me that black

people were never collectively given a chance to decide whether they wanted to be American citizens or not. After the Civil War, for example, there was no plebiscite putting the question of American citizenship to a vote. Therefore, implicit in the turn-of-the-century controversy between Washington and DuBois is the idea that black people are a nation—a separate nation apart from white America. Around 1897, the idea was more a part of Washington's thinking than DuBois'; but it was to haunt DuBois until the day he died (in Ghana).

The educational ideas of both Washington and DuBois were doomed to failure. Both ideas, within the context of American values, were merely the extension of another kind of oppression. Only, now it was an oppression of the spirit. Within the context of a racist America, both were advocating a "colonialized" education; that is, an education equivalent to the kind the native receives, in Africa and Asia, under the imperialists. The fundamental role of education in a racist society would have to be to "keep the niggers in their place."

All of the Negro colleges in this country were, and, are even now, controlled by white money—white power. DuBois recognized this after he was dismissed from Atlanta University. In 1934, he further proceeded to advocate the establishment of independent "segregated" institutions and the development of the black community as a separate entity. The advocacy of such ideas led to a break with the NAACP, which was committed to a policy of total integration into American society. Here then, is the tension, the ambiguity between integration and segregation, occurring in the highest ranks of a well-established middle-class organization. Hence, in 1934, DuBois had not really advanced, at least not in terms of the ideas postulated above, but was merely picking up the threads of arguments put forth by Washington and Marcus Garvey. And the double-consciousness dominated his entire professional life.

He had been everything that was demanded of him: scholar, poet, politician, nationalist, integrationist, and finally in old age, a Communist. His had been a life full of controversy. He knew much about human nature, especially that of his people, but he did not understand Garvey—Garvey—who was merely his own double-consciousness theory personified in a very dynamic and forceful manner. Garvey was, in fact, attempting the destruction of that very tension which had plagued all of DuBois' professional career.

It involved knowing and deciding who and what we are. Had Garvey an organizational apparatus equivalent to the NAACP's, the entire history of the world might have been different. For Garvey was more emotionally cohesive than DuBois, and not as intellectually fragmented. DuBois, for all of his commitment, was a somewhat stuffy intellectual with middle-class hangups, for which Garvey constantly attacked him. The people to whom Garvey appealed could never have understood DuBois. But Garvey understood them, and the life-force within him was very fundamental to them. The NAACP has never had the kind of fervent appeal that the Garvey Movement had. It has rarely understood the tension within the black masses. To them, Garvey was a fanatic. But are these the words of a fanatic, or of a lover?

The N.A.A.C.P. wants us all to become white by amalgamation, but they are not honest enough to come out with the truth. To be a Negro is no disgrace, but an honor, and we of the U.N.I.A. do not want to become white. . . . We are proud and honorable. We love our race and respect and adore our mothers.

And, in a letter to his followers from prison:

My months of forcible removal from among you, being imprisoned as a punishment for advocating the cause of *our real emancipation* [emphasis mine], have not left me hopeless or despondent; but to the contrary, I see a great ray of light and the bursting of a mighty political cloud which will bring you complete freedom. . . .

We have gradually won our way back into the confidence of

the God of Africa, and He shall speak with a voice of thunder,
that shall shake the pillars of a corrupt and unjust world, and
once more restore Ethiopia to her ancient glory. . . .

Hold fast to the Faith. Desert not the ranks, but as brave
soldiers march on to victory. I am happy, and shall remain so, as
long as you keep the flag flying.

So in 1940, Garvey died. He died in London, an exile.
He was a proud man whose real fault was not lack of intense
feeling and conviction, but an inability to tailor his nationalism to the realities of the American context. And also he
was a threat to Europe's colonial designs in Africa, a much
greater threat than the Pan-African conferences DuBois used
to organize. Garvey wanted a nation for his people. That
would have meant the destruction of British, French and
Portuguese imperialism in Africa. And since it was a movement directed by blacks here in this country, it would also
have internally challenged American imperialism as it existed
at that time.

But Garvey was no Theodor Herzl or Chaim Weizmann,*
with their kind of skills and resources behind him. Had he
been, he might have brought a nation into existence. But
neither he nor his people had those kinds of resources, and,
worse, the black bourgeoisie of the period did not understand him with the same intensity as the masses.

In 1940, the year Garvey died, Malcolm Little was fifteen
years old. He caught a bus from Lansing, Michigan, and
went to Boston to live with his sister Ella Collins, who is
now head of the organization Malcolm started when he
broke with the Nation of Islam. It is probably the most important bus ride in history.

---

* NOTE: Herzl (1860–1904) and Weizmann (1874–1952) are two important
thinkers in the history of Jewish Zionism. During the 19th century, Jewish
intellectuals began to describe analytically the problem of the Jews since what
is called the Diaspora—the dispersion of the Jews among the Gentiles after
the Exile. The efforts of these two men and many others culminated in the
erection of Israel. Because Garvey also advocated a "return," some writers
have called his movement "Black Zionism."

Malcolm X, whose father had been a Garveyite, was destined to confront the double-consciousness of Black America. But his confrontation would be a modern one, rooted in the teachings of the Nation of Islam and in the realities of contemporary politics. That is to say, his ideas would be a synthesis of black nationalism's essential truths as derived from Martin Delaney, DuBois, Garvey, the honorable Elijah Muhammed, Fanon, and Richard Wright. And his speech would be marked by a particular cadence, a kind of "hip" understanding of the world. It was the truth as only the oppressed, and those whose lives have somehow been "outside of history," could know it.

Civil rights and brotherhood were in vogue when Malcolm started "blowing"—started telling the truth in a manner only a deaf man would ignore. And many of us *were* deaf, or if not, in a deep sleep. He shot holes through the civil rights movement that was the new "in" for the white liberals. James Baldwin was also "in," pleading for a new morality to people who saw him as another form of entertainment. And there were sit-ins, pray-ins, sleep-ins, non-violence, and the March on Washington. And the voice of Malcolm cut through it all, stripping away the sham and the lies. He was the conscience of Black America, setting out, like a warrior, to destroy the double-consciousness. He did not eschew dialogue. He attempted, instead, to make it more meaningful by infusing some truth into it. For this reason, it was both painful and beautiful to listen to him.

Malcolm covered everything—nationhood, manhood, the family, brotherhood, history, and the Third World Revolution. Yet it always seemed to me that he was talking about a revolution of the psyche, about how we should see ourselves in the world.

But, just as suddenly as he was thrust among us—he was gone. Gone, just as Black America was starting to understand what he was talking about. And those who killed him, did so for just that reason. For Malcolm wanted to make real the internationalism of Garvey and DuBois. Our problem had ceased to be one of civil rights, he argued, but is, instead, one of human rights. As such—he extended the argument— it belongs in an international context. Like Garvey and DuBois before him, he linked the general oppression of Black America to that of the Third World. Further, he strongly advocated unity with that world, something few civil rights leaders have dared to do.

Hence, what has come to be known as Black Power must be seen in terms of the ideas and persons which preceded it. Black Power is, in fact, a synthesis of all of the nationalistic ideas embedded within the double-consciousness of Black America. But it has no one *specific* meaning. It is rather a kind of feeling—a kind of emotional response to one's history. The theoreticians among us can break down its components. However, that will not be enough, for like all good theories, it can ultimately be defined only in action—in movement. Essentially, this is what the "New Breed" is doing— defining itself through actions, be they artistic or political.

We have attempted through these historical judgments to examine the idea of nationhood, the idea, real or fanciful, that black people comprise a separate national entity within the dominant white culture. This sense of being separate, especially within a racist society with so-called democratic ideas, has created a particular tension within the psychology of Black America. We are saying, further, that this sense of the "separate" moves through much of today's black literature.

There is also a concomitant sense of being at "war." Max Stanford explains that this sense began the minute the first slaves were snatched from their lands. These two tensions, "separation" and "war," are pressing historical realities; both are leading to a literature of Armageddon.

We must face these ideas in all of their dimensions. In some cases, the literature speaks to the tension within, say, the family; or it deals with the nature of black manhood.

At other times, especially in something like Jimmy Garrett's play *We Own The Night*, the "war" seems directed against an unseen white enemy; it is, in fact, an attack on the Uncle Tomism of the older generation.

The tension, or double-consciousness, is most often resolved in violence, simply because the nature of our existence in America has been one of violence. In some cases, the tension resolves in recognizing the beauty and love within Black America itself. No, not a new "Negritude," but a profound sense of a unique and beautiful culture; and a sense that there are many spiritual areas to explore *within* this culture. This is a kind of separation but there is no tension about it. There is a kind of peace in the separation. This peace may be threatened by the realities of the beast-world, but yet, it is lived as fully as life can be lived. This sense of a haven in blackness is found most often in the poetry selections.

But history weighs down on all of this literature. Every black writer in America has had to react to this history, either to make peace with it, or make war with it. It cannot be ignored. Every black writer has chosen a particular stance towards it. He or she may tell you that, for them, it was never a problem. But they will be liars.

Most contemporary black writing of the last few years, the literature of the young, has been aimed at the destruction of the double-consciousness. It has been aimed at consolidating the African-American personality. And it has not been essentially a literature of protest. It has, instead, turned its attention inward to the internal problems of the group. The problem of living in a racist society, therefore, is something that lurks on the immediate horizon, but which can not be dealt with until certain political, social and spiritual truths are understood by the oppressed themselves—inwardly understood.

It is a literature primarily directed at the consciences of

black people. And, in that sense, it is a literature that is somewhat more mature than that which preceded it. The white world—the West—is seen now as a dying creature, totally bereft of spirituality. This being the case, the only hope is some kind of psychic withdrawal from its values and assumptions. Not just America, but most of the non-colored world has been in the process of destroying the spiritual roots of mankind, while not substituting anything meaningful for this destruction.

Therefore, many see the enslavement of the Third World as an enslavement of the Spirit. Marxists carefully analyze the *material* reasons for this kind of oppression, but it takes a Fanon to illustrate the spiritual malaise in back of this enslavement. I tend to feel that the answer lies outside of historical materialism. It is rooted in how man sees himself in the spiritual sense, in what *he construes existence to mean.* Most Western philosophical orientations have taken the force of meaning out of existence.

Why this has happened is not really known, at least not in any sense that is final. We do know that the Western mind construes reality differently from that of the rest of the world. Or should I say, *feels* reality differently? Western mythological configurations are even vastly different from other configurations. Such configurations lead to the postulation of certain ideas of what art is, of what life is (see Jimmy Stewart's essay in this book).

Let us take, for example, the disorientation one experiences when one sees a piece of African sculpture in a Madison Avenue art gallery. Ask yourself: What is it doing there? In Africa, the piece had ritual significance. It was a spiritual affirmation of the connection between man and his ancestors, and it implied a particular kind of ontology—a particular sense of being. However, when you see it in that gallery, you must recognize that no African artist *desired* that it be placed there. Rather, it was stolen by force and placed there. And the mind that stole it was of a different nature from the mind that made it.

In the gallery or the salon, it is merely an *objet d'art*, but for your ancestors, it was a bridge between them and the spirit, a bridge between you and your soul in the progression of a spiritual lineage. It was art, merely incidentally, for it was essentially functional in its natural setting. The same goes for music, song, dance, the folk tale and dress. All of these things were coalesced, with form and function unified. All of these were an evocation of the spirit which included an affirmation of daily life, and the necessity of living life with honor.

The degree to which the artists among us understand some of these things is the degree to which we shall fashion a total art form that speaks primarily to the needs of our people. The temptation offered by Western society is to turn from these essential truths and merge with the oppressor for solace. This temptation demands, not merely integration of the flesh, but also integration of the spirit. And there are few of us for whom this would not have dire consequences. Further, the tension, the double-consciousness of which we have already spoken, cannot be resolved in so easy a manner, especially when, within the context of the racist society, the merger has little chance of being a healthy one.

In an essay entitled, "Blue Print for Negro Writing," Richard Wright attempted to define all aspects of the writer's role—especially as it is related to his status as an oppressed individual. Wright saw the problem in the following manner: The black writer had turned to writing in an attempt to demonstrate to the white world that there were "Negroes who were civilized." I suppose, here, he meant people like Charles Chestnutt and William Braithwaite. The writing, Wright attempted to prove, had become the voice of the educated Negro pleading with white America for justice. But

it was "external to the lives of educated Negroes themselves."
Further, much of this writing was rarely addressed to black
people, to their needs, sufferings and aspirations.

It is precisely here that almost all of our literature had
failed. It had succumbed merely to providing exotic entertainment for white America. As Wright suggests, we had yet
to create a dynamic body of literature addressed to the needs
of our people. And there are a myriad of socio-economic
reasons underlying this failure. The so-called Harlem Renaissance was, for the most part, a fantasy-era for most black
writers and their white friends. For the people of the community, it never even existed. It was a thing apart. And when
the money stopped, in 1929, to quote Langston Hughes:
". . . we were no longer in vogue, anyway, we Negroes. Sophisticated New Yorkers turned to Noel Coward. Colored actors
began to go hungry, publishers politely rejected new manu-
scripts, and patrons found other uses for their money. The
cycle that had charlestoned into being on the dancing heels
of *Shuffle Along* now ended in *Green Pastures* with De Lawd.
. . . The generous 1920's were over." For most of us, they had
never begun. It was all an illusion, a kind of surrealistic
euphoria.

Wright insisted on an approach to literature that would
reconcile the black man's "nationalism" and his "revolutionary aspirations." The best way for the writer to do this,
he wrote in "Blue Print," was the utilization of his own
tradition and culture—a culture that had developed out of
the black church, and the folklore of the people:

Blues, spirituals, and folk tales recounted from mouth to mouth;
the whispered words of a black mother to her black daughter on
the ways of men; the confidential wisdom of a black father to his
black son; the swapping of sex experiences on the street corners
from boy to boy in the deepest vernacular; work songs sung under
blazing suns—all these formed the channels through which the
racial wisdom flowed.

And what of the nationalism about which we spoke earlier? Here again, the tension arises. The question of nationalism occurs repeatedly in the works of Wright. Like DuBois and other intellectuals, Wright found that he could not ignore it. Within Wright himself, there was being waged a great conflict over the validity of nationalism. In the essay under discussion, he forces the question out into the open, asserting the necessity of understanding the function of nationalism in the lives of the people:

Let those who shy at the nationalistic implications of Negro life look at the body of folklore, living and powerful, which rose out of a common fate. Here are those vital beginnings of a recognition of a value in life as it is lived, a recognition that makes the emergence of a *new culture in the shell of the old.* [emphasis mine] And at the moment that this process starts, at the moment when people begin to realize a *meaning* in their suffering, the civilization that engenders that suffering is doomed. . . .

A further reading of this essay reveals that Wright was not trying to construct a black ideology, but was, instead, attempting a kind of reconciliation between nationalism and Communism. The essay was written in 1937. By then, the Communists had discarded the "nation within a nation" concept and were working to discourage black nationalism among the Negro members of the Party. Wright was trying to re-link nationalism and Communism, but the two were incompatible. The Communists discouraged the construction of a black theoretical frame of reference, but did not substitute a theory that was more viable than the one some of its black Party members proposed. Hence, the double-consciousness was not resolved. Wright ended up splitting with the Party to preserve his own identity.

Even though he had failed, Richard Wright was headed in the right direction. But the conditions under which he labored did not allow success. The Party, for example, had never really understood the "Negro question" in any manner that was finally meaningful to black people. Further, the nationalistic models which Wright and a contemporary of his, Ralph Ellison, saw around them were too "brutal" and "coarse" for their sensibilities (Ras, in Ellison's novel). Ultimately, the tension within Wright forced him to leave America, to become a voluntary exile.

The last years of his life were spent explaining the psychology of the oppressed throughout the Third World. In *White Man Listen!*, he attempted to analyze, much like Fanon, the malaise accompanying the relationship between the oppressed and the oppressors. And the double-consciousness never left him. *White Man Listen! Black Power*, and *The Color Line* are Wright's attempt to understand his own racial dilemma by placing it in an international context, thus linking it to the general affects of colonialism on the psychology of the oppressed. Therefore, these works, historically, link Wright with Garvey and DuBois, as well as foreshadow the ideas of Fanon and Brother Malcolm. To be more germane to our subject, these latter works are certainly more pertinent to the ideas of the "New Breed" youth, than say, *Native Son*.

They are especially more pertinent than Ralph Ellison's novel, *Invisible Man*, which is a profound piece of writing but the kind of novel which, nonetheless, has little bearing on the world as the "New Breed" sees it. The things that concerned Ellison are interesting to read, but contemporary black youth feels another force in the world today. We know who we are, and we are not invisible, *at least not to each other*. We are not Kafkaesque creatures stumbling through a white light of confusion and absurdity. The light is black (now, get that!) as are most of the meaningful tendencies in the world.

. . . Let us waste no time in sterile litanies and nauseating mimicry. Leave this Europe where they are never done talking of Man, yet

murder men everywhere they find them, at the corner of every one
of their own streets, in all corners of the globe. For centuries they
have stifled almost the whole of humanity in the name of a so-
called spiritual experience. Look at them today swaying between
atomic and spiritual disintegration.

> FRANTZ FANON—*The Wretched of The Earth*

Our literature, our art and our music are moving closer to
the forces motivating Black America. You can hear it everywhere, especially in the music, a surging new sound. Be it
the Supremes, James Brown, the Temptations, John Coltrane,
or Albert Ayler, there is a vital newness in this energy. There
is love, tension and spiritual togetherness in it. We are
beautiful—but there is more work to do, and just being
beautiful is not enough.

We must take this sound, and make this energy meaningful to our people. Otherwise, it will have meant nothing,
will have affected nothing. The force of what we have to say
can only be realized in action. Black literature must become
an integral part of the community's life style. And I believe
that it must also be integral to the myths and experiences
underlying the *total* history of black people.

New constructs will have to be developed. We will have
to alter our concepts of what art is, of what it is supposed to
"do." The dead forms taught most writers in the white man's
schools will have to be destroyed, or at best, radically altered.
We can learn more about what poetry is by listening to the
cadences in Malcolm's speeches, than from most of Western
poetics. Listen to James Brown scream. Ask yourself, then;
Have you ever heard a Negro poet sing like that? Of course
not, because we have been tied to the texts, like most
white poets. The text could be destroyed and no one would
be hurt in the least by it. The key is in the music. Our
music has always been far ahead of our literature. Actually,
until recently, it was our only literature, except for, perhaps,
the folktale.

Therefore, what we are asking for is a new synthesis; a new sense of literature as a *living* reality. But first, we must liberate ourselves, destroy the double-consciousness. We must integrate with *ourselves*, understand that we have within us a great vision, revolutionary and spiritual in nature, understand that the West is dying, and offers little promise of rebirth.

All of her prophets have told her so: Sartre, Brecht, Camus, Albee, Burroughs and Fellini, have foretold her doom. Can we do anything less? It is merely what we have always secretly known—what Garvey, DuBois, Fanon and Malcolm knew: The West is dying, as it must, as it should. However, the approach of this death merely makes the power-mad Magog's of the West more vicious, more dangerous —like McNamara with his computing machines, scientifically figuring out how to kill more people. We must address ourselves to this reality in the sharpest terms possible. Primarily, it is an address to black people. And that is not protest, as such. You don't have to protest to a hungry man about his hunger. You have either to feed him, or help him to eliminate the root causes of that hunger.

What of craft—the writer's craft? Well, under terms of a new definition concerning the function of literature, a new concept of what craft is will also evolve. For example, do I not find the craft of Stevie Wonder more suitable than that of Jascha Heifetz? Are not the sensibilities which produced the former closer to me than the latter? And does not the one indicate a way into things absent from the other?

To reiterate, the key to where the black people have to go is in the music. Our music has always been the most dominant manifestation of what we are and feel, literature was just an afterthought, the step taken by the Negro bourgeoisie who desired acceptance on the white man's terms. And that is precisely why the literature has failed. It was the case of one elite addressing another elite.

But our music is something else. The best of it has always

operated at the core of our lives, forcing itself upon us as in a ritual. It has always, somehow, represented the collective psyche. Black literature must attempt to achieve that same sense of the collective ritual, but ritual directed at the destruction of useless, dead ideas. Further, it can be a ritual that affirms our highest possibilities, but is yet honest with us.

Some of these tendencies already exist in the literature. It is readily perceivable in LeRoi Jones's *Black Mass*, and in a recent recording of his with the Jihad Singers. Also, we have the work of Yusuf Rahman, who is the poetic equivalent of Charlie Parker. Similar tendencies are found in Sun–Ra's music and poetry; Ronald Fair's novel, *Many Thousand Gone*; the short stories of Henry Dumas (represented in this anthology); the poetry of K. Kgositsile, Welton Smith, Ed Spriggs, and Rolland Snellings; the dramatic choreography of Eleo Pomare; Calvin Hernton's very explosive poems; Ishmael Reed's poetry and prose works which are notable for a startling display of imagery; David Henderson's work, particularly "Keep On Pushin'," where he gets a chance to sing. There are many, many others.

What this has all been leading us to say is that the poet must become a performer, the way James Brown is a performer—loud, gaudy and racy. He must take his work where his people are: Harlem, Watts, Philadelphia, Chicago and the rural South. He must learn to embellish the context in which the work is executed; and, where possible, link the work to all usable aspects of the music. For the context of the work is as important as the work itself. Poets must learn to sing, dance and chant their works, tearing into the substance of their individual and collective experiences. We must make literature move people to a deeper understanding of what this thing is all about, be a kind of priest, a black magician, working juju with the word on the world.

Finally, the black artist must link his work to the struggle for his liberation and the liberation of his brothers and sisters.

But, he will have executed an essential aspect of his role if he makes even a small gesture in the manner outlined. He will be furthering the psychological liberation of his people, without which, no change is even possible.

The artist and the political activist are one. They are both shapers of the future reality. Both understand and manipulate the collective myths of the race. Both are warriors, priests, lovers and destroyers. For the first violence will be internal—the destruction of a weak spiritual self for a more perfect self. But it will be a necessary violence. It is the only thing that will destroy the double-consciousness—the tension that is in the souls of the black folk.

Contributors

AHMED LEGRAHAM ALHAMISI is a corresponding editor for *Journal of Black Poetry*. He is also editor of a magazine published in Detroit, *Black Arts*.

CHARLES ANDERSON is a revolutionary brother in exile. Brother Charles, please get in touch!

S. E. ANDERSON: "My writing began at Pratt Institute, but didn't become stylized until I went to Lincoln University in 1962. A group of students and I formed a controversial black literary magazine called *Axiom*. I have been an activist in such organizations as the Student Nonviolent Coordinating Committee, the National Student Movement, The Black Arts (Harlem) and the Black Panther Party. My work has appeared in the *Liberator* magazine and *Negro Digest*. I am United States Editor of the *New African Magazine*."

KUWASI BALAGON, twenty-one years old, feels that it isn't necessary to give a biography of himself, his poetry speaks for him.

LINDSAY BARRETT was born in Jamaica and has lived in England and France. A very prolific writer, he has published a novel, *Song for Mumu*, and has had a number of plays produced in Nigeria, where he lectures on the roots of Africa and Afro-American literature. He has also worked as a journalist and been guest lecturer at the University of Ibadan in Nigeria.

BOB BENNETT: "Born and died August 13, 1947. Reborn sometimes in the last three years as black. Miseducated in the Jersey City school system, continuing at Fordham University in New York. I began to write in order to put some of my blackness and soul in ink for myself and my people."

LEBERT BETHUNE: "Born 1937, studied at New York University and Sorbonne, travelled extensively throughout Europe and the mid-east. Worked in East Africa as a film maker for the Tanzanian government. Author of a collection of poems *Juju of My Own*. At present I am working on a long novel about Africa and the Caribbean, and a new collection of poems."

HART LEROI BIBBS: "Aquarius, privately published poetry book *Poly-Rhythms to Freedom*. I am published in *Liberator*, *Negro Digest*, *Writer's Forum*, *Literary Times*, *Theo*, *Free-lance Poets*, *Jet* and *Kauri*."

JAMES BOGGS: "Revolutionary theoretician, was born in Marion Junction, Alabama, where white folks are gentlemen by day and Ku Klux Klanners at night. After graduating from Dunbar High School in Bessamer, Alabama, he bummed his way through the western part of the country, working in the hop fields of Washington state, cutting ice in Minnesota, and finally in Detroit with the W.P.A. At the start of World War II he became an auto worker, and has been one ever since, and a rebel for as long as he can remember. He is the author of *The American Revolution*, translated in Latin America, France and Japan, and has published articles on Black Power in Italy and Argentina."

FREDERICK JAMES BRYANT, JR. was born in Philadelphia in 1942. He was discharged from the U.S. Navy in June 1963. He entered Lincoln University (Pennsylvania) in September of the same year, and two years later was awarded the Eichelburger Prize for prose writing. The following year he was designated as Poet Laureate of Lincoln University. His one-act play, *Lord of the Mummy Wrappings*, was staged at Lincoln in April, 1967.

ED BULLINS is a playwright, and a co-founder of the Black Arts/West in San Francisco's Fillmore District, patterned after LeRoi Jones' Black Arts Repertory Theater/School in Harlem. He is a member of Black Arts Alliance, assisting LeRoi Jones in film making in San Francisco and Los Angeles. Presently he is resident playwright of the New Lafayette Theater in Harlem.

BEN CALDWELL is a playwright and graphic artist. His play the *Militant Preacher* has been performed on several occasions by the Spirit House Movers, a repertoire group led by LeRoi Jones, always to enthusiastic audiences. Mr. Caldwell's works have been published by the Jihad Press. He lives in Newark, New Jersey.

STOKELY CARMICHAEL was formerly chairman of the Student Nonviolent Coordinating Committee. He has been a field organizer in the South, and is co-author with Charles Hamilton of *Black Power*.

CHARLIE COBB is twenty-four and a field secretary for SNCC, based in Washington, D.C. He attended Howard University in 1961, but dropped out to work with SNCC in Mississippi. He is currently working with SNCC in the development of a network of liberation schools.

JOHN HENRIK CLARKE has studied writing at New York and Columbia Universities. With an interest in the history of people of African descent worldover, he has written many articles on the subject, including "Reclaiming the Lost African Heritage," published in *The American Negro Writer* by the American Society of African Culture in 1960. Mr. Clarke is the editor of *Harlem: A Community in Transition* (1964) and *Harlem, U.S.A.*, and has been associated with *Freedomways Magazine* since 1962.

STANLEY CROUCH is a West Coast correspondent for *The Cricket*, a magazine of Black music. Brother Crouch is a musician and music critic. His poetry has been published in *Liberator* and *Black Dialogue*.

HAROLD CRUSE was born in Petersburg, Virginia and raised in New York City. A member of the Harlem radical movement of the early 1950's, Mr. Cruse began his writing career as a film and drama critic, and has published articles in *Studies on the Left*, *Le Temps Moderne, Liberator*, and is the author of *The Crisis of the Negro Intellectual*.

SAM CORNISH, "a native of West Baltimore, dropped out of Douglass High School after his first semester in 1952, taking his education into his own hands. I have published three books, *In This Corner, People Under the Window*, and *Generations*, as well as having individual poems published in small magazines througout the country. I am editor of *Mimeo* and employed by the Enoch Pratt Library."

VICTOR HERNANDEZ CRUZ was born in Puerto Rico in 1949 and came to New York City when he was four. Magazines in which his work has been published include *Evergreen Review, For Now, Down Here* and *Umbra*. In the autumn of 1968 Random House will publish a book of his poems, *Snaps*.

WALT DELEGALL is a native of Philadelphia. He studied at Howard University, where he was a member of the Dasien Literary Group. He has been published in *New American Poets* and *Beyond the Blues*.

RONALD DRAYTON: "I wrote one play, *Black Chaos*, and adapted *Dope*. I am now working with the New Drama Workshop, which will do a production of my play *The Conquest of Africa in the Memory of Antoine Artaud* at the Village Gate, and with the Wayne Grice Drama Workshop. I have written an unpublished novel, *Morning Before the Dawn*, and numerous poems."

HENRY DUMAS: "Born in Arkansas, came up to Harlem age of 10, Air Force and all that—spent a year in the great Arabian

Peninsula—lived in New Jersey while attending Rutgers University. I am published in *Freedomways*, *Negro Digest*, *Umbra*, Hiram College *Poetry Review* and *Trace*. I have just finished my first novel which is long overdue. I am very much concerned about what is happening to my people and what we are doing with our precious tradition." Henry Dumas was shot and killed by a white policeman in New York City in late May, 1968.

RONALD L. FAIR was born in Chicago, Illinois, on October 27, 1932. Following his graduation from high school in Chicago he spent three years in the United States Navy as a hospital corpsman. He is the author of *Many Thousand Gone: An American Fable* and *The Hog Butcher*. He is published in the *Chicago Daily Defender* and *The Chat Noir Review*, a Chicago quarterly.

JULIA FIELDS was born in Uniontown, Alabama, in 1938. Her work has appeared in *New Negro Poets*, *Beyond the Blues*, *Massachusetts Review* and *Negro Digest*.

CLARENCE FRANKLIN: "Born in a small hole in the road named Racetrack, near Jackson, Miss., in 1932. Father a sharecropper who jumped the land several times because at the end of the year he always owed the 'boss.' Encouraged by my English teacher, attempted to study writing. Quit school to work as pinsetter to help at home. Read a lot. Attempted to write novels about justice and law à la E. Stanley Gardner because of a vague desire to be a lawyer . . . wrote *Stranger on a Train* . . . fizzled out."

AL FRASER is a graduate of Howard University. He holds a M.A. in political science. He was a member of the Dasien Group while he was in college. He has written extensively on African political affairs and history.

CAROL FREEMAN was born in 1941 in Rayville, Louisiana. She has attended numerous schools including Oakland City College and the University of California. Philosophy—"revolutionary black nationalist."

C. H. FULLER, JR., is a native of Philadelphia. He was a founder along with Jimmy Stewart, Larry Neal, and Marybelle Moore of

Kuntu, an organization of Black writers and artists. He is a novelist and a playwright. His play on the life of Marcus Garvey will be performed in Philadelphia. His work is published in *Liberator* magazine and *Black Dialogue*. He has also edited numerous literary newspapers in the Philadelphia area.

JIMMY GARRETT: "I'm 24, born in Dallas, Texas, reared in Los Angeles, California. . . . A black writer has the responsibility of collecting, distilling, clarifying and directing the energies of black people leading toward purposeful, meaningful action. Black action that is the black writer's individualism and his life. . . . Am living now in San Francisco attending State College and helping to prepare myself and my people for ultimate confrontations." Jimmy Garrett has worked with SNCC in Mississippi and Los Angeles.

LETHONIA GEE (LEE GEE) "is a beautiful soul sister from the Bronx. All love."

JOE GONCALVES, born in Boston, Mass., 1937. Resident off and on of San Francisco since 1948. Presently, Editor of *Journal of Black Poetry* and Poetry Editor for *Black Dialogue*.

LEROY GOODWIN: "I was born and raised in Los Angeles, California (Watts of course), and am now working in the Baltimore anti-poverty program."

D. L. GRAHAM lives in Gary, Indiana. He was formerly a student at Fisk University, where he studied under John Killens.

RUDY BEE GRAHAM is a Harvard drop-out. Besides writing poetry, he has written several plays, two of which were performed by the New Lafayette Theater. He is published in *Negro Digest* and *Black Dialogue*.

KIRK HALL: "An Afro-American with no illusions about the last part of that term, 'cause it doesn't mean citizenship, or civilized characteristics, or any kind of liberating thing—it means 'bad news.'" Born May 13, 1944, Montclair, New Jersey. B. A. Sociology, Virginia Union University, 1967.

BOBB HAMILTON lives in New York City. Sculptor and poet, he is also East Coast Editor of *Soulbook*.

Q. R. HAND, JR: "I believe poetry should produce behavioral change and is an active participatory two-way process. Poetry must also at this point in time-space-history help clarify humanizing values, and 'turn people on' to the fact that they have within themselves the power to change, if necessary, destroy the present national political-economic system. And to engage oneself in this process of change is necessarily humanizing, especially for Black Americans." Born 1937, Brooklyn, New York. Grew up in Bedford-Stuyvesant and Harlem. Presently attending Goddard College.

NATHAN HARE began life on a sharecropper's farm near Slick, Oklahoma. He received his B. A. from Langston University and an M.A. and Ph. D. in sociology from the University of Chicago. During his senior year in college he won the novice Golden Gloves championship in his division and fought professionally as "Nat Harris" while teaching at Howard University, as he does now. Nathan Hare has published articles in many magazines, including *Crime and Delinquency, Negro History Bulletin, Civil Liberties Bulletin, The Saturday Evening Post,* and is the author of *The Black Anglo Saxons.* At this time he is working on *A Black Primer,* a book on White America, and a work of satire.

ALBERT E. HAYNES, JR., is an artist and poet. He was one of the founders of the original *Umbra.* His work has appeared in *Liberator* magazine and *Soulbook.* He is very active in the struggle for human rights. He has participated in numerous poetry readings in the Black community.

DAVID HENDERSON'S work is widely anthologized. He has been published in *Liberator, Negro Digest,* and *Kulchur.* He is a member of the Teacher's and Writers' Collaborative at Columbia University. A book of his poems, *Felix and the Silent Forest,* has been published by the Poets Press. He is currently teaching at the City College of New York, and is editor of *Umbra* magazine.

CALVIN C. HERNTON is the author of one book of verse, *The Coming of Chronos to the House of Nightsong,* and two volumes of essays, *Sex and Racism* and *White Papers for White Americans.* He is a co-founder of *Umbra* magazine, and has contributed essays and poems to many periodicals. Mr. Hernton holds an M.A. in sociology from Fisk University and has worked as a shoe shine boy, pinsetter, market researcher, garment worker, book reviewer and factory hand. "Now floating around in Europe, working on a novel (yet untitled), finding that only a handful of white men in the whole world are capable of ever treating a black man or woman as a human being. When I left America I was to the left of Martin Luther King; when I return, for I shall, and soon, I will be to the left of Malcolm X and Fannon."

YUSEF IMAN is a singer, actor and poet. He is a member of the Spirit House Movers. He has performed in numerous plays in the Black community, particularly the work of LeRoi Jones. Some of his work has been published by Jihad Publications in Newark. Brother Yusef can be heard on the Jihad recording *Black and Beautiful*.

MARVIN JACKMON (NAZZAM AL FITNAH) is a San Francisco playwright and poet. His plays, *Come Next Summer* and *Flowers for the Trashman*, have been performed in the San Francisco Bay area and southern California. He is one of the founders of Black Arts West. His plays, poems, and essays have appeared in *Black Dialogue, Journal of Black Poetry* and *Soulbook*. He is a contributing editor to *Journal of Black Poetry*.

LANCE JEFFERS was a member of the Dasein Group while at Howard University. He has been a teacher in the Midwest.

RAY JOHNSON was born in Harlem. "Made the lower-Eastside with painters William White and the now deceased Bob Thompson."

LEROI JONES, poet, social critic, and dramatist, was born in Newark, New Jersey, in 1934. He is the author of, among other works, *Dutchman, Home, Tales*, and *Black Music*.

NORMAN JORDAN, twenty-eight years old, was born in Ansted, West Virginia. "Dropped out of high school and went into the Navy where I travelled both in this country and abroad for four years. My poetry has been read in such places as: Karamu, *An Evening with Jordan*, The Well, The Gate, and the New School of Afro-American Thought. I have stopped trying to have my poetry published about five years ago nor do I send my plays anywhere; as long as I am having my work produced here for black people, my black people, I am happy. I am married, have two children and live in Cleveland."

KEORAPETSE WILLIAM KGOSITSILE: "Poetry, like any other art form, is meaningless, i.e., has no use, unless it be a specific act actual as dance or childbirth; carved bleeding from history. Tears scorched to deep tracks on the mine laborer's back recording the national epitaph. Walls and what shapes people your memory. Clarity is not a thought process but a way of life." Born in Johannesburg, South Africa, 1938. Lincoln University, Columbia University, University of New Hampshire, the New School. Poems and essays published here and abroad.

PETER LABRIE has worked with the Department of Urban Renewal in Oakland, California. He attended the University of California at Berkeley where he took a B. A. in political science and earned a master's degree in city planning. He has been published in *Negro Digest* and *Black Dialogue*.

LESLIE ALEXANDER LACY spent three years in Ghana. He is the co-author of "The Sekondi-Tackoradi Strike" (a study of trade unionism in Ghana) in *Politics in Africa*. He is finishing a book on Ghana called *Politics and Labor in Ghana: 1921–1966*.

REGINALD LOCKETT: "One must be turned on to his Blackness and deep in it. My role as a Black writer is to convey how this is essential for BLACK PEOPLE. Long Knife (the white man) must be taught that his death and destruction is near. White-minded 'Knee-grows' must know this too. That is, if they don't straighten up and fly right they will perish with the Long Knives." Born 1947, Berkeley, California. Presently attending San Francisco State College.

DAVID LLORENS is a poet-essayist. He was formerly assistant editor of *Negro Digest*. He worked also with the SNCC Mississippi project. He is currently an assistant editor of *Ebony* magazine.

BILL MAHONEY was born October 1, 1941. "Was miseducated in the Montclair, New Jersey, school system until 1959, when Howard University took over the job. My education ended when

I was expelled from Howard University (they say I was not expelled but was suspended; a tricky legal point) for refusing to take my final ROTC course. As for philosophy, I am now trying to complete a novel where a bit of that may be revealed to myself and friends who are kindly probing me to finish the thing."

GASTON NEAL: "Born Cancer, deadborn 1934, reborn 1961. My home is Pittsburgh, Pa., Black Hill District—thrown out of high school from the reformatory into the army. Soon I was called *undesireable* by the army thrown out again then bummed around the country. My philosophy is simply to purge myself of the whiteness within me and link completely with my Black brothers in the struggle to destroy the enemy and rebuild a Black Nation. I am director of the New School of Afro-American Thought in Washington, D.C., and editing a volume of poetry of my time spent in St. Elizabeth Hospital.

LARRY NEAL was born in 1937 in Atlanta, Georgia, and was reared in Philadelphia. He received a B.A. from Lincoln University and did graduate work at the University of Pennsylvania. Mr. Neal was formerly the Arts Editor of *Liberator* magazine, and is currently an editor of *The Cricket* and a contributing editor of *Journal of Black Poetry*. He believes that poetry and art should contribute to making a revolution in America. Larry Neal and his wife, the former Evelyn Rodgers of Birmingham, Alabama, live in New York City.

ODARO (BARBARA JONES) was born June 22, 1946. "Poems have appeared in *Three Shades of Humanism*, *We Speak* and *Pacesetter*, Harlem Youth Unlimited Quarterly, also I have appeared in poetry readings around Harlem."

CHARLES PATTERSON: "I was born October 29, 1941, in Fayetteville, N.C. We migrated to the 'Big Apple' when I was about two years old. Educated in the New York City public schools (too poor to attend college). I started my love affair with literature when I found it the best means to express myself and the bitterness which engulfed my soul. Worked with LeRoi Jones and the Black Arts Repertory Theater School, which produced two plays of mine: *Black Ice* and *The Super*. Recorded a record for WBAI with the *Umbra* poets."

YUSEF RAHMAN: "Once slaved-named ronald stone re-incarnated to eternal life as a most willing slave of Allah, Universal and Almighty."

CLARENCE REED lives in Harlem. "Is a painter, photographer, and political activist. Worked with the Black Arts Theater in Harlem and was a member of the Harlem Black Panther Party. Jihad Publications has published a book of his poems entitled *Forever Tears.*"

SONIA SANCHEZ: "Am thirty-one years old, born Birmingham, Alabama, a graduate of Hunter College. My philosophy is my ole man CHUCK who has brought me to where i am now. He made me viscerally aware that black people do not have the luxury to indulge in factions cus the 'Man' has his shit straight and will use it, and it's apt time for black people to get theirs down and allow brothers and sisters to keep on pushing in their own way, or we ain't gonna make it!! I teach 5th grade children in n.y.c. have written 2 one act plays. I have a beautiful 9 year old daughter who is artistically bent—I'd like to have two more children—am working at the latter."

BARBARA SIMMONS, "a native of Washington, D.C. now living in New York City, makes her first appearance in print in this anthology. She has just recorded 'Soul-Theme One,' with Jackie McLean for his record date with Blue Note Record Company."

LEFTY SIMS is a pianist. He is heavily influenced by the teachings of Islam.

WELTON SMITH: "Lives in new york in temporary exile from his home, san francisco. He left frisco in protest of his own growing insensitivity which he later discovered to be rooted in new york. It is clear at this point that either welton smith or new york must go, and smith ain't getting up off nothing. He was born in Houston, Texas—Sagittarius in Sagittarius."

JEAN WHEELER SMITH was born in 1942 in Detroit, Michigan. She earned a full, four-year scholarship at Howard University and was graduated in June, 1965, with honors and a Phi Betta Kappa key. She joined the civil rights movement in June,

1963, in Albany, Georgia, and Greenwood, Mississippi, as a SNCC field worker. She and her husband, a SNCC field secretary from Georgia, have worked with the Child Development Group of Mississippi-Headstart, Strike City near Leland, Mississippi, and in the preparation of adult literacy materials for the movement.

ROLLAND SNELLINGS (ASKIA MUHAMMAD TOURE): A former staff-member of *Liberator* magazine, he is now editor of *Black Dialogue*. His work has appeared in *Negro Digest, Freedomways, Umbra, Black America* and *Chalk Circle*. He is one of the prime movers of the new spirit in Black Art. He is an extremely active poet, reading his works wherever Black people gather.

A. B. SPELLMAN: "I was born of school-teaching parents August 7, 1934, in Elizabeth City, North Carolina. I attended Howard University where I earned a B.A. degree in Political Science and also did post graduate work in Law and English Literature. I came to New York in 1959 and I have lived there ever since. I have published one book of poems, *The Beautiful Days*, and a study of four jazz personalities, *Four Lives in the Bebop Business*. I have published essays on history, politics and jazz in *Nation, Jazz, Downbeat*; my poetry has been published in many 'little' magazines. My poems have also appeared in *Beyond the Blues, New Negro Poets* and *Negro Poets*."

EDWARD S. SPRIGGS is the East Coast editor of *Black Dialogue*. He is also a contributing editor to *Journal of Black Poetry*. He is active in the current movement to make art more relevant to the Black community.

JAMES STEWART: "Our guiding musical and aesthetic philosophy might be spoken of as being a kind of Black American expression of the kuntu category of African aesthetics. We believe our Black creative orientation is consistent with that principle." His essay "Revolutionary Nationalism and the Black Artist" was published in the Winter, 1966, edition of *Black Dialogue* magazine. His artwork has appeared in various exhibits of Black painters in Philadelphia, where he lives. He is an altoist-baritonist with several bands.

SUN RA is a musician-philosopher. "Some people are of this world, others are not. My natural self is not of this world because this world is not of my not and nothingness, alas and happily, at last I can say this world is this unfortunate planet." Sun Ra is the leader of one of the most important bands in the history of music—The Myth Science Arkestra. He began writing and playing seriously several years ago in Chicago. He has recorded on the Saturn and ESP labels. Some of his albums are *The Magic City*, *Heliocentric Worlds*, *Planet Earth*, *When Sun Comes Out*, and *When Angels Speak of Love*."

LORENZO THOMAS lives in Jamaica, New York. Is a student at Queens College where he was formerly co-editor of *Omnivore*. His poems have appeared in *Kulchur*, *New Poems*, *Umbra*, *Liberator* and *Eastside Review*.

RICHARD THOMAS, born April 2, 1939, Detroit, Michigan. "Graduated from high school in 1957, after the Marine Corps, I took writing seriously. Met Ron Milner and Margaret Danner in 1960, with their help and inspiration I got myself together. Became a Baba'i in 1962. For the first time in my angry bag, was able to see what Black poets could do with an eye big as the earth. I am published in *Scimitar and Song*, *Zeitgeist*, *Snapdragon* and a few mimeographs."

JACQUES WAKEFIELD, nineteen years old, is an actor as well as a poet. He appeared in the C.B.S. television production of *Lenox Avenue Sunday* under the direction of hip Barbara Ann Teer. He has also appeared in Miss Teer's adaptation of *Black Spirit and Power of LeRoi Jones*.

RON WELBURN: "I began shaping my socio-aesthetic interests while in high school, becoming familiar with available jazz music, also playing the cornet and alto saxophone. I entered Lincoln University in 1964. My foremost intentions in life are 1. explore the aesthetic value of human feelings; 2. advance the stature of Afro-American culture through literature and music."

JOSEPH WHITE was born in Philadelphia and is thirty-three years old. He was awarded a John Hay Whitney Fellowship for

1963–1964 and has published several pieces of fiction, most recently in *Liberator*.

CHARLES E. WILSON was born in New York thirty-six years ago, has attended numerous colleges and universities and has completed a Masters Education of Psychology as well as most of the course credits for a Masters degree in Public Administration. His material has been published by the *Liberator* magazine, *Liberation*, *Negro Digest*, *Jewish Currents*, and others. He lives in Brooklyn, New York.

TED WILSON is currently editor of *Pride* magazine. He grew up in Harlem and has been active in community organization. He was formerly on the staff of *Liberator* magazine. He is a frequent contributor to the Associated Negro Press.

JAY WRIGHT was born in Albuquerque, New Mexico, in 1935 and spent his early youth in California. He holds a B. A. from the University of California at Berkeley, an M.A. from Rutgers University (1966), and spent one semester at Union Theological Seminary. He has held several fellowships, including a Rockefeller Brothers Theological fellowship, has written two plays, and has published poetry in *Yale Review, New Negro Poets, Poetry Review* and other magazines.

In Memoriam 2007

A number of contributors to *Black Fire* have made their transition including my co-editor, Larry Neal. I have noted those whose passing I am aware of. It is possible that I've missed others. If you know of others that have passed and are not listed below, please help us pay tribute and respect by emailing their information to *publisher@blackclassicbooks.com*.

- Amiri

Kuwasi Balagon
Hart Leroi Bibbs
James Boggs
John Henrik Clarke
Harold Cruse
Walt Delegall
Henry Dumas
Kirk Hall
Q.R. Hand, Jr.
Calvin C. Hernton
Yusef Iman
Lance Jeffers
David Llorens
Gaston Neal
Larry Neal
Sun Ra
Clarence Reed
Barbara Simmons
Welton Smith
James Stewart
Lorenzo Thomas
Kwame Ture (Stokely Carmichael)

Amiri Baraka

Larry Neal

AMIRI BARAKA, born in 1934 in Newark, New Jersey, is the author of over 40 books of essays, poems, drama, and music history and criticism. He is a poet icon and revolutionary political activist who has recited poetry and lectured on cultural and political issues extensively throughout the USA, the Caribbean, Africa, and Europe.

Baraka is renowned as the founder of the Black Arts Movement in Harlem during the 1960s that became, though short-lived, the virtual blueprint for a new American theater aesthetics. His published and performance work, such as the signature study on African-American music, *Blues People* (1963), and the play *Dutchman* (1963), practically seeded "the cultural corollary to black nationalism" of that revolutionary American milieu.

Other titles range *from Selected Poetry of Amiri Baraka/LeRoi Jones* (1979), to *The Music* (1987), a fascinating collection of poems and monographs on Jazz and Blues authored by Baraka and his wife and poet Amina, and his boldly sortied essays, *The Essence of Reparations* (2003).

Baraka's many awards and honors include an Obie, the American Academy of Arts & Letters award, the James Weldon Johnson Medal for contributions to the arts, Rockefeller Foundation and National Endowment for the Arts grants, Professor Emeritus at the State university of New York at Stony Brook, and the Poet Laureate of New Jersey.

Baraka lives in Newark with his wife and author Amina Baraka; they have five children. Baraka and Amina head the word-music ensemble, Blue Ark: The Word Ship, and co-direct Kimako's Blues People, the "artspace" housed in their theater basement for some fifteen years.

LARRY NEAL was born in Atlanta, Georgia in 1937 and attended Lincoln University and the University of Pennsylvania for his undergraduate and graduate degrees. Neal relocated to New York in 1964, where he became a major catalyst for the Black Arts Movement. That same year, along with Amiri Baraka, he opened the Black Arts Repertory Theater in Harlem. Neal also served as a music and literary critic, writing essays about the works of Ralph Ellison, Zora Neal Hurston, Charlie Parker and others. He also wrote what are considered groundbreaking essays defining the Black Arts Movement. Neal was an instructor at the City College of New York, Wesleyan and Yale Universities. He also served as the Executive Director for the District of Columbia Commission on the Arts and Humanities. The commission has honored him by creating a writing award in his name. Neal died prematurely of a heart attack in 1981.

RELATED TITLES FROM BLACK CLASSIC PRESS

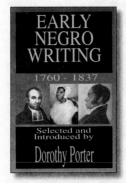

Early Negro Writing 1760-1837

ED. DOROTHY PORTER

A RARE AND INDISPENSABLE collection of writing with literary, social and historical importance. Included are documents from mutual aid and fraternal organizations, arguments about emigration, and selected narratives, poems, and essays.

ISBN 0-933121-59-8. 1971*, 1995. 660 pp. Paper $24.95.

Survey Graphic (March 1925), Harlem Mecca of the New Negro

ED. ALAIN LOCKE

HARLEM MECCA is an indispensable aid toward gaining a better understanding of the Harlem Renaissance. The contributors to this edition include W.E.B. DuBois, Arthur Schomburg, James Weldon Johnson, Langston Hughes and Countee Cullen.

ISBN 0-933121-05-9. 1925*, 1980. 92 pp. illus. Paper $14.95

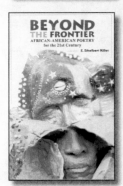

Beyond the Frontier

ED. E. ETHELBERT MILLER

ONE OF THE largest collections of Black poetry ever published, *Beyond the Frontier* is a vibrant compilation of 354 poems written by 175 of today's most provocative new voices. Miller, the editor, is also a poet and intentional anthologist. He has made a career as a nurturer of Black writers and works tirelessly to ensure the survival of African American poetry. This collection confirms his intentions.

ISBN 1-57478-017-4. 2002. 572 pp. Paper. $24.95

Continuum: New and Selected Poems

MARI EVANS

DISTINGUISHED POET and contributor to the Black Arts Movement, Evans writes unabashedly for and about African Americans. *Continuum* is full of her brilliance, humor, and musical language. Included are signature poems such as "I Am A Black Woman" and "Celebration" alongside new works.

ISBN 978-1-57478-038-3. 2007. 155 pp. Paper. $14.95

ALSO AVAILABLE FROM BLACK CLASSIC PRESS

Restoring the Queen
LAINI MATAKA,
$8.95.

Never As Strangers
LAINI MATAKA,
$8.95.

Bein' A Strong Black Woman Can Get U Killed
LAINI MATAKA,
$11.95.

Whispers, Secrets & Promises
E. ETHELBERT MILLER, $10.95.

First Light: New and Selected Poems
E. ETHELBERT MILLER, $11.95.

When Divas Laugh: The Diva Squad Poetry Collection
ED. CHEZIA THOMPSON-CAGER, $16.95.

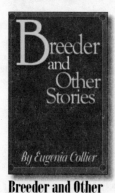

Breeder and Other Stories
EUGENIA COLLIER, $11.95.

Gone Fishin'
WALTER MOSLEY, $22.00.

Hand Me My Griot Clothes
PETER J. HARRIS, $8.95.